"I've never counted bars. I don't count bars. You start the verse
and then you let it close on its own, whenever you feel like it's
done. Sometimes it's short; sometimes it's long. I haven't been
rhymin' much recently, so maybe a lot built up or something and
now the verses have been longer. It harks back to when me and Big
Boi first met Organized Noize. We were rhymers. We wouldn't even
think chorus. We weren't thinking songs. We were just verses. When
we met Rico from Organized Noize in front of his job—and Gipp from
Goodie Mob had his truck out there and was playin' a beat—Rico
said, 'Let me hear how y'all rhyme.' And me and Big Boi just kept
rhymin' and rhymin' and didn't ever stop."

— —

ANDRÉ 3000

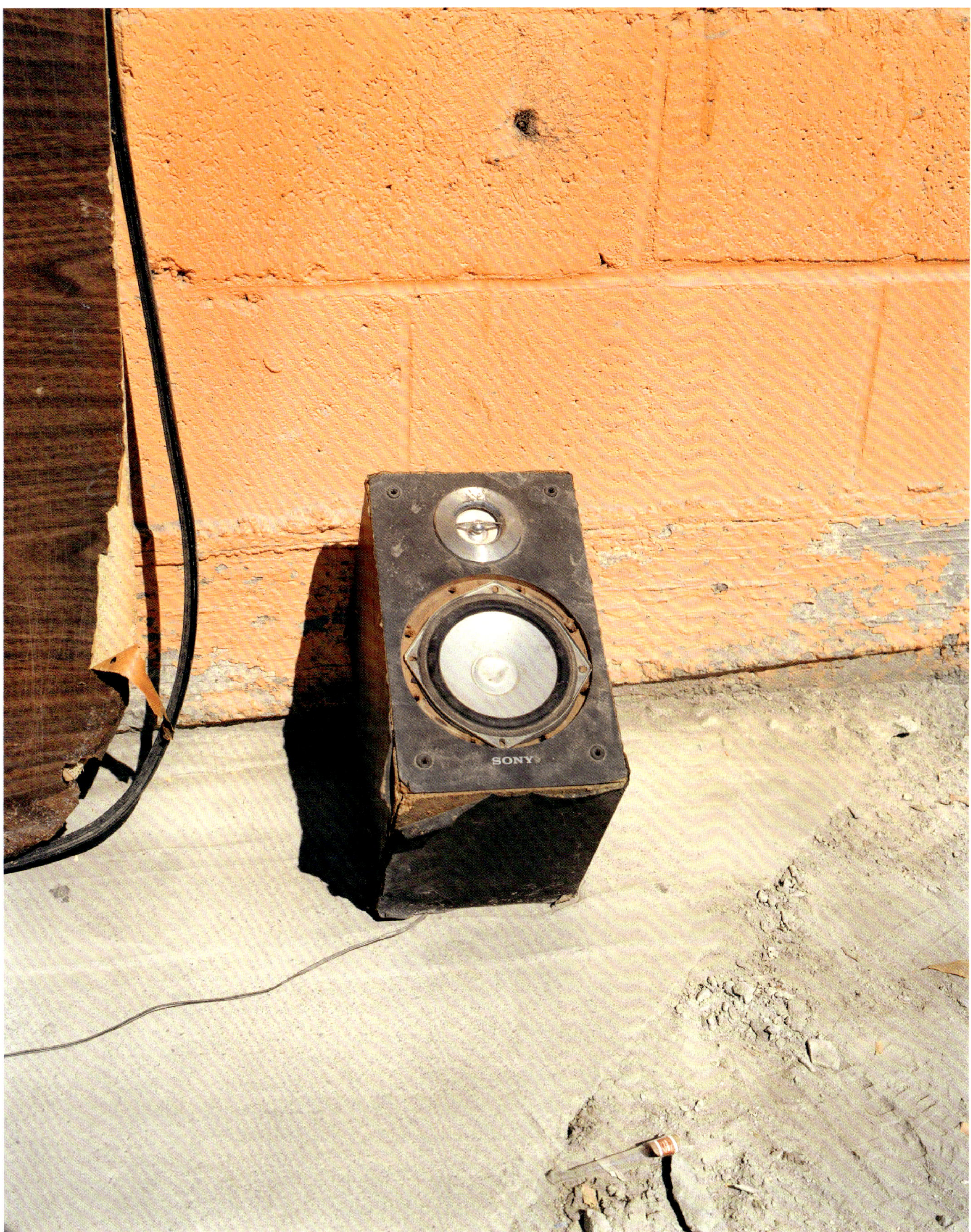

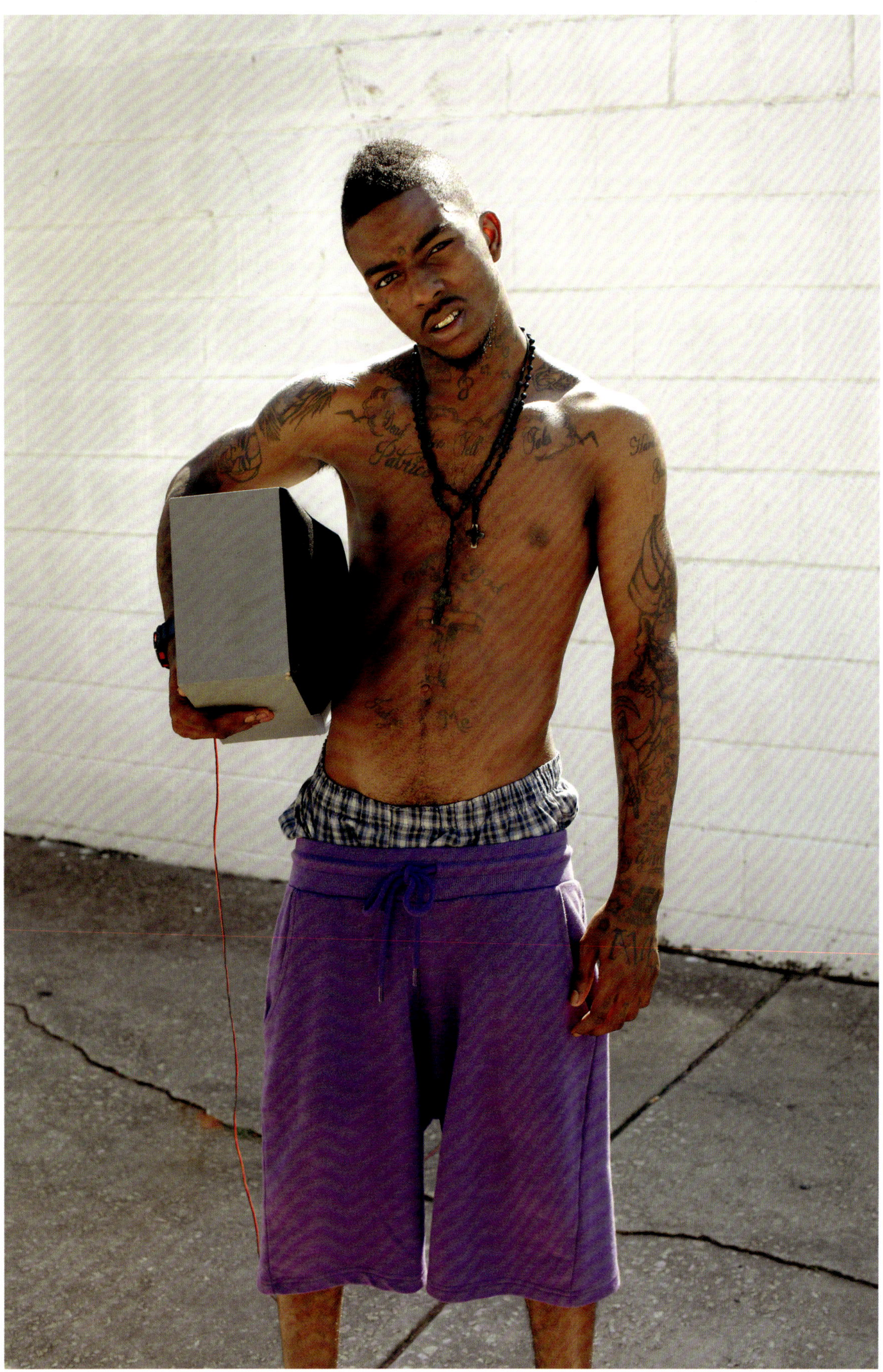

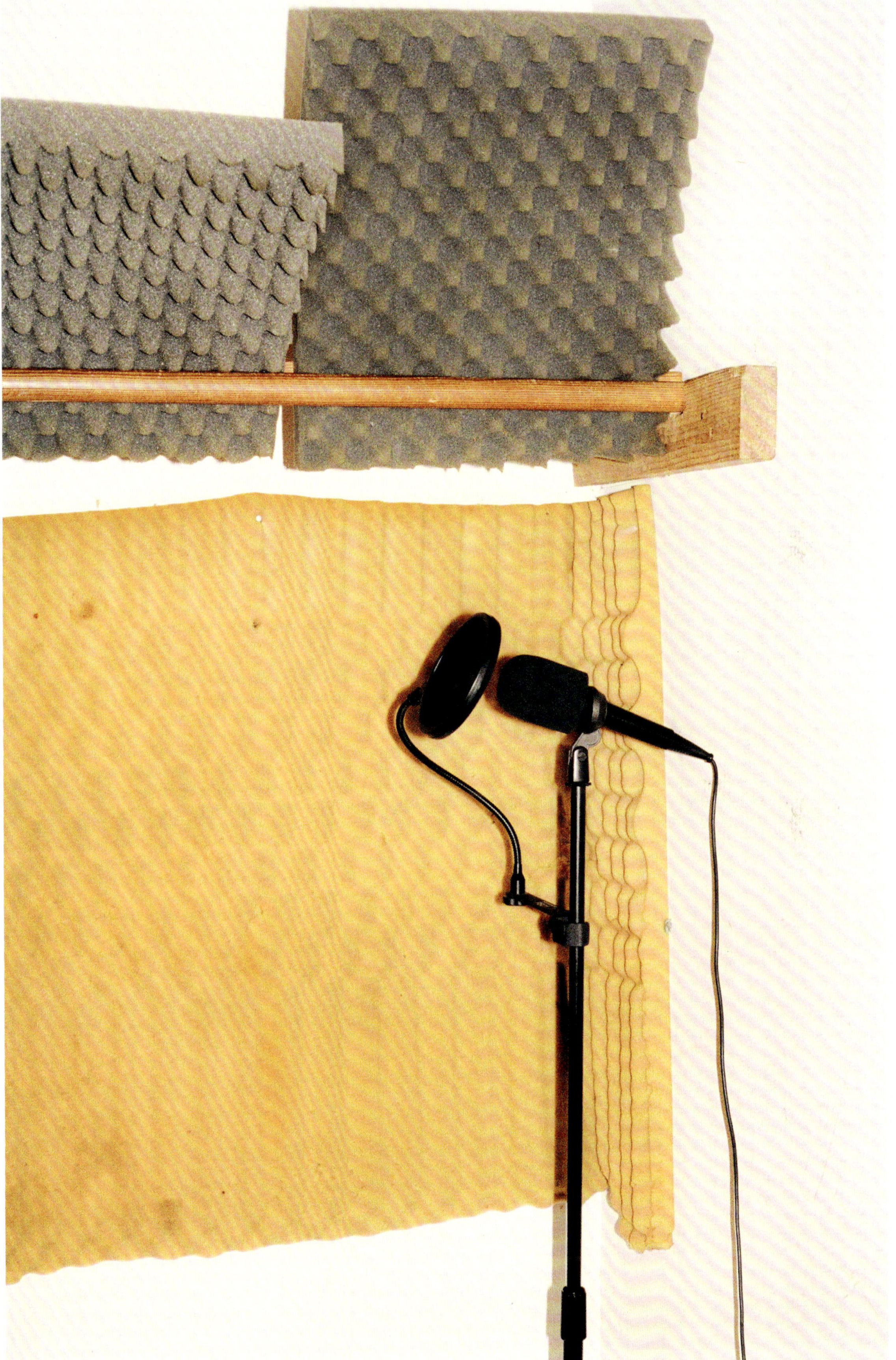

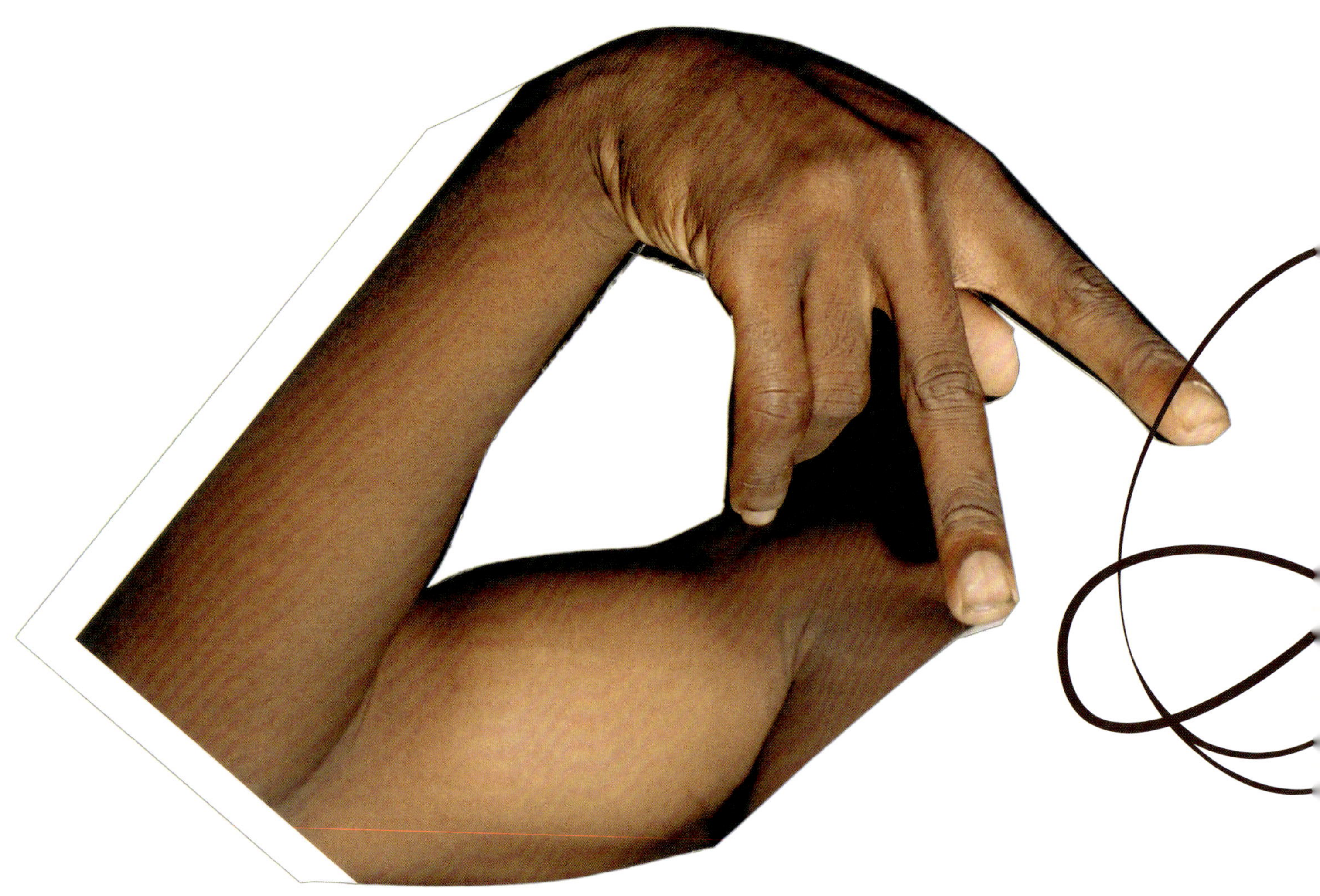

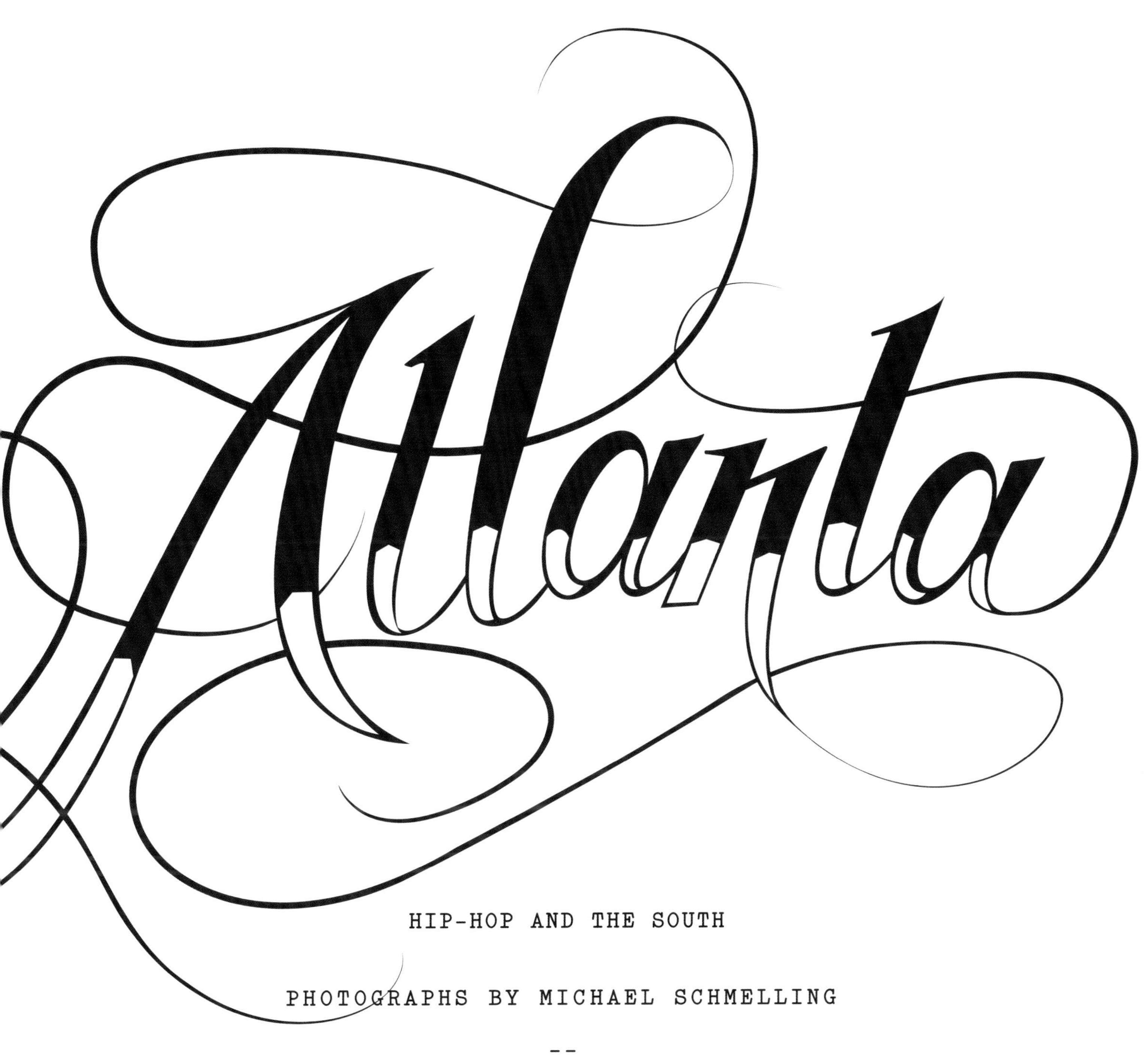

HIP-HOP AND THE SOUTH

PHOTOGRAPHS BY MICHAEL SCHMELLING

--

TEXT BY KELEFA SANNEH

INTERVIEWS BY WILL WELCH

CHRONICLE BOOKS · SAN FRANCISCO

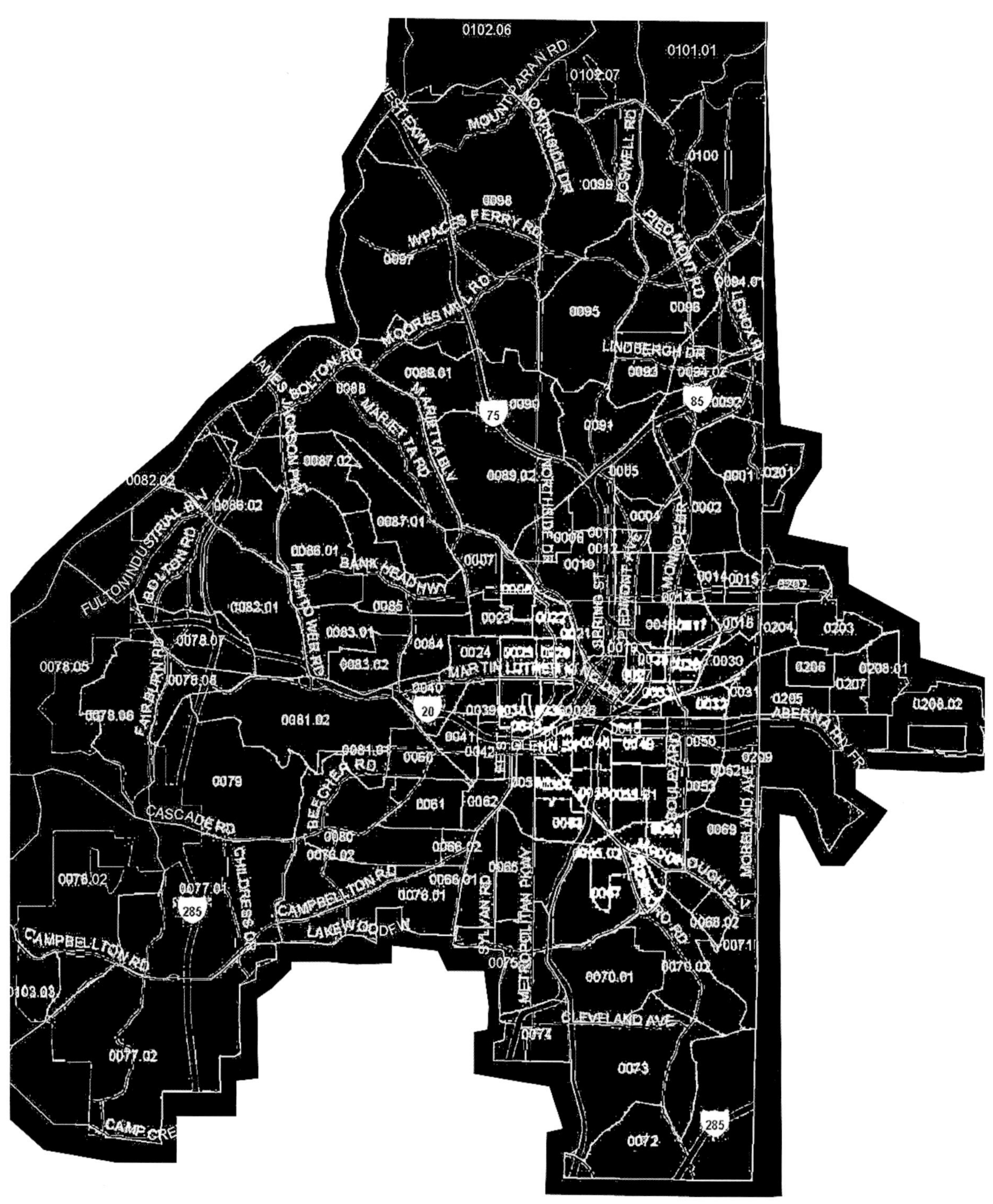

Atlanta, Georgia - 132.4 Square Miles - Population 5.1 Million Approx

campbellton road
old national highway
bankhead
head land and delowe
285   75/85   20 E/W
cleveland avenue
moreland | memorial
jonesboro road
hollywood road
mcdaniel

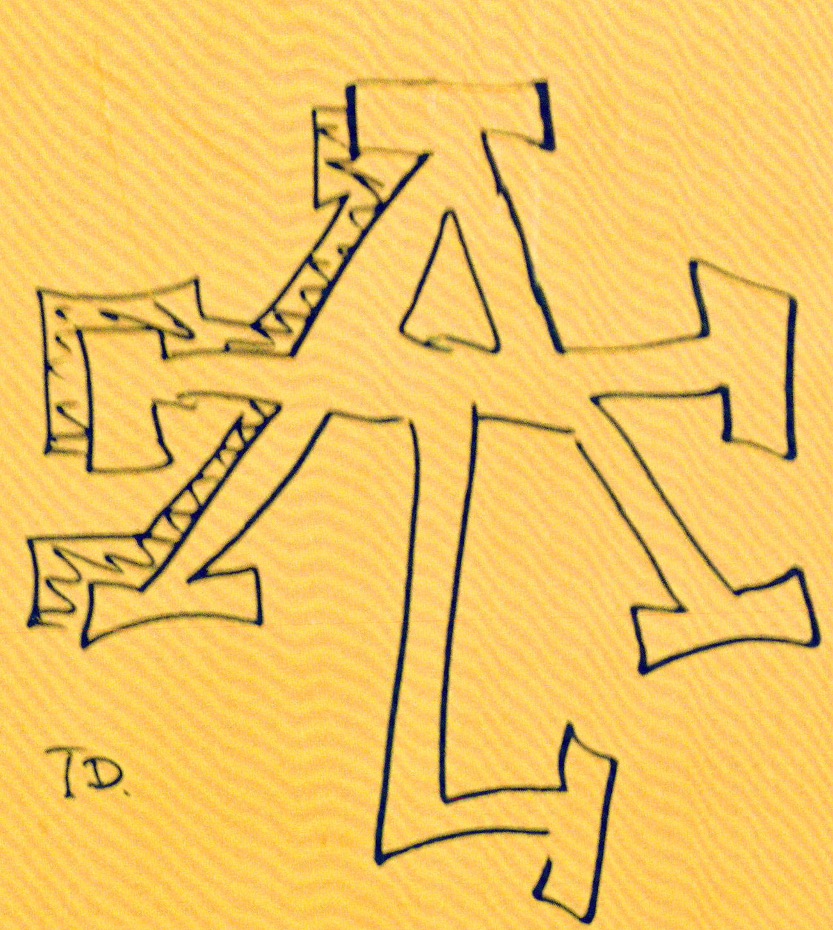

TD.

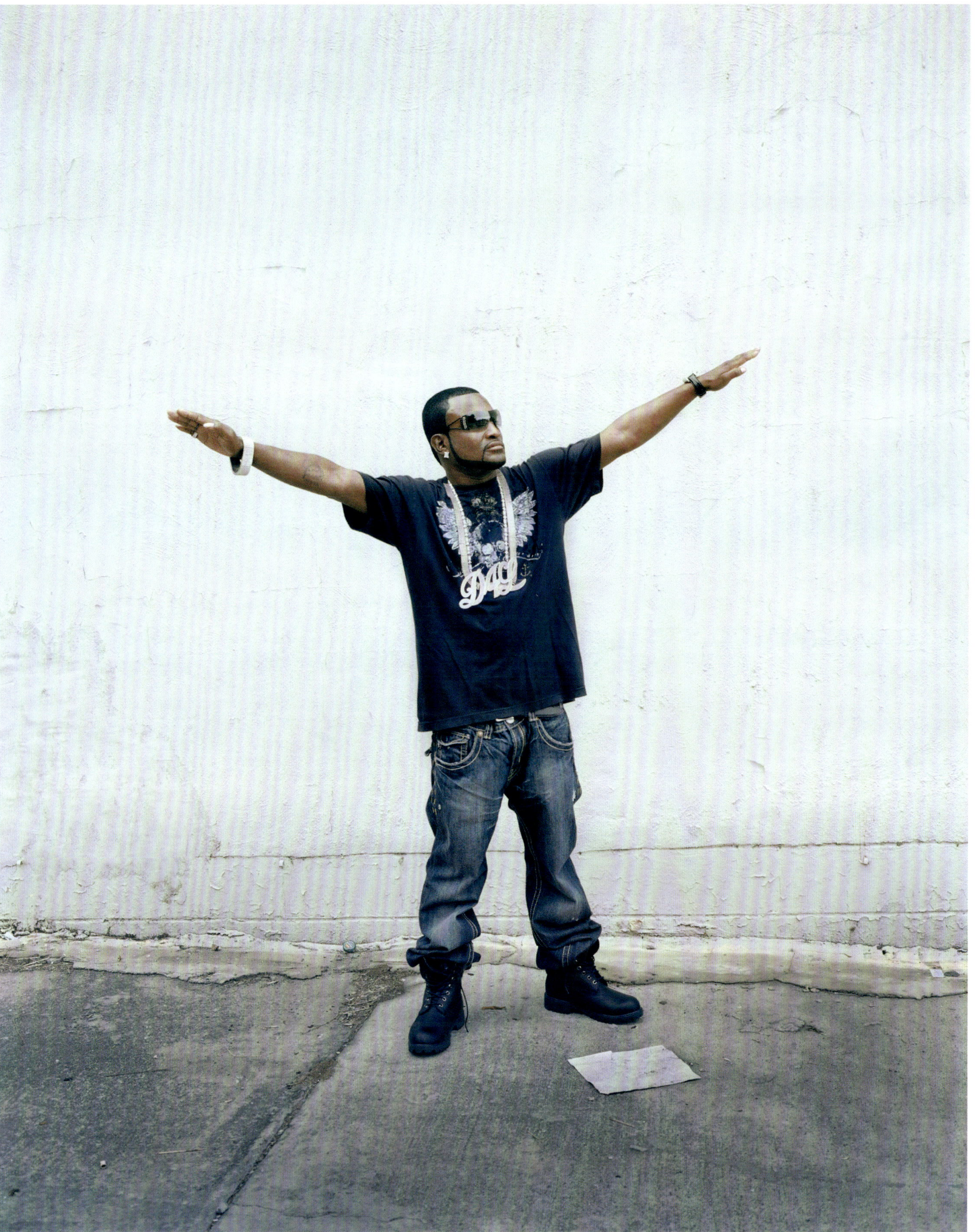

South side stand up
East side stand up
West side stand up
North side stand up
This is from The A

--

LIL TEXAS

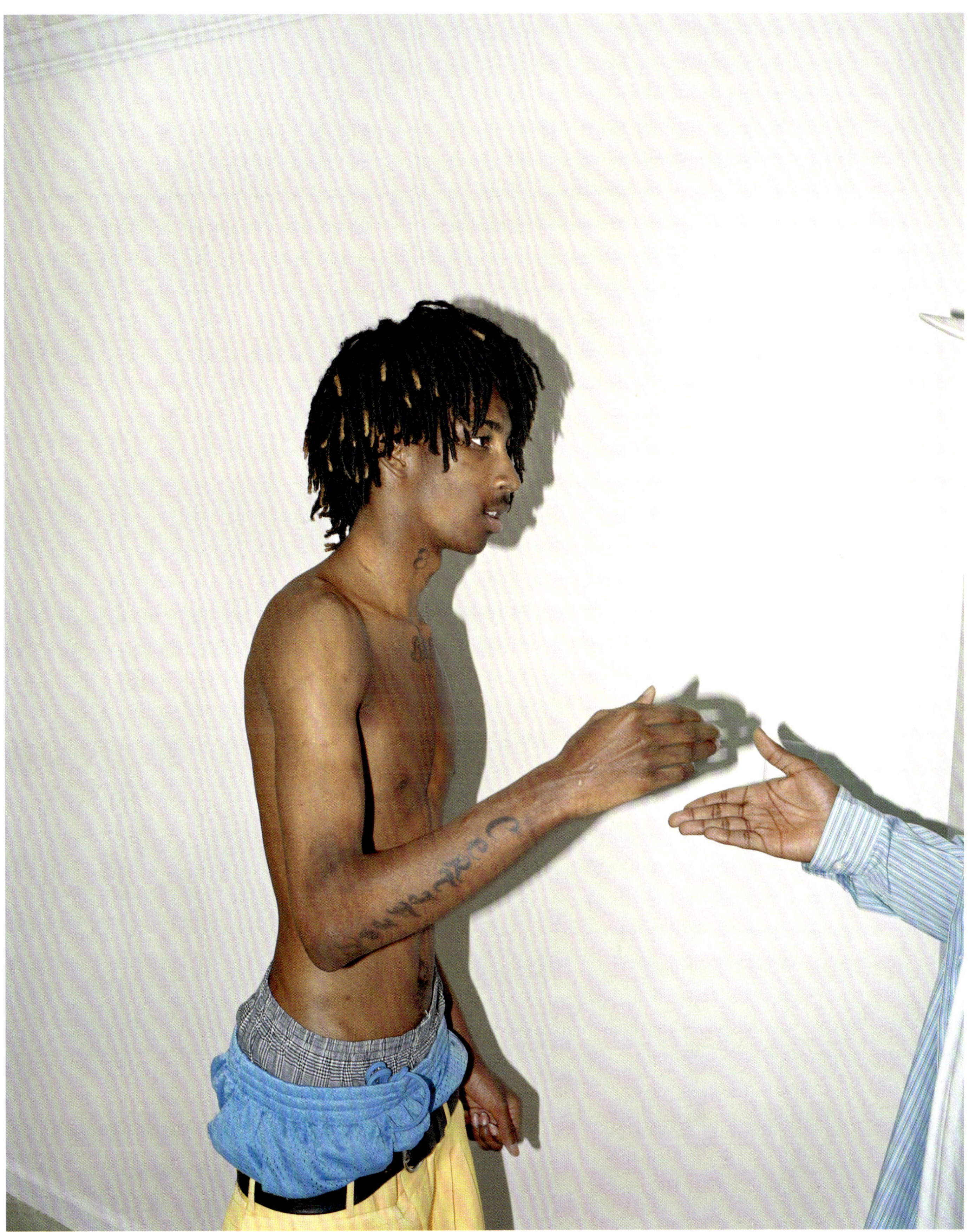

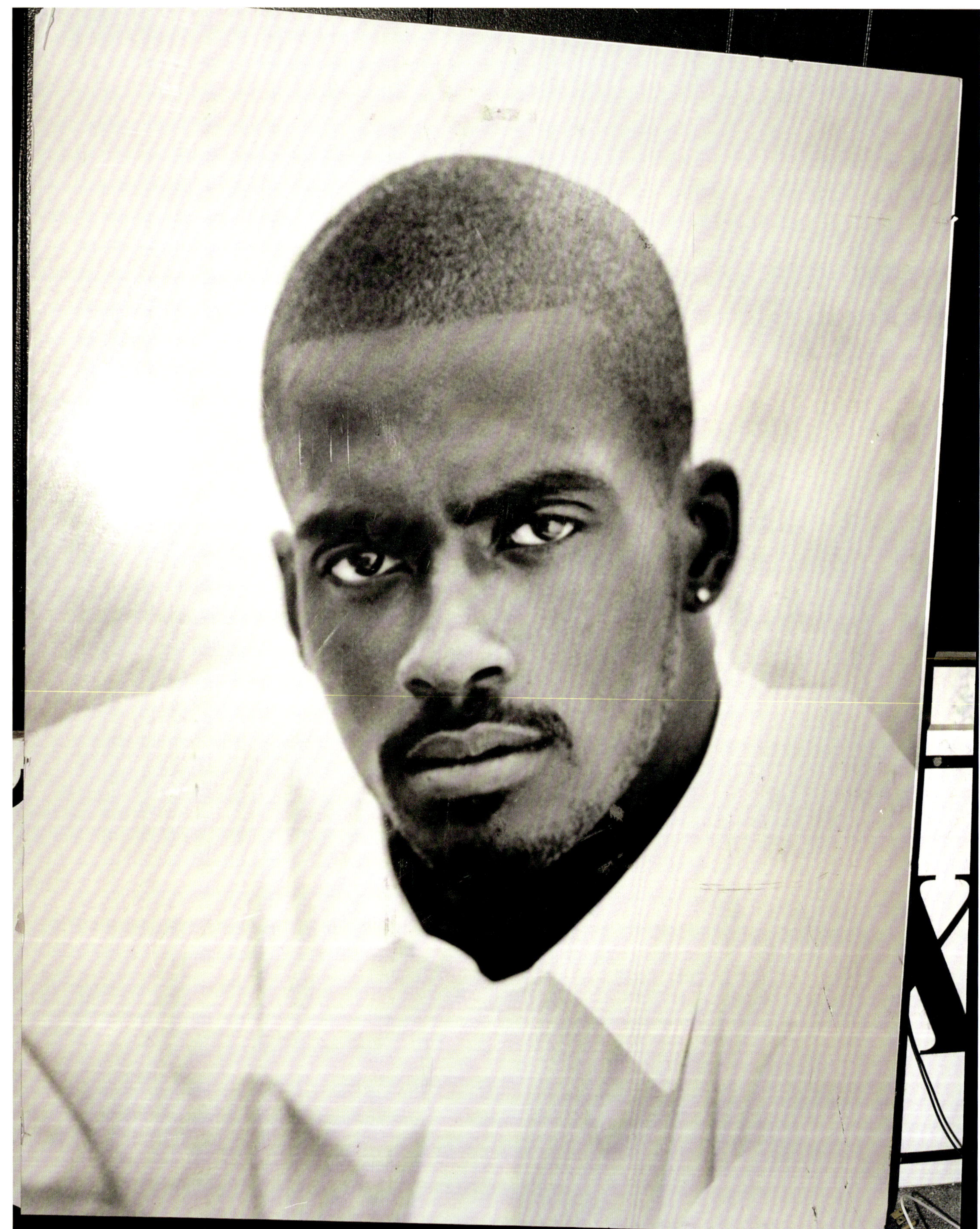

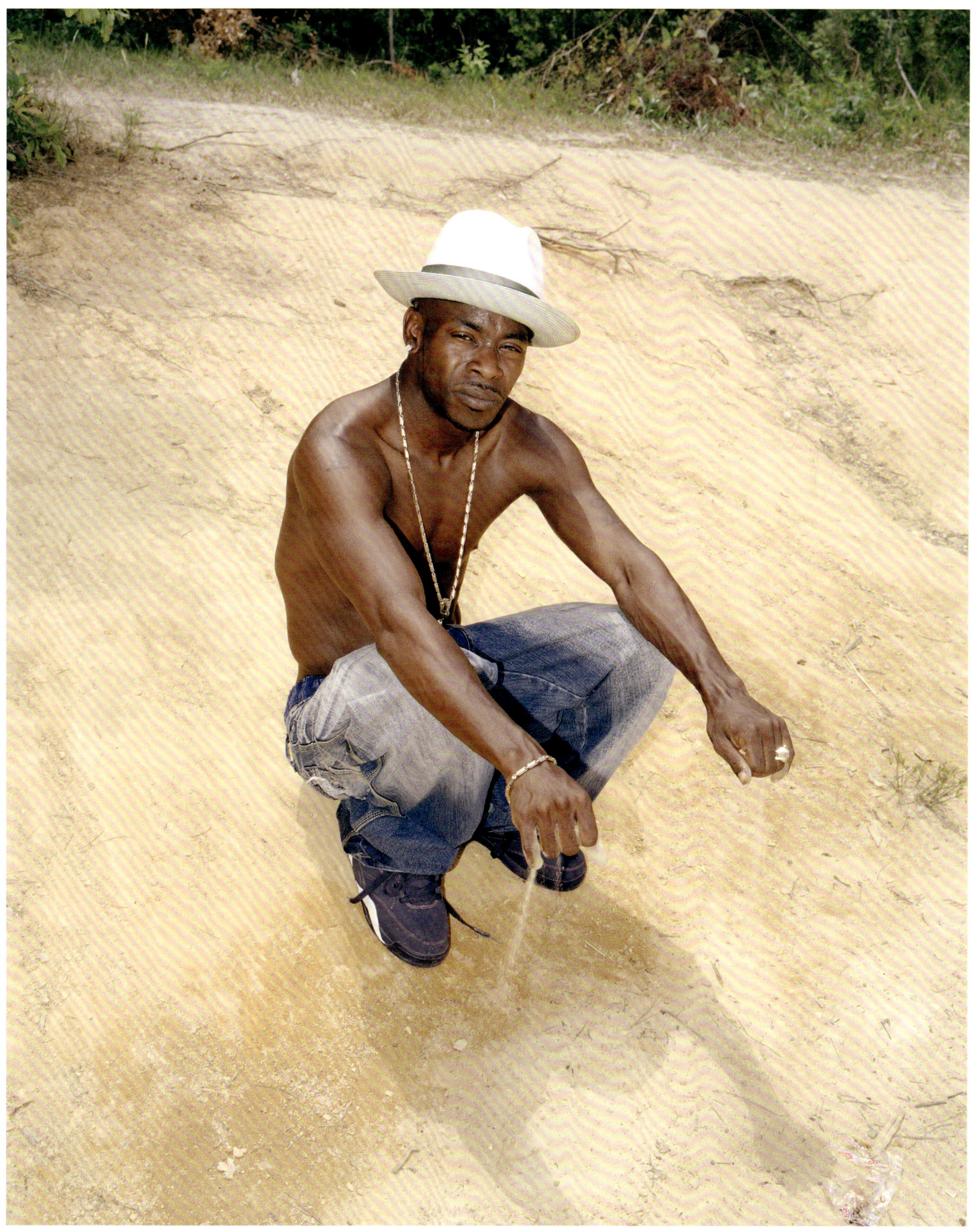

Less than ten minutes into OutKast's 1994 debut album, *Southernplayalisticadillacmuzik,* the rapping stops and a tour guide takes over. "I'd like to welcome you to Atlanta," he says, and he lists some local landmarks: the Hawks, the Braves, the Falcons, and the Georgia Dome—"which, by the way, still flies the Confederate battle flag." The album was its own kind of battle flag: an Atlanta hip-hop manifesto, by turns fond and defiant. André 3000 was just a kid known as Dré back then, and he came out swinging: "I rip shit with pimp shit, I'm slangin' it from the South/Talk bad about the A-Town, I'll bust you in your fuckin' mouth."

But who were they talking to? Who was being welcomed to Atlanta? Who needed to be told not to talk bad about the A-Town? Dré and Big Boi, the two members of OutKast, were proud Atlantans, even though Big Boi grew up in Savannah, and Dré spent some time in Decatur. Their local pride was deeply felt, but it was also deeply self-conscious; they knew (or hoped) that their debut album would be heard all over the country, and they knew that hip-hop listeners from out of town, particularly New Yorkers, sometimes didn't take the South seriously. New York was hip-hop's historic birthplace, and the city's taste-makers caricatured Southern hip-hop as simplistic, crude, lowbrow, insubstantial—which is pretty much what the music industry elite once said about New York hip-hop.

To fight back, Dré and Big Boi dug in, filling their intricate rhymes with references to local streets, local traditions, even the local subway system. (Hardly anyone besides Dré has ever rapped about riding the MARTA.) The third OutKast album, *Aquemini,* was released in 1998; by then, Dré and Big Boi were rap stars, and hip-hop's center of gravity was moving south. And yet the album ended on another note of defiance: a snippet from the 1995 Source Awards, held in New York, during which OutKast was named best new

artist and was nearly booed off the stage. During his brief speech, Dré seems close to losing his composure. "The South got something to say," he shouts—as if any reasonable person could disagree.

The Atlanta rappers who followed in OutKast's wake didn't have to struggle so mightily against geographic chauvinism, though plenty of chauvinism remained. In the '00s, Ludacris and T.I. and Young Jeezy became mainstream stars, and it never seemed to occur to them that the South might not have something to say. Meanwhile, Atlanta's up and coming rappers, like many of the ones photographed in this book, made music that was local in a different sense. Instead of addressing outsiders, the way OutKast did, these kids made music for their fellow Atlantans, without apology or explanation, seemingly oblivious to nonlocal listeners, who might not know the difference between "Zone 4" and "Zone 6" (they're police jurisdictions attached to different groups of neighborhoods), or what "white-boy swag" means (it's complicated). In other words, these are kids are secure in the knowledge that Atlanta is the center of the hip-hop universe. Outsiders are welcome—but not, of course, necessary.

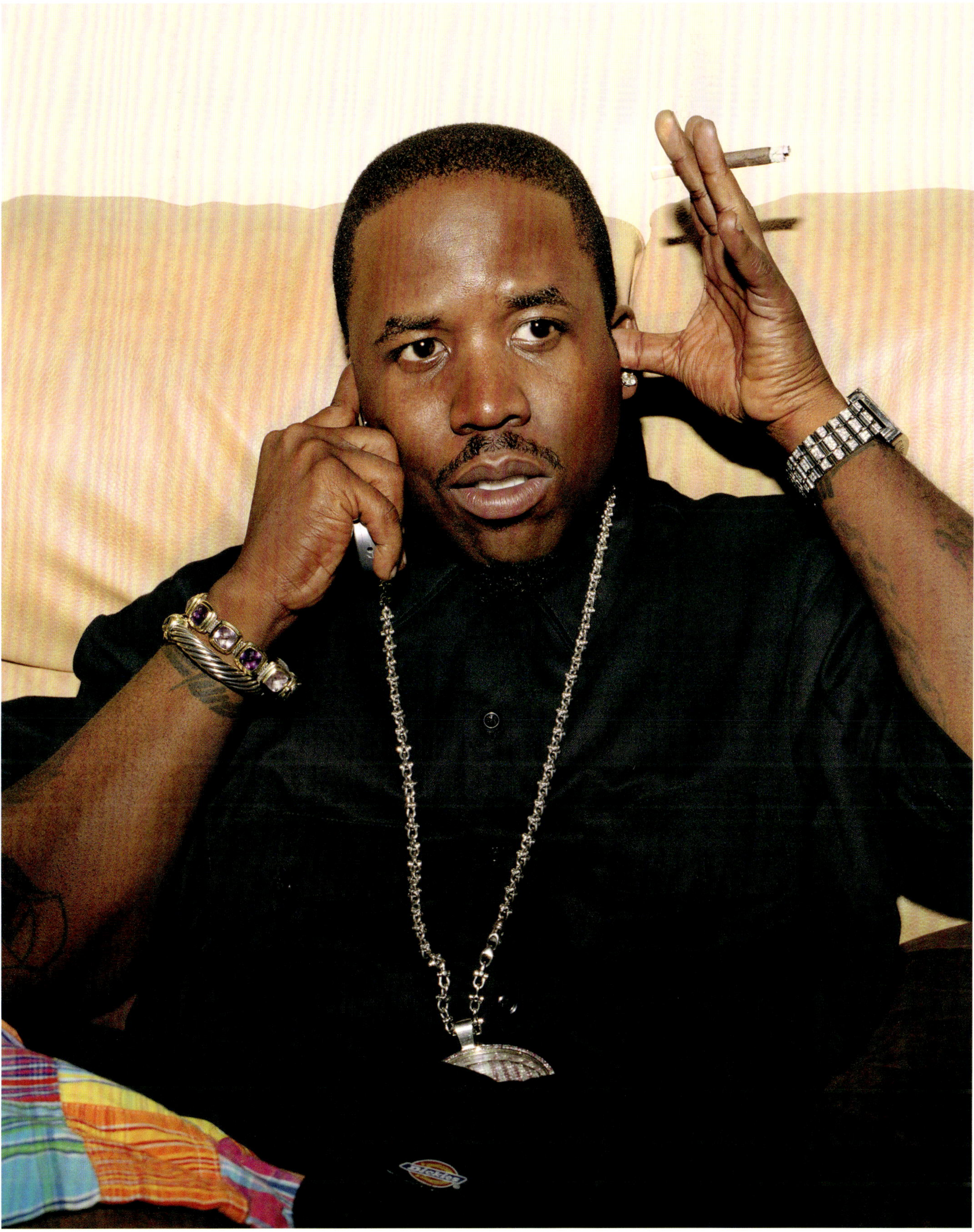

Outkast

<u>A</u>quemini

In-Stores September 29th

Includes

Skew It On The Bar - B

featuring Raekwon

Rosa Parks (Hush That Fuss)

GREG STREET TOP 8@8

8) Break up - Mario Gucci

7) Halle Berry - Hurrican Chris

6) Plenty Money - Plies

5) Every Girl - Young Money

4) DADDY - Twista

3) What's up - Rich Kids

2) EGO - Beyonce (Remix)

1) Best I Ever HAD - Drake

DATE: 7/1/09

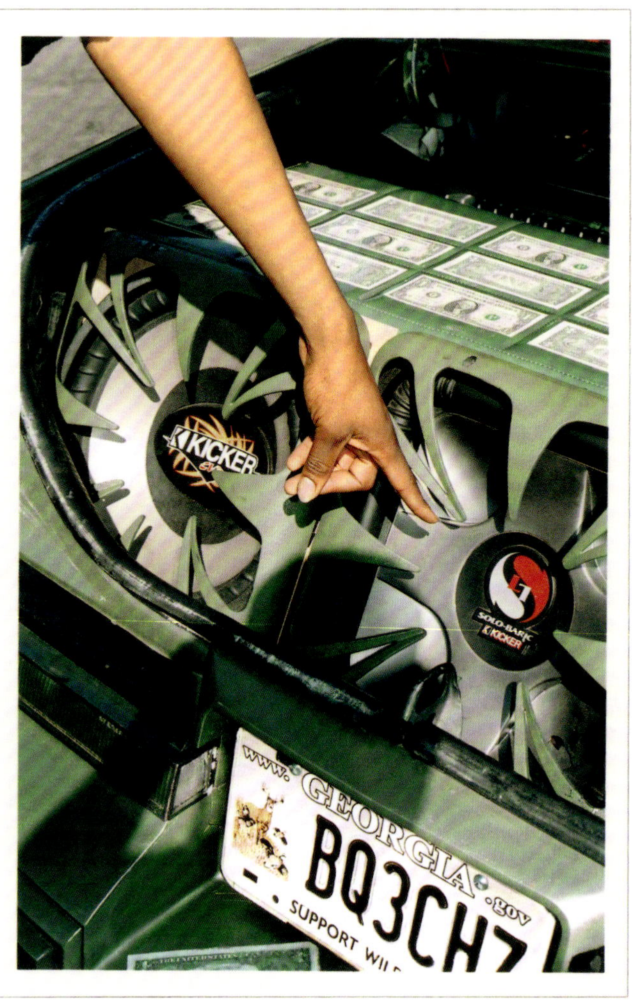

KICKER
SOLO-BARIC
KICKER
www. GEORGIA .gov
BQ3CH7
SUPPORT WILD

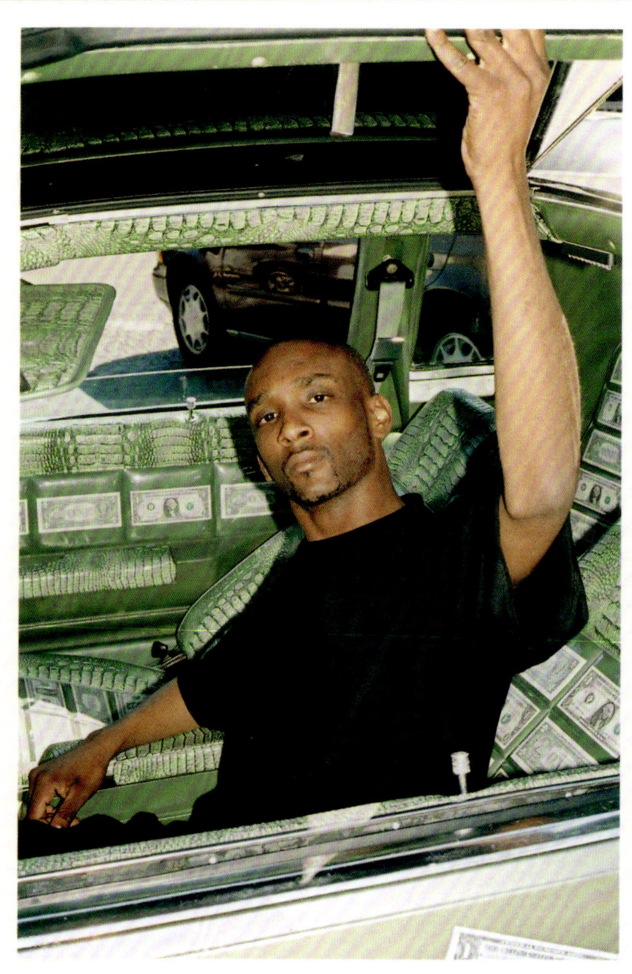

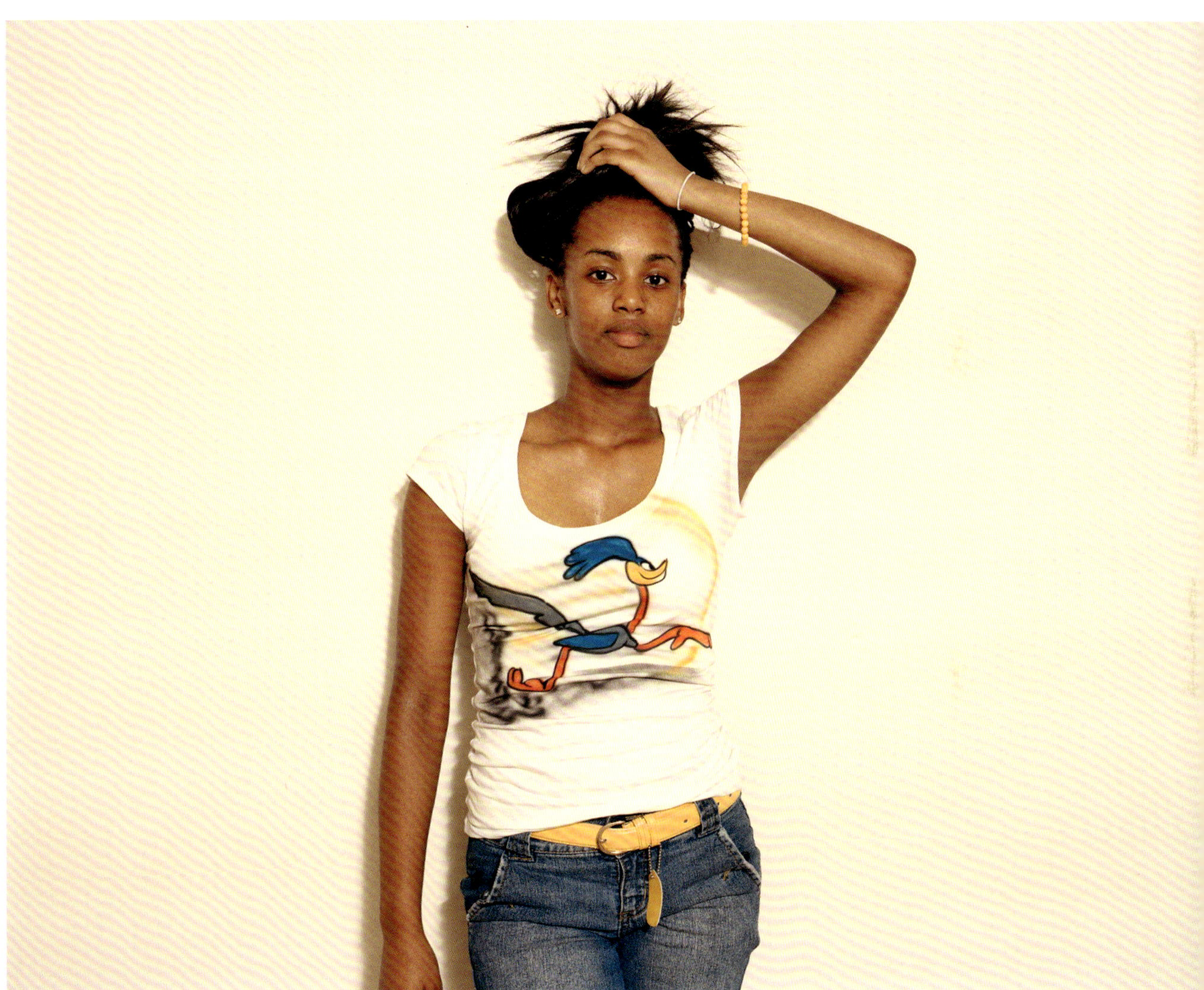

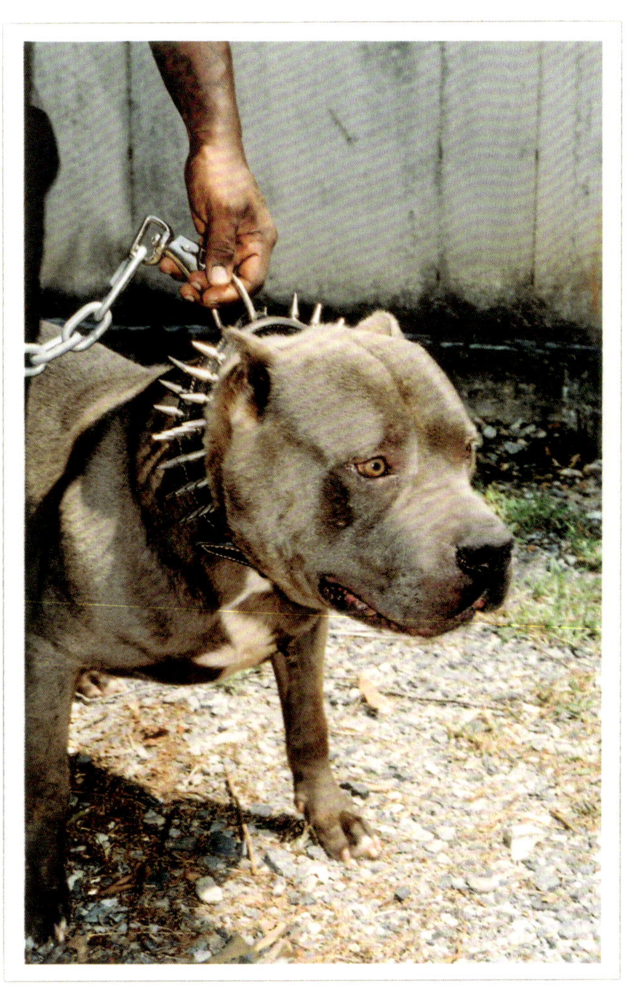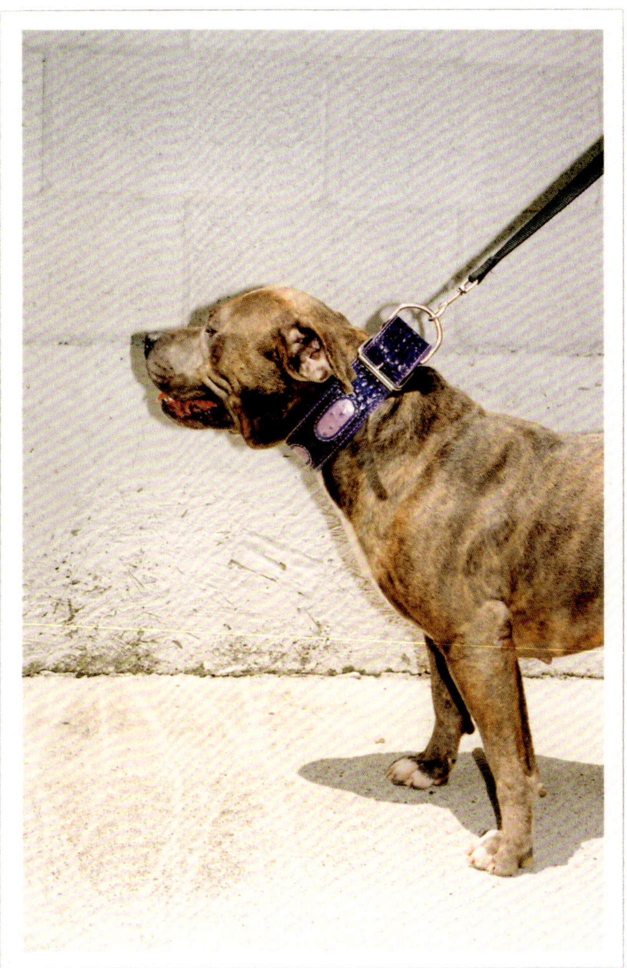

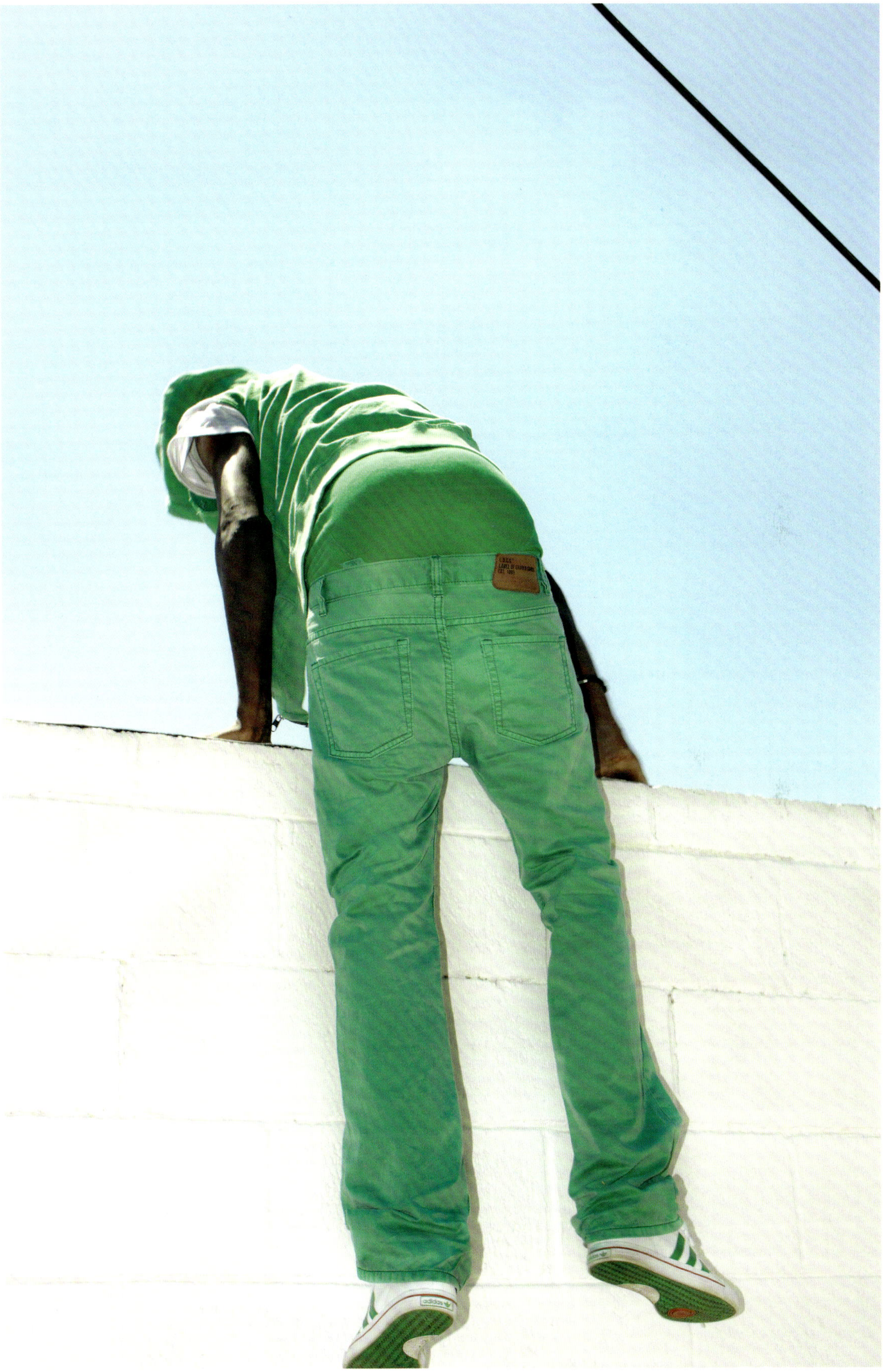

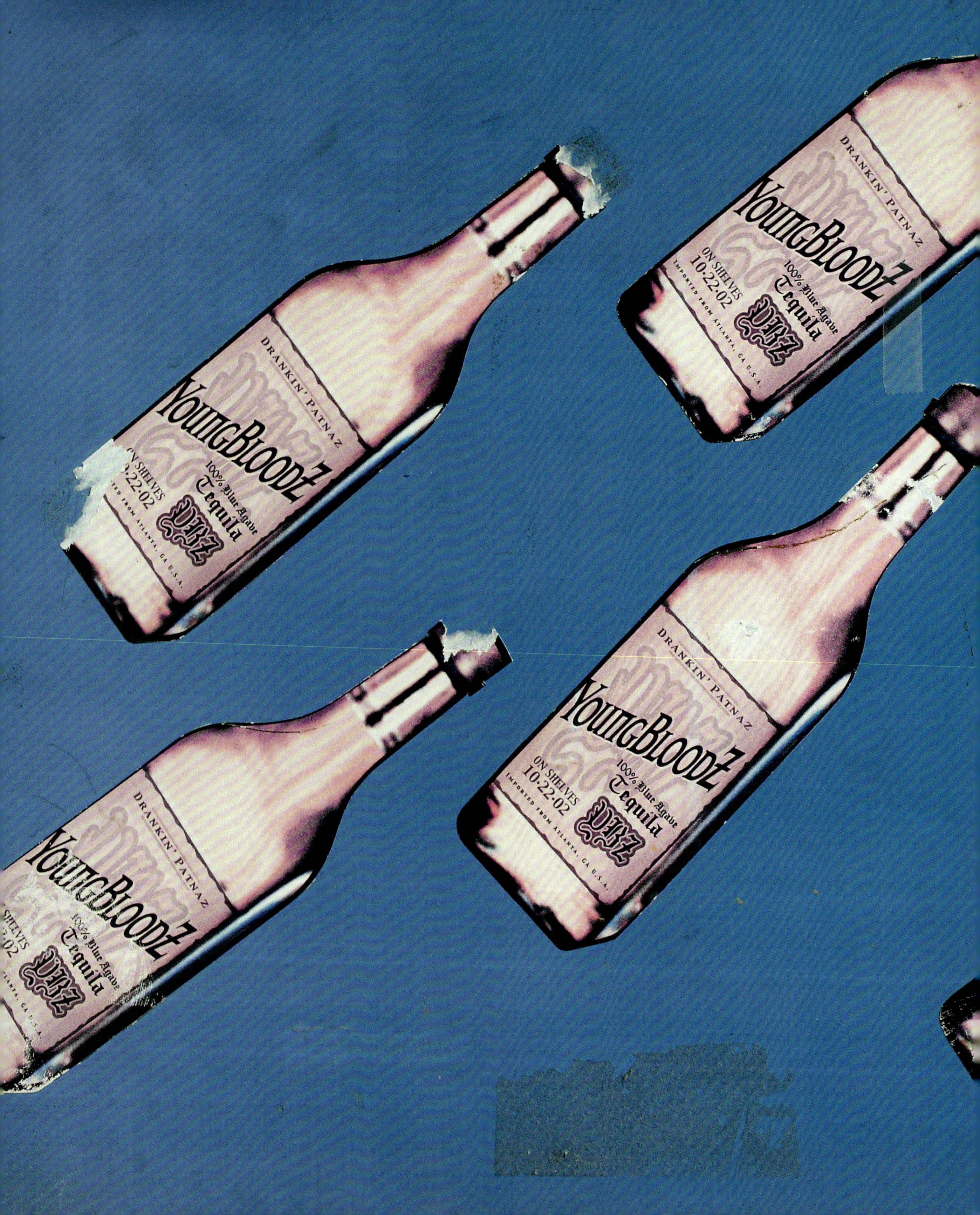

DRANKIN' PATNAZ
YoungBloodZ
100% Blue Agave
Tequila
YBZ
ON SHELVES
10.22.02
IMPORTED FROM ATLANTA, CA U.S.A.

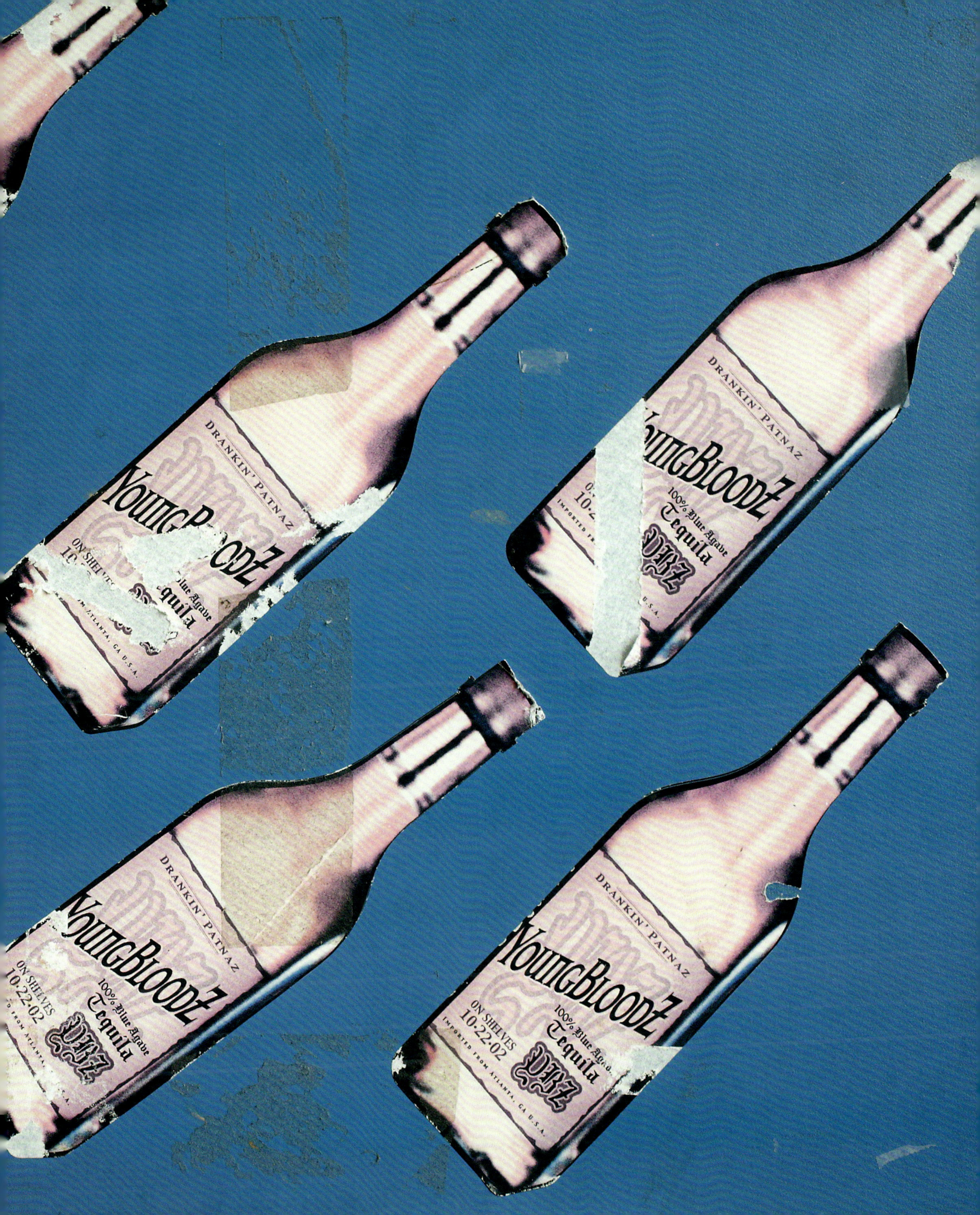

DRANKIN' PATNAZ
YoungBloodZ
100% Blue Agave
Tequila
DRBZ
ON SHELVES
10·22·02
IMPORTED FROM ATLANTA, GA U.S.A.

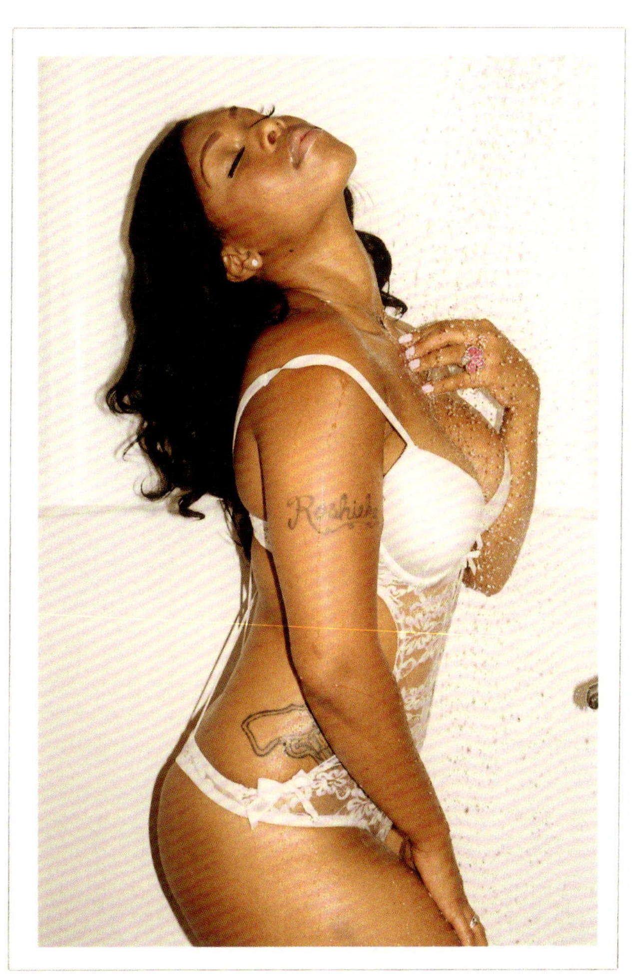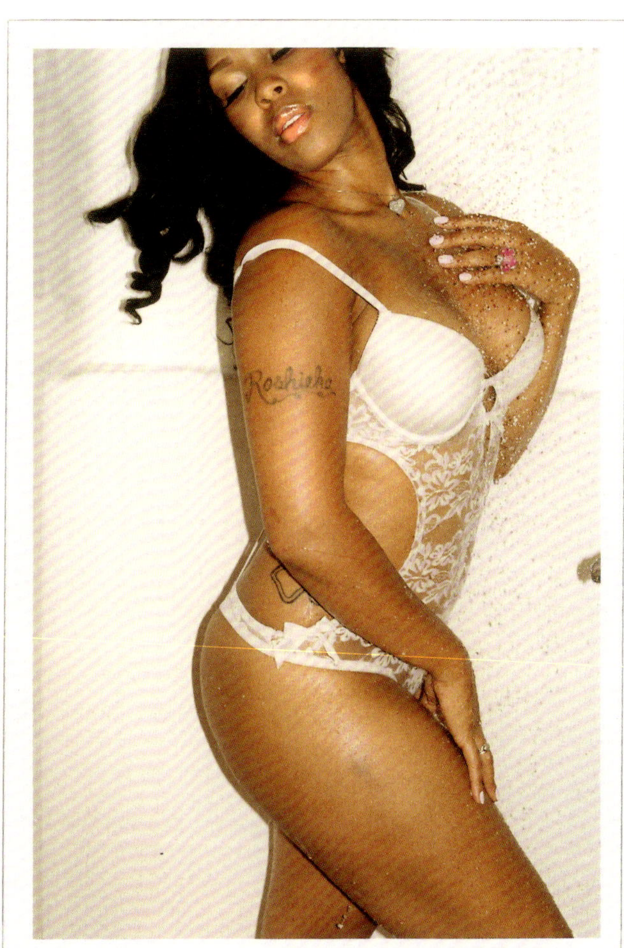

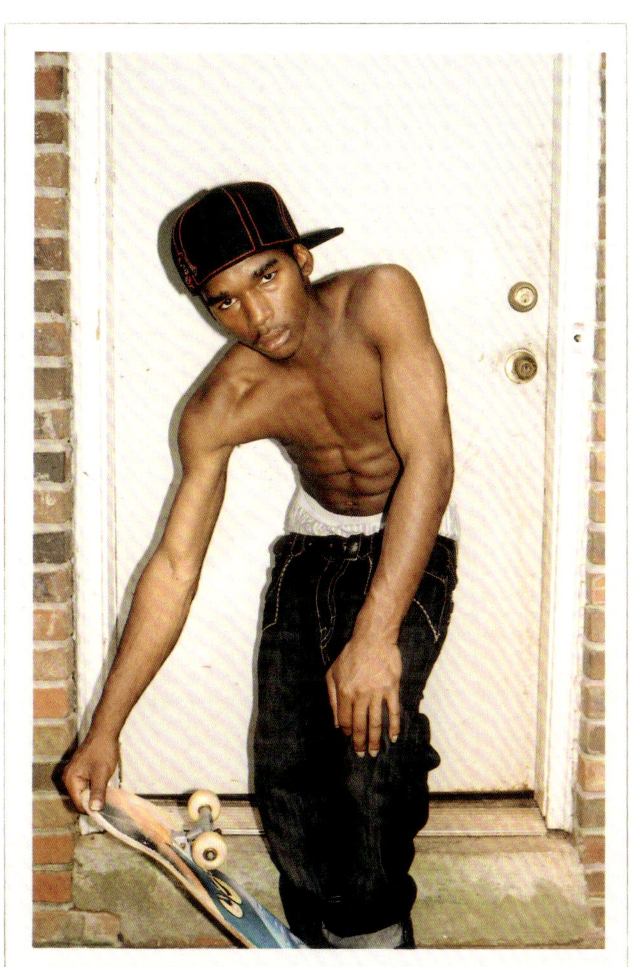
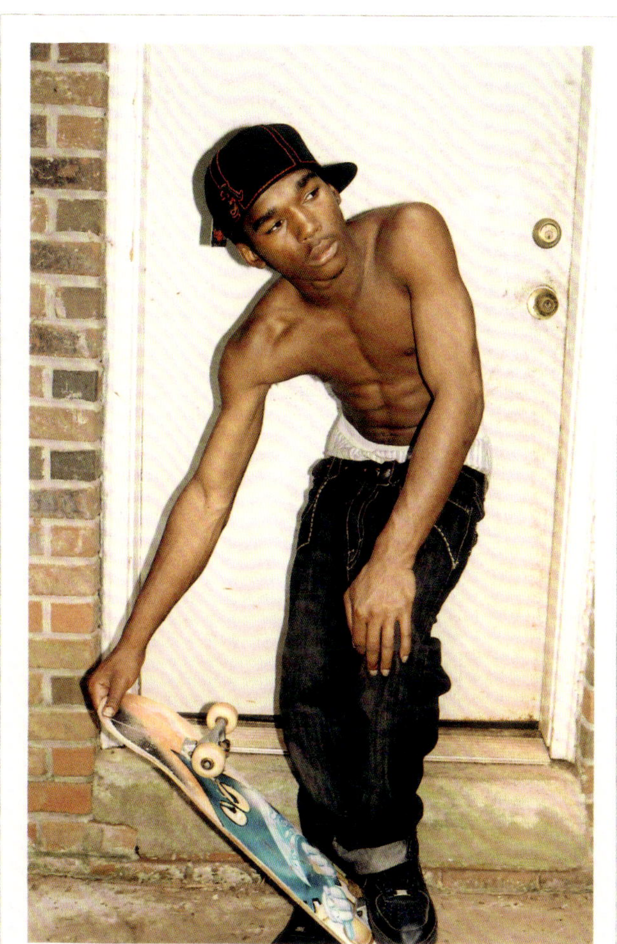

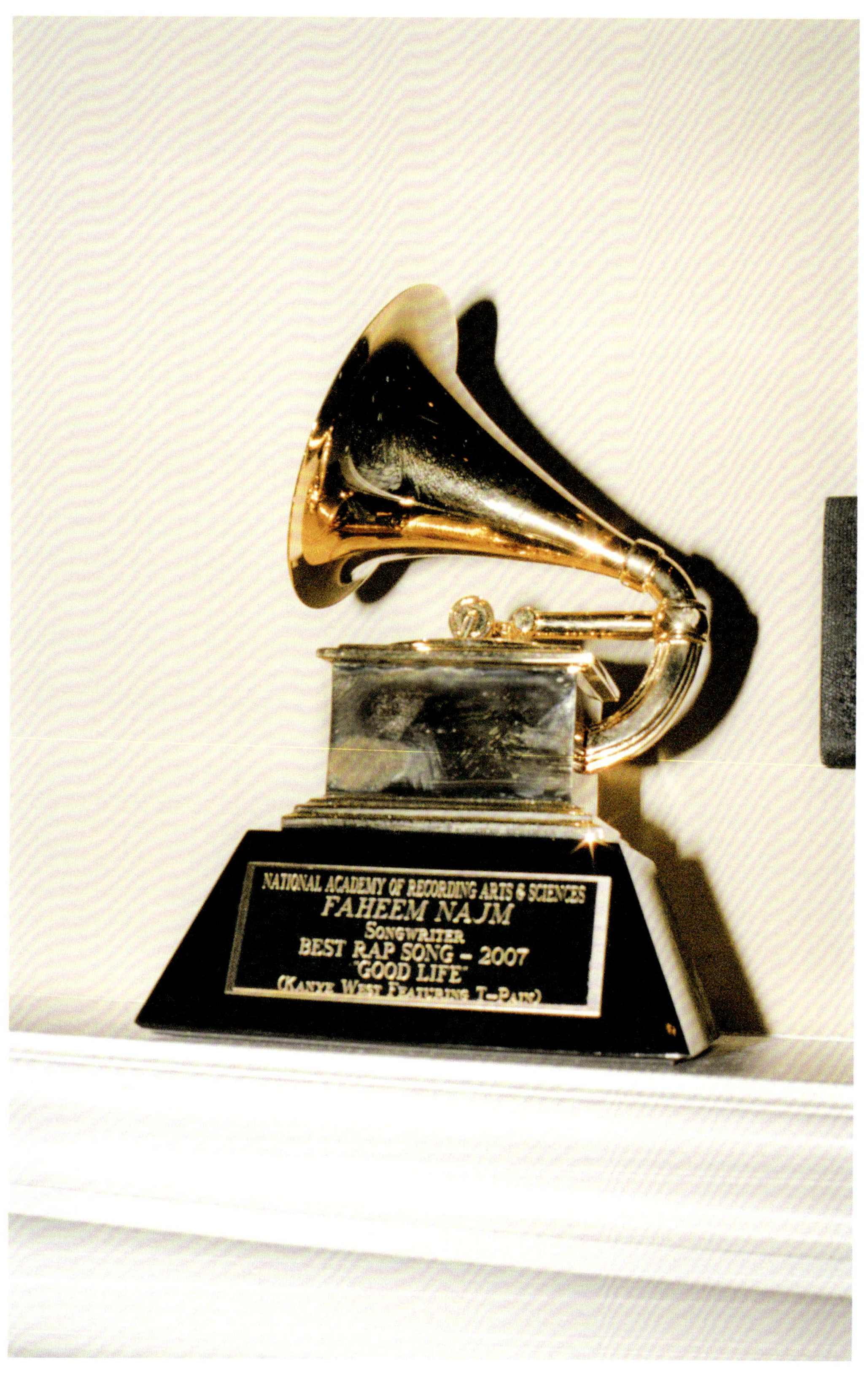

NATIONAL ACADEMY OF RECORDING ARTS & SCIENCES
FAHEEM NAJM
Songwriter
BEST RAP SONG – 2007
"GOOD LIFE"
(KANYE WEST FEATURING T-PAIN)

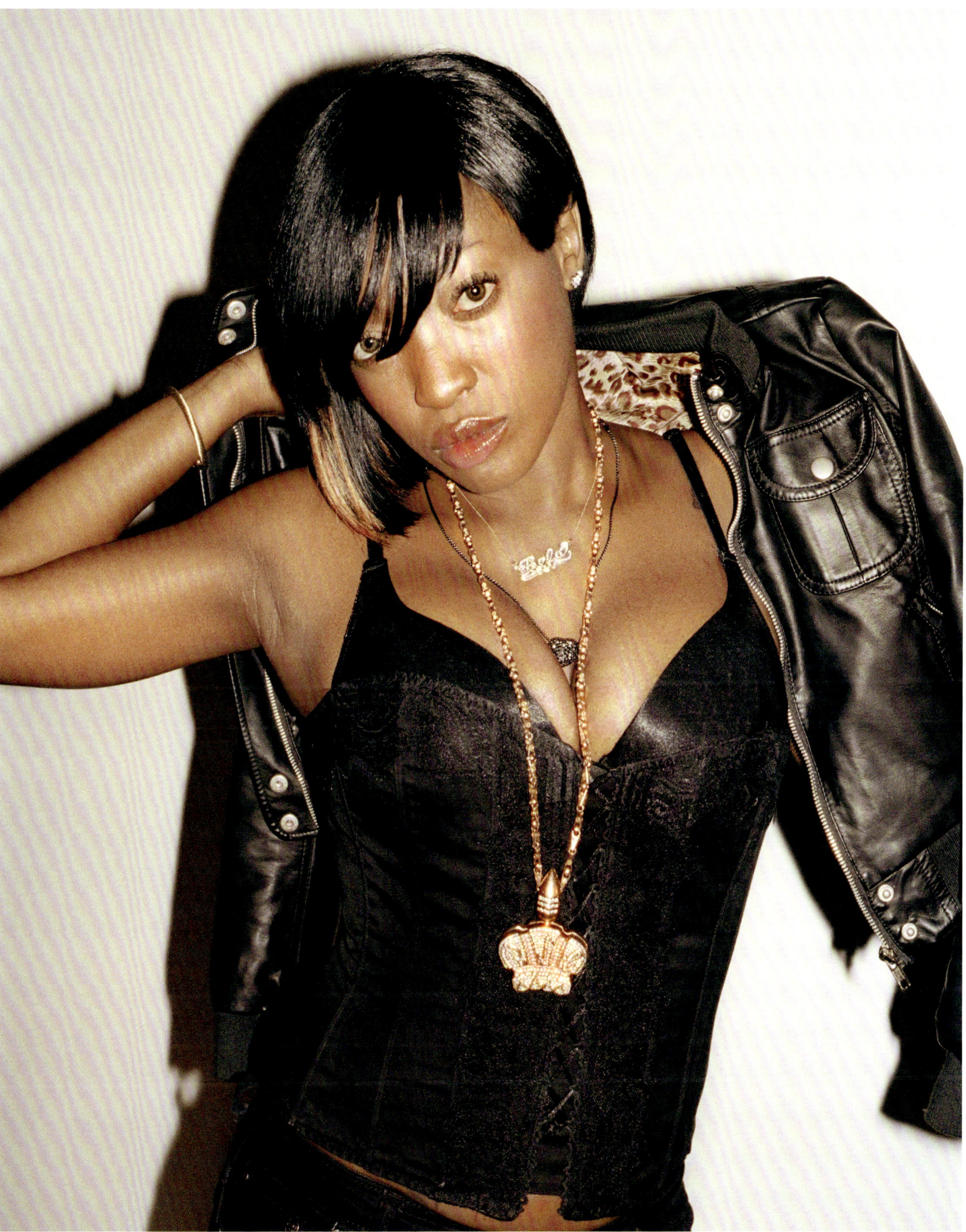

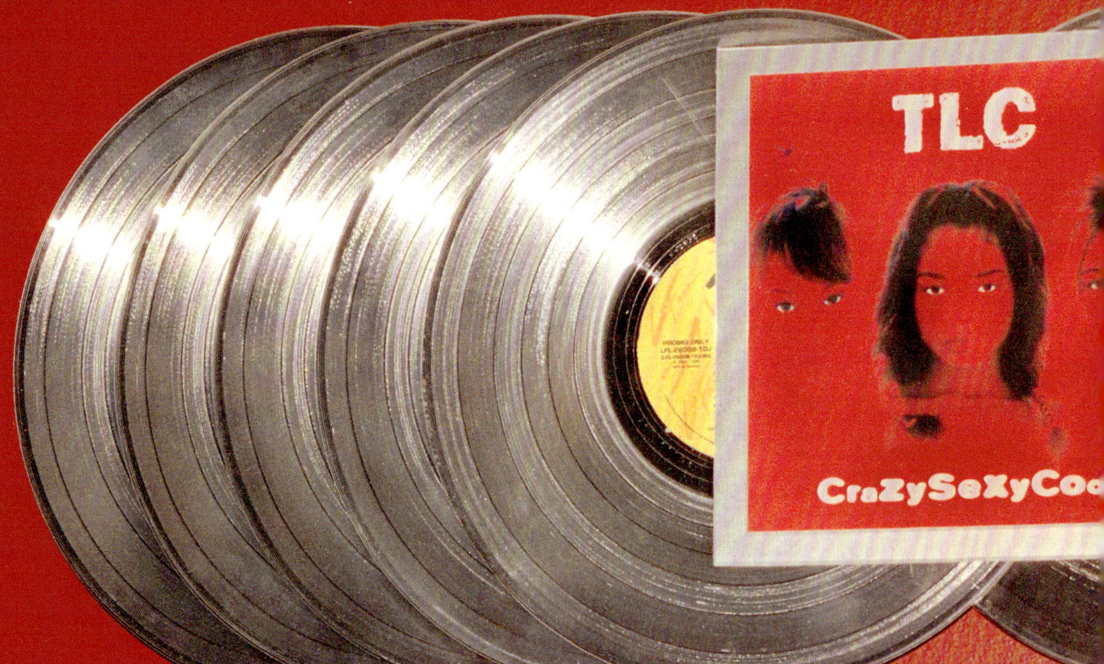
TLC
CraZySeXyCoo
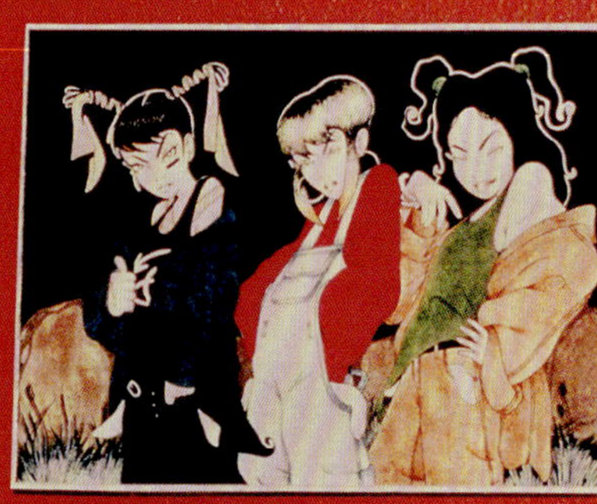
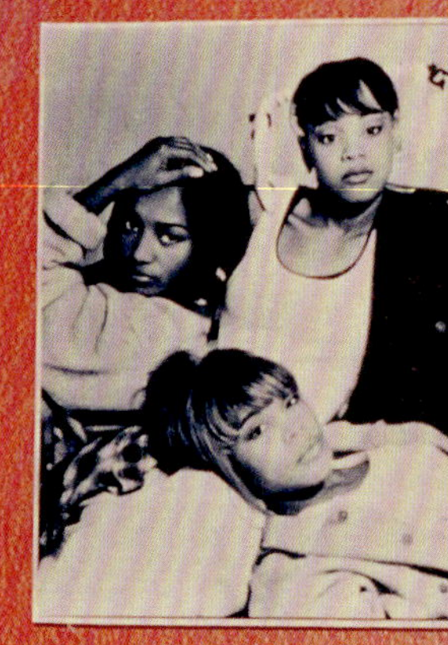
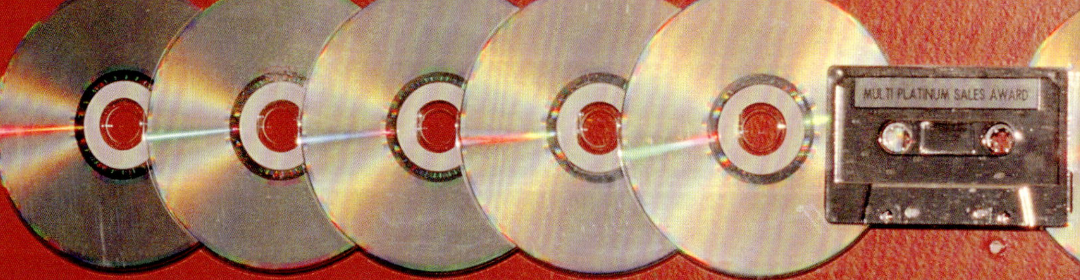
MULTI PLATINUM SALES AWARD
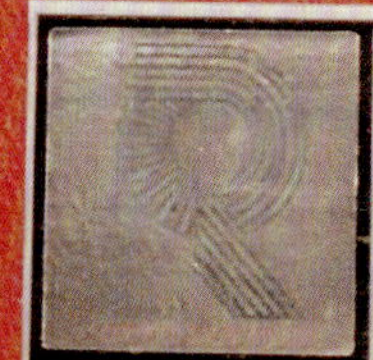
PRESENTED TO
RAYMON MURR
TO COMMEMORATE THE SALE
10,000,000 COPIES O
LAFACE RECORD
ALBUM, CASSETTE AN
"CRAZYSEXYCOO

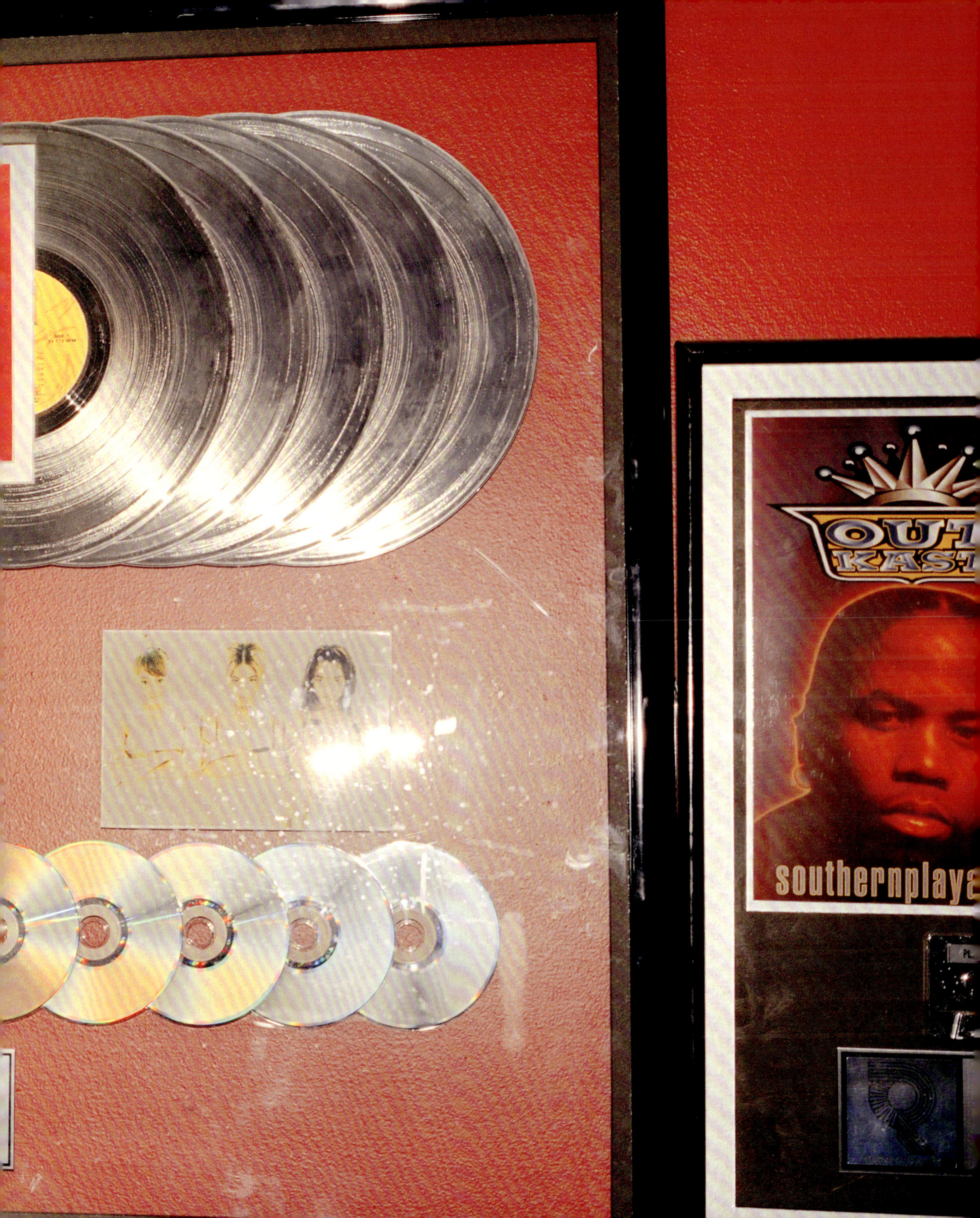

OUT
KAS
southernplaya
PL

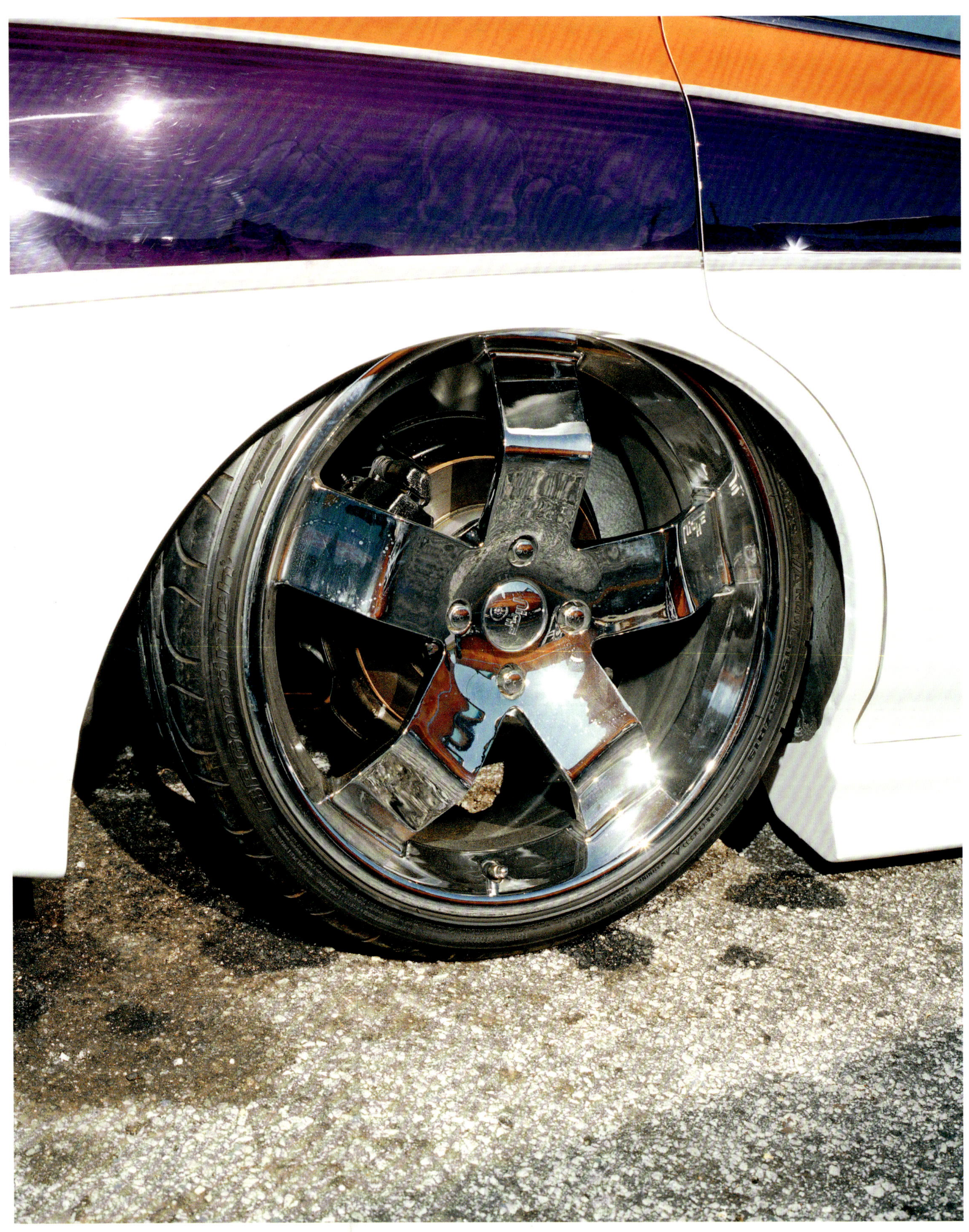

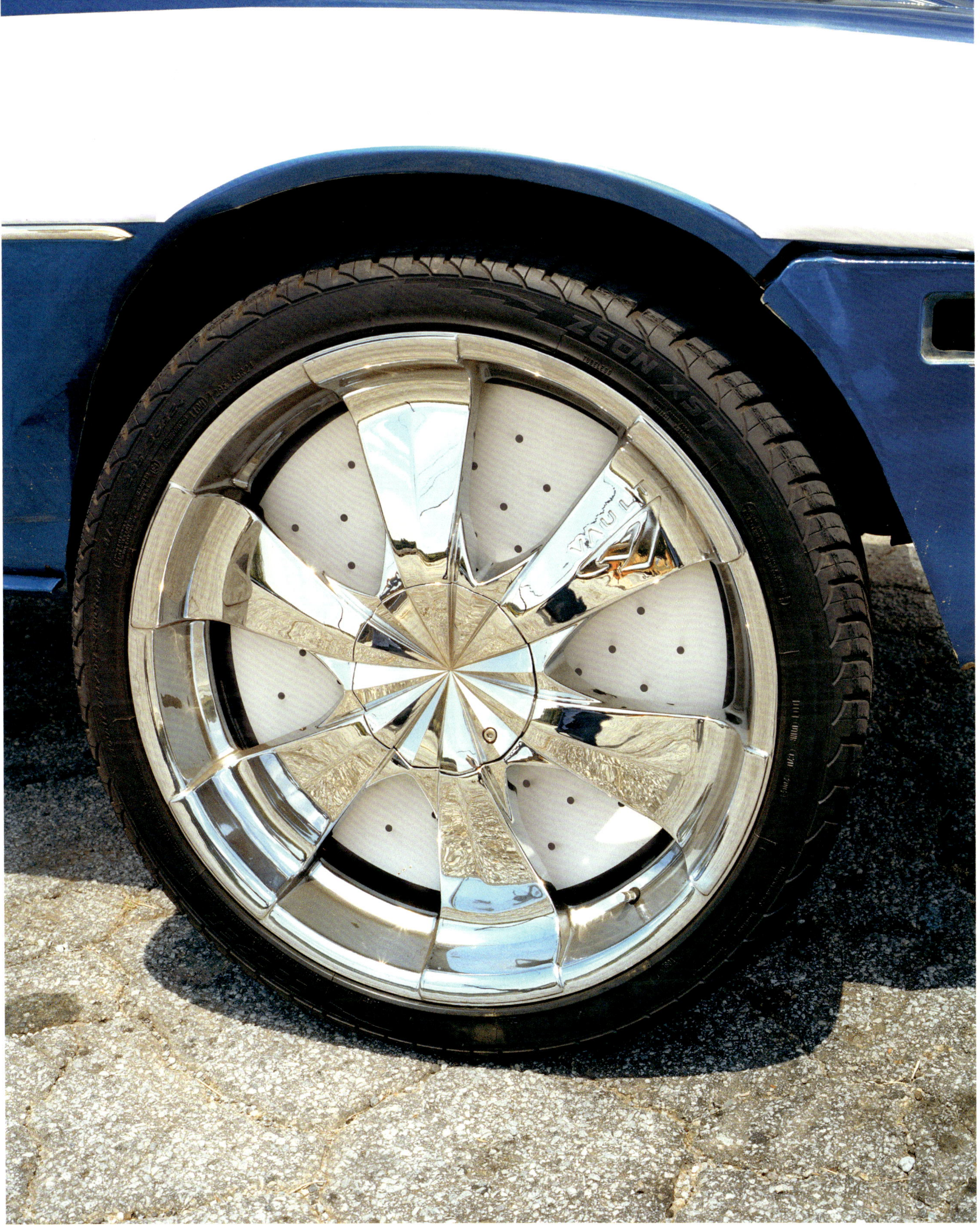

ZEON XST
VAU LT

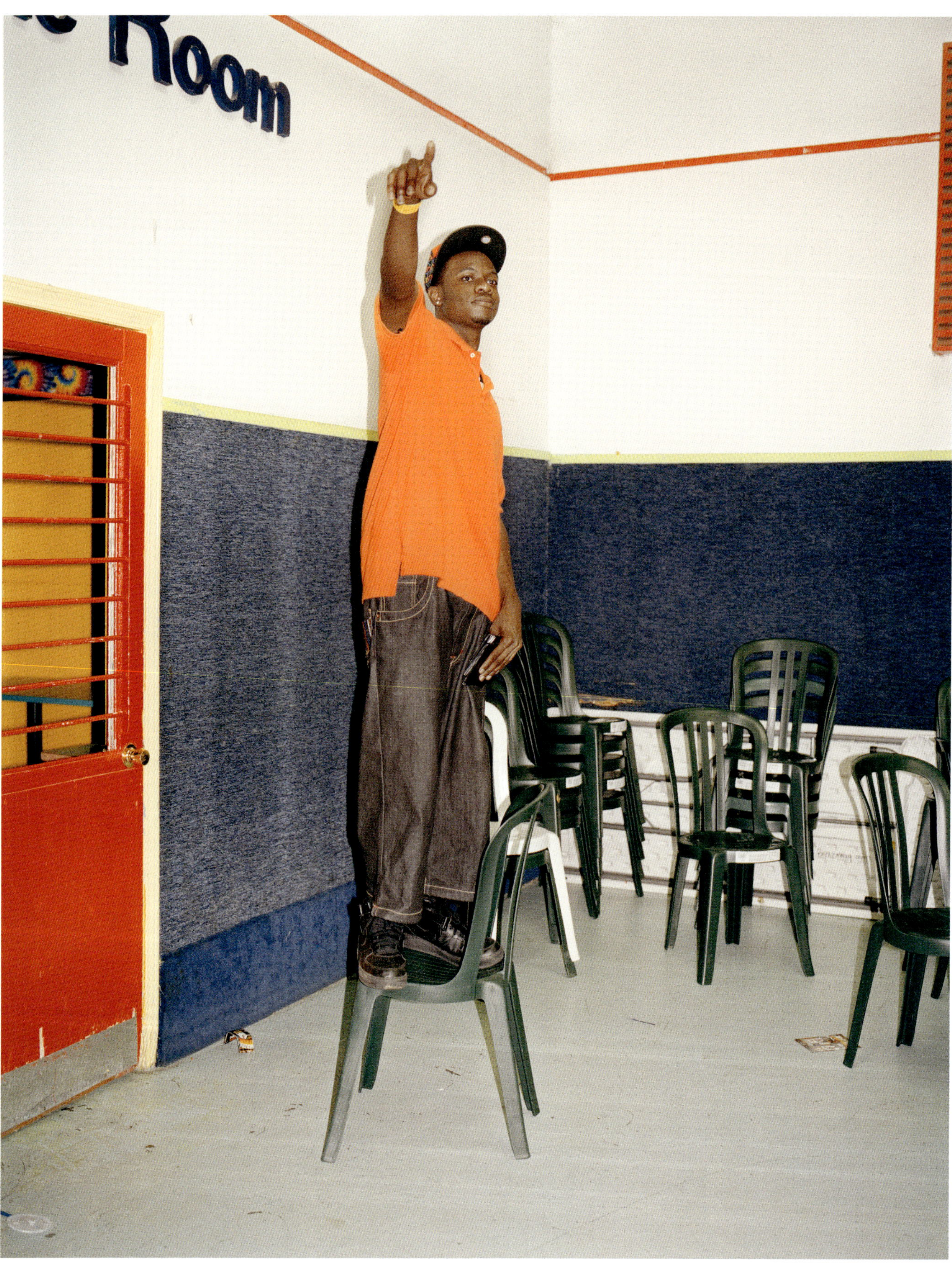
Room

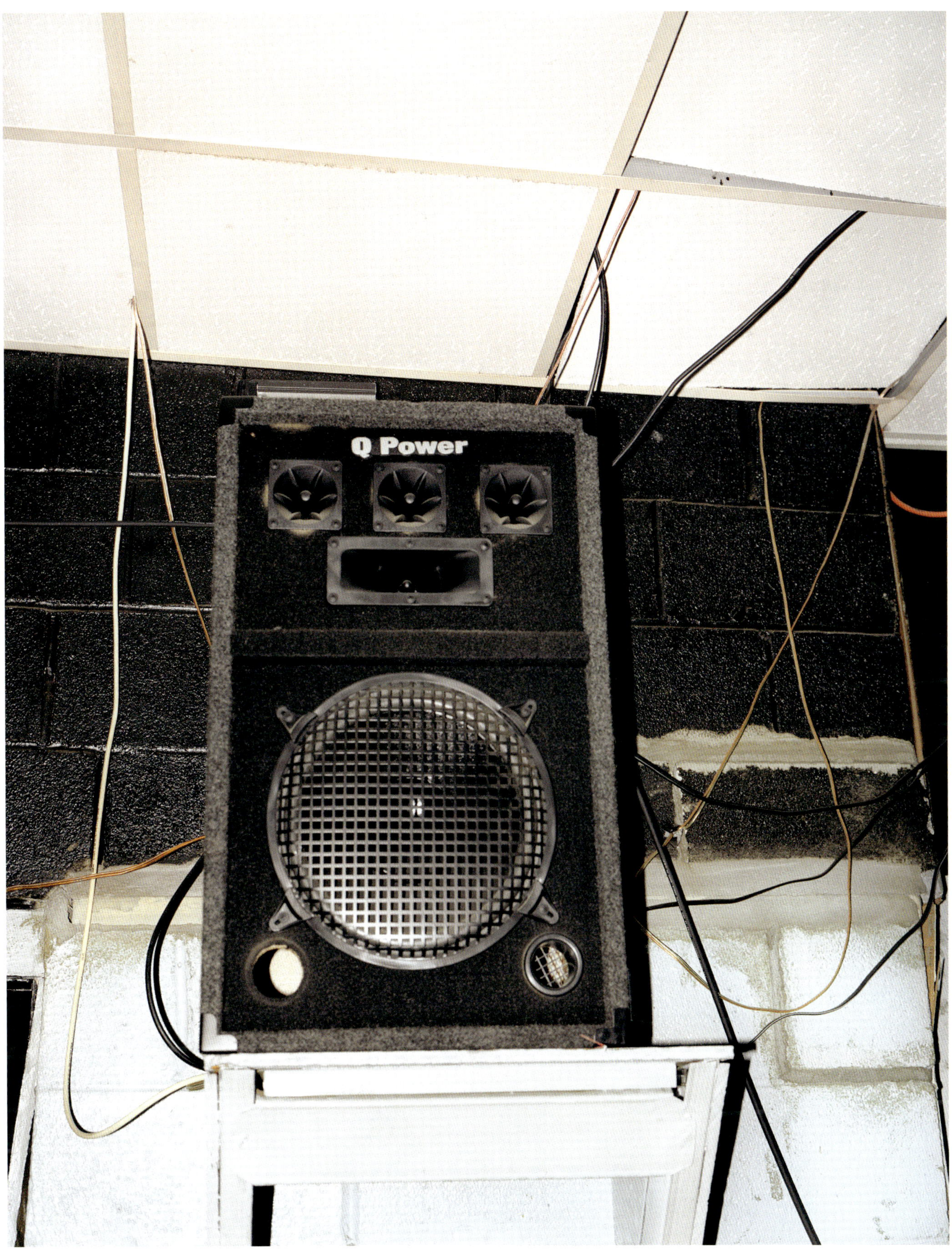

Q Power

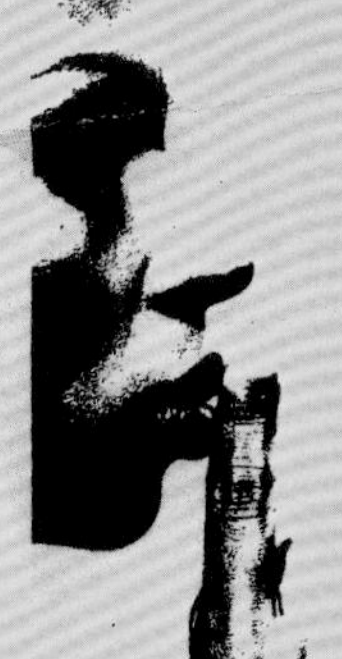

TOP OF DA LINE/ TRAPPED OUT ENT.

PRESENTS

SECRET
SPOT

Sexy Bikini
FRIDAY

FREE! 11pm until... Open mic Only $10 to perform!!

735 CENTER HILL AVE.

ATLANTA, GA 30318

right off Bankhead...on the WESTSIDE!!

With Dj Lil Rascal on the 1's and 2's!!

STUPID FOOD AND DRANKS ON DECK!!!!!

More Info:
678-754-6948
404-438-9126

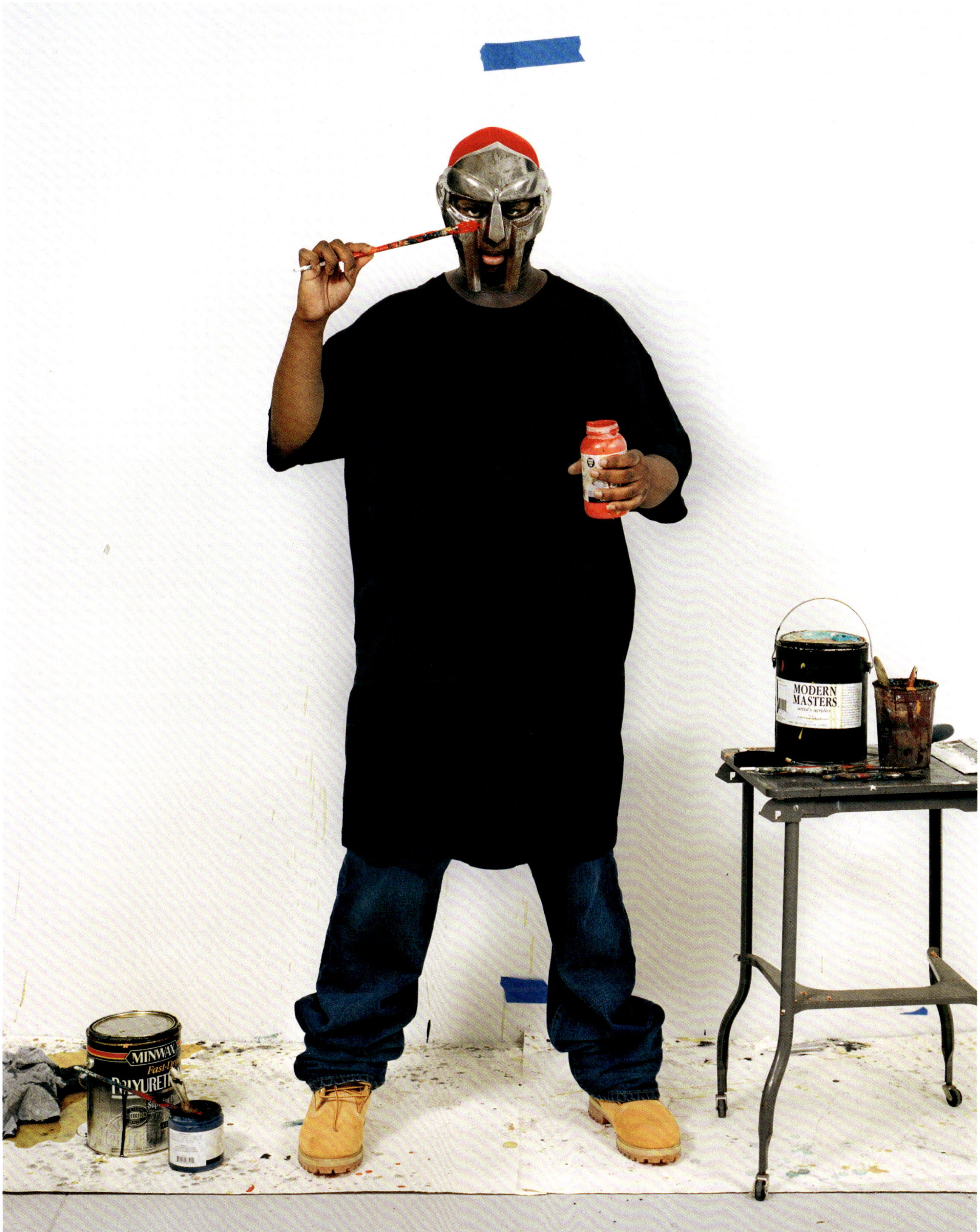

THE MUSIC BOX

- MIXTAPES
- T-SHIRTS
- XXX DVDS
- MAGAZINES
- SOCKS
- HOOD DVDS

678 997 8047

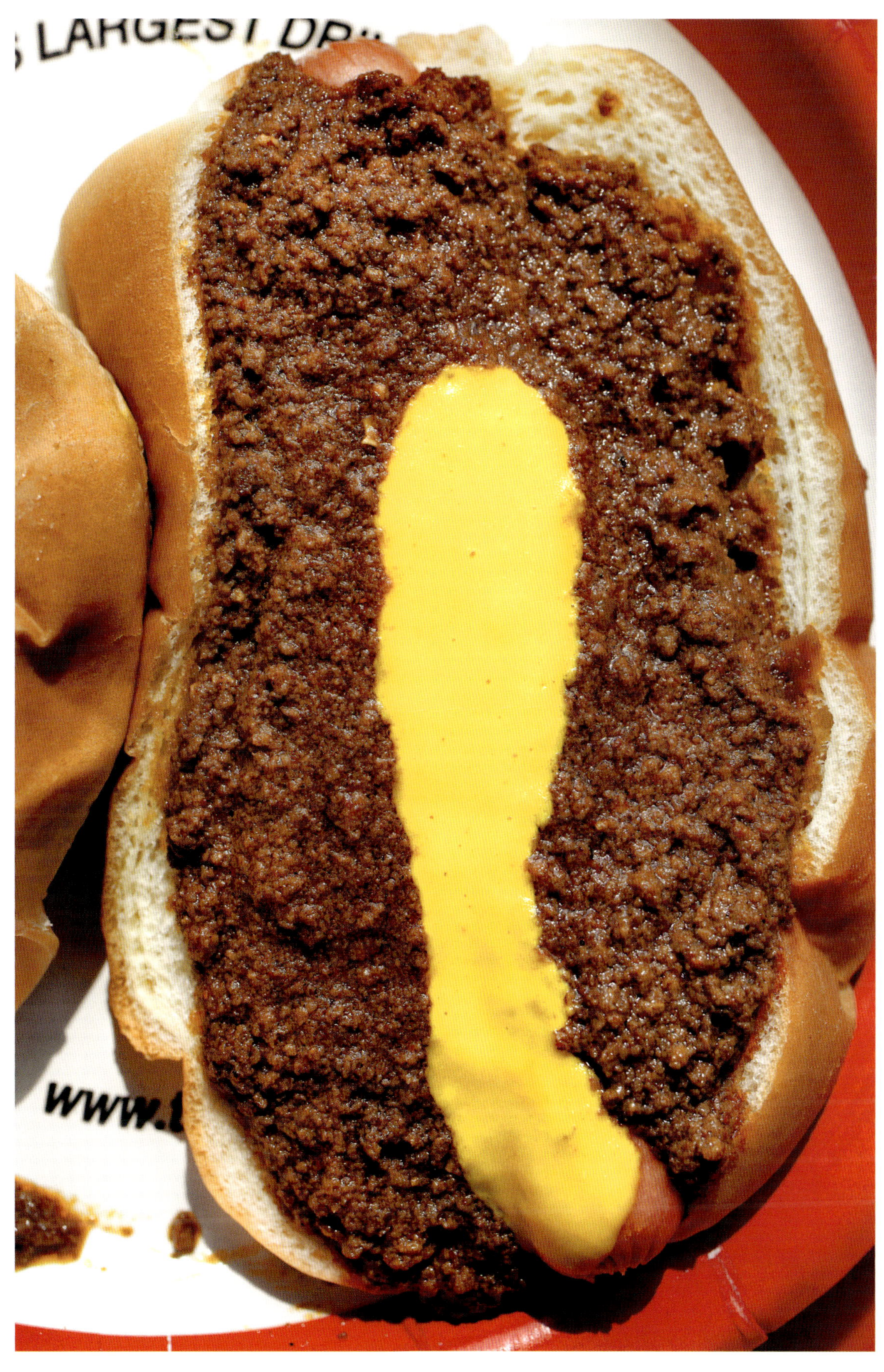
LARGEST DR
www.t

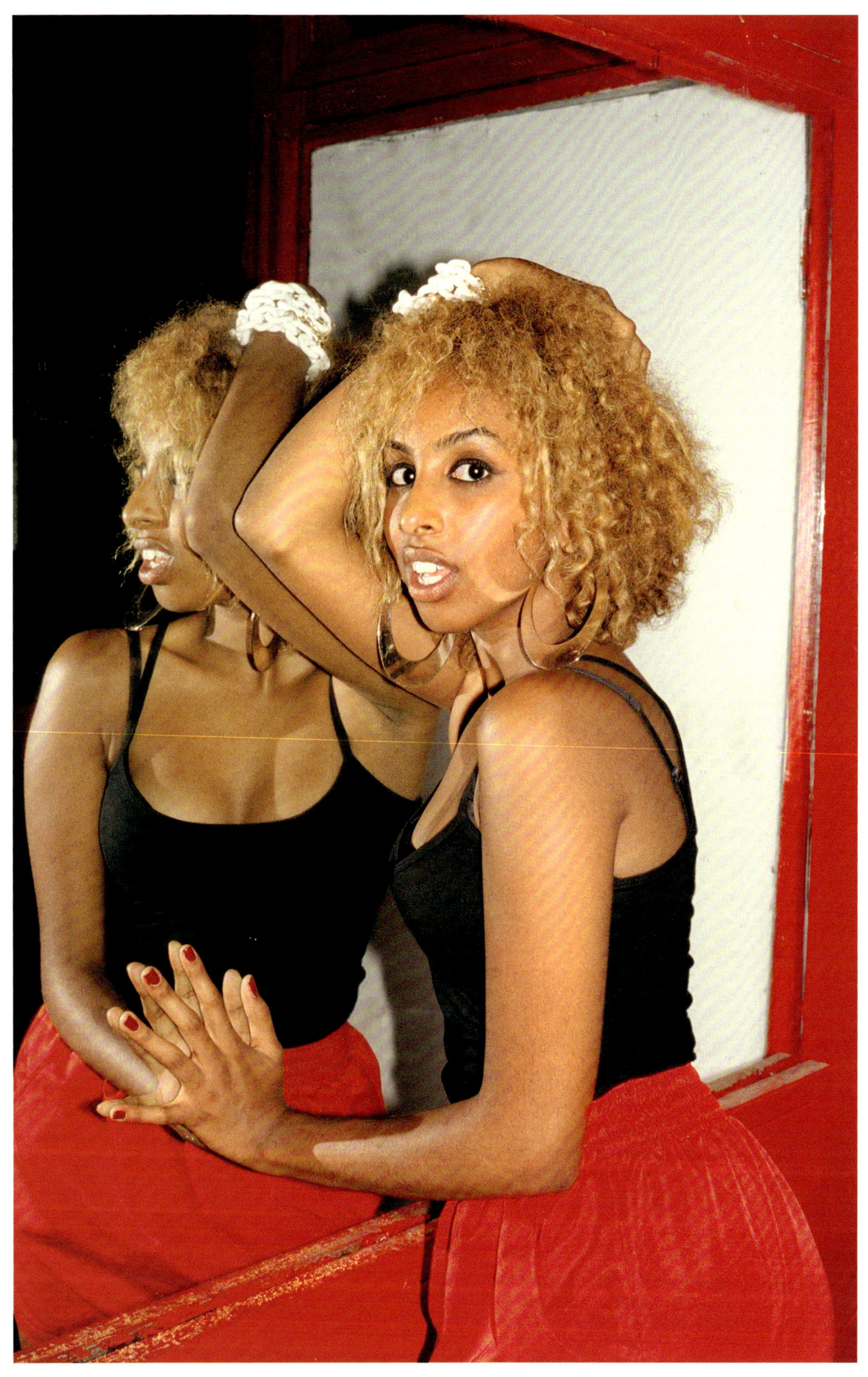

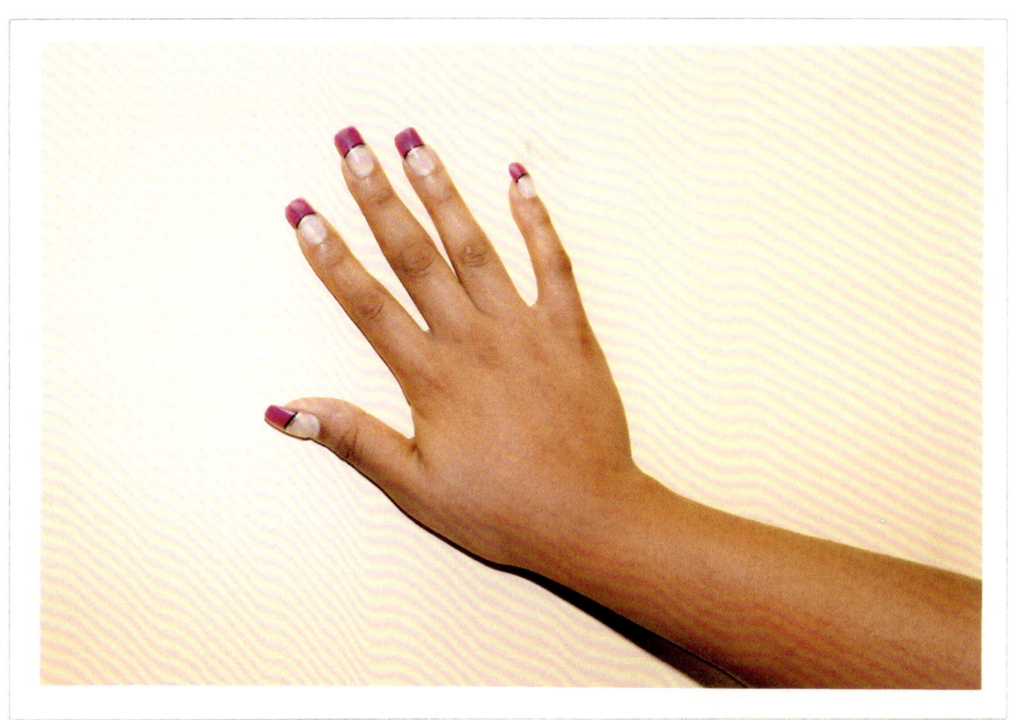

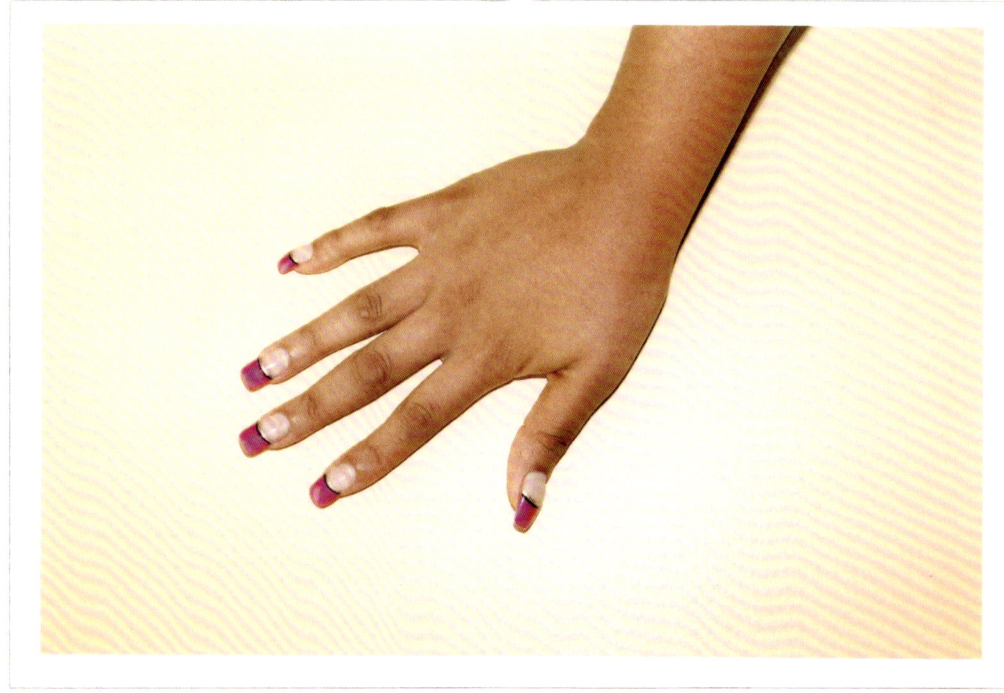

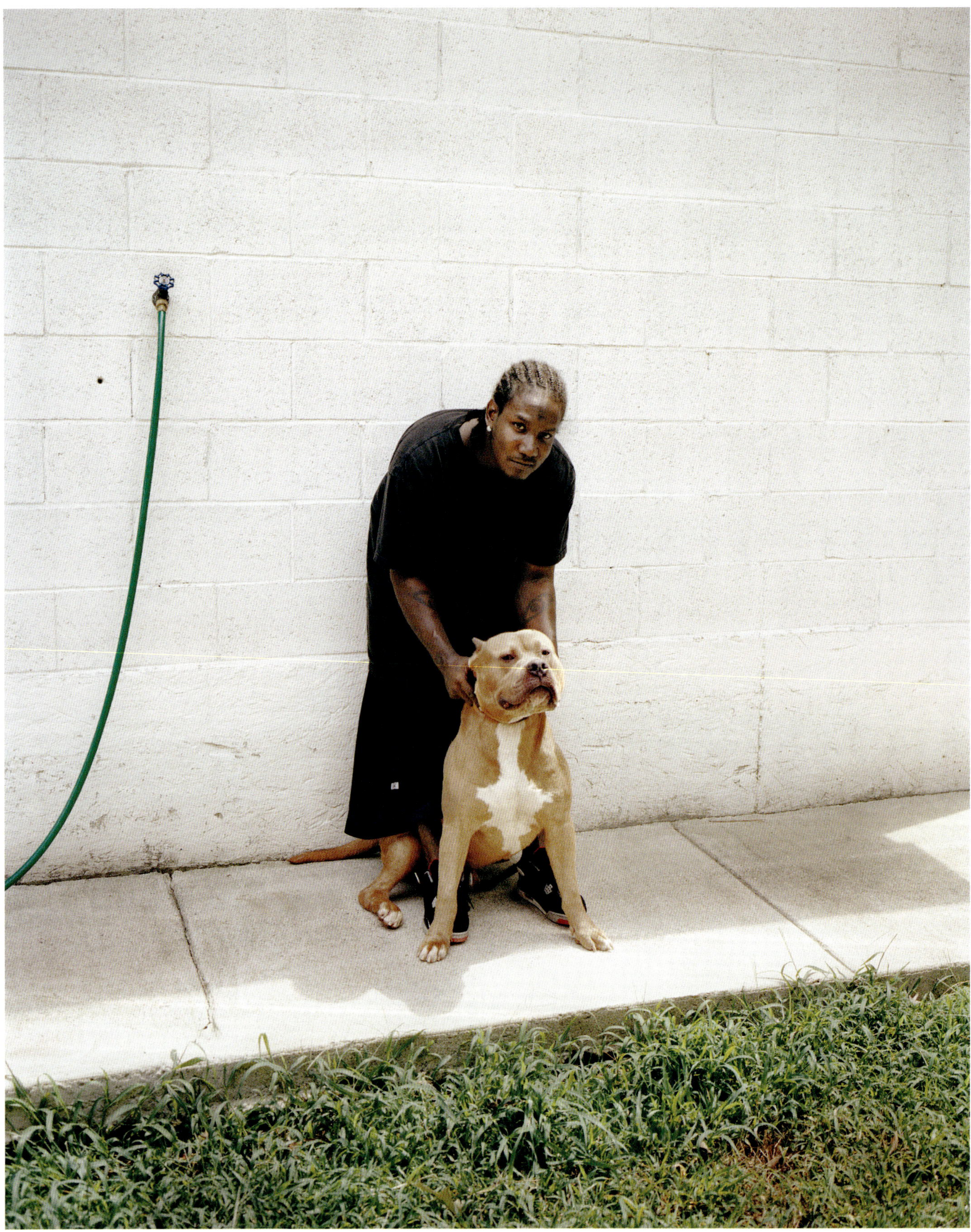

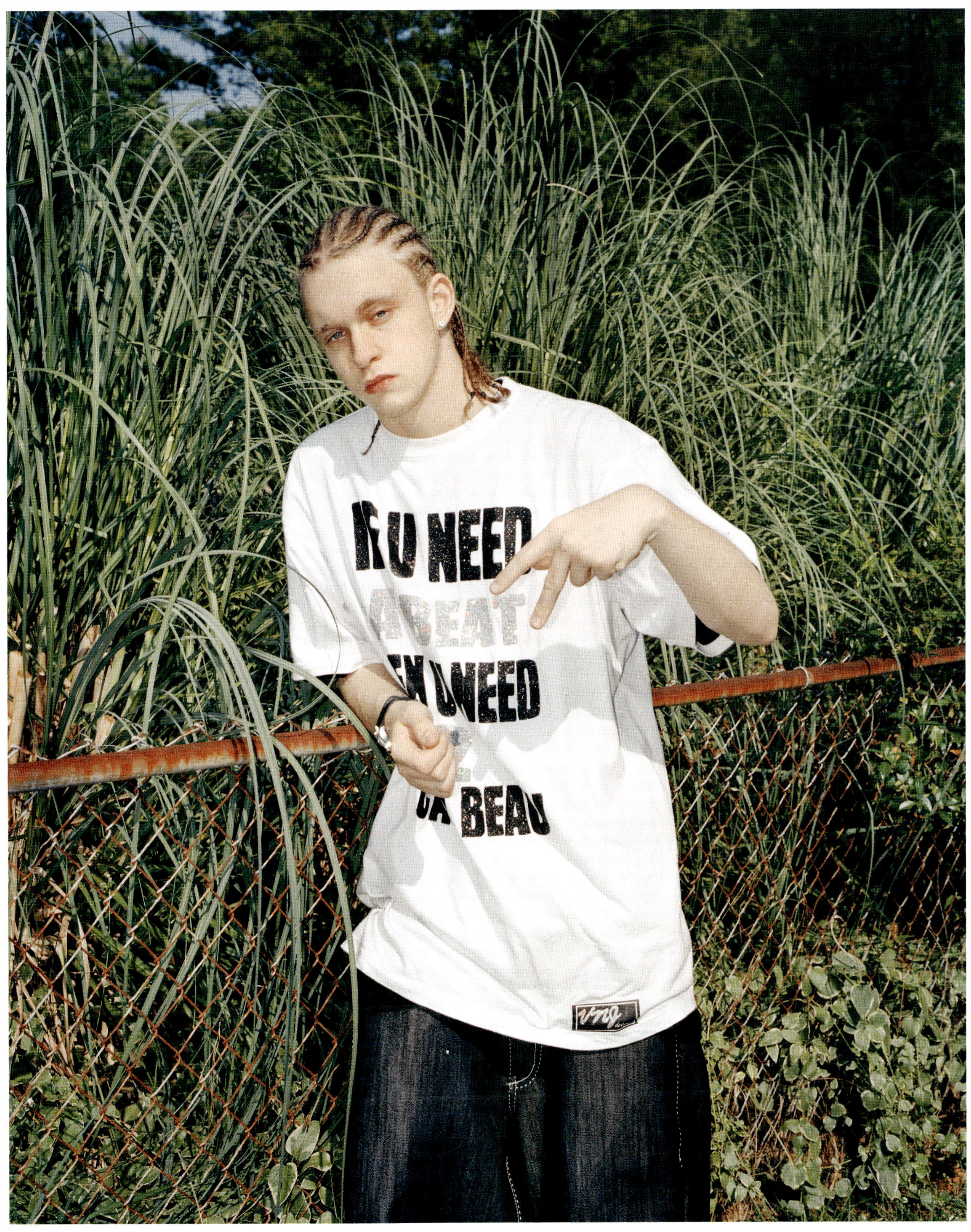
IF U NEED
A BEAT
THEN U NEED
DA BEAU

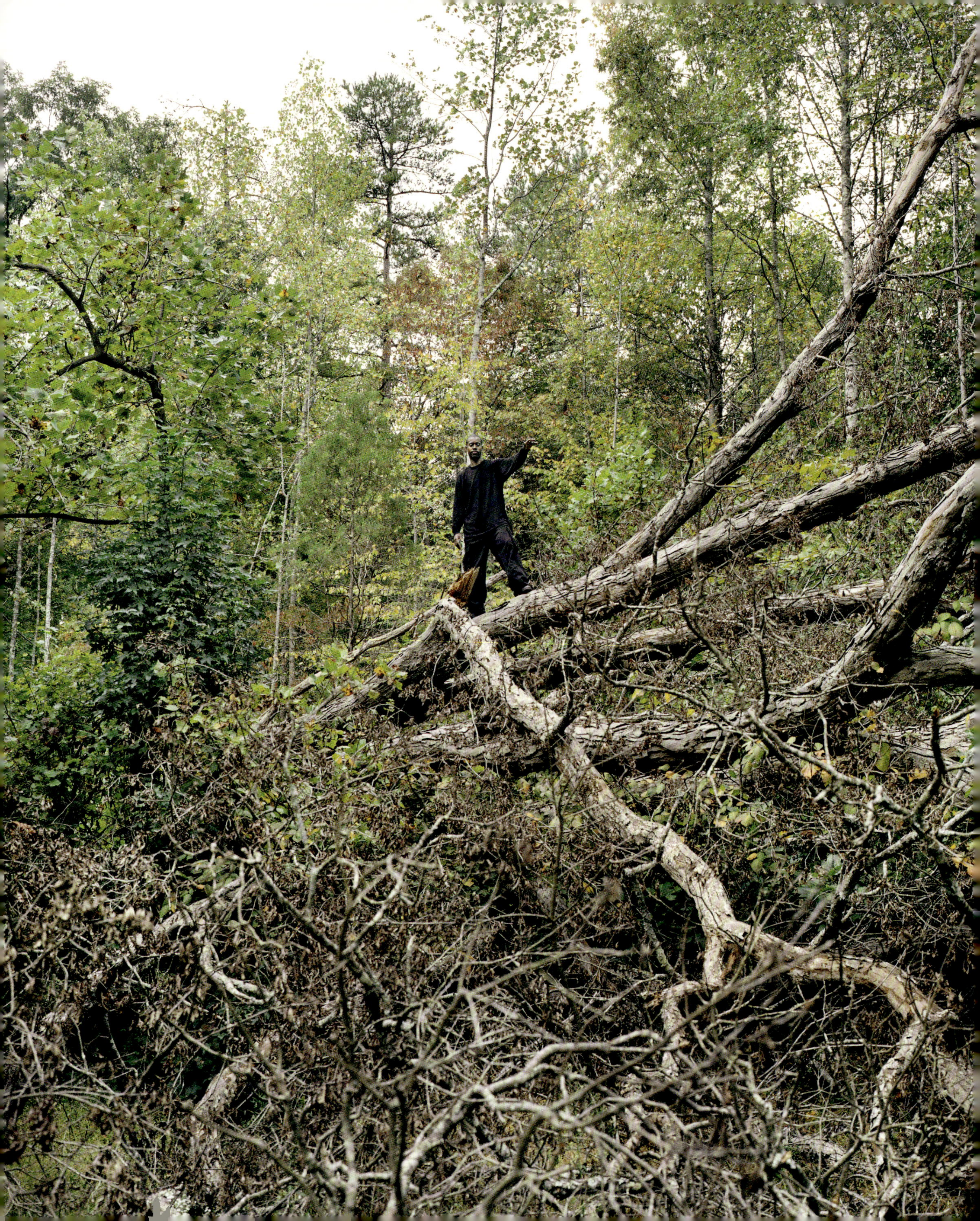

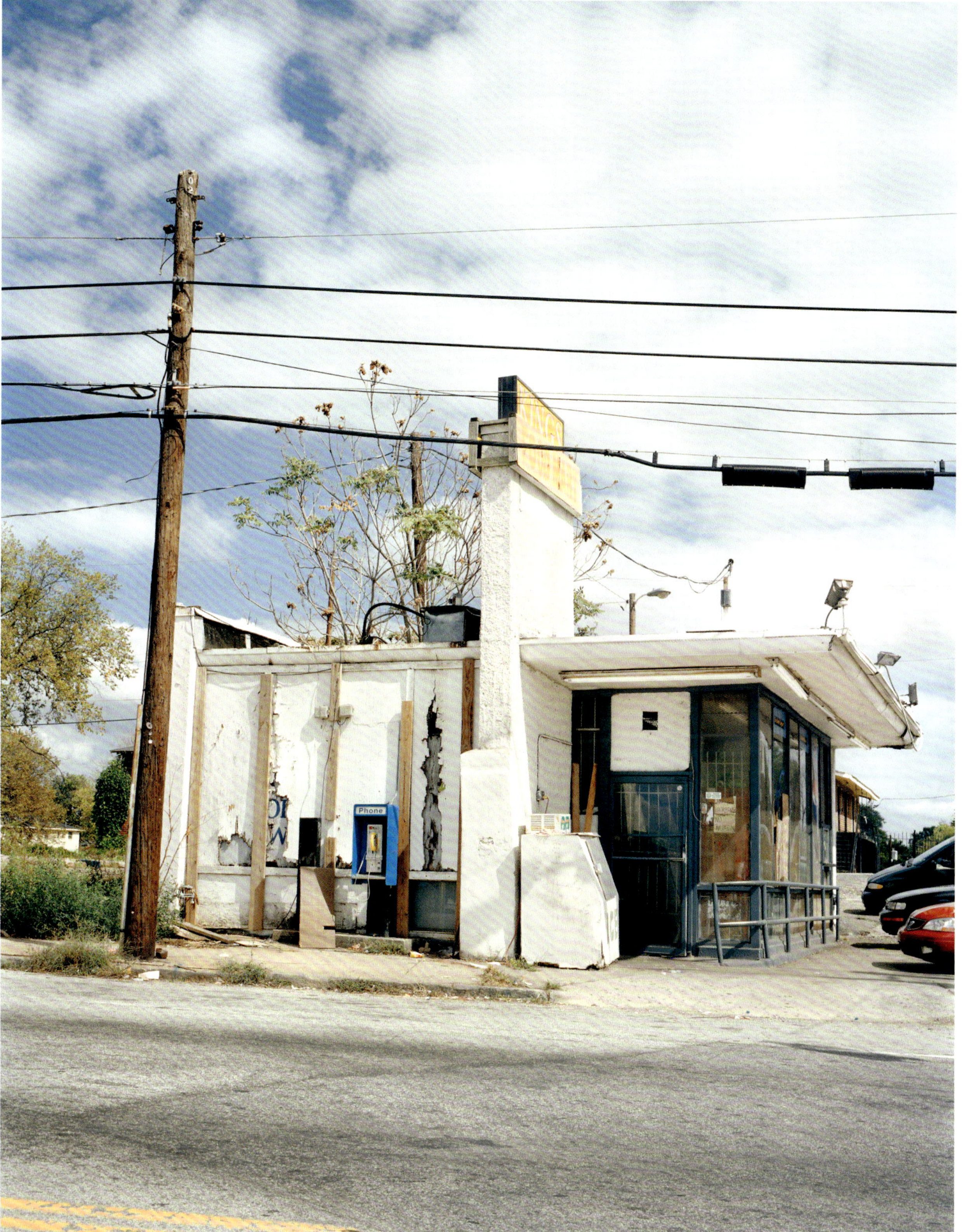
Phone

From the mid-1980s until the mid-1990s, lots of hip-hop fans seemed to agree on what a great rapper's voice should sound like: rich and resonant, with plenty of bass, like Rakim or Chuck D or KRS-One or Ice Cube or Scarface or Tupac Shakur or Bun B or the Notorious B.I.G. Rappers wanted to sound authoritative, wanted to be taken seriously, wanted to be heeded or feared or trusted or believed—above all, respected. There were exceptions (like Snoop Dogg, whose reedy rasp set him apart), but it seemed normal, then, that hip-hop should be ruled by booming voices.

Jay-Z helped change that, starting in 1996; his voice was untheatrical, sometimes even ugly (it had a distinctly adolescent quality, as if it hadn't quite broken), which made his rhymes sound less like performances and more like conversations. Eminem rapped in a pinched, nasal tone—a parody of white speech patterns, and a redemption of them. And part of Atlanta's appeal was the way its rappers found new ways to depart from the declamatory style that was once the hip-hop orthodoxy.

Young Jeezy popularized a radical new approach, casual but not at all conversational: he rapped slowly and breathily, dragging out the vowels and filling in empty spaces with interjections —"Yeeeah" or "Thaaat's right"— that were sometimes more memorable than the lines they followed; you could hear the hot air in his rhymes. The Florida transplant T-Pain, who called his first album *Rappa Ternt Sanga*, helped convert the city (and the country) to Auto-Tune, the pitch correction software that makes tuneless humans sound like tuneful cyborgs; soon there were plenty more "rappas ternt sangas." And toward the end of the decade, as the city's hip-hop grew more playful, the voices got more trebly, as if to signal their distance from the sonorous old guard. OJ da Juiceman raps as if he's straining to push his voice into a higher register, and he supplements his verses with falsetto interjections—"Ay!"; Yung LA wields an adenoidal singing voice and a whispery rapping voice; the kids from Travis Porter and Rich Kids strive to sound as thin and bratty as possible. They probably think it's hilarious. Mostly, it is.

Sometimes it sounds as if these kids are just turning the old equation upside down: if deep voices meant deep thoughts and deep music, then high, nasal voices must mean high spirits and high times. They're inviting listeners to take them lightly, and plenty of listeners—even some in Atlanta—have obliged. Ali, from Travis Porter, barely considers himself a rapper at all. "I try to sing, but I can't sing," he says. "Like, I just harmonize." But no rapper wants to be a laughingstock, and so even the most fun-loving tracks usually contain warnings for listeners or rivals who might be tempted to make assumptions. In Ali's words: "Don't take me wrong/What you think they call me Ali for? I'll crack your dome."

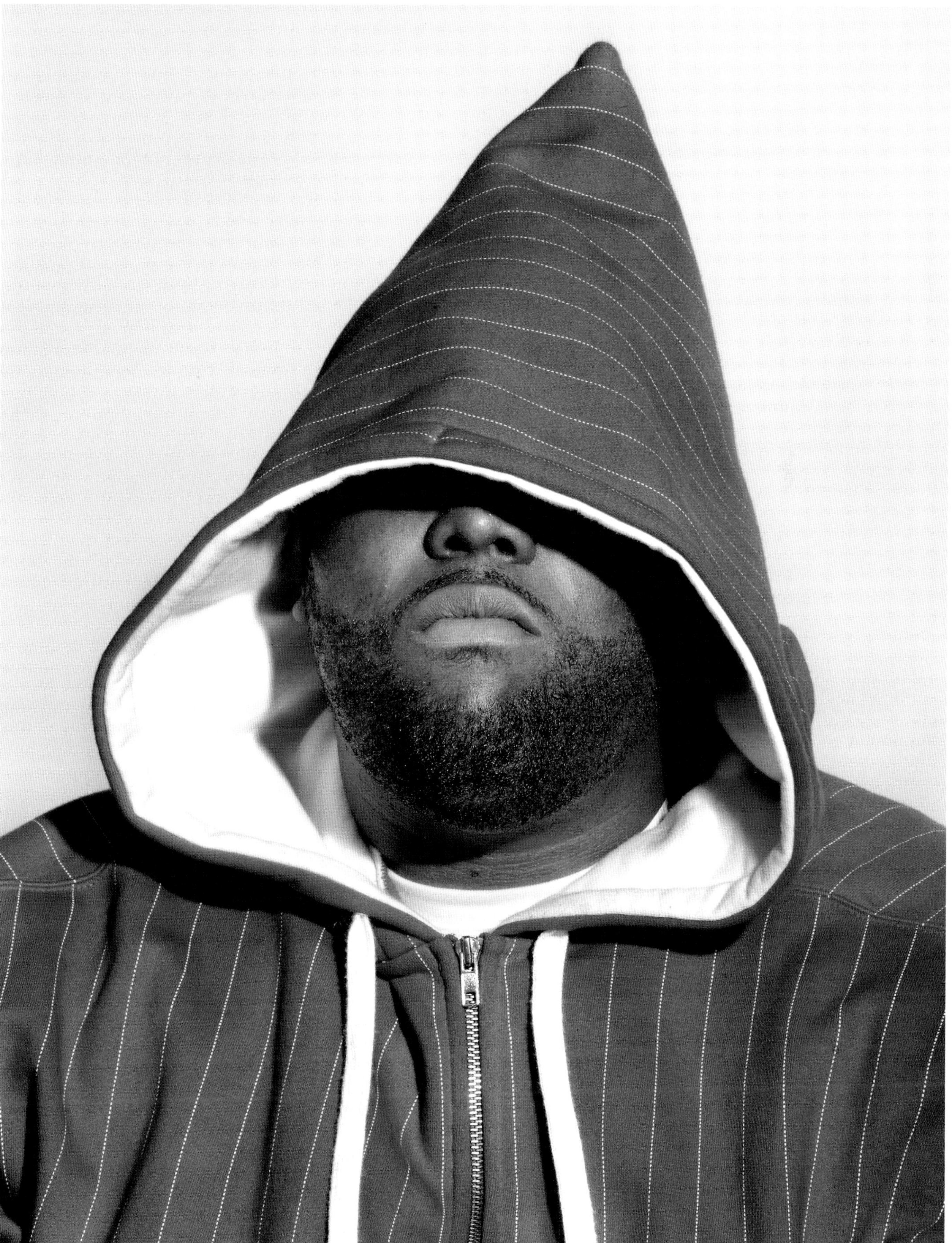

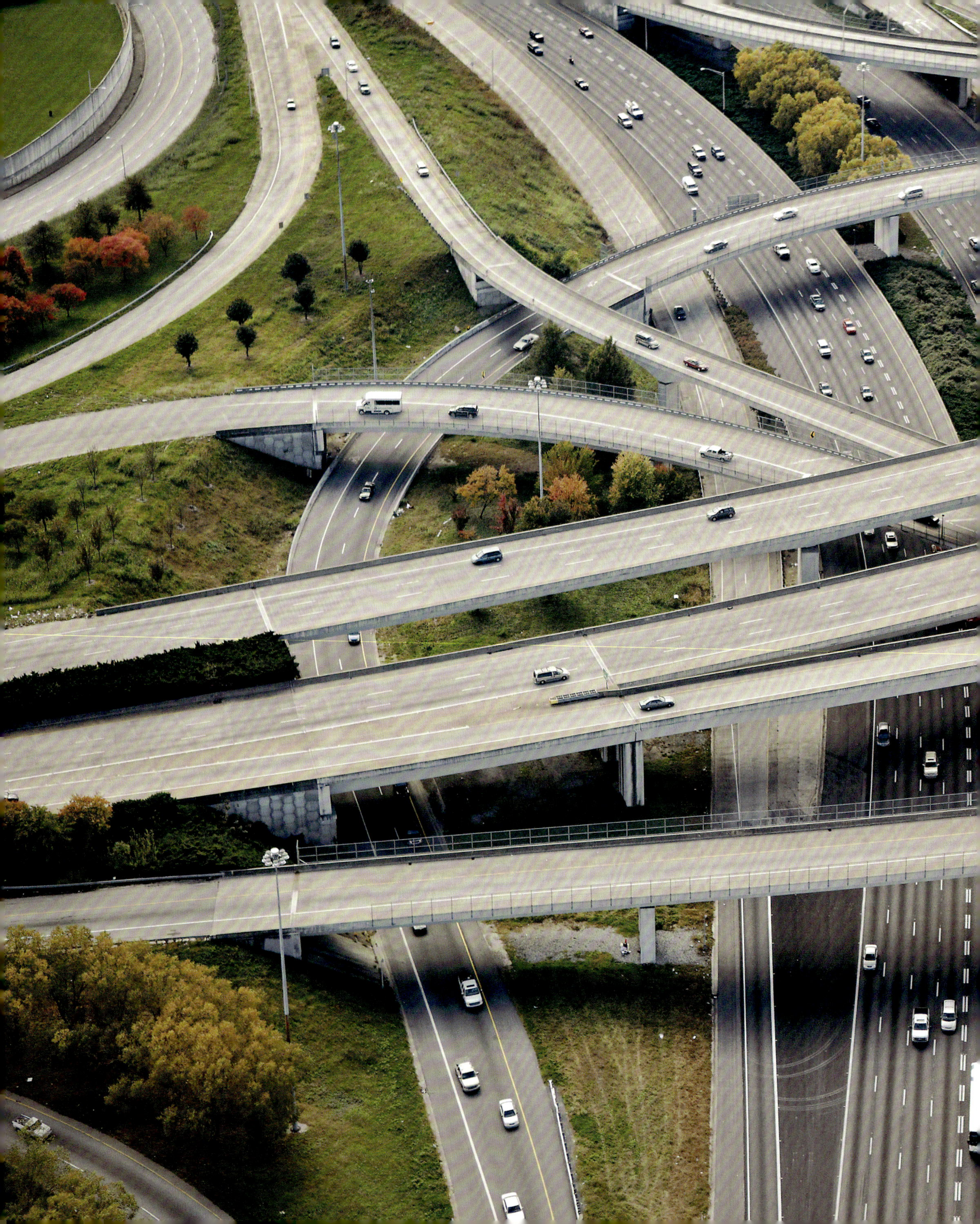

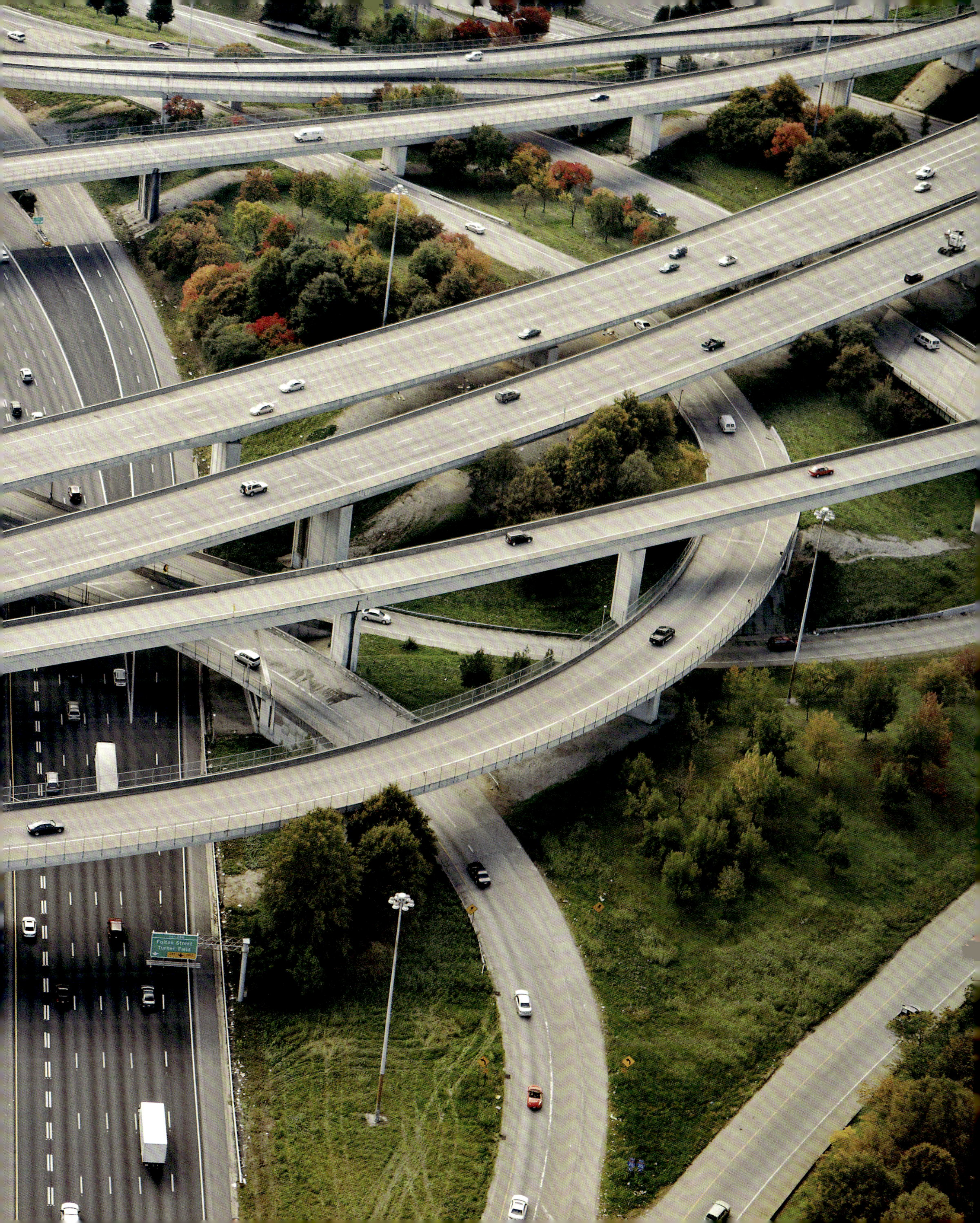
Fulton Street
Turner Field

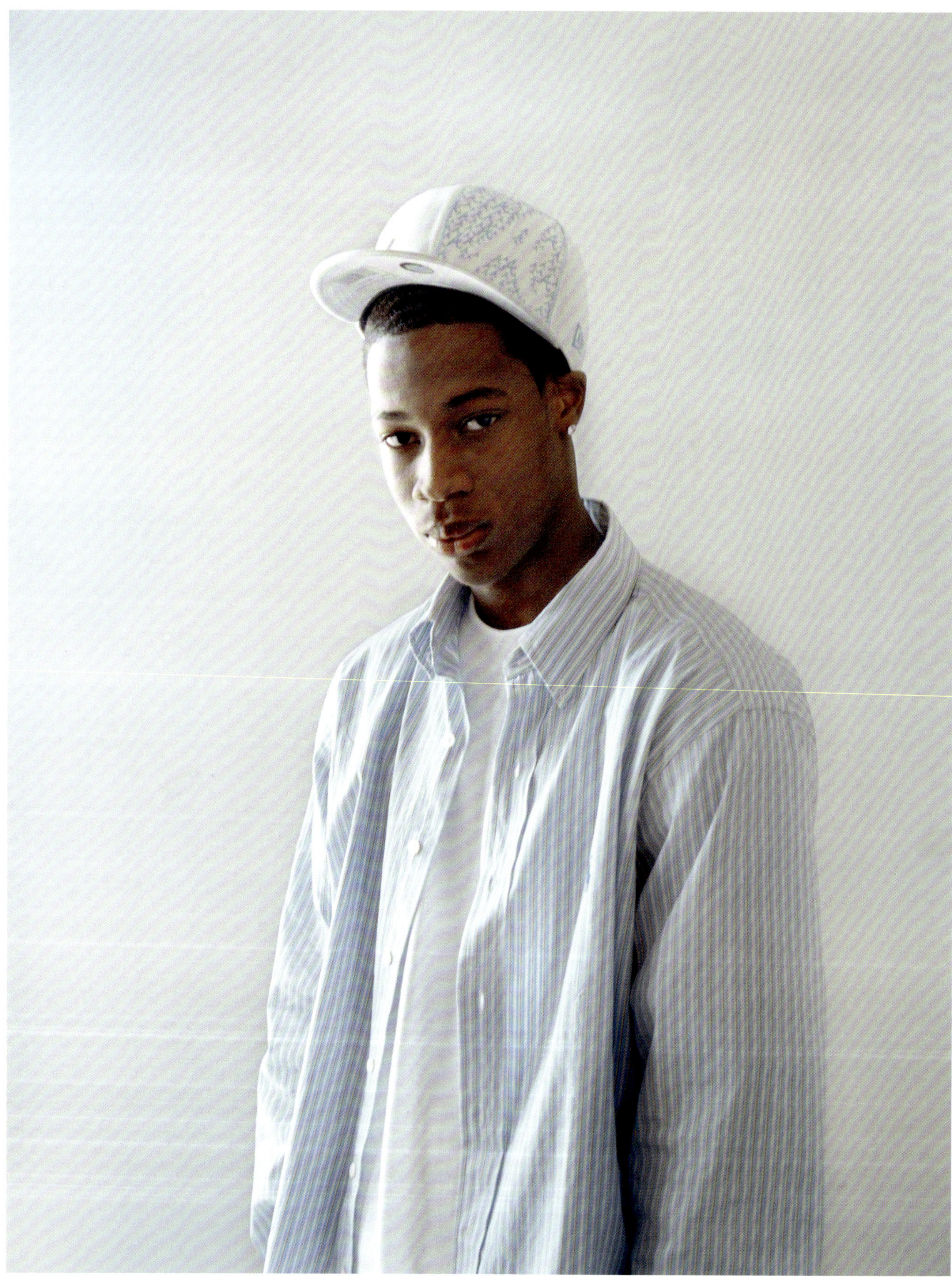

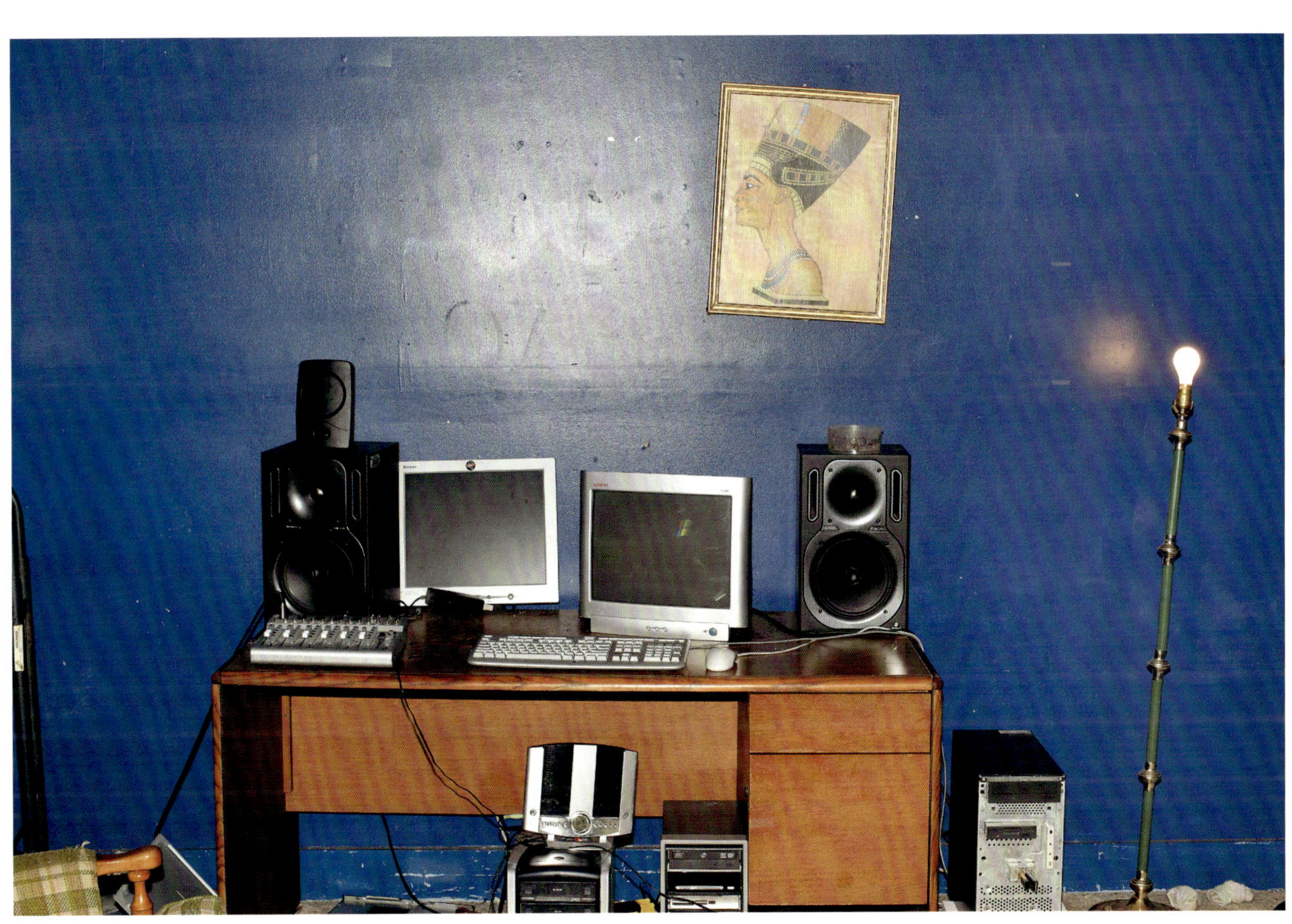

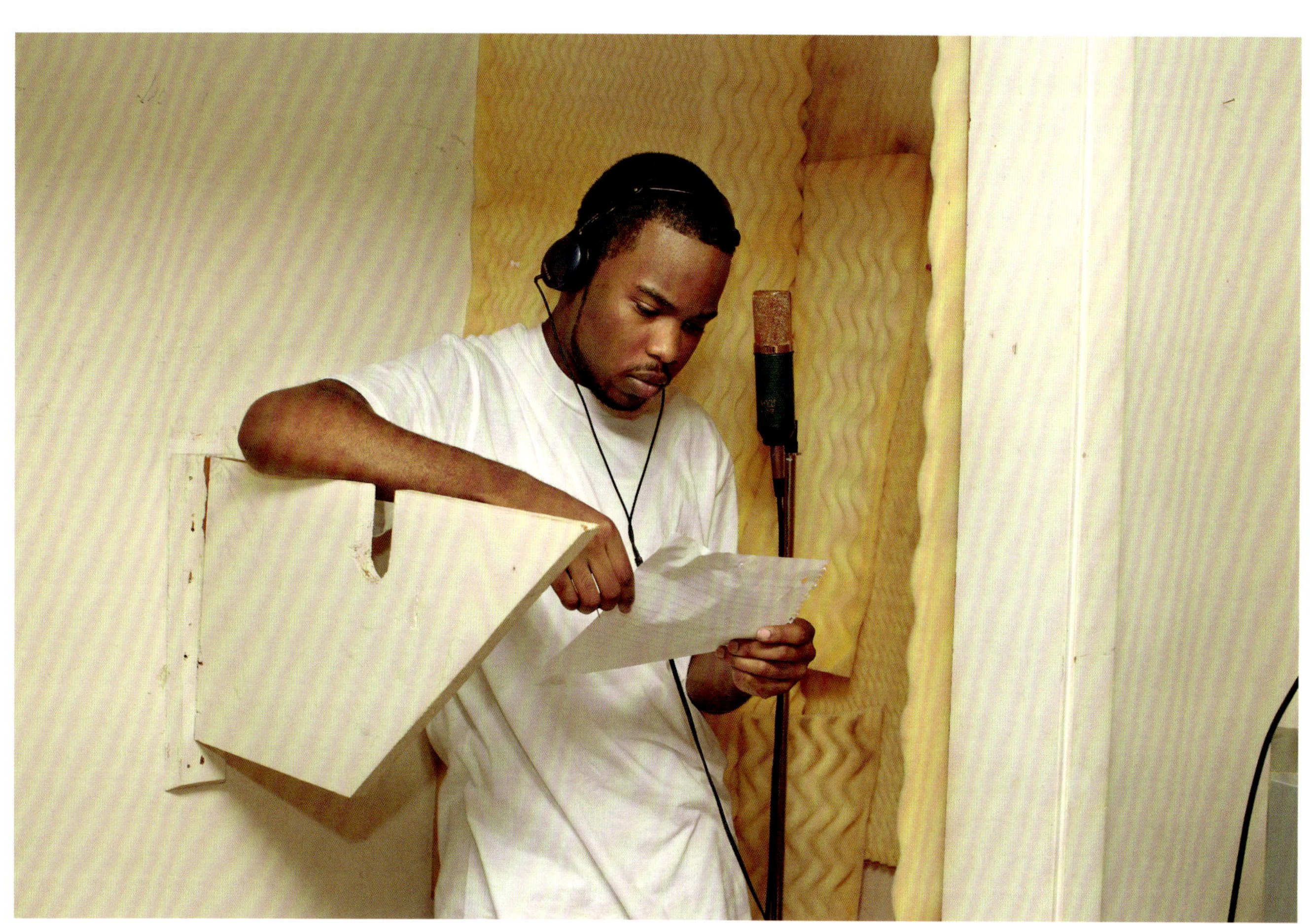

- Yungster - I set how
- ~~don't guess~~
. So da money comin 2
. all I kno is how to ad.
and multiply my Mathematics.
- Em Neva tricka off ~~today~~
~~Cause~~ ~~you'll~~ certified pimp'n
What!. you'll Neoa ~~catch~~ me tricken.
why . Tricks are 4kins hoho.. you Silly Rabb

- Money, Im bout dat, Money, I got du
- doctors Say I got ch
problem.. "I admit I got
it b.d
- ever since ah addlense ~~address~~
- Moneys been da only subject
And nothing comes b.4 it
- So quit wit all dat sh.
- Shhh..
- ~~I grind hard~~
- ~~I hold~~ money makes da world go
around watch me cs I
- 50 watch you betta orb.t
- heed of tha states So you
can call call me president
Mr. Bens my only friend. So why do
you Round me dry

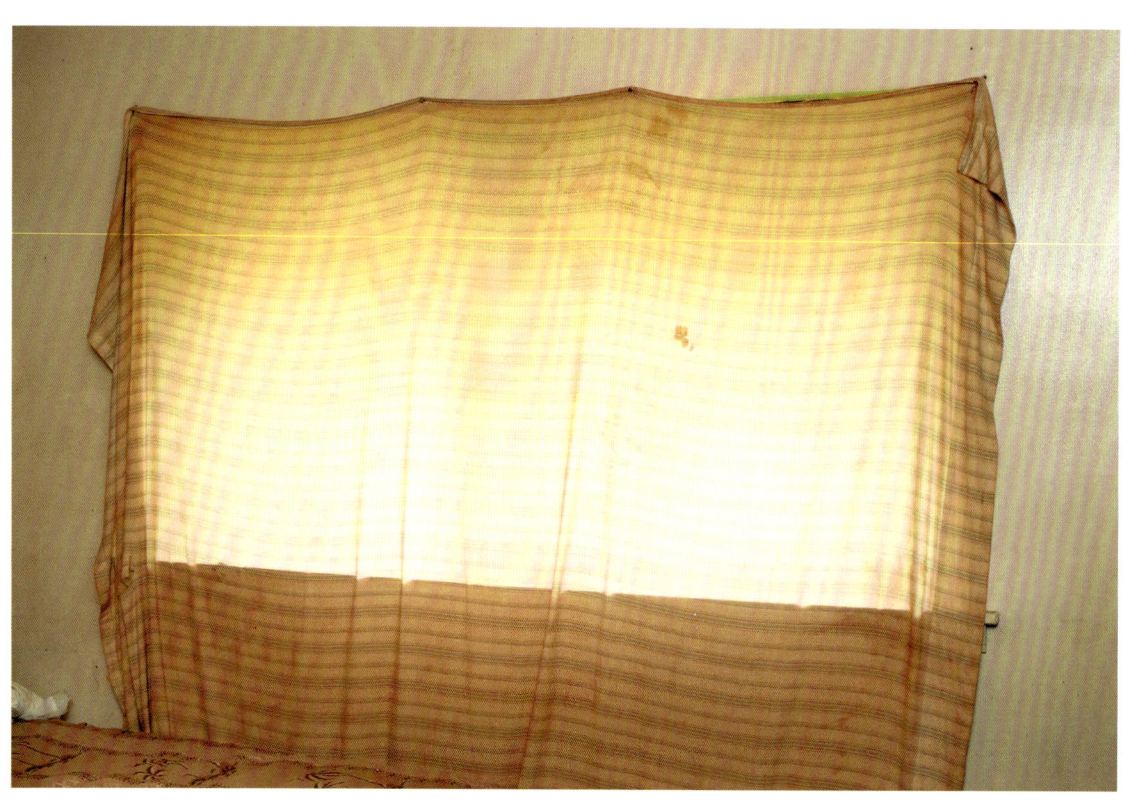

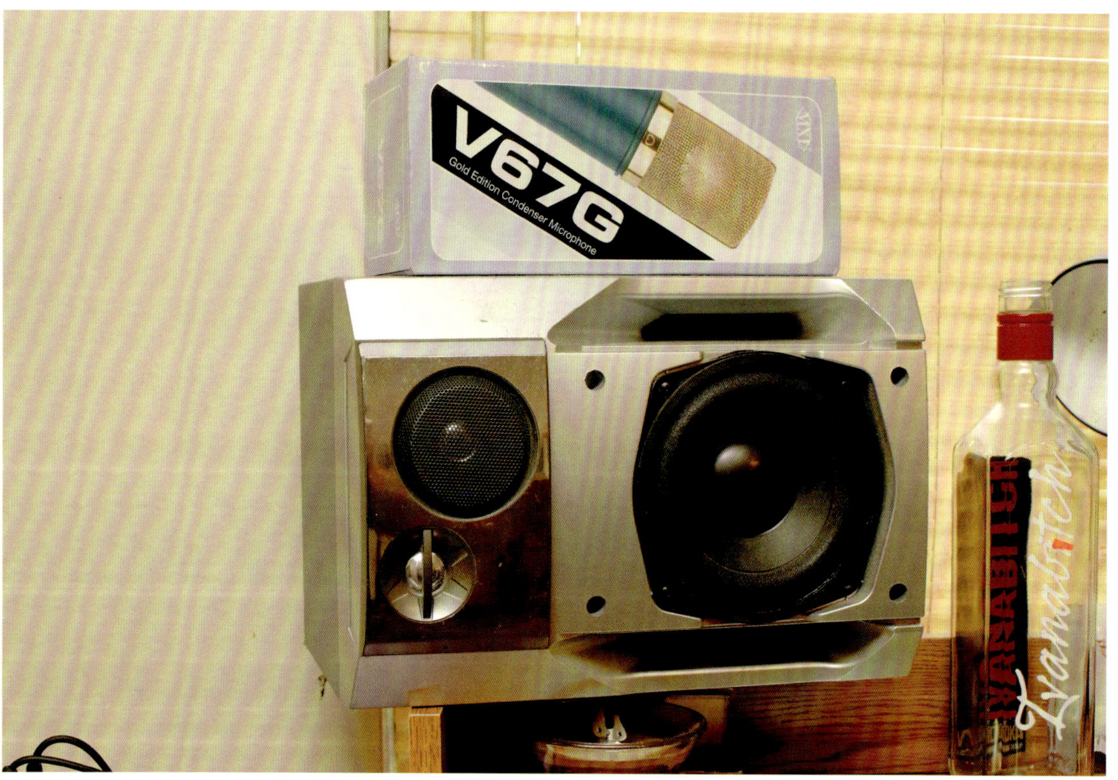
MXL
V67G
Gold Edition Condenser Microphone
KARABILIR

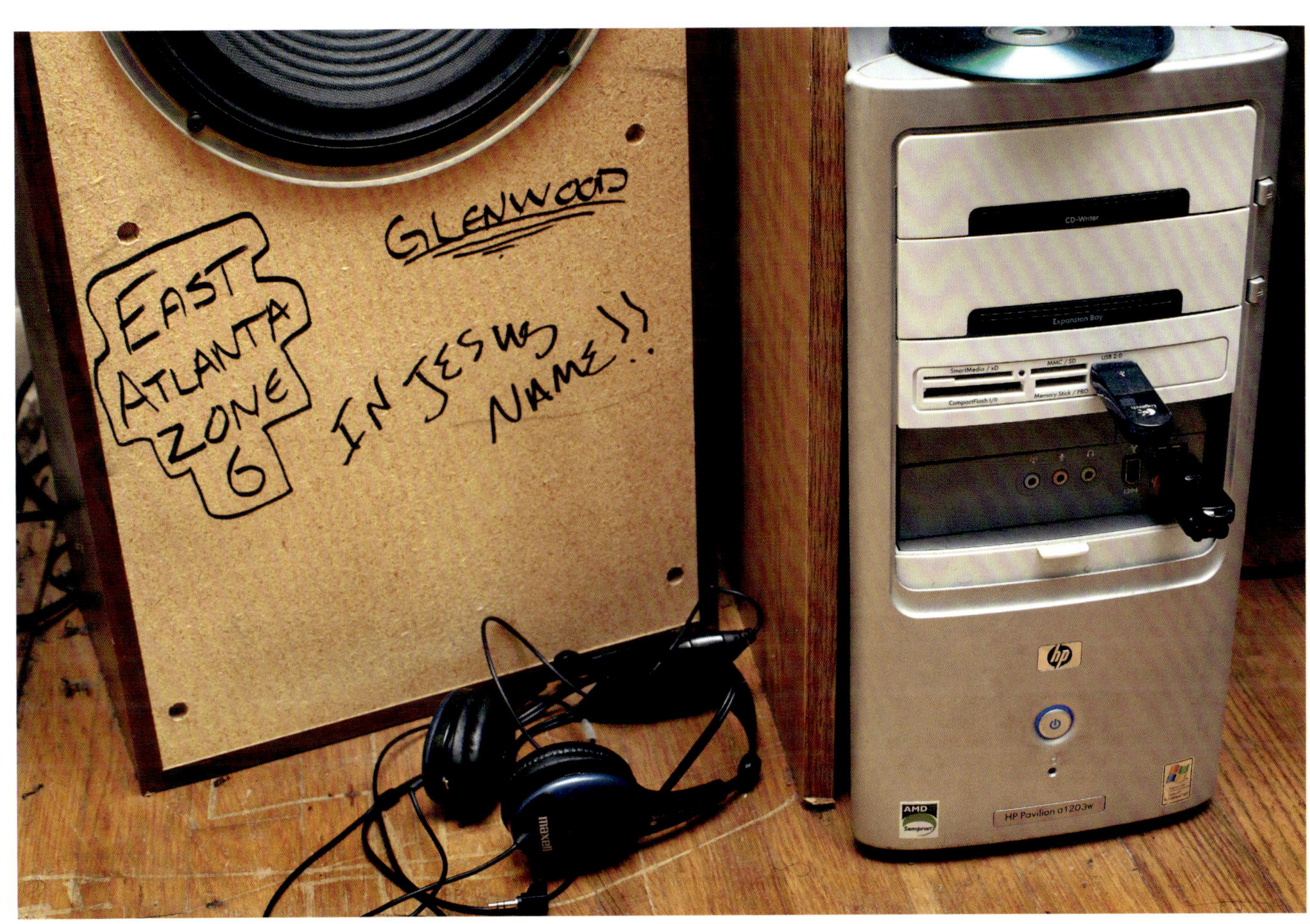

GLENWOOD
EAST ATLANTA ZONE 6
IN JESUS NAME!!

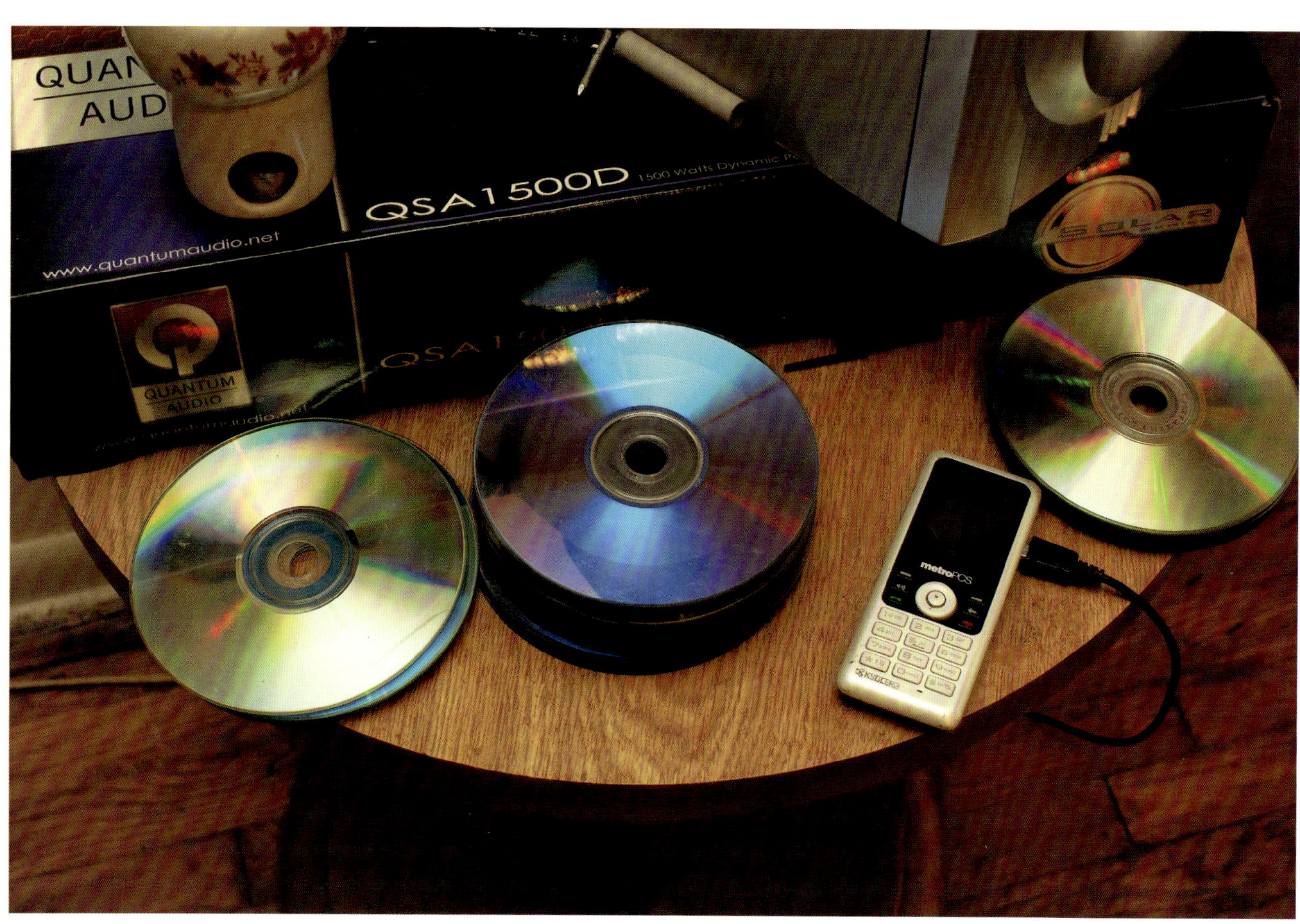
QUAN
AUD
QSA1500D 1500 Watts Dynamic Pe
www.quantumaudio.net
QUANTUM
AUDIO
SOLAR
metroPCS
KYOCERA

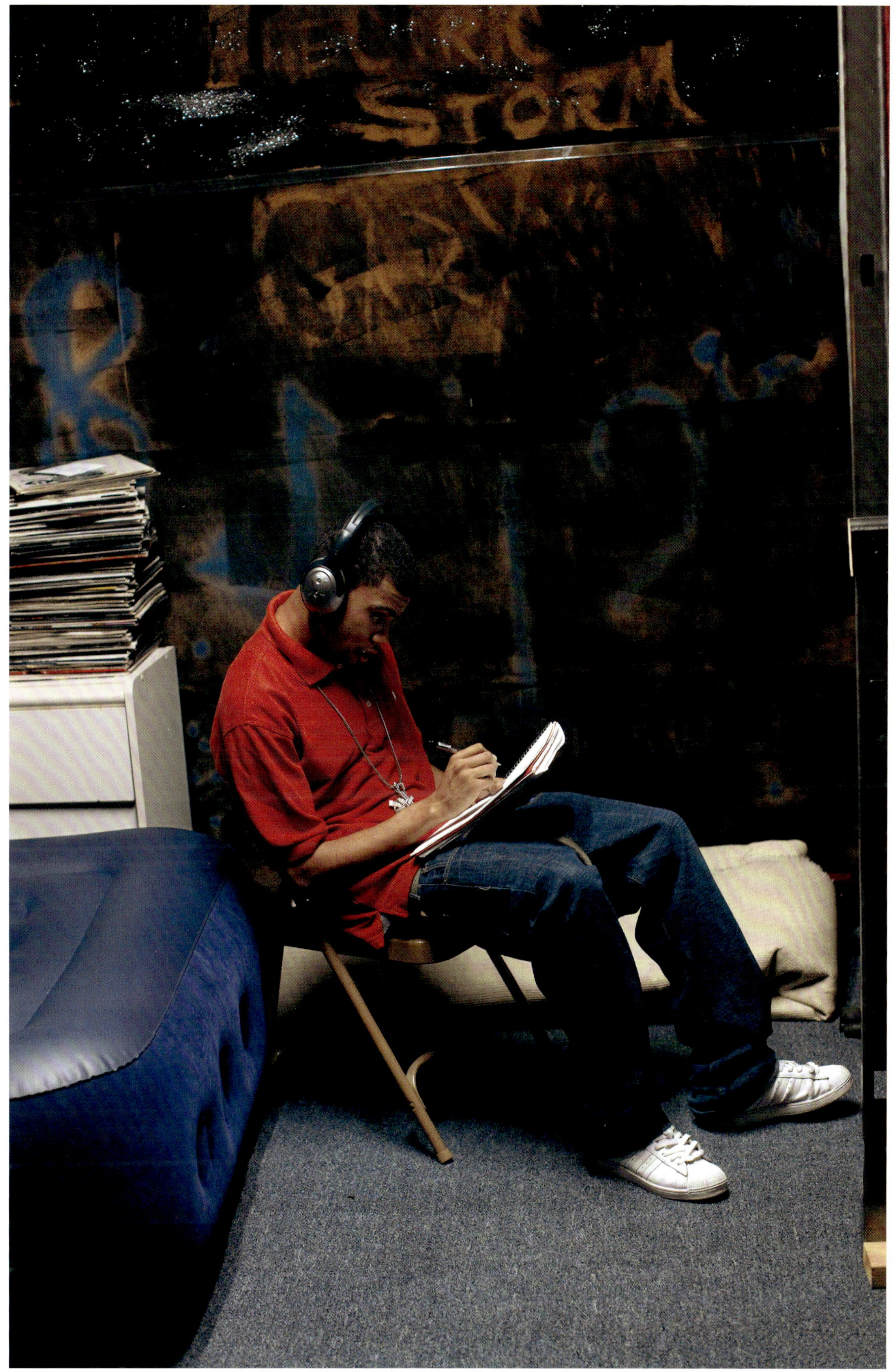

STORM

look at

look at her ass "ooh" look at her boots
Dam look at her Body "Aye" watch how she move
look at her   look at her   she be dancin on da pole too
look at her   look at her   she ~~is~~ dancin on my whole ce...

~~I wanna see you baby~~ it open soon as it ~~work this doll~~
~~and Baby if y~~

Everytime I see her dance I jus wonder can she fuck wit dat
If I thorow dis money baby tell me can you throw it back
I be diggin all her tats so I be gettin all her sace
Plus she go both ways ~~I~~ like two way streets she brought
a model back,
She ~~told me~~ she will swallow dat den asked me where
dem dollars at,
I said it's in yo pocket baby share sum of yo profit lace
you should see ~~how she~~ her naked ~~you should see her on the pole~~
If I like da way she pop if you gon love her on the pole
She like to wind it up slow then she make dat ass clap
Baby if you give it to me you cant have dat ass back
It's official Mr. pimpin call me Goldie I'm a mac
Told her bring it here let me show you wat to do wit dat

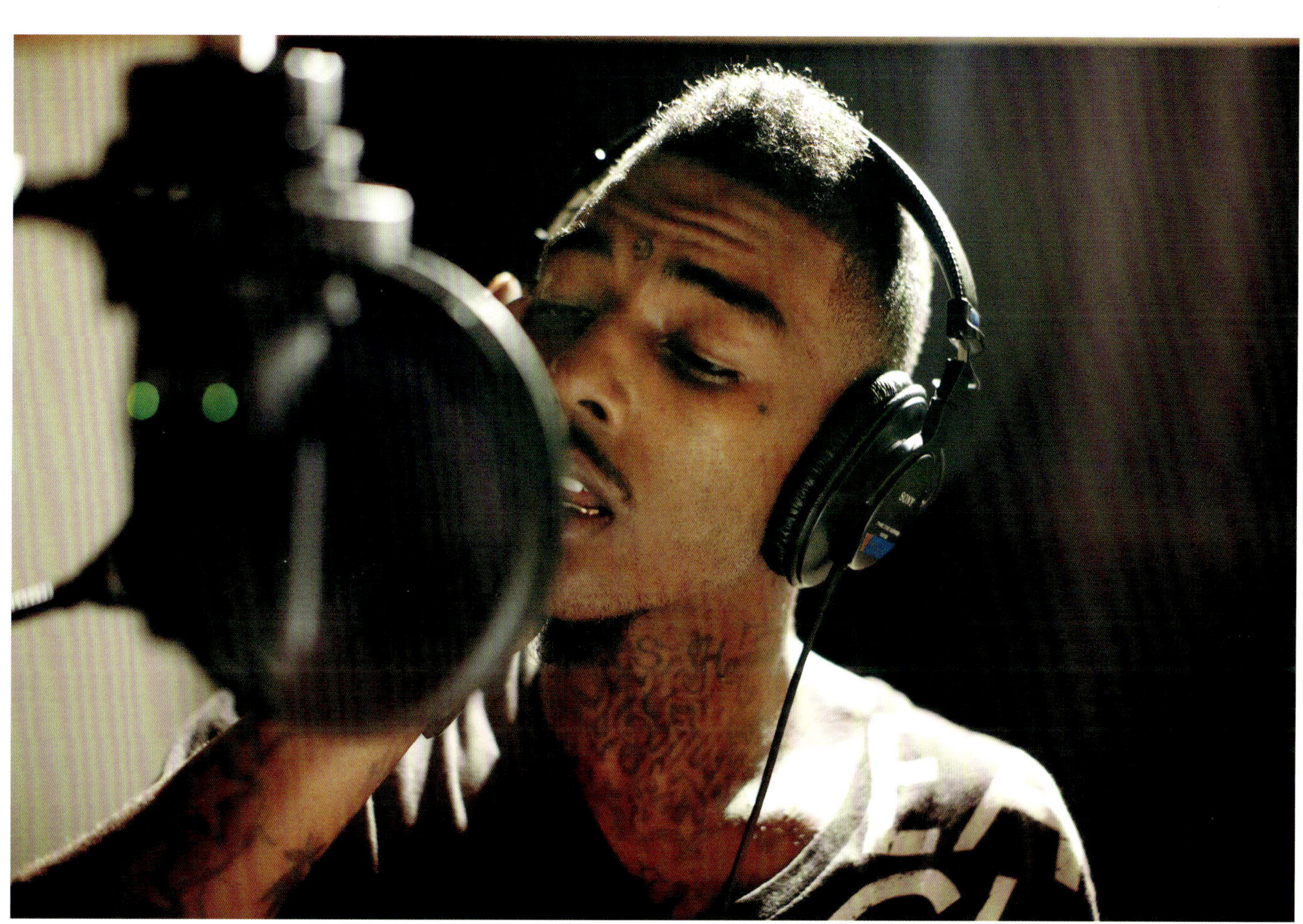

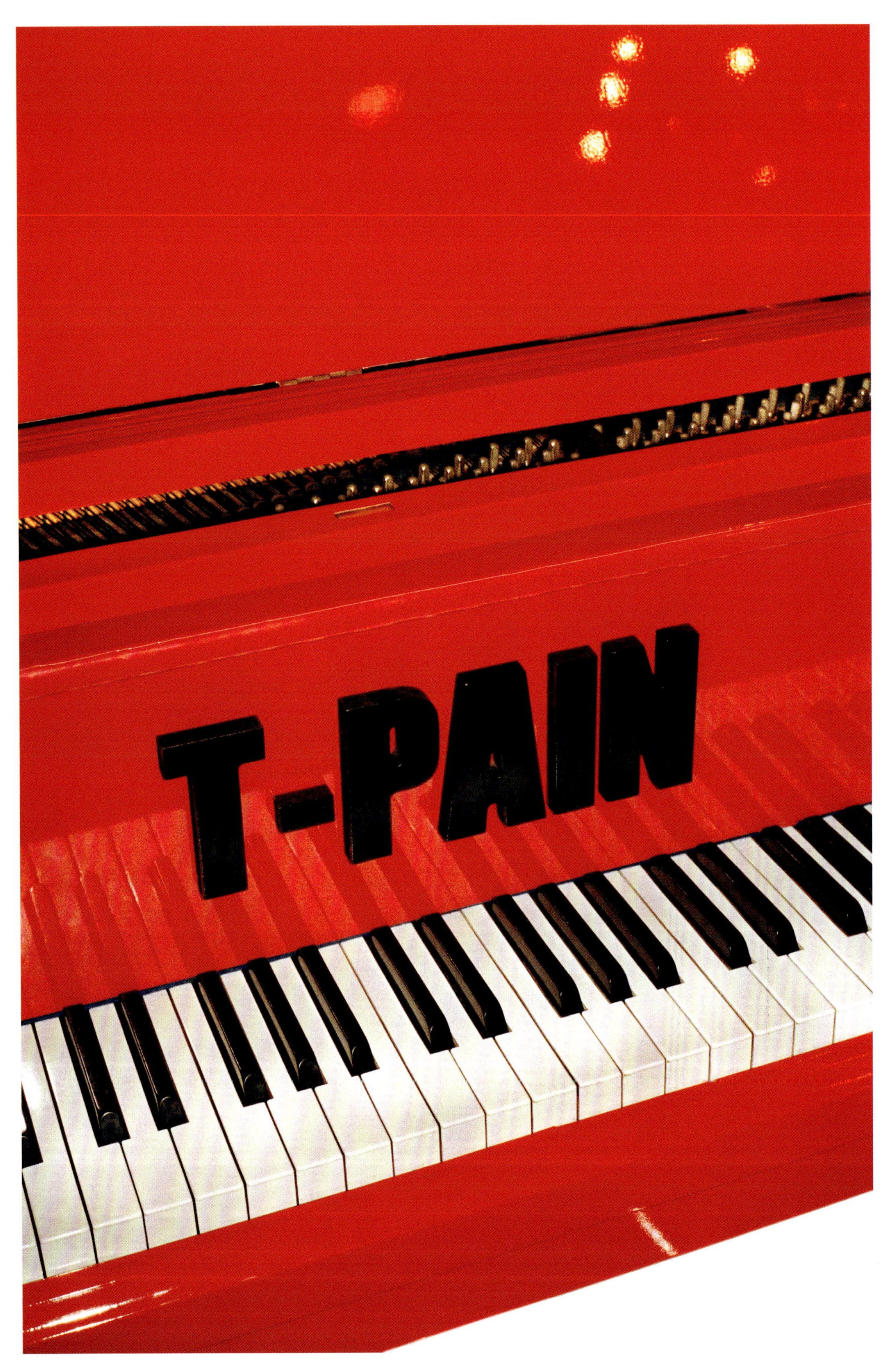

T-PAIN

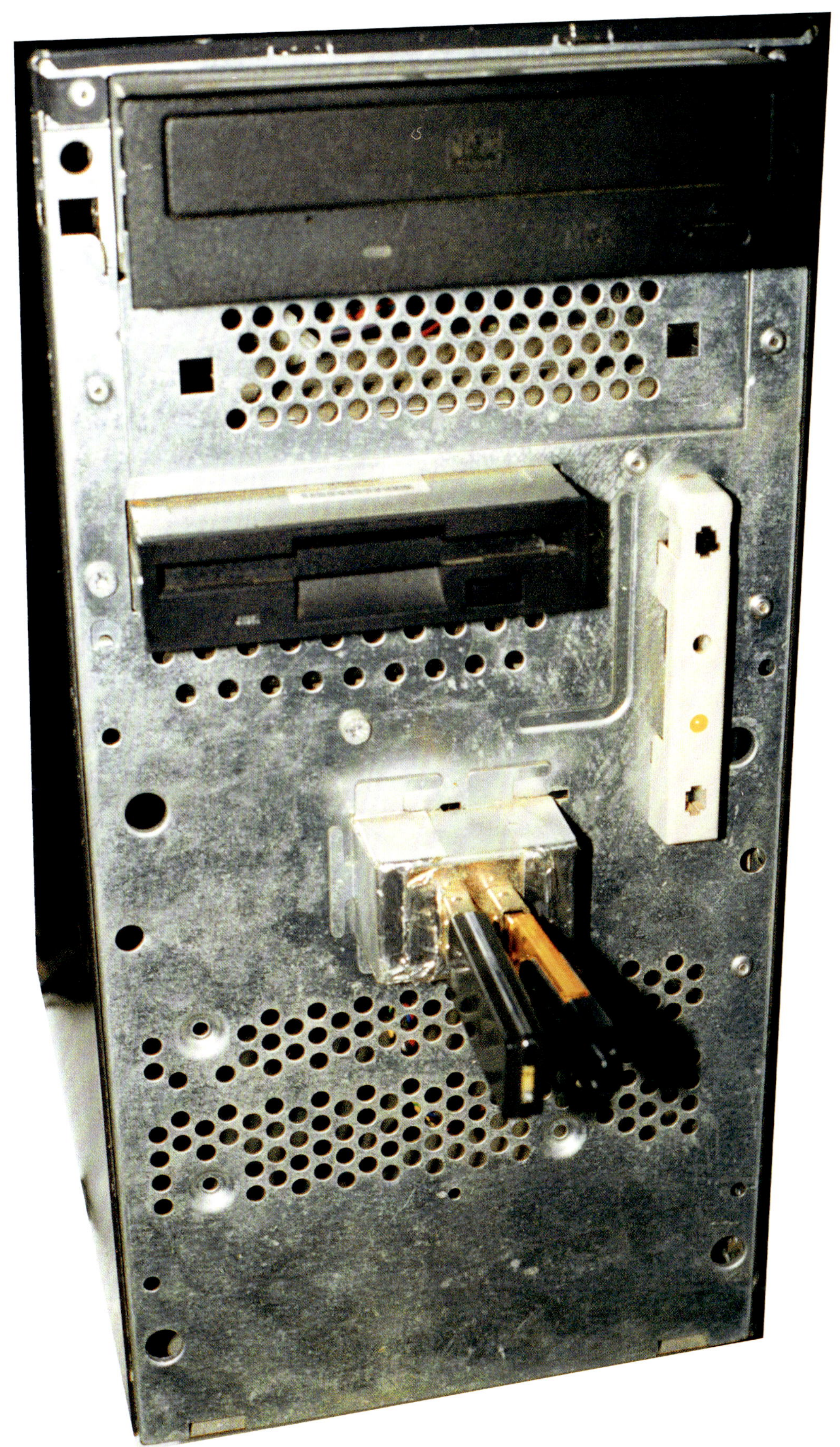

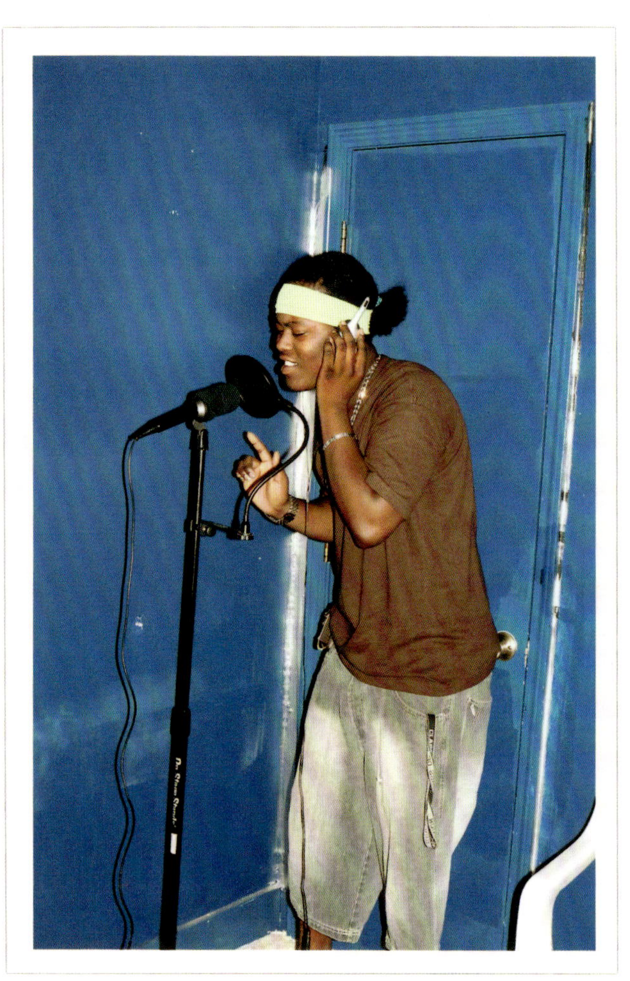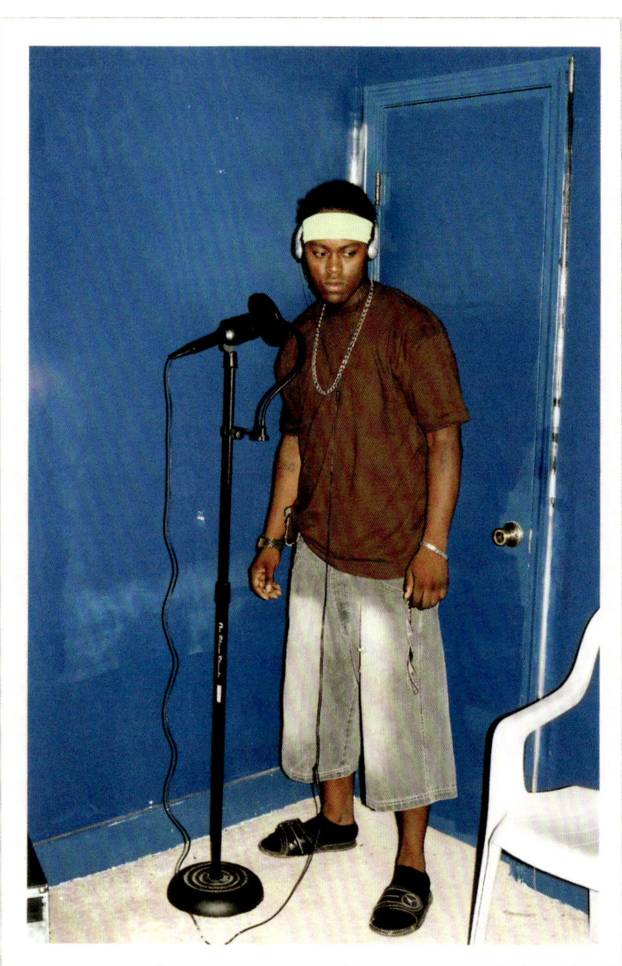

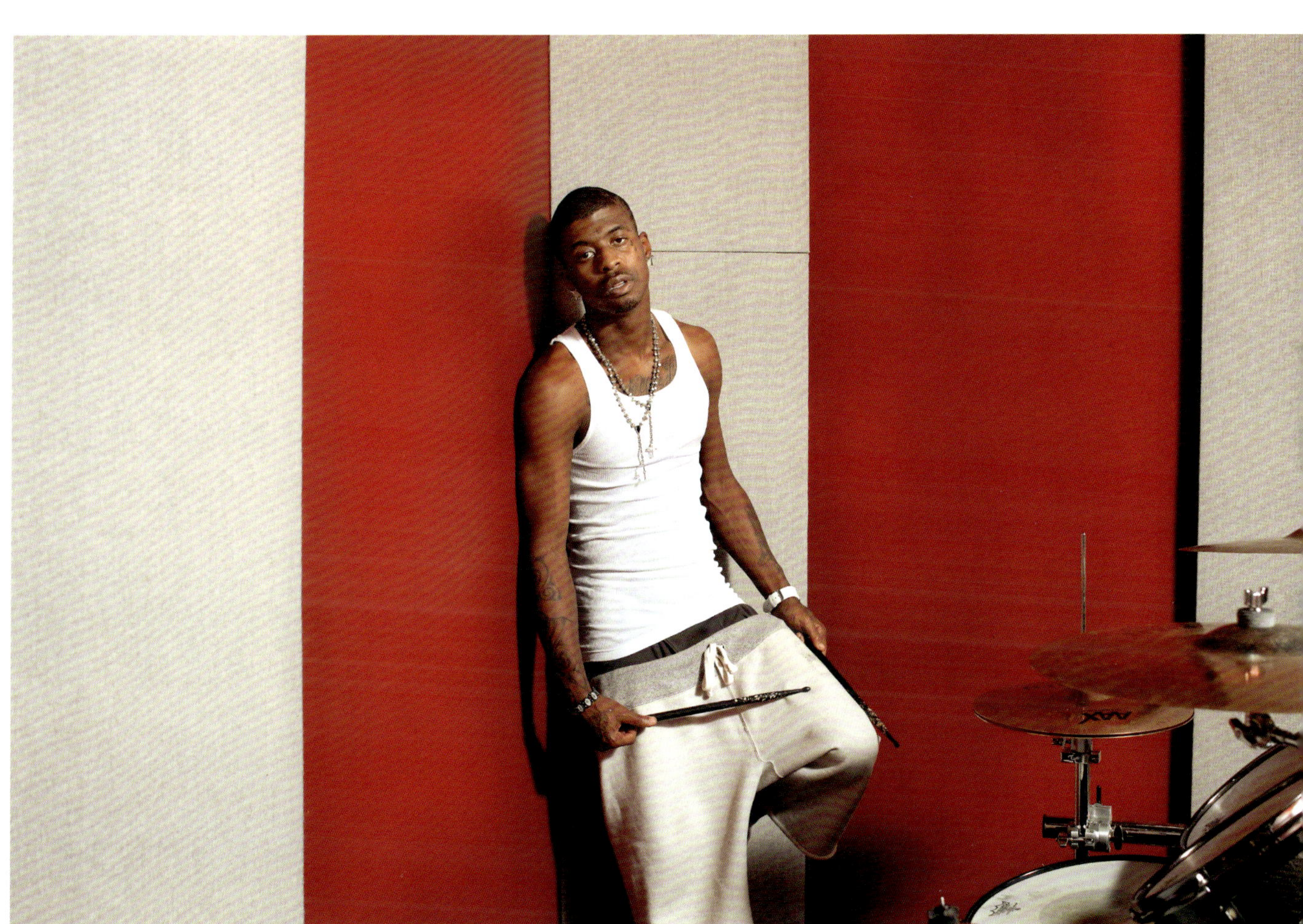

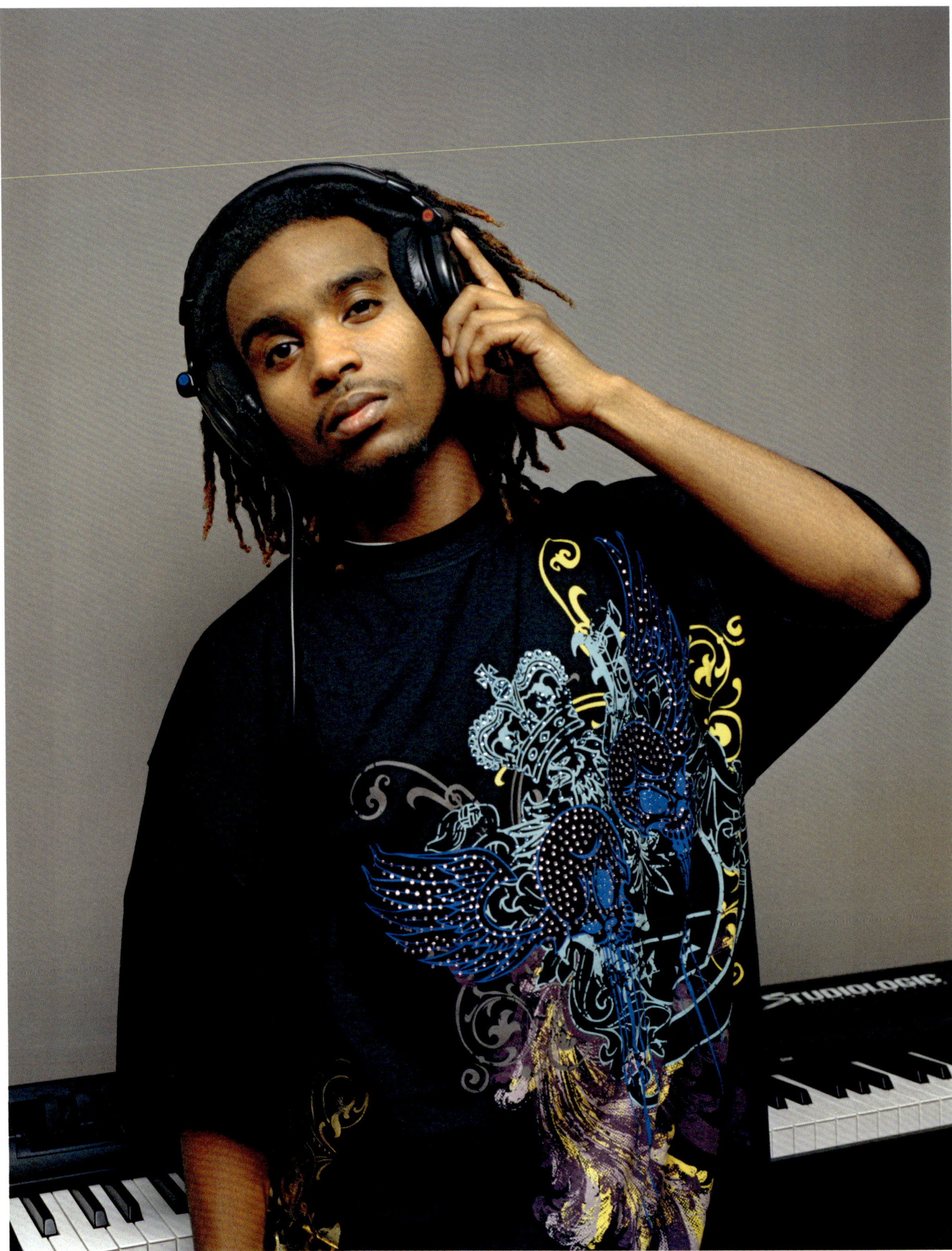

STUDIOLOGIC.

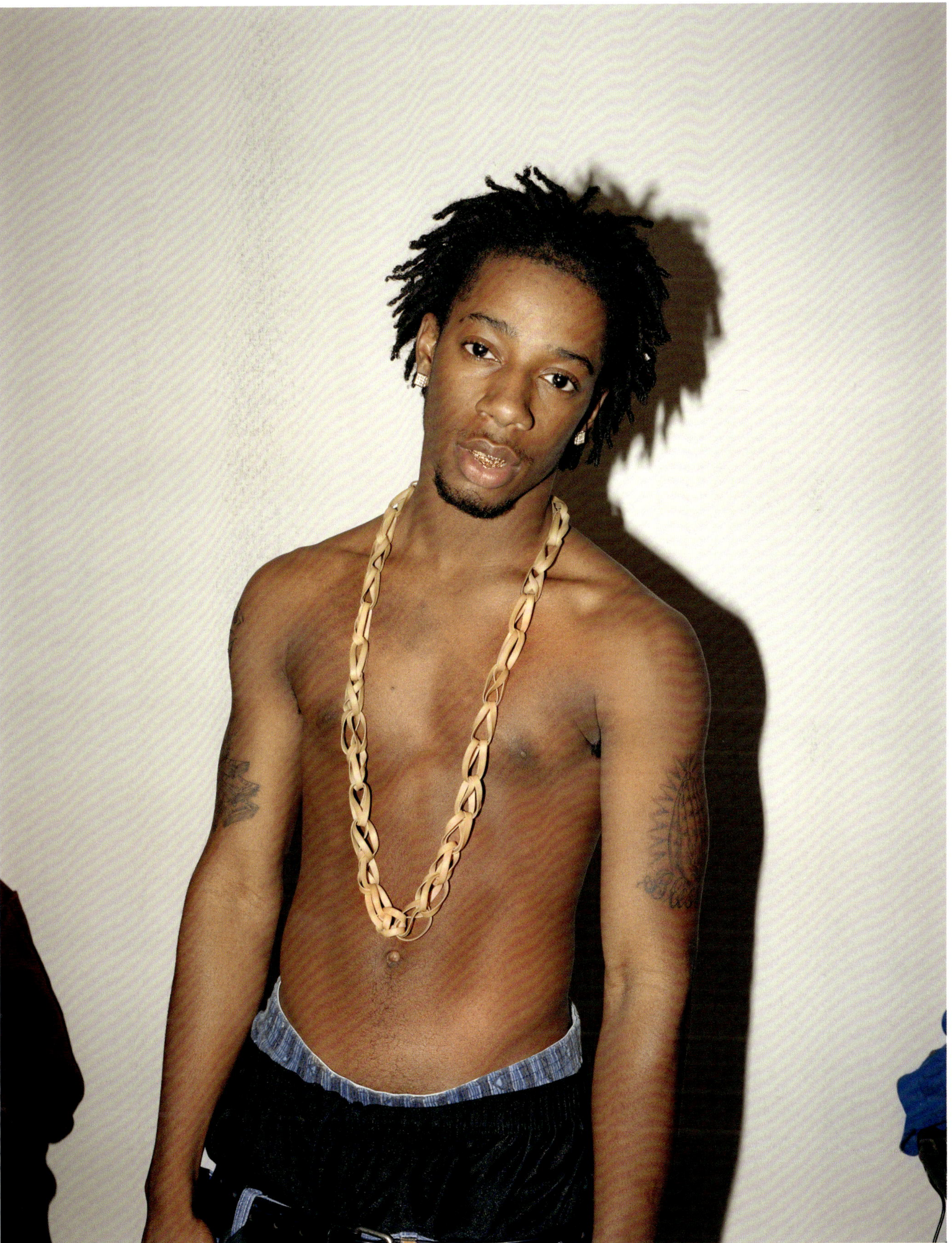

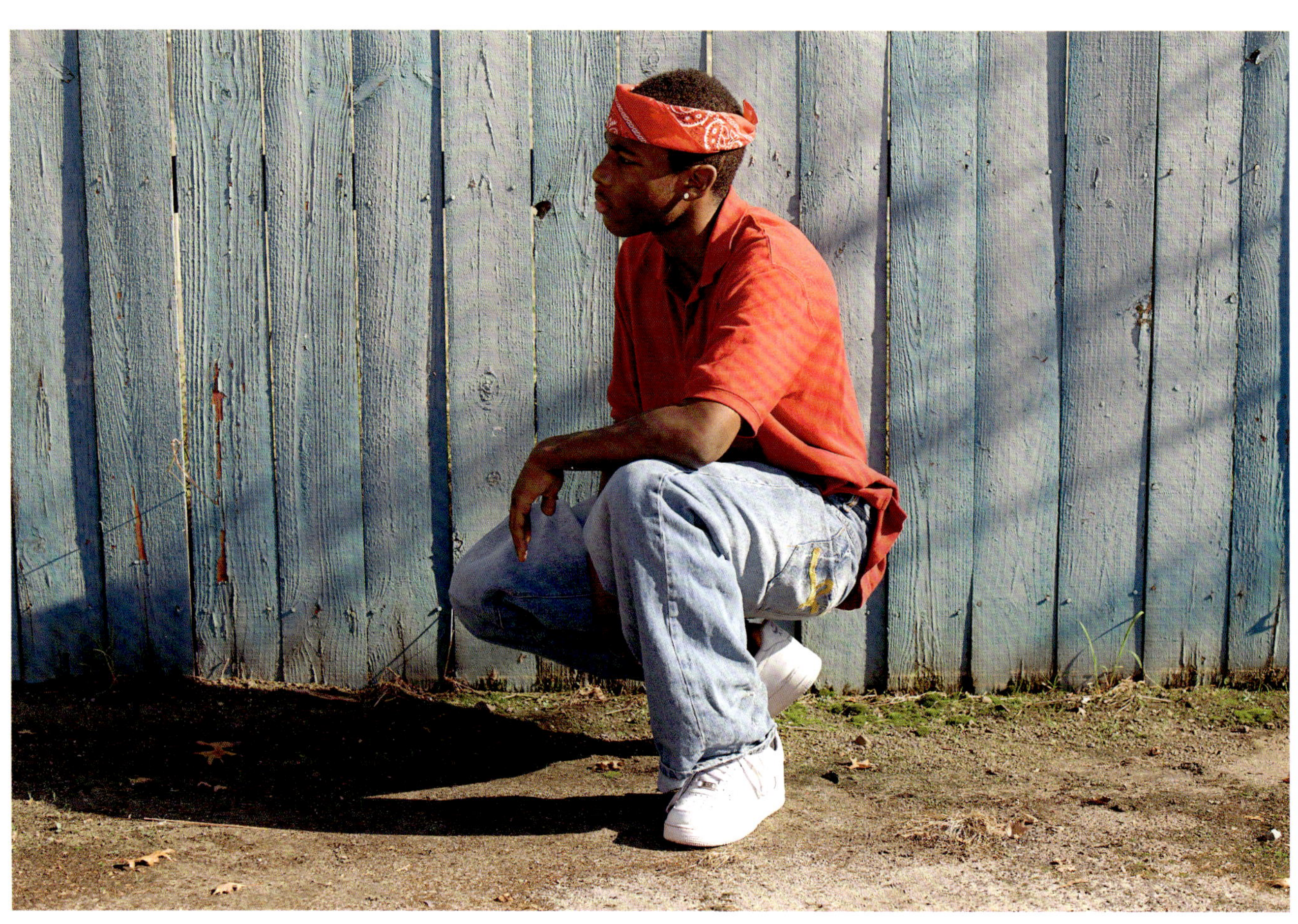

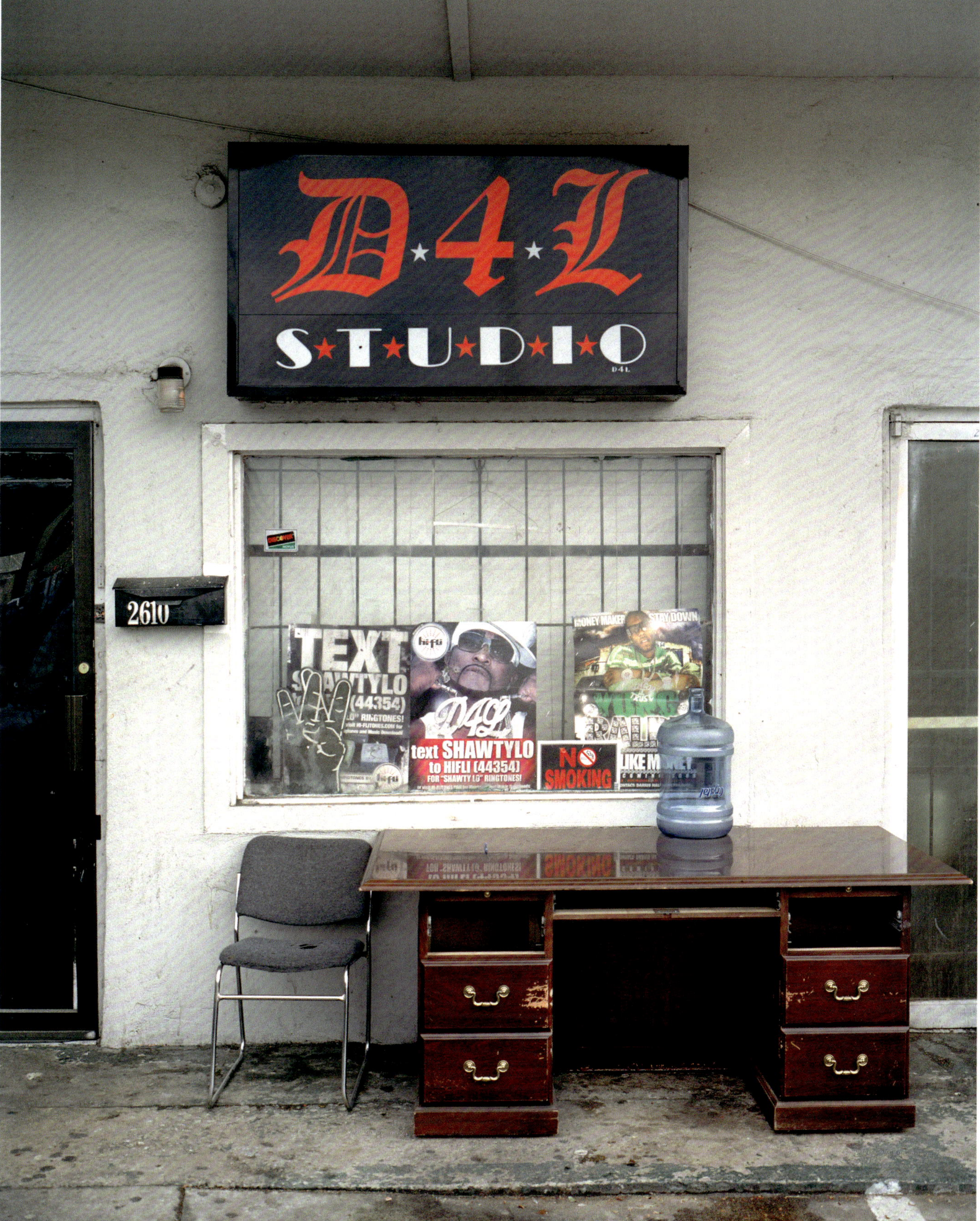
D·4·L
STUDIO
D 4 L
2610
TEXT
SHAWTYLO
(44354)
"LO" RINGTONES!
hi-fli
text SHAWTYLO
to HIFLI (44354)
FOR "SHAWTY LO" RINGTONES!
MONEY MAKER   STAY DOWN
NO SMOKING
LIKE MONEY

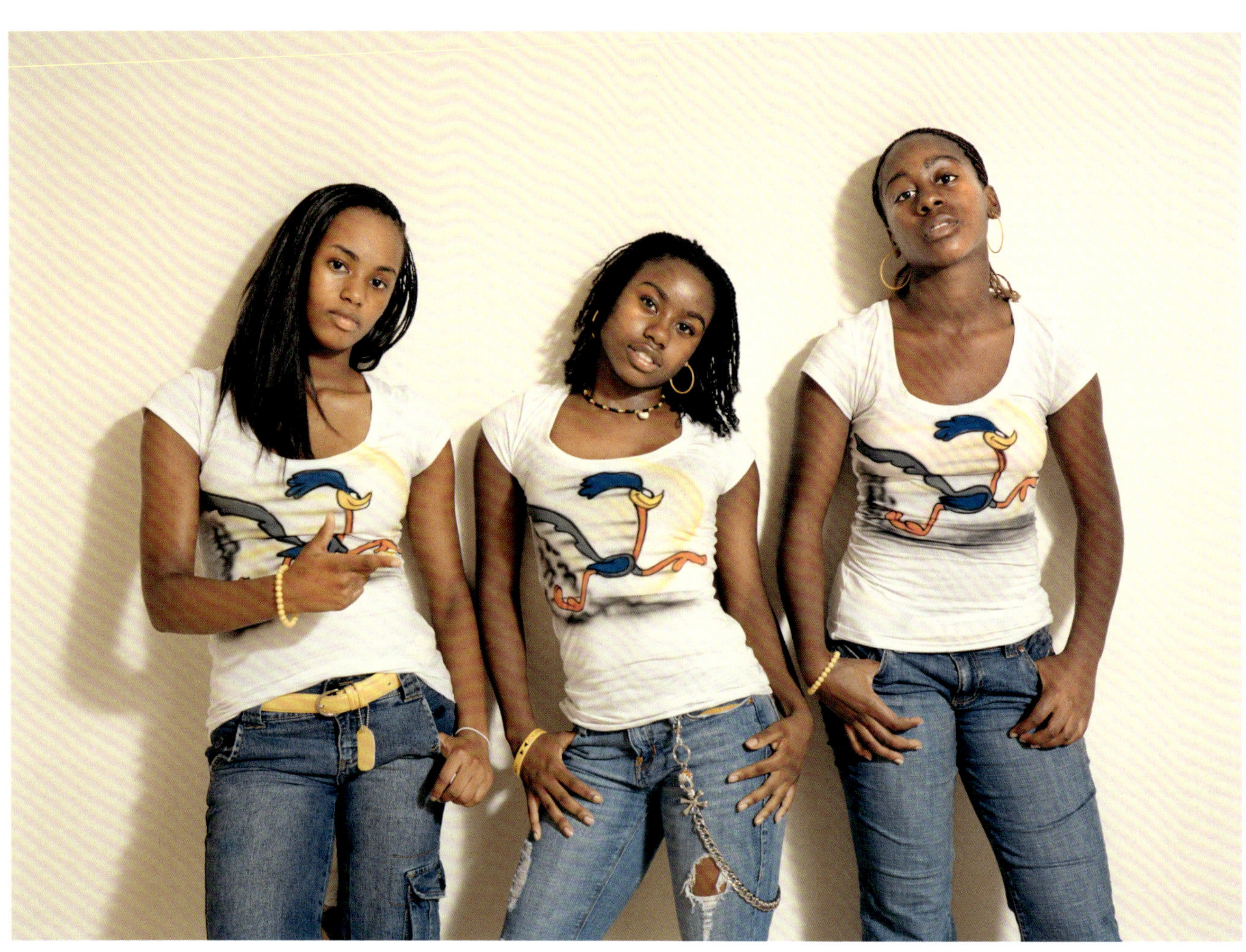

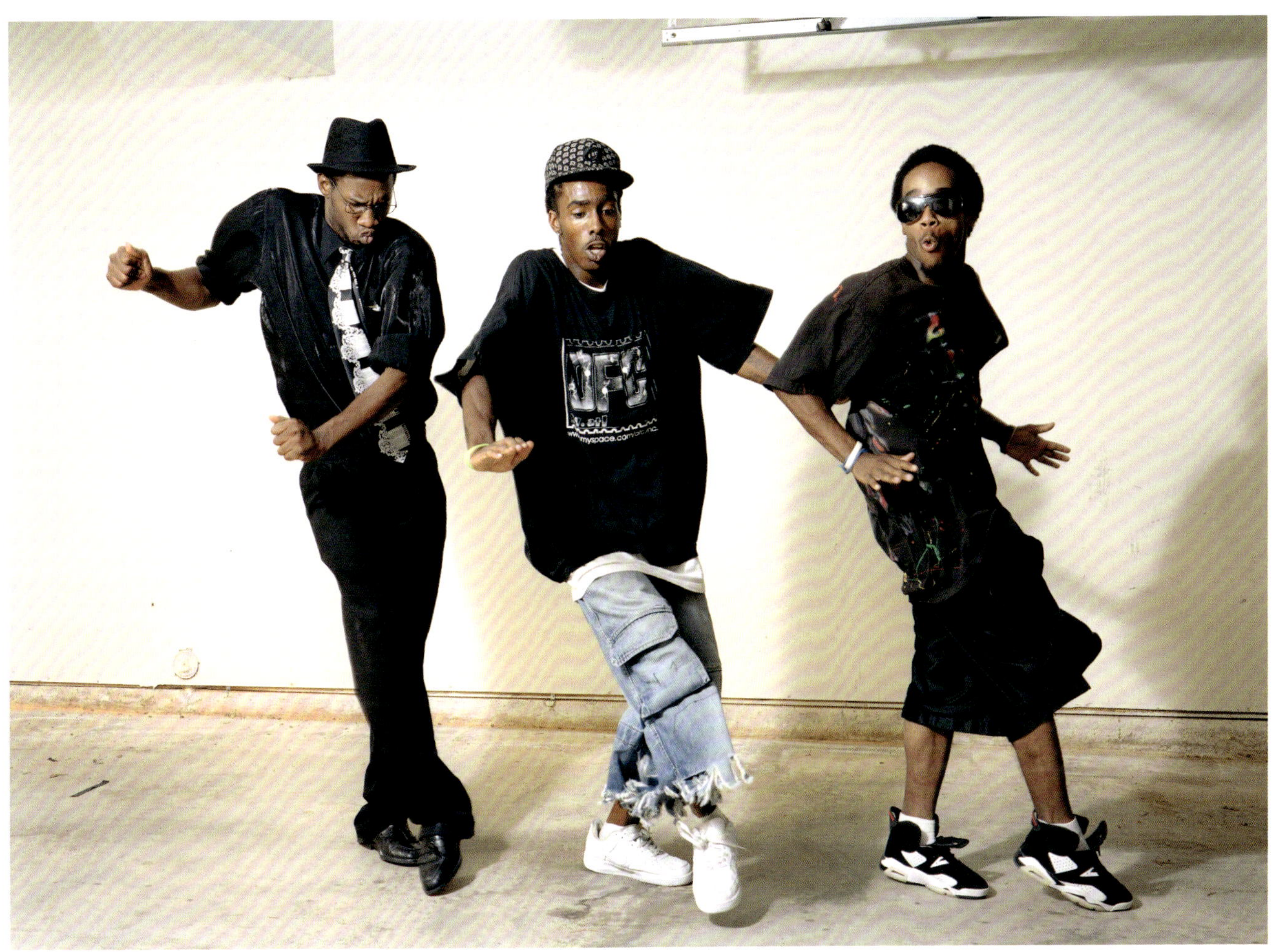

THE THING ABOUT SNAP
--

"Snap music," lightweight and aerodynamic, born in the clubs of Bankhead, on Atlanta's west side. In 2005 and 2006, snap went pop, spinning off national hits—"Laffy Taffy," by D4L; "Lean Wit It, Rock Wit It," by Dem Franchize Boyz; "Do It to It," by Cherish; "It's Goin' Down," by Yung Joc—each with its own moves. (Snap exploded at the same time as YouTube, which made it infinitely easier for kids around the world to watch each other dance.)

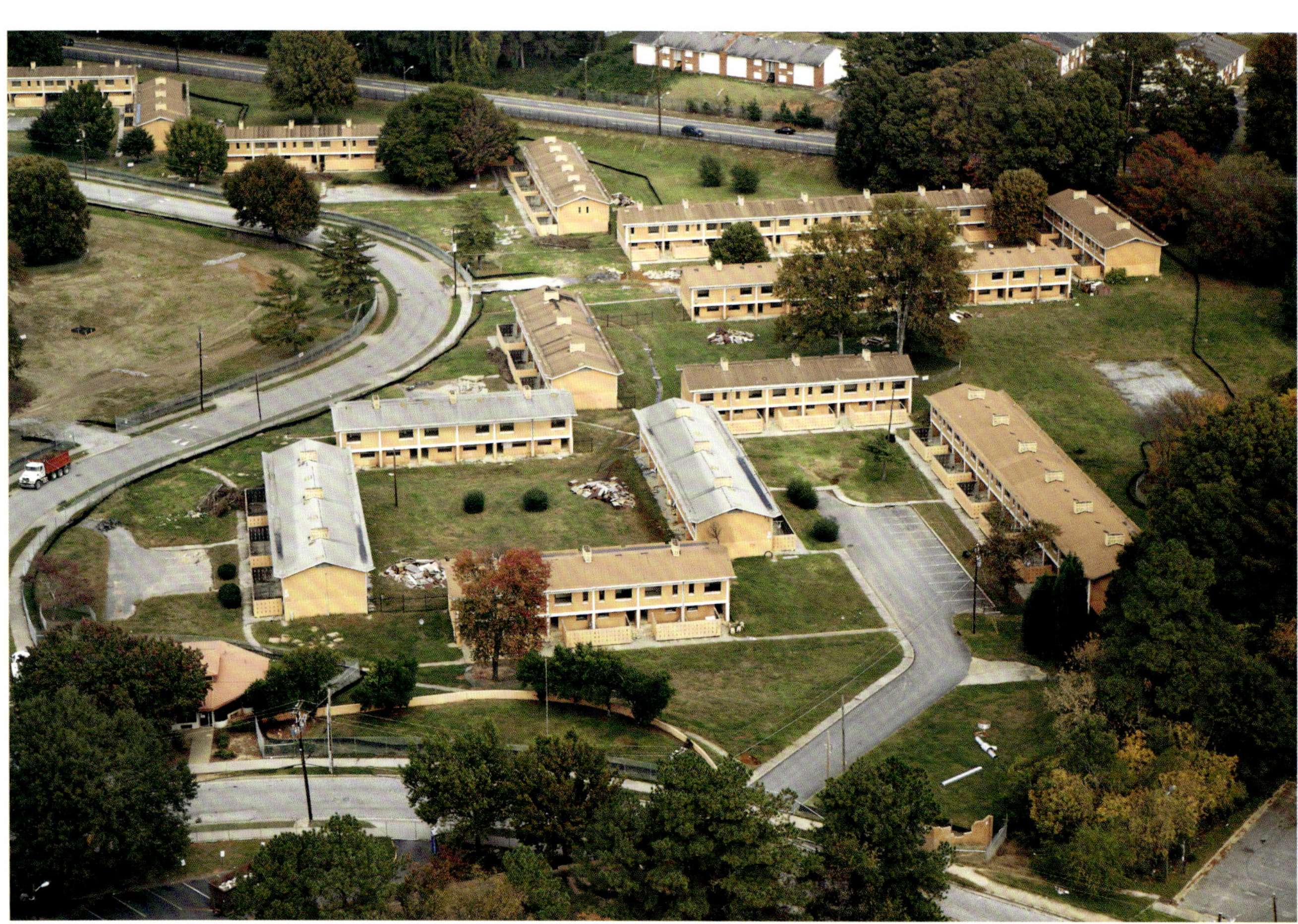

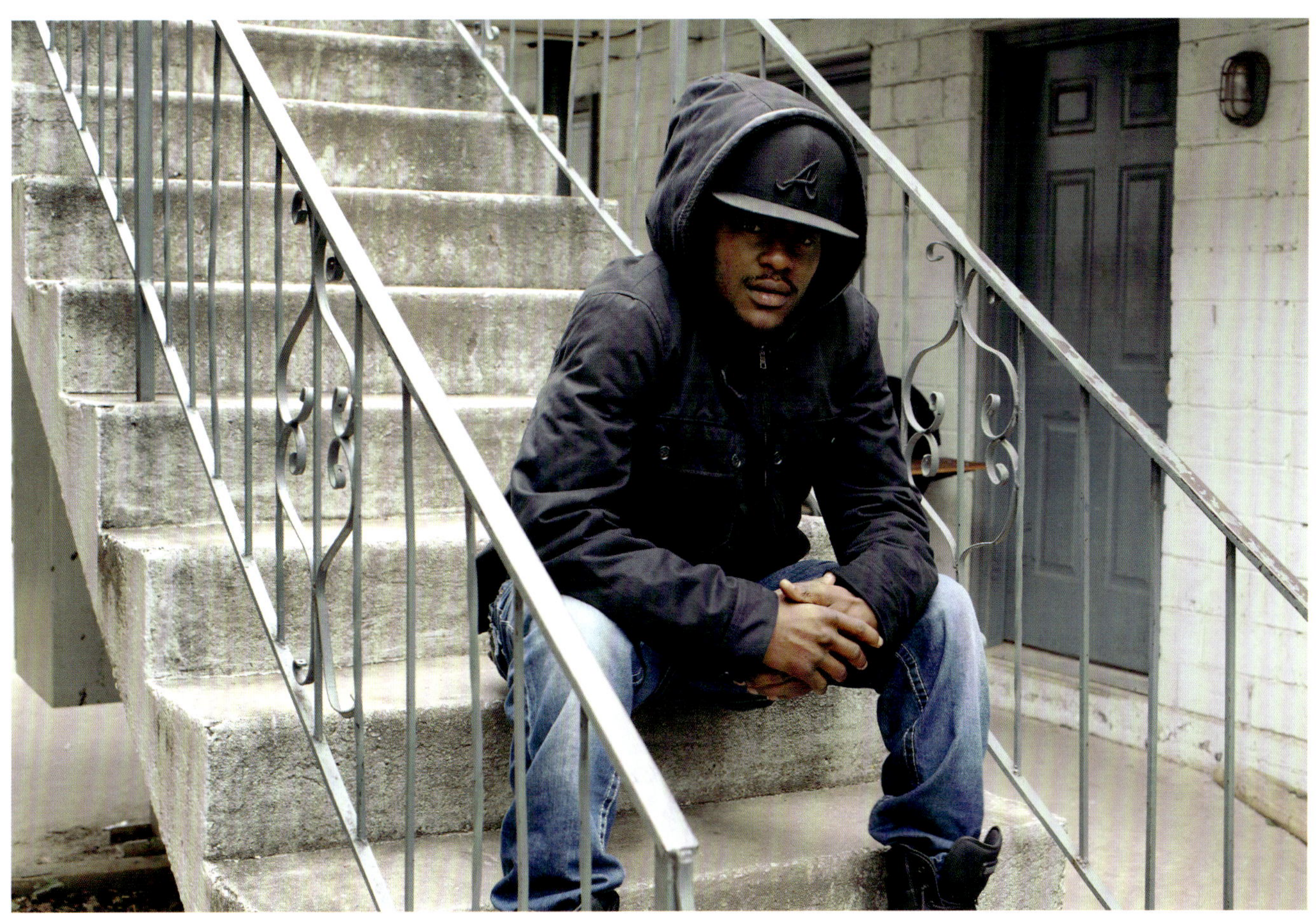

Trap: a noun (a place where drugs are sold), a verb (to sell drugs), and sometimes a subgenre; T.I. staked his claim in 2003, with *Trap Muzik*, his second album, and so did Young Jeezy, with his 2005 mixtape, *Trap or Die*. Unsmiling dudes rapping in the first person about the drug trade—in cities with less fertile musical scenes, they just call that "hip-hop."

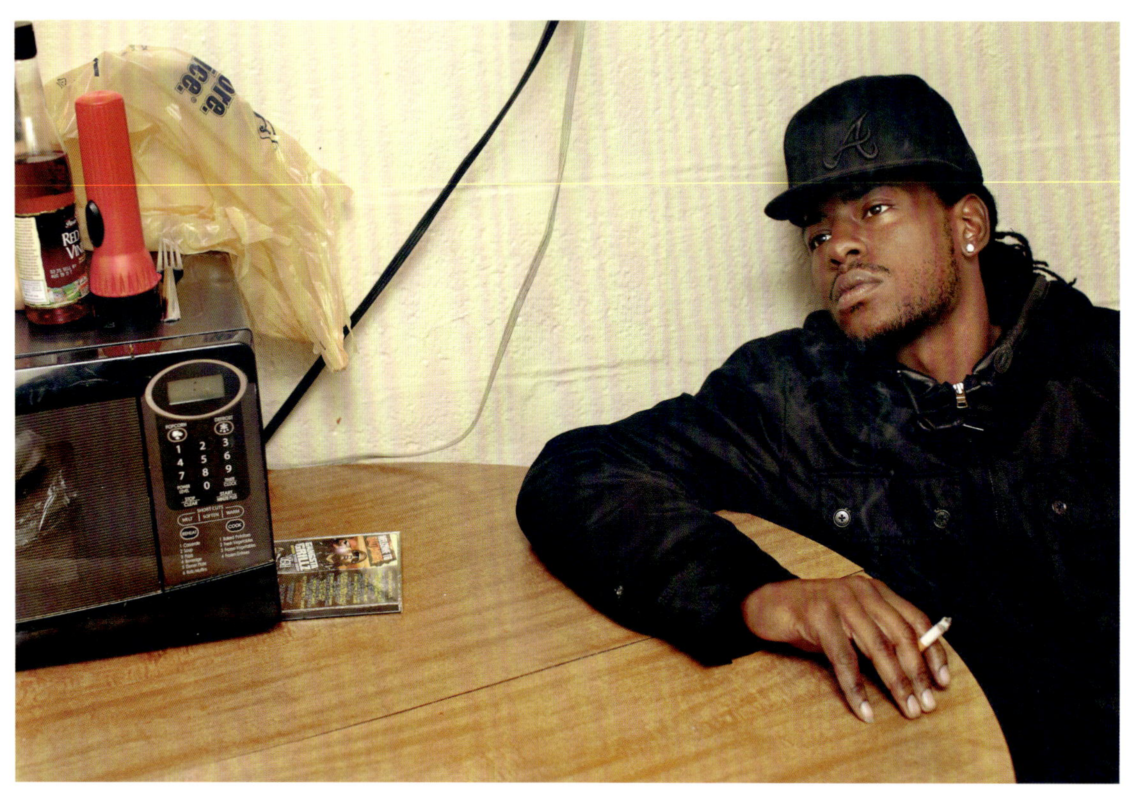

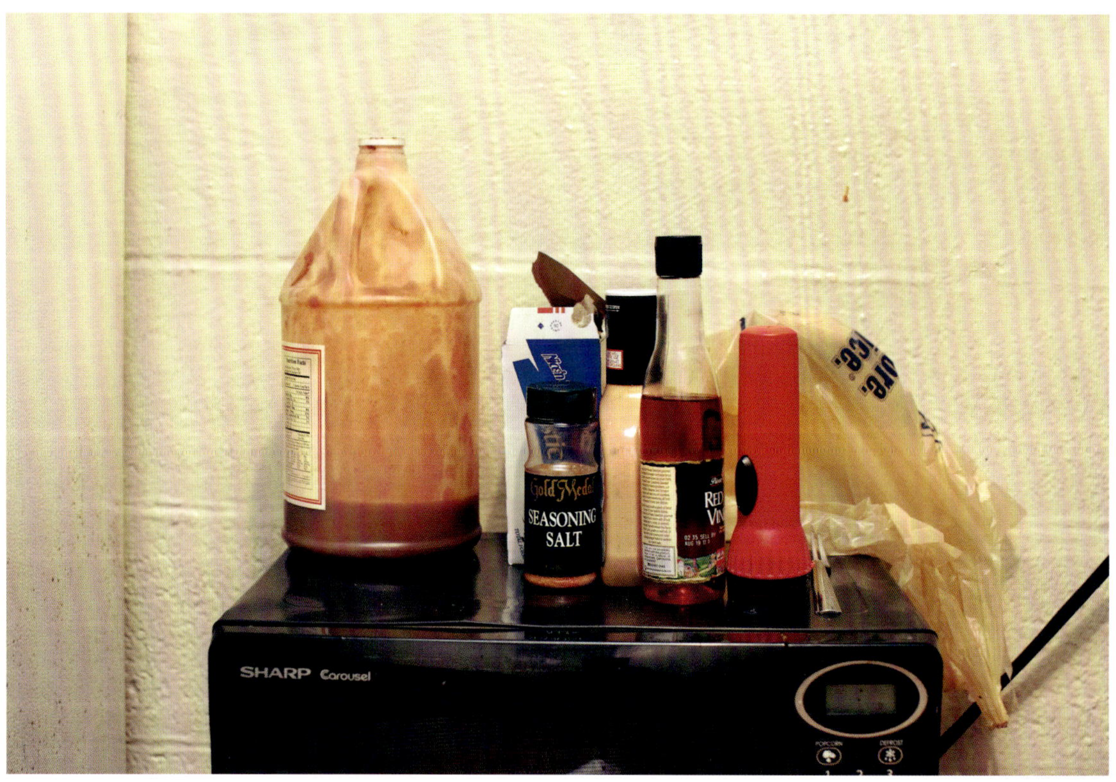
SHARP Carousel
Gold Medal
SEASONING
SALT

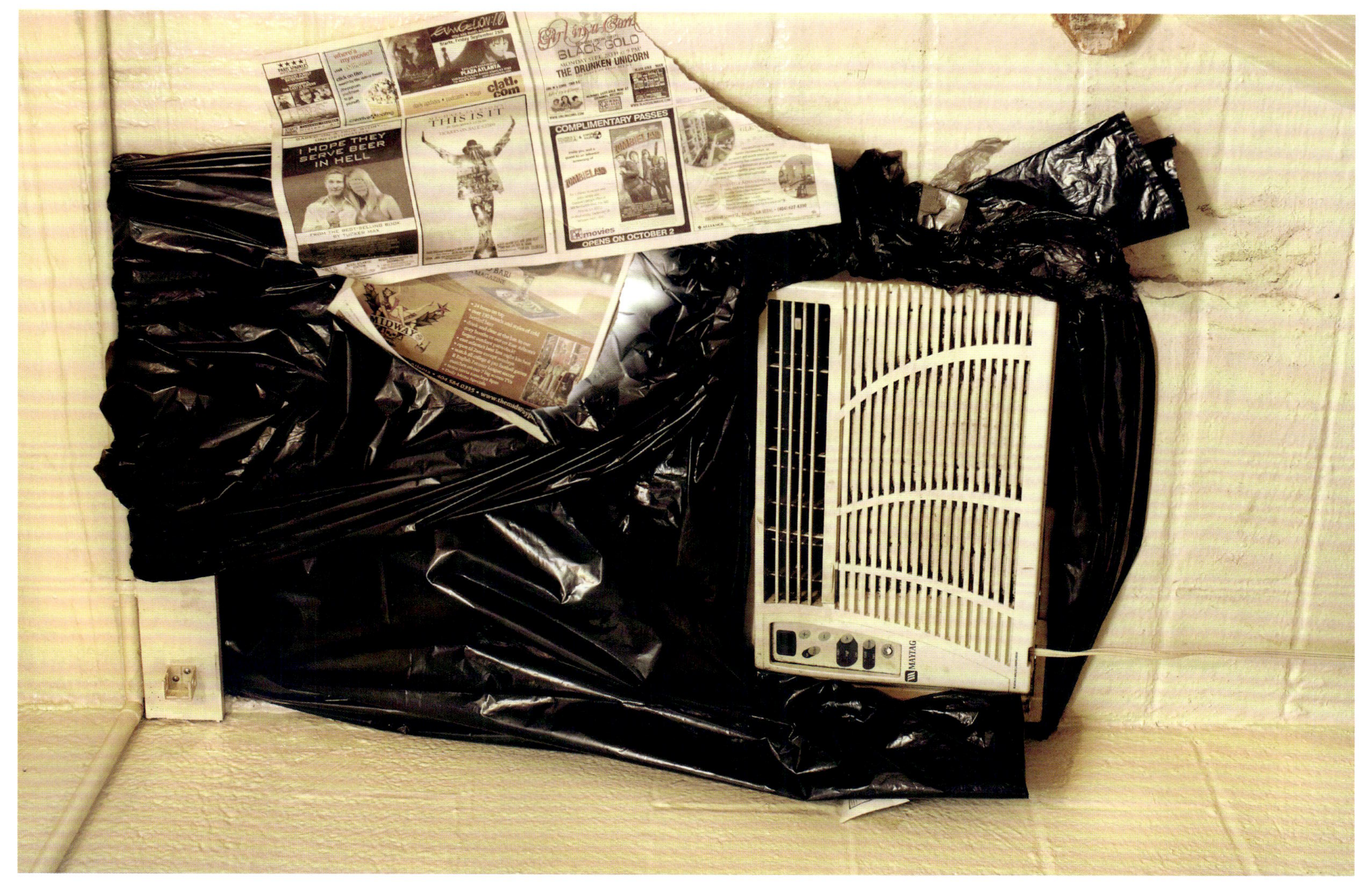
EVANGELION:1.0
where's my money?
clati.com
PLAZA ATLANTA
THIS IS IT
I HOPE THEY SERVE BEER IN HELL
FROM THE BEST-SELLING BOOK BY TUCKER MAX
BLACK GOLD
THE DRUNKEN UNICORN
COMPLIMENTARY PASSES
ZOMBIELAND
movies
OPENS ON OCTOBER 2
MAYTAG

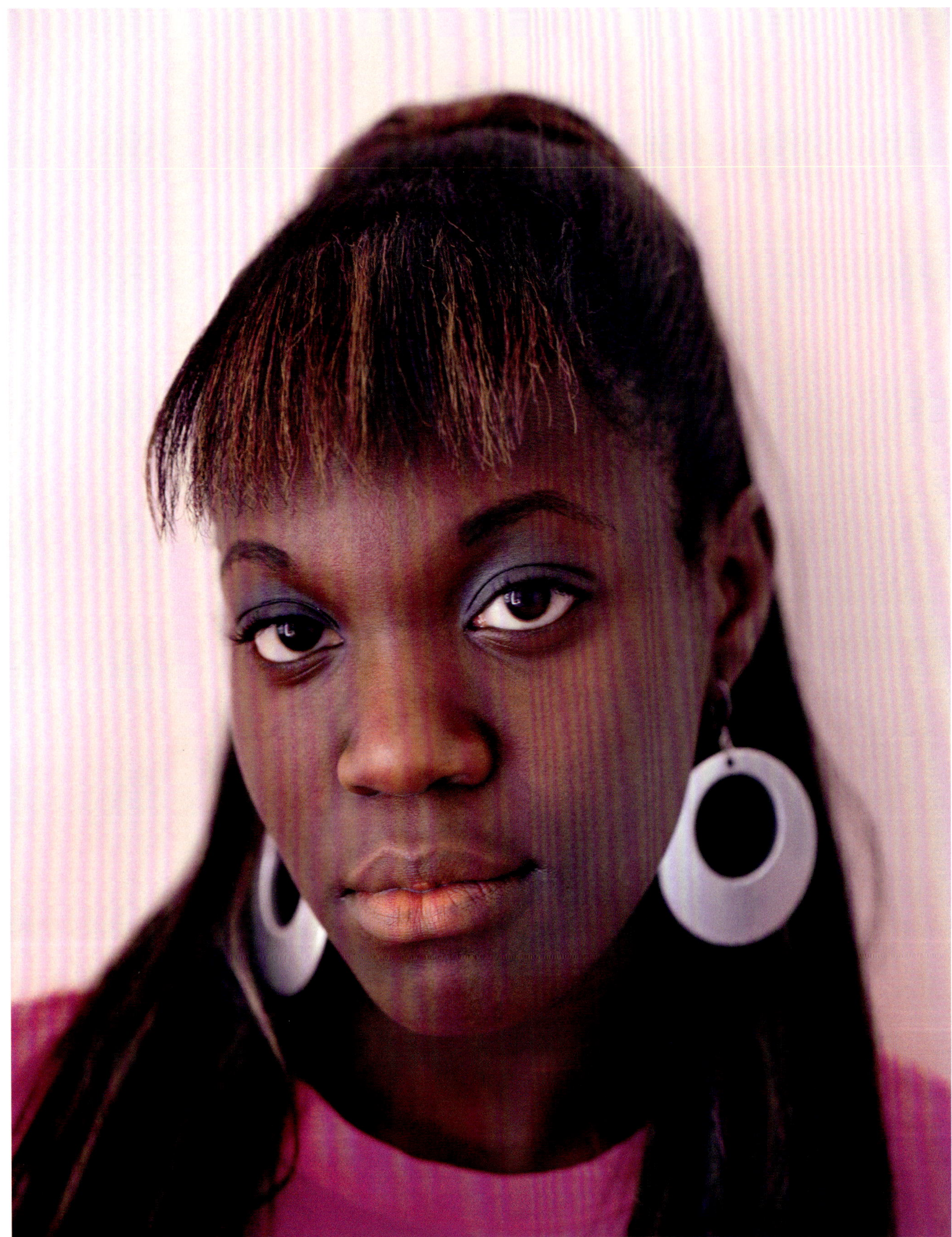

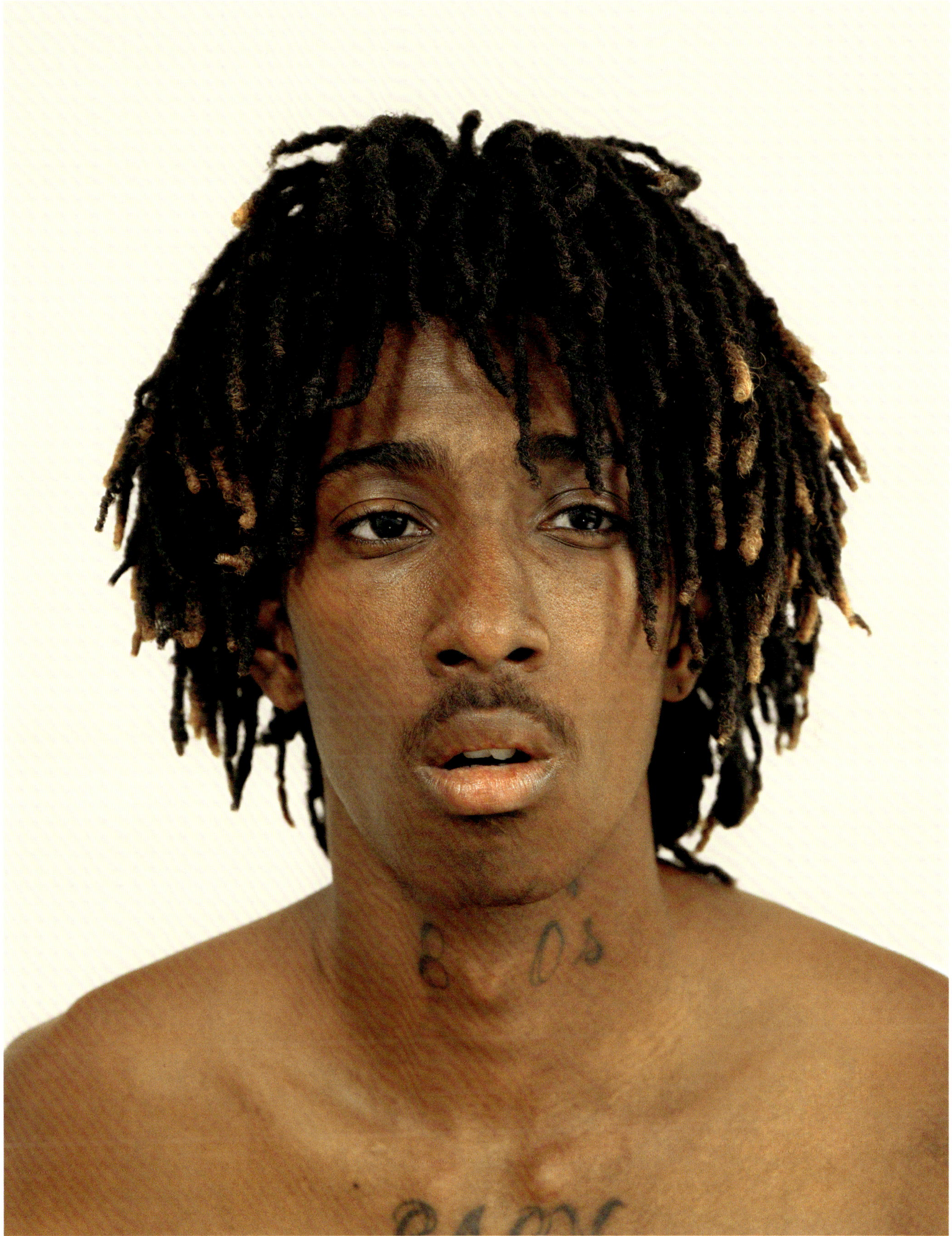

cartoen Shawty Ralph lauren fo de
flow homes 9 thousand dallas worth
al clothes on 500 thousand dallas worll of gold
on over 500 diamonds in my do chain in
hunderd 45 thousand on Both arms
Right wrist hundred grand watch
Coc don Ebbocs on da belf thats ah
dope arm 2 gloss on da stuff I be so
armed DRo JuAn while you flipping out
and dissing me Imma award hustle
thing peep da Authenticity Prison G
Isnt he bearing em like Grizztey Martin
luther King in da Melann up at Busy Bee
J.T.G. illy Philly mills meek's either G
Me and charlie mack arrest the cardiac
fill he no breathe he know me Shawty say
he wild But Im wilder Ricky chown Simpson
40 pounds on da prowler DRo

DRO Heep ah pocket full lah do da down
thang money got da mad face an cash
aint ah damn thang funny I can datt em
me ah jet I got dat airplane money fish
scale gray blocs this is Rare caine honey
tell em meet me in ahova when I get off
get out de shower Im in de trump tower
Pine apple Prowlen I use to tickle den hoes
till dem hoes went sour they say that drop
Rose on dim 4s meant Power long bread ball head
Just like Ron howard you aint selling weight till
you got Metro ton Powder BMF neache left
Shit n on dim like Bowels trap a yay whale weight
face point is drizzoe game iteed up slam dunking
Bricks so dwight Beame howard hondred shot
Aikin till yo Patruk say he coward

"Shoulder Lean," by Young Dro, topped the rap charts in 2006. The chorus (delivered by T.I.) went, "Let me see you bounce, right to left, and let your shoulder lean," but somehow this wasn't really a dance track—it was too woozy, for one thing. Young Dro's voice was about as thick as his drawl; he sounded as if he had a cold and hated terminal consonants. And the more he rapped, the stranger things got; sometime after the two-minute mark, he announced, "Pearl Bent,' cockin' hammer, Arm & Hammer propaganda/Bitches think I'm pimpin' and leanin' in salamander sandals." Young Dro is some kind of genius, and also a classicist, in his way: a believer in the power of syllables, neatly stacked and precisely delivered; a believer in the power of telling details (he's obsessed with seafood) and unexpected references. But he's not a crank or a crusader; he seems to like being slightly out of place in a scene, and a city, where word-nerds don't rule. He made a mixtape with Yung LA and they called it *Black Boy White Boy*. Yung LA rapped and sang in a ridiculous "Wayne's World" voice, and Young Dro delivered his absurd but precise couplets—they made a pretty good team. By 2009, Dro had emerged as a hometown favorite: a mentor to emerging acts, and one of Atlanta's favorite rappers, even though the rest of the country mainly knew him as the "Shoulder Lean" guy. Which might mean that he skipped straight from rookie to veteran without ever quite becoming a star.

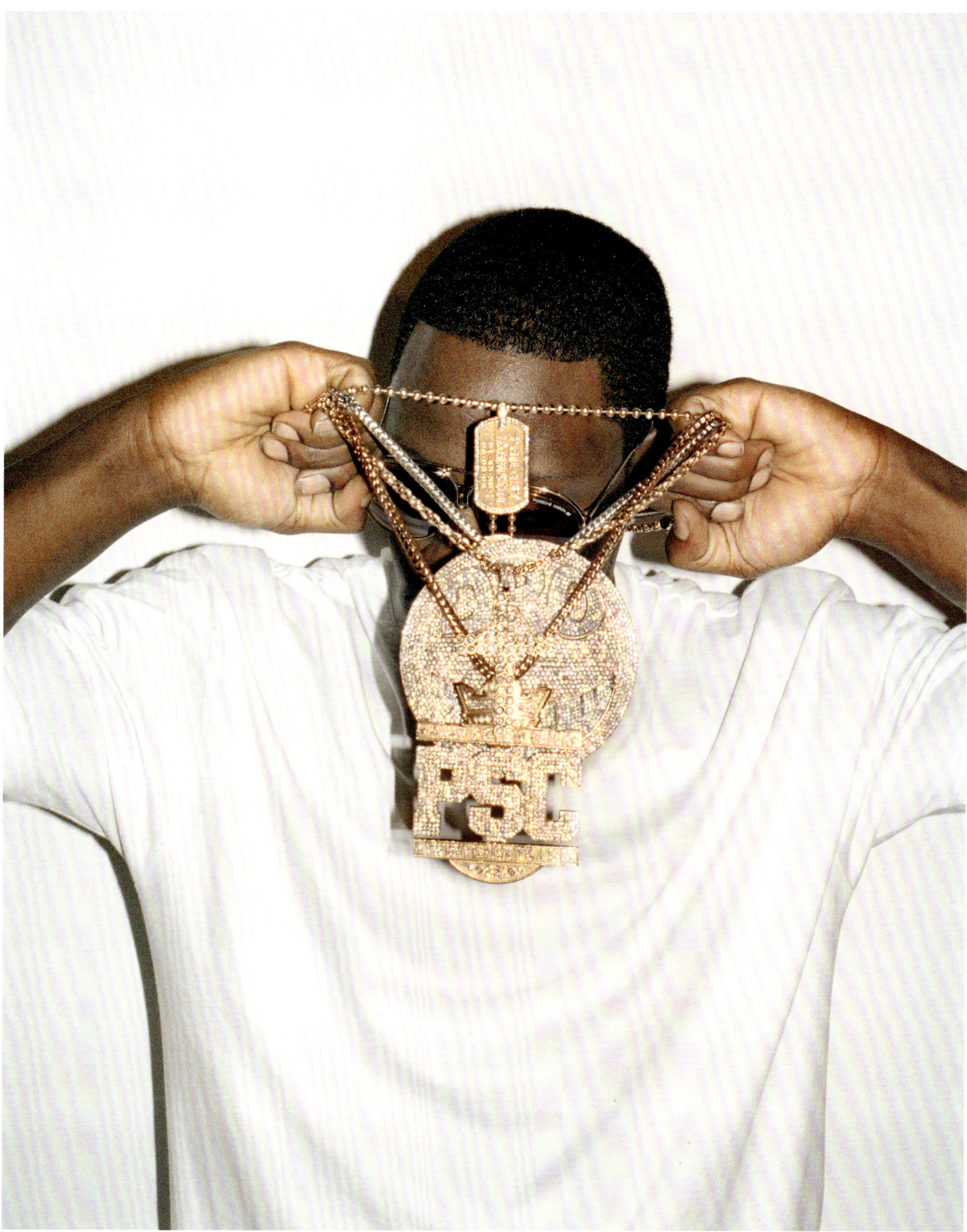

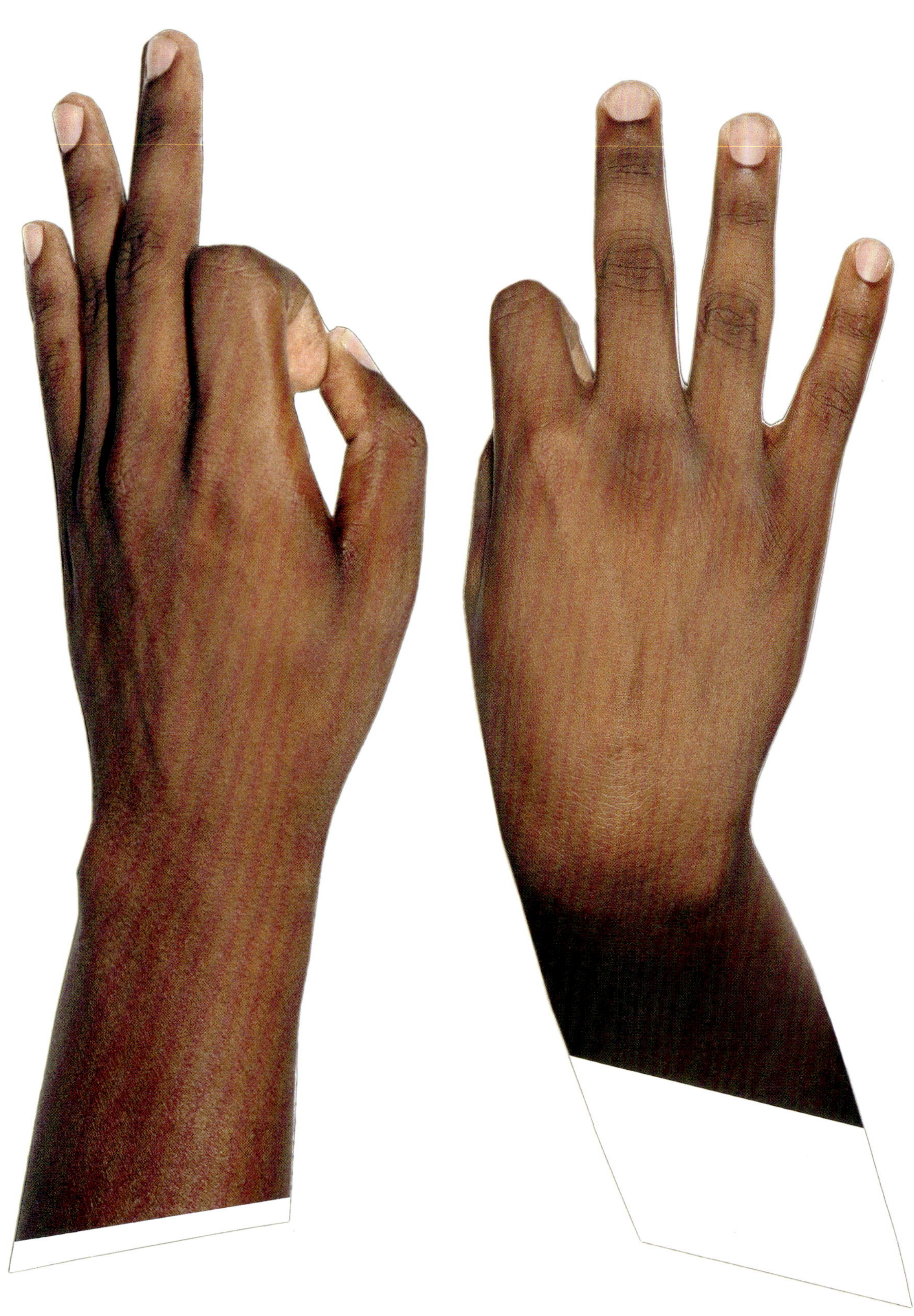

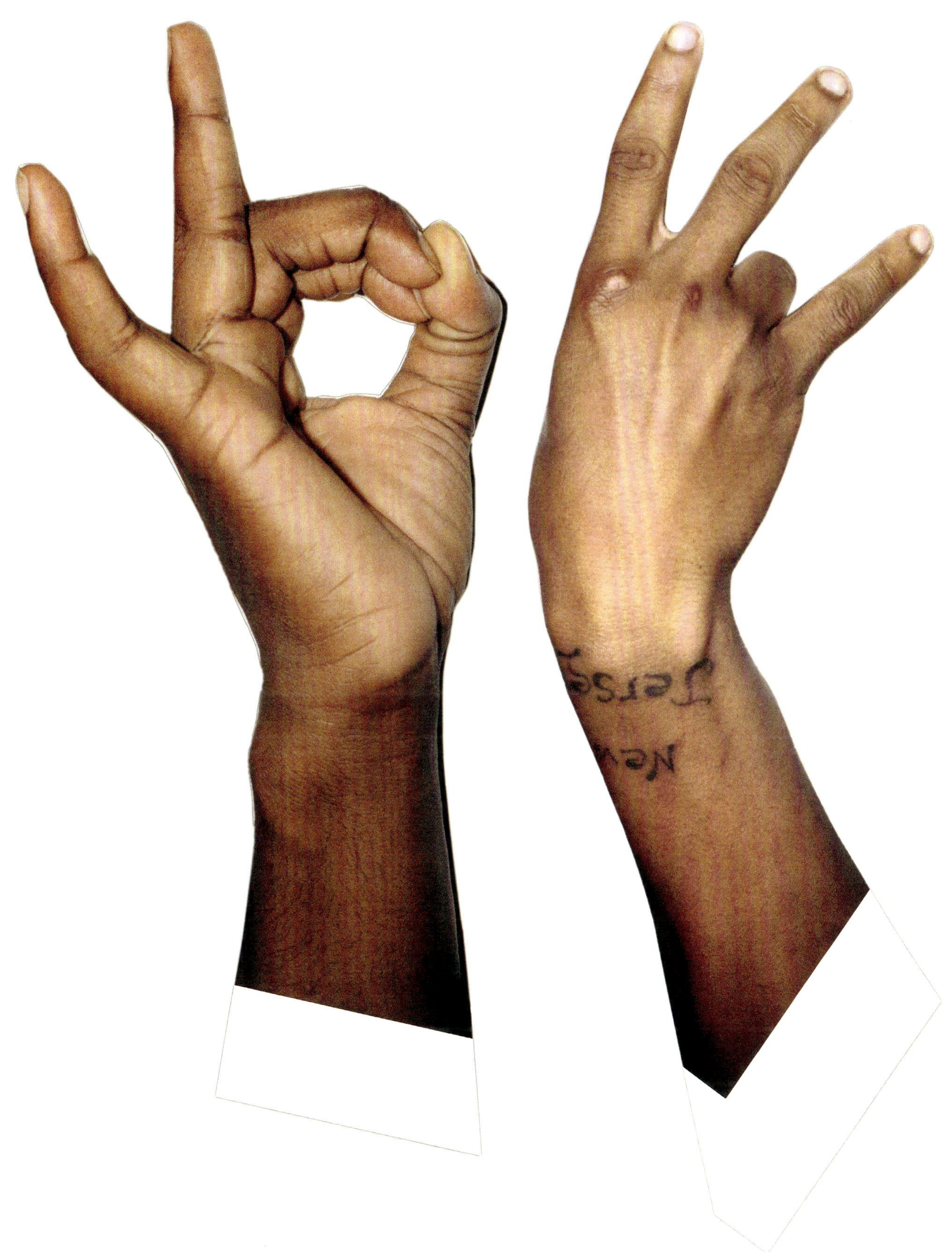
New Jersey

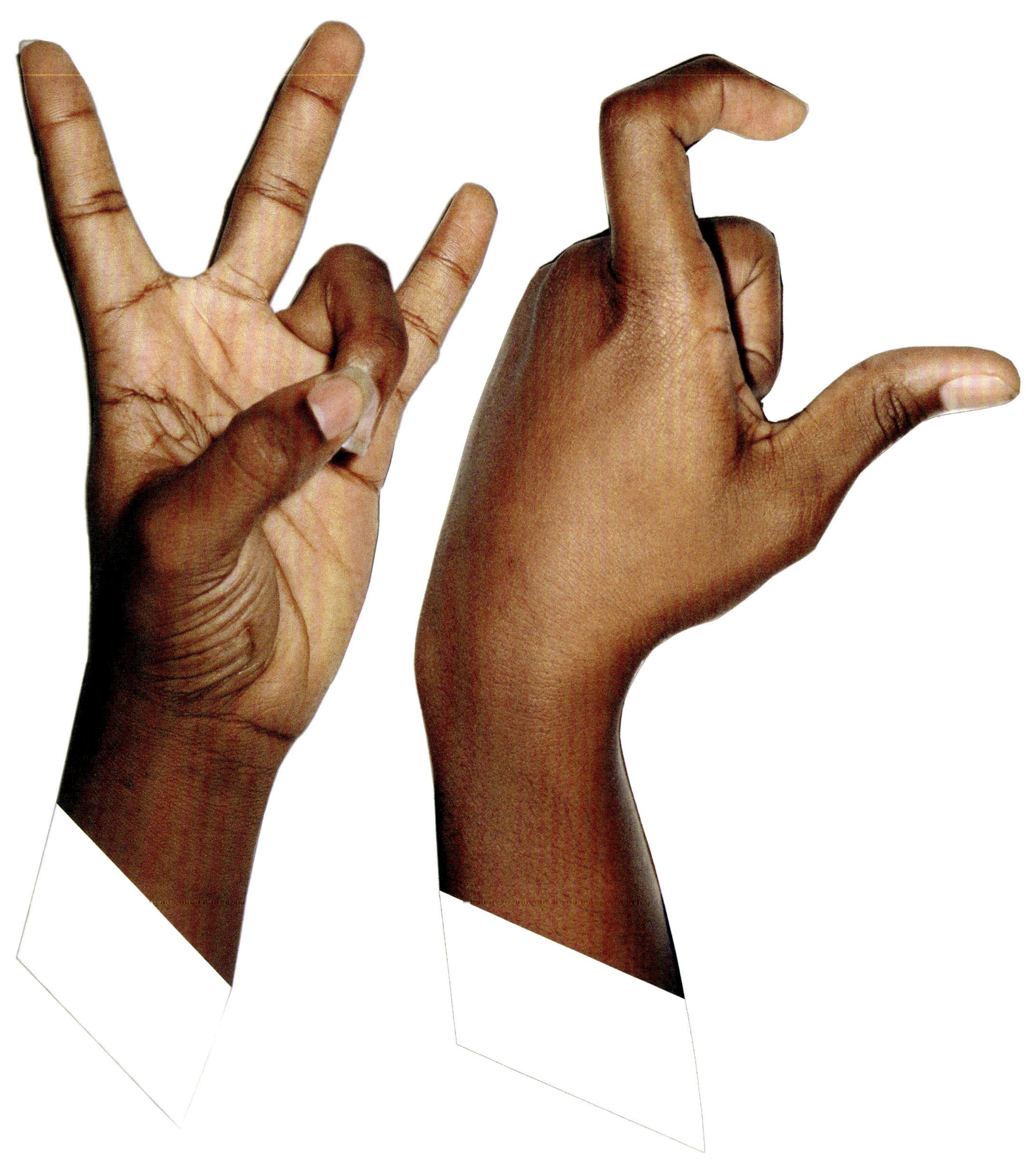

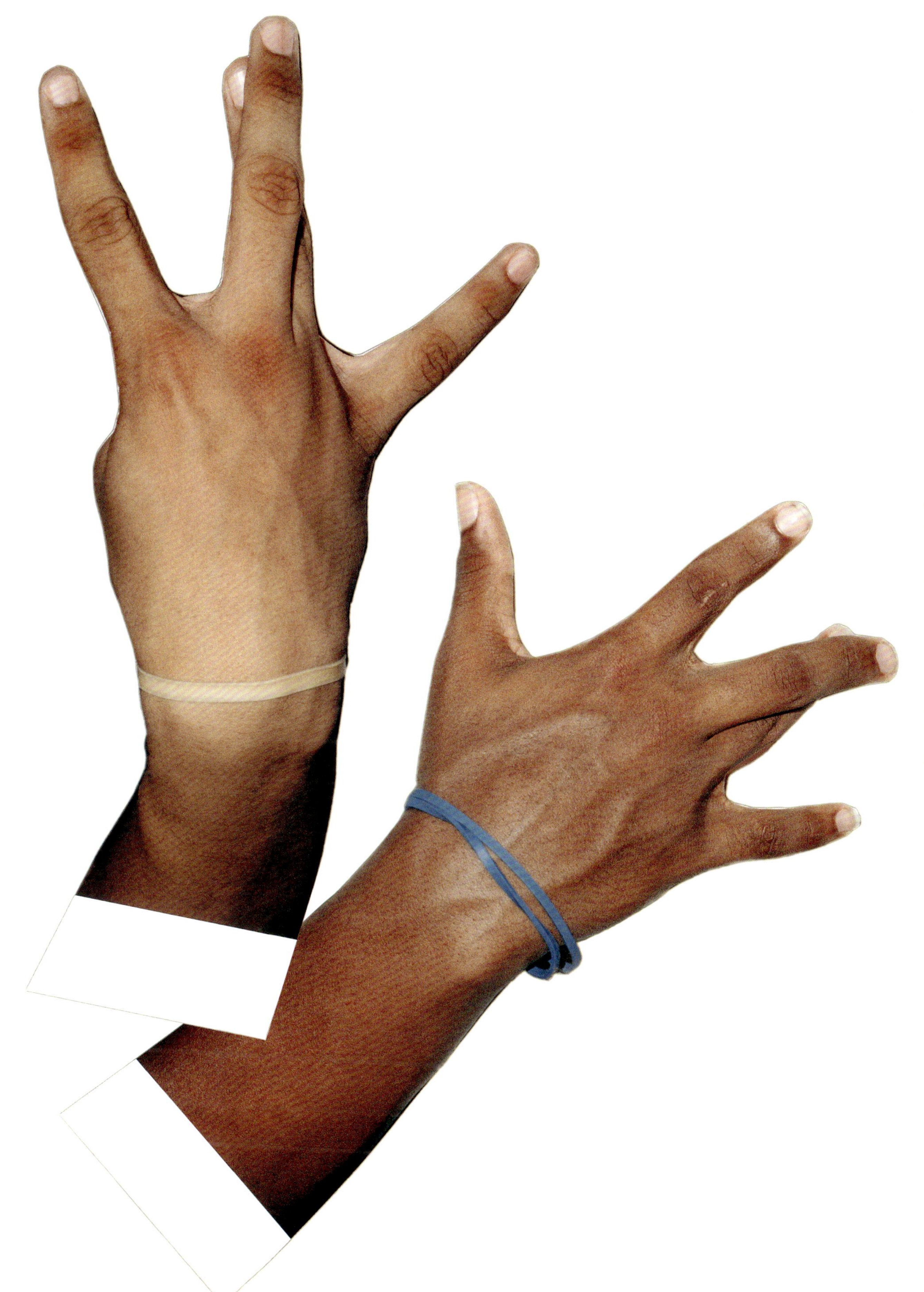

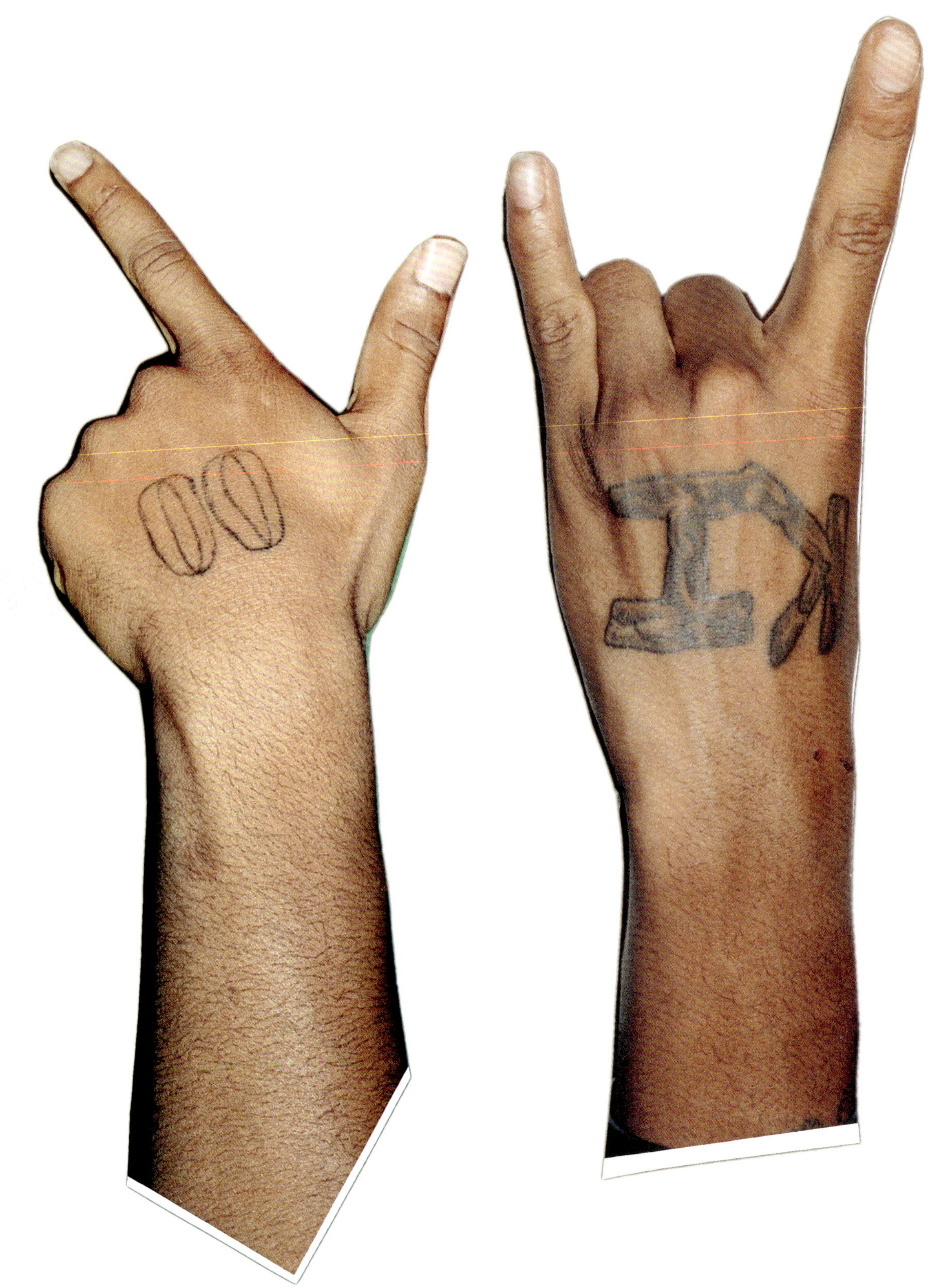

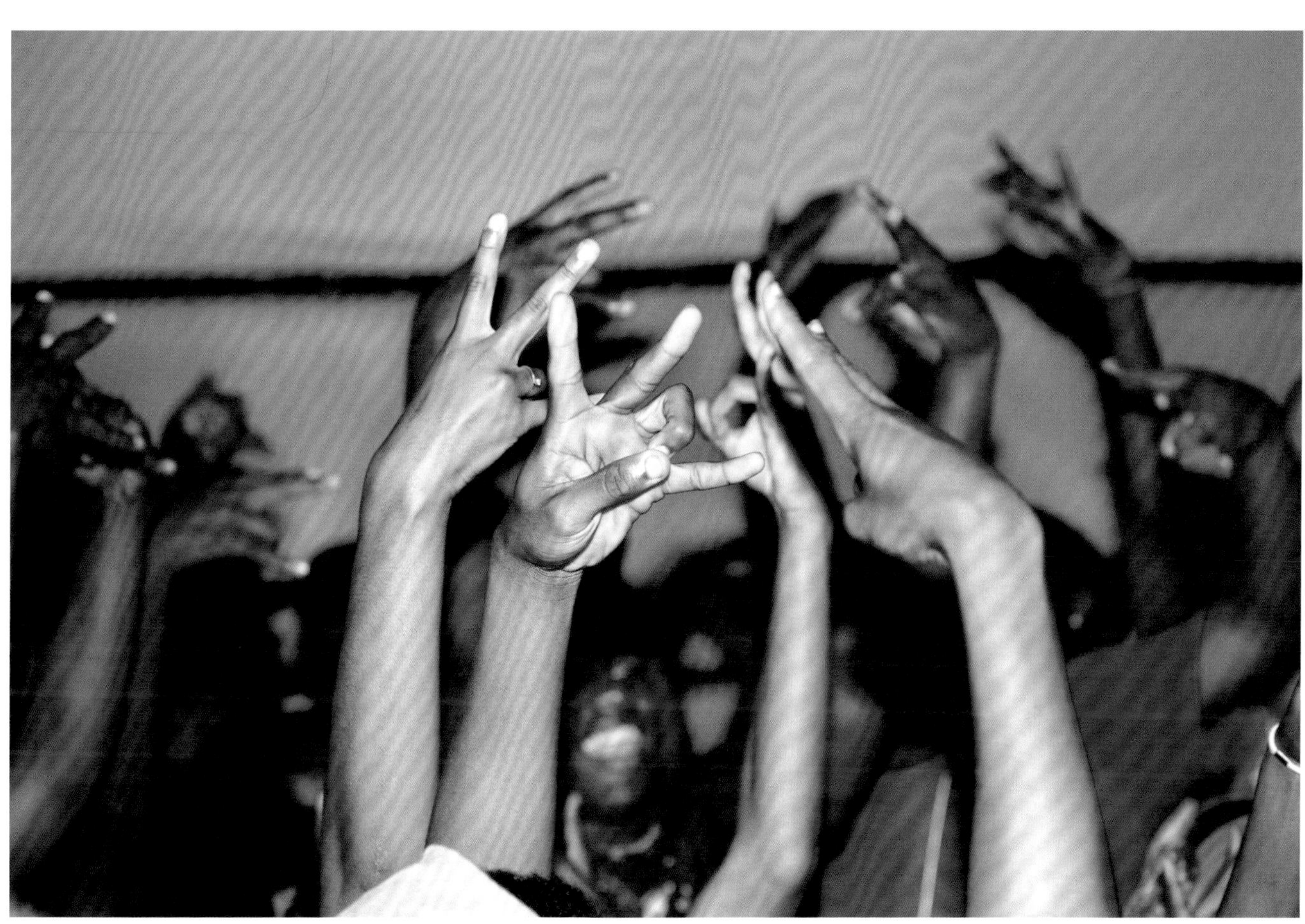

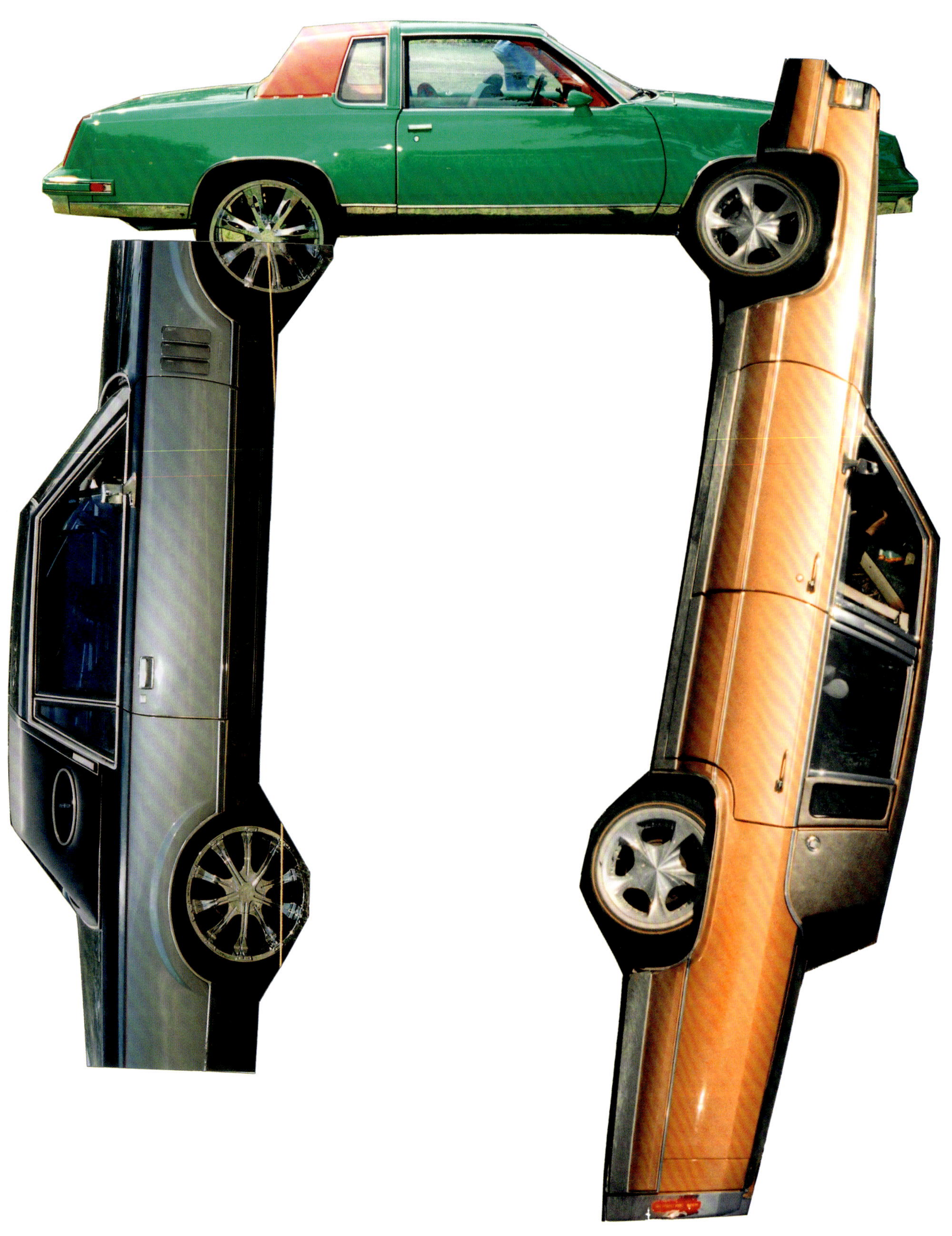

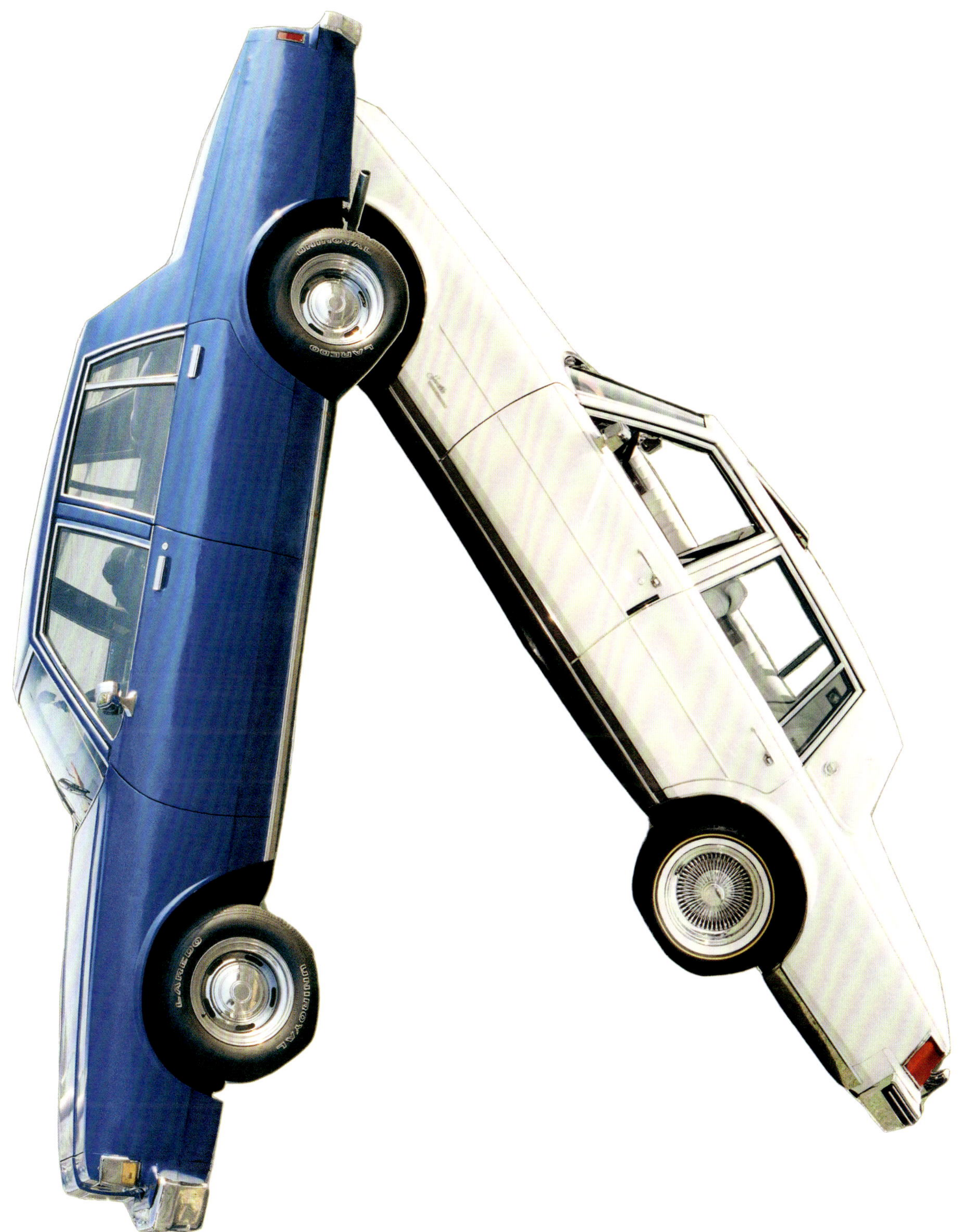

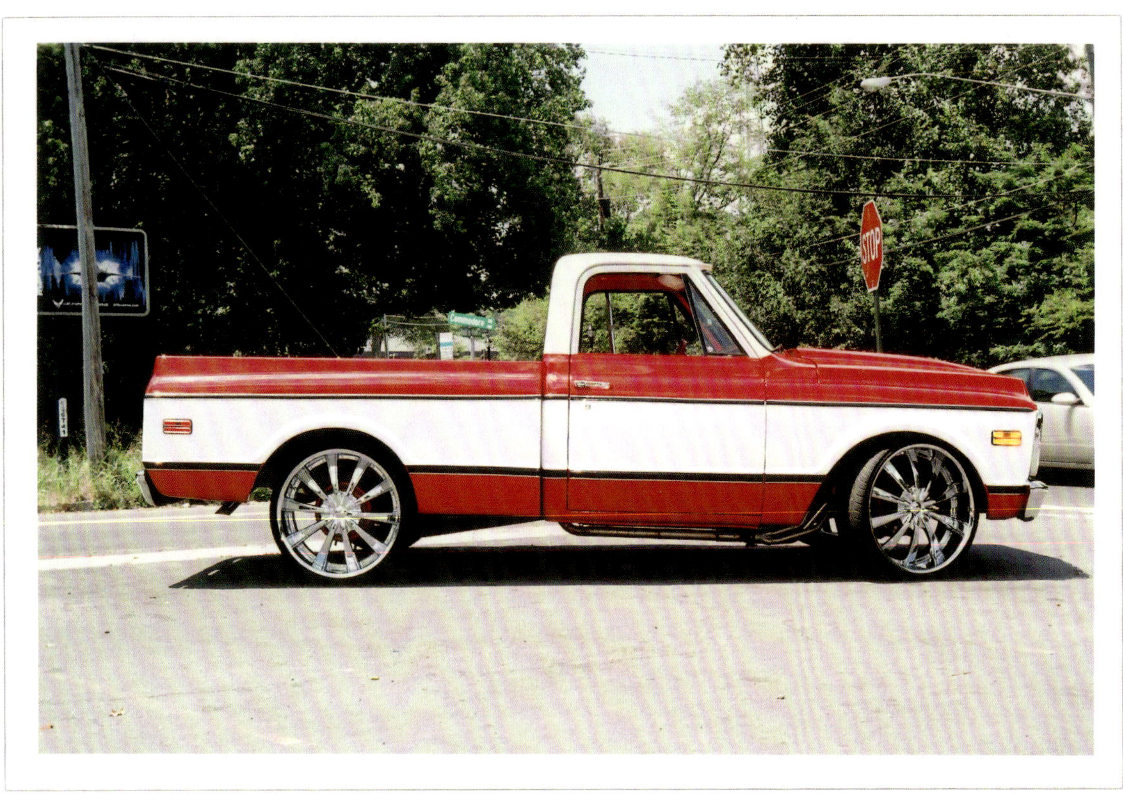

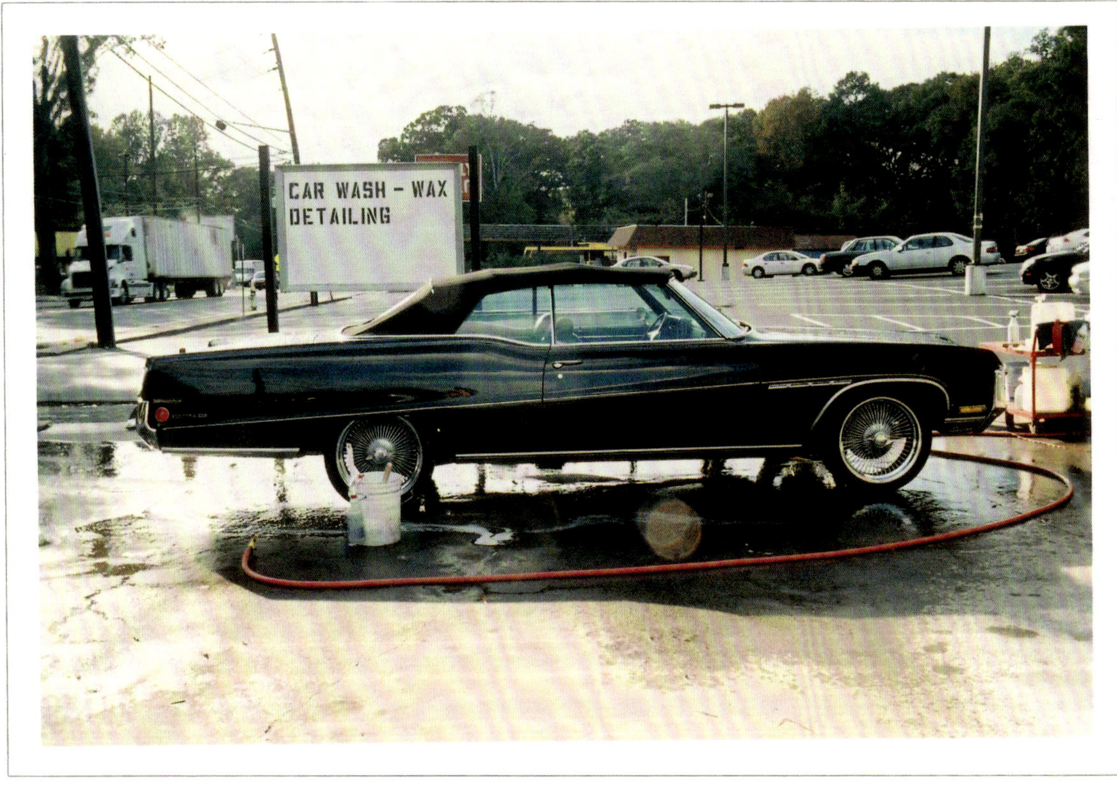

CAR WASH - WAX
DETAILING

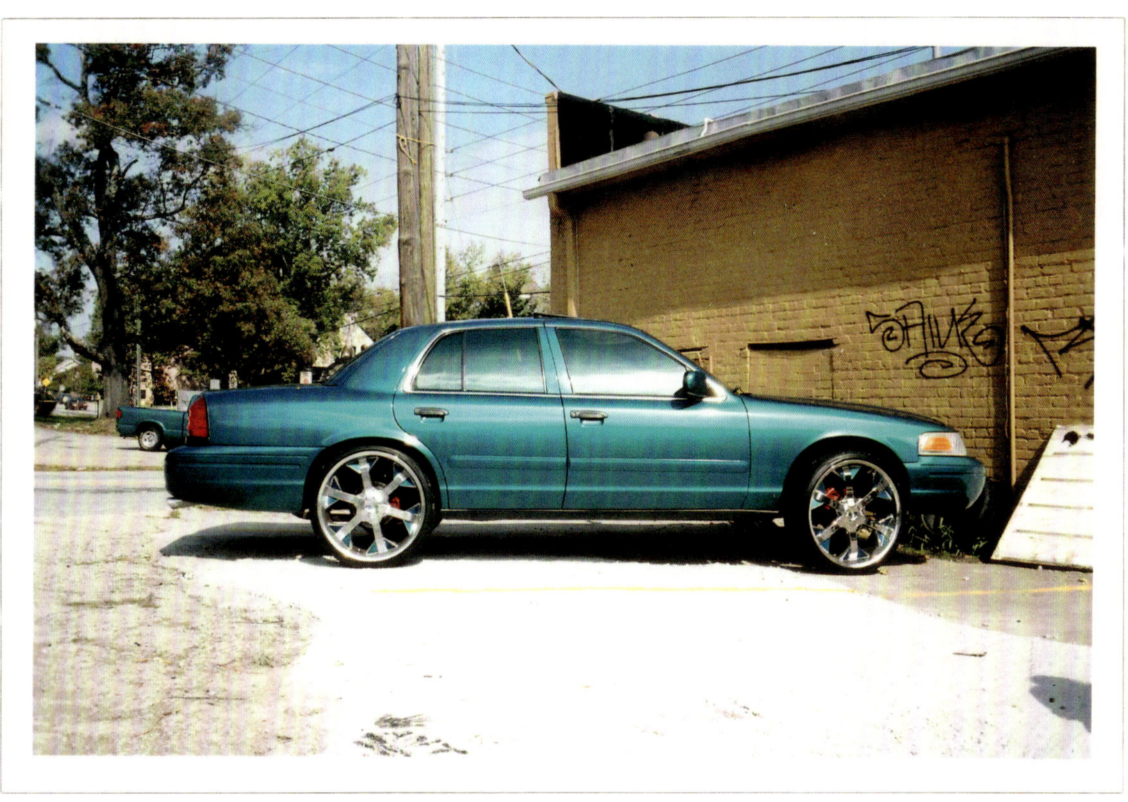

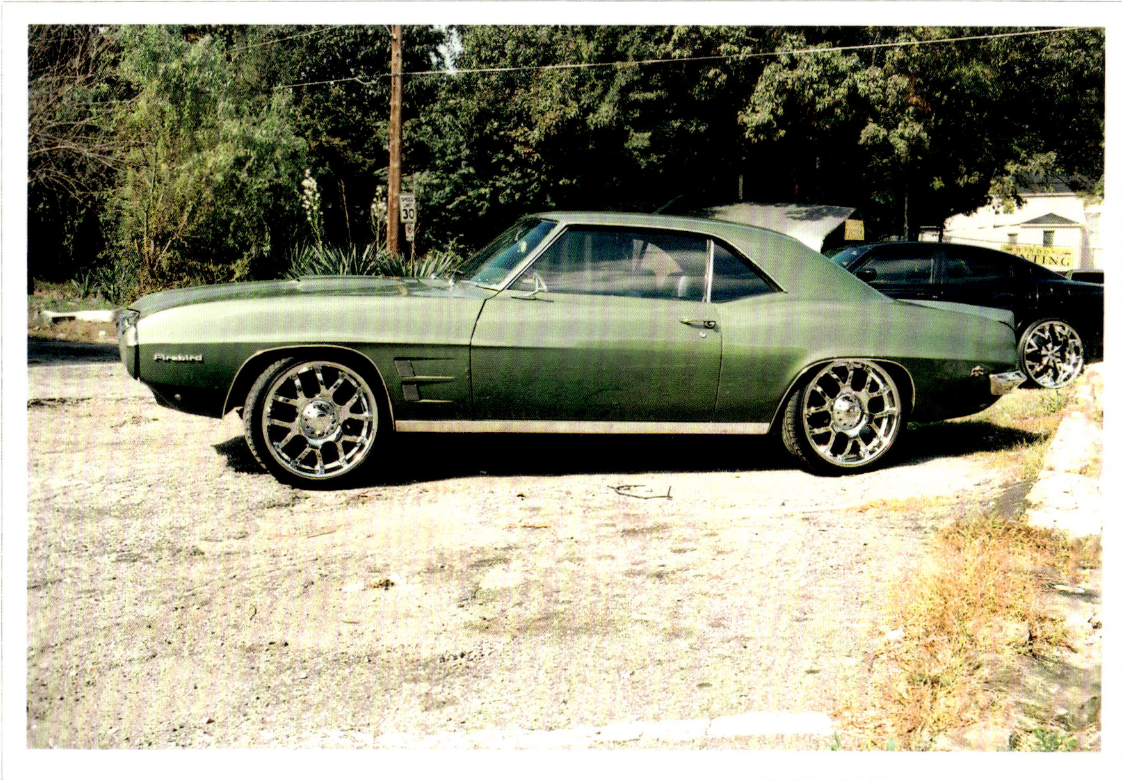

MOMO
BAZO
KOBO
DUB

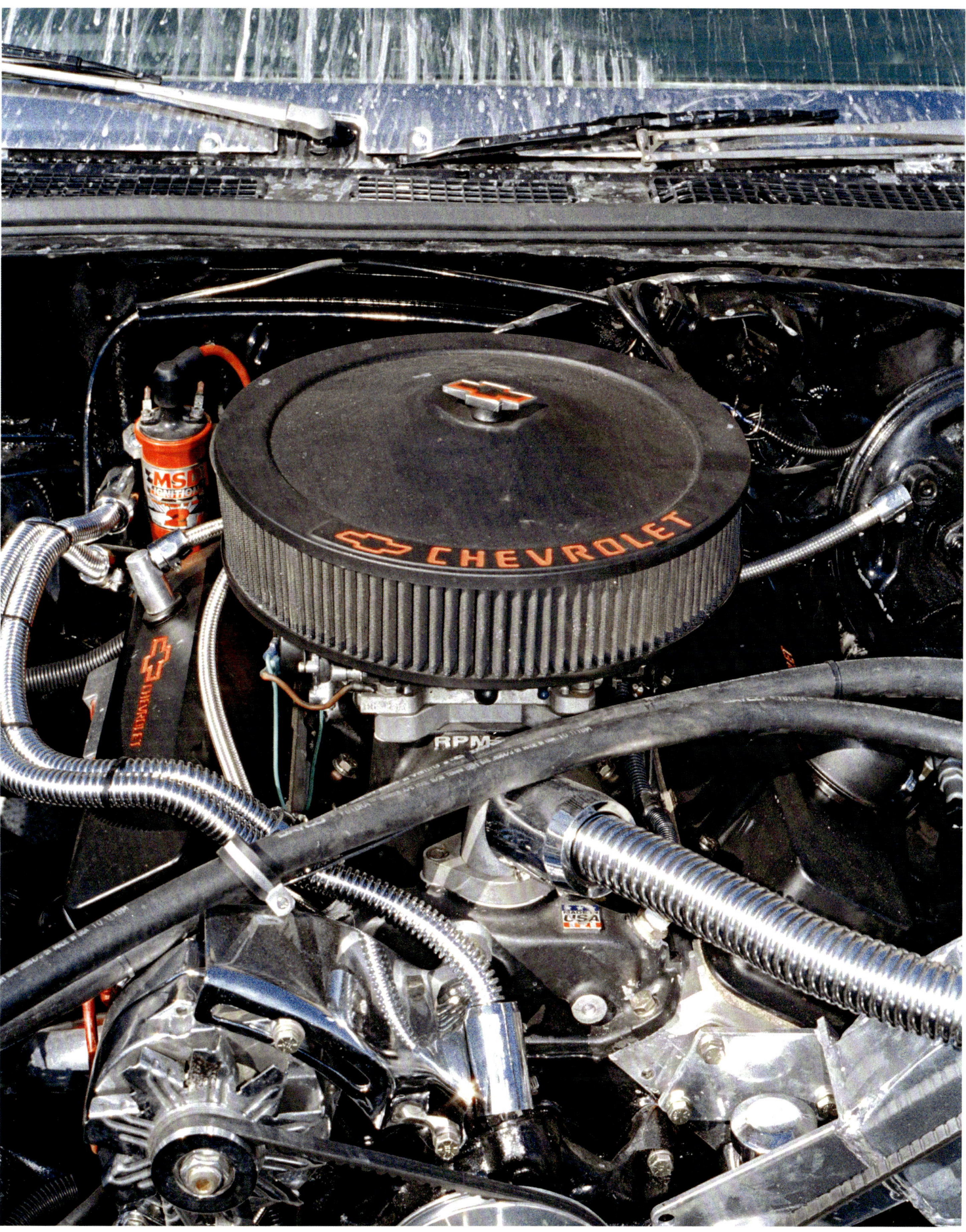

MSD IGNITION
CHEVROLET
CHEVROLET
RPM
USA

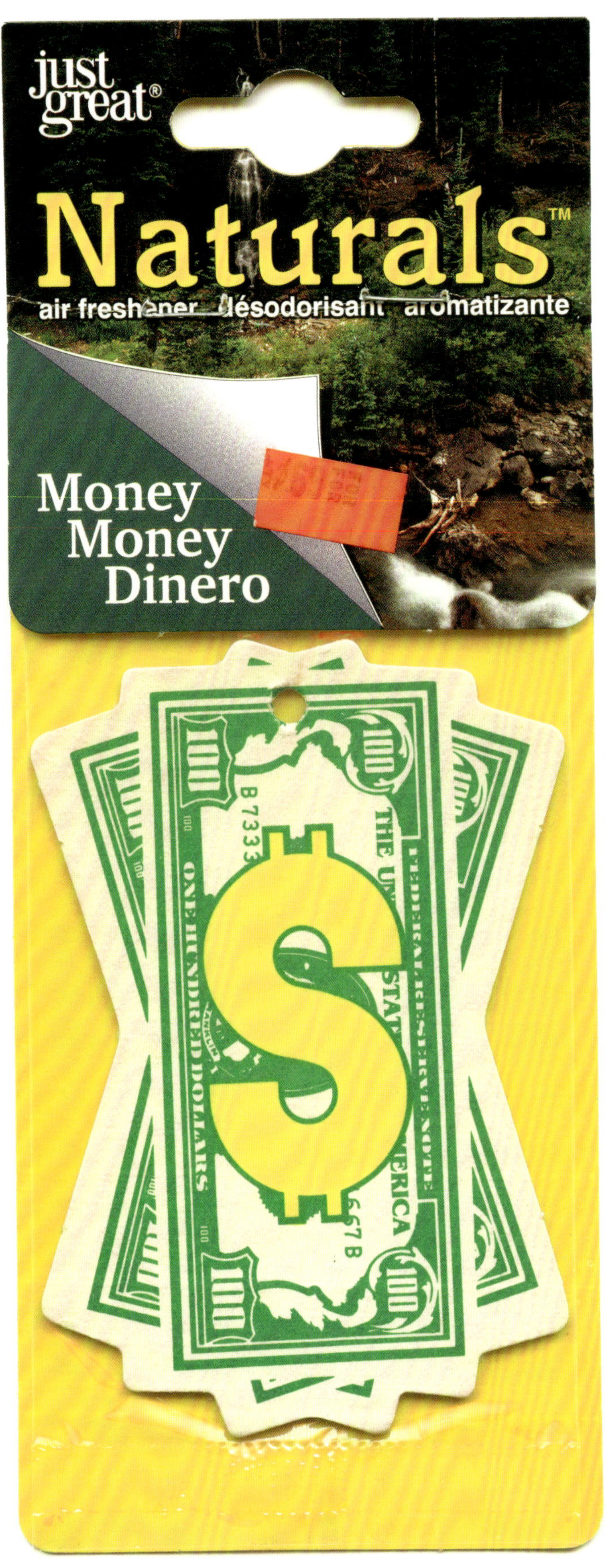
just great®
Naturals™
air freshener désodorisant aromatizante
Money
Money
Dinero
100
B 7333
THE UNITED STAT
ONE HUNDRED DOLLARS
$
667 B
100

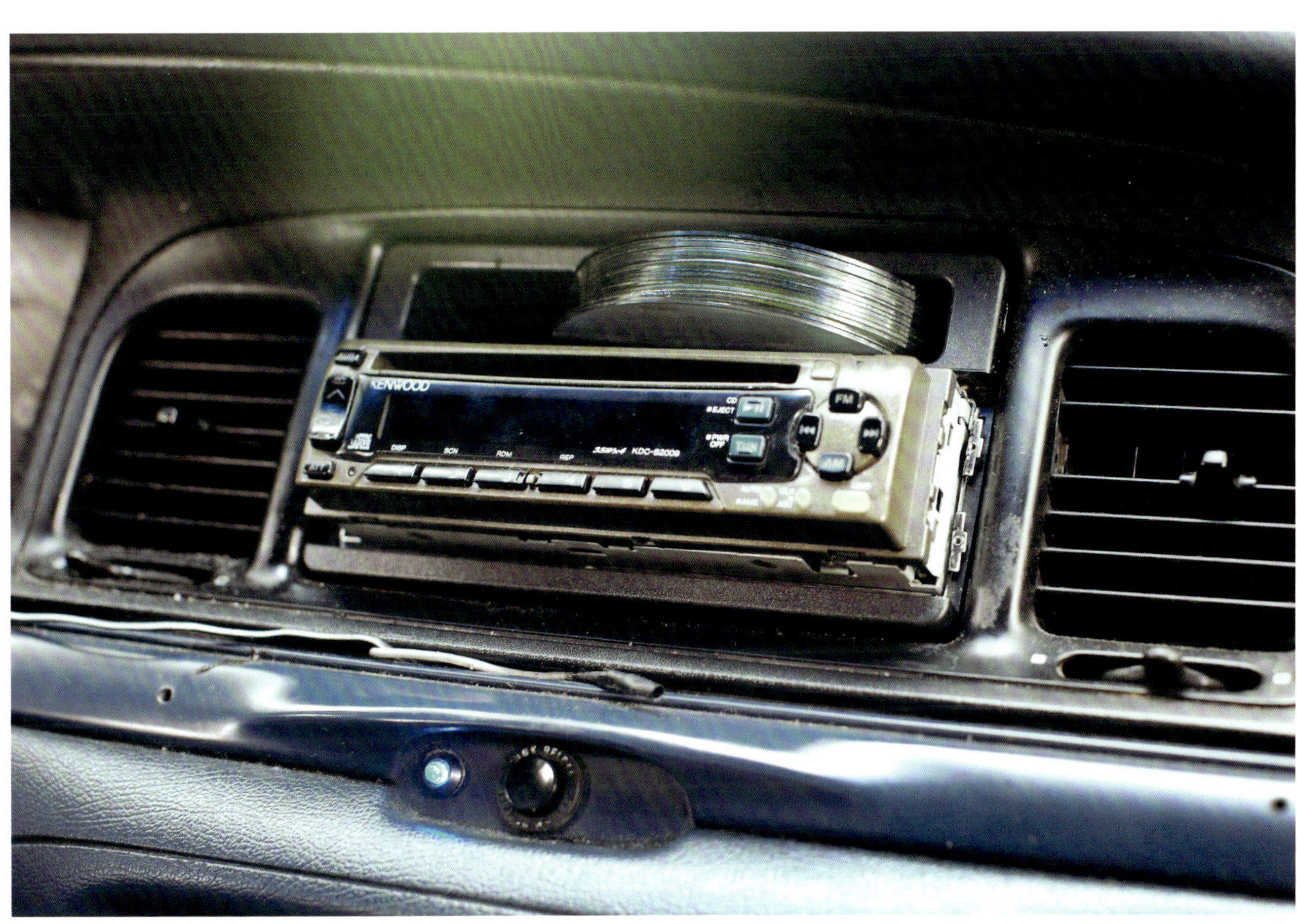

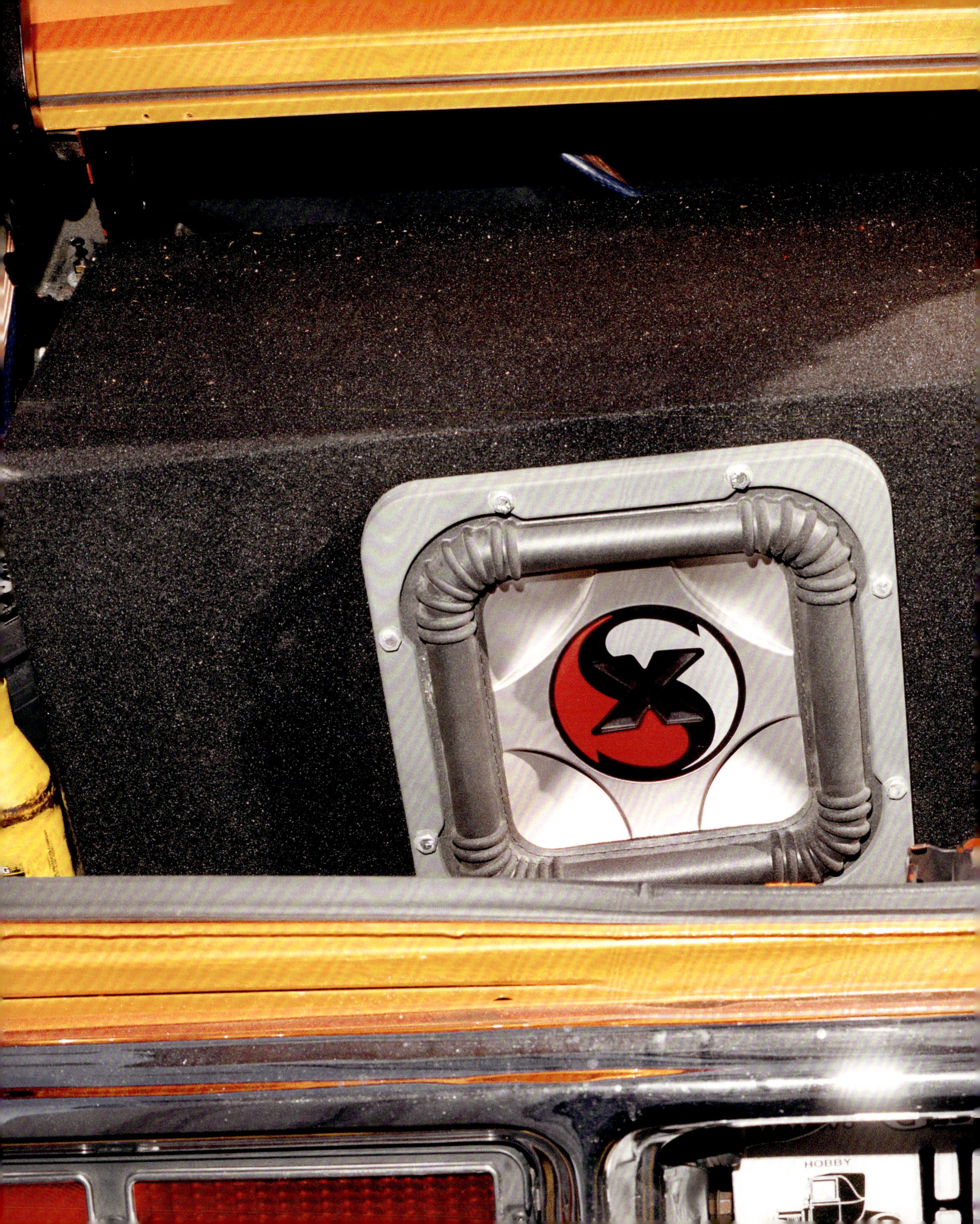

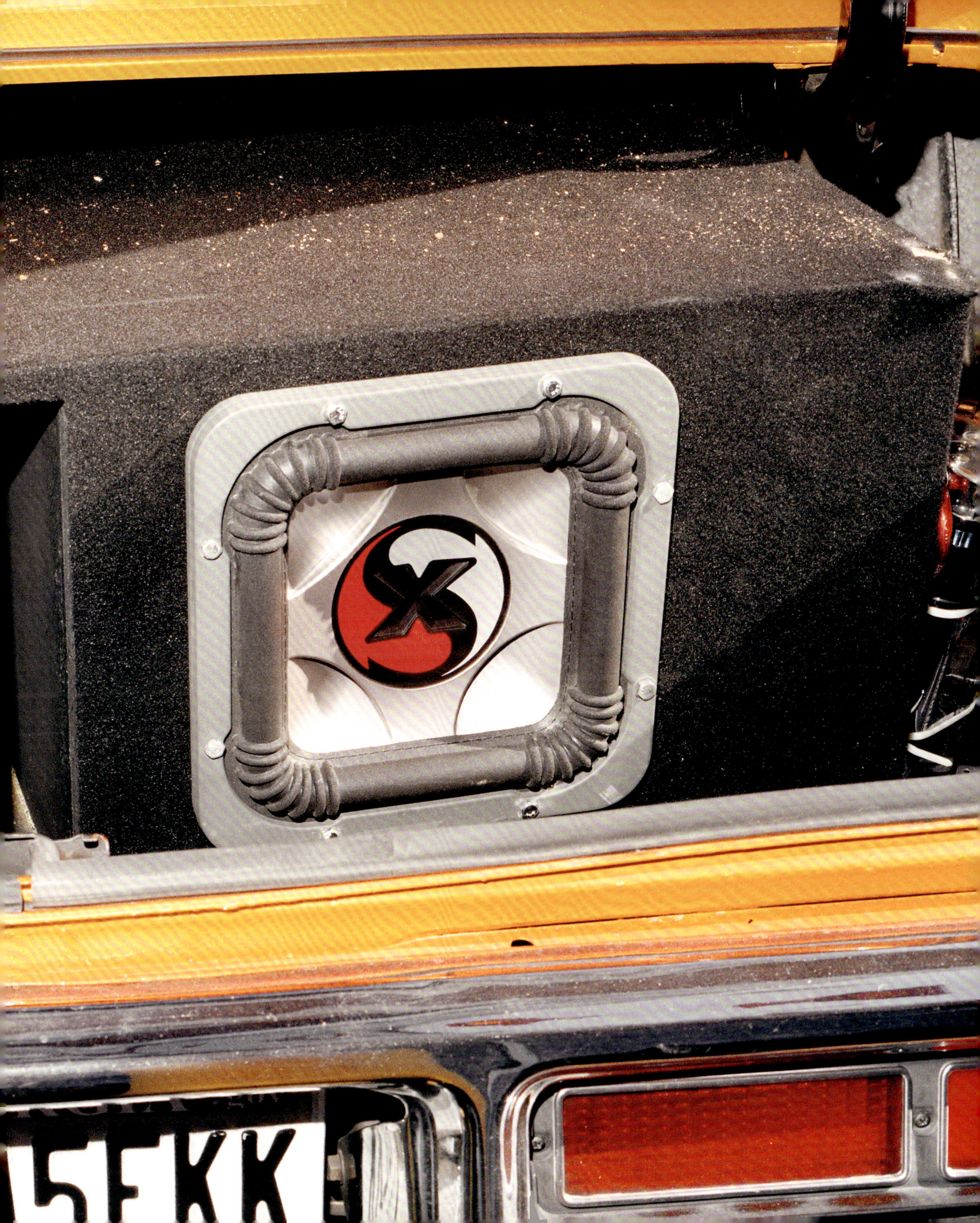

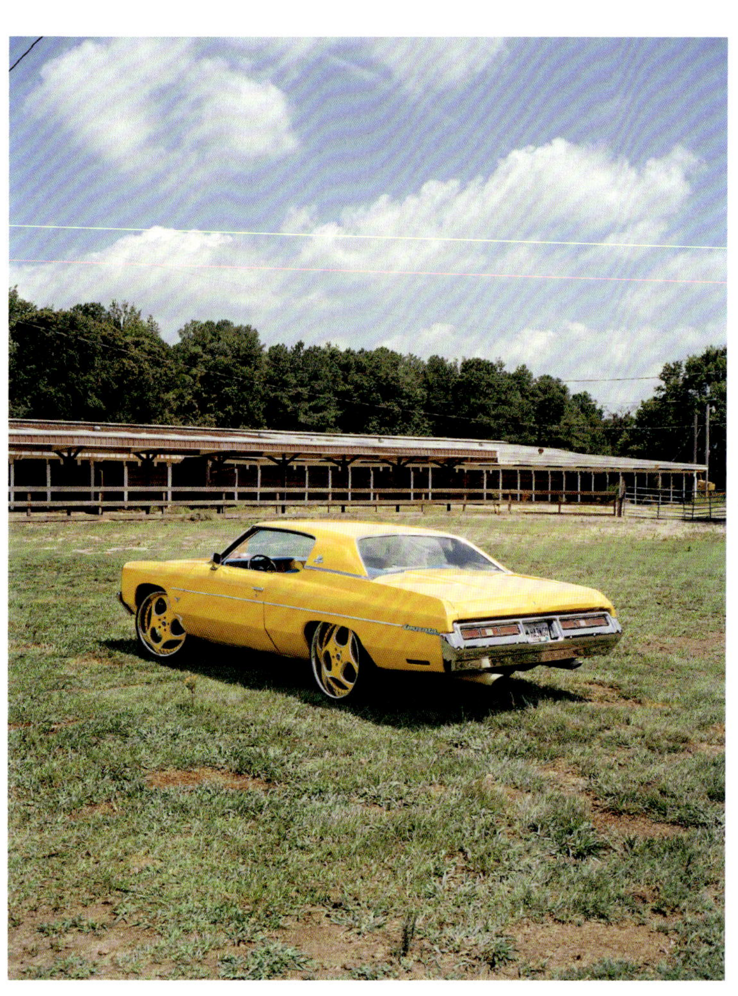

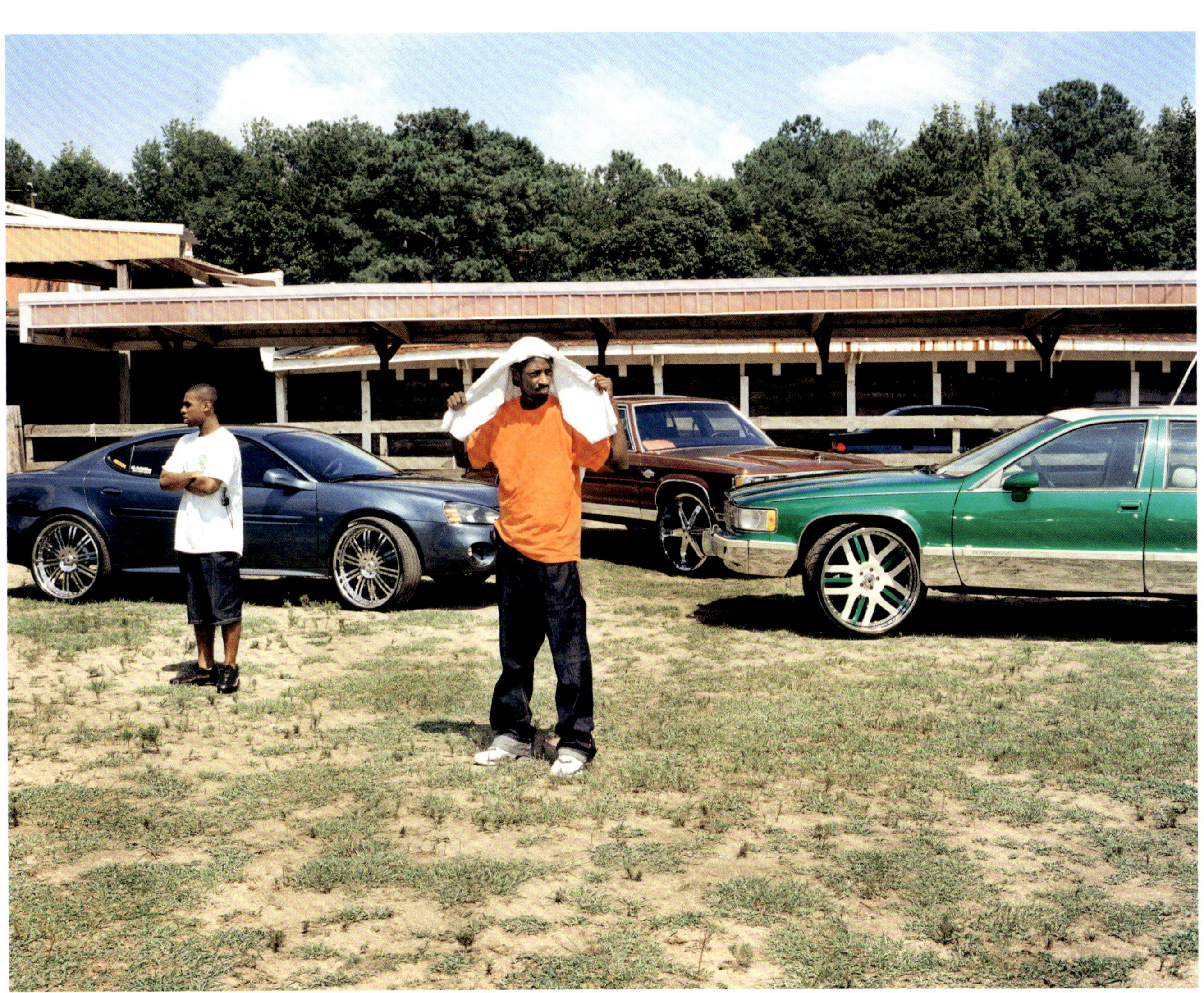

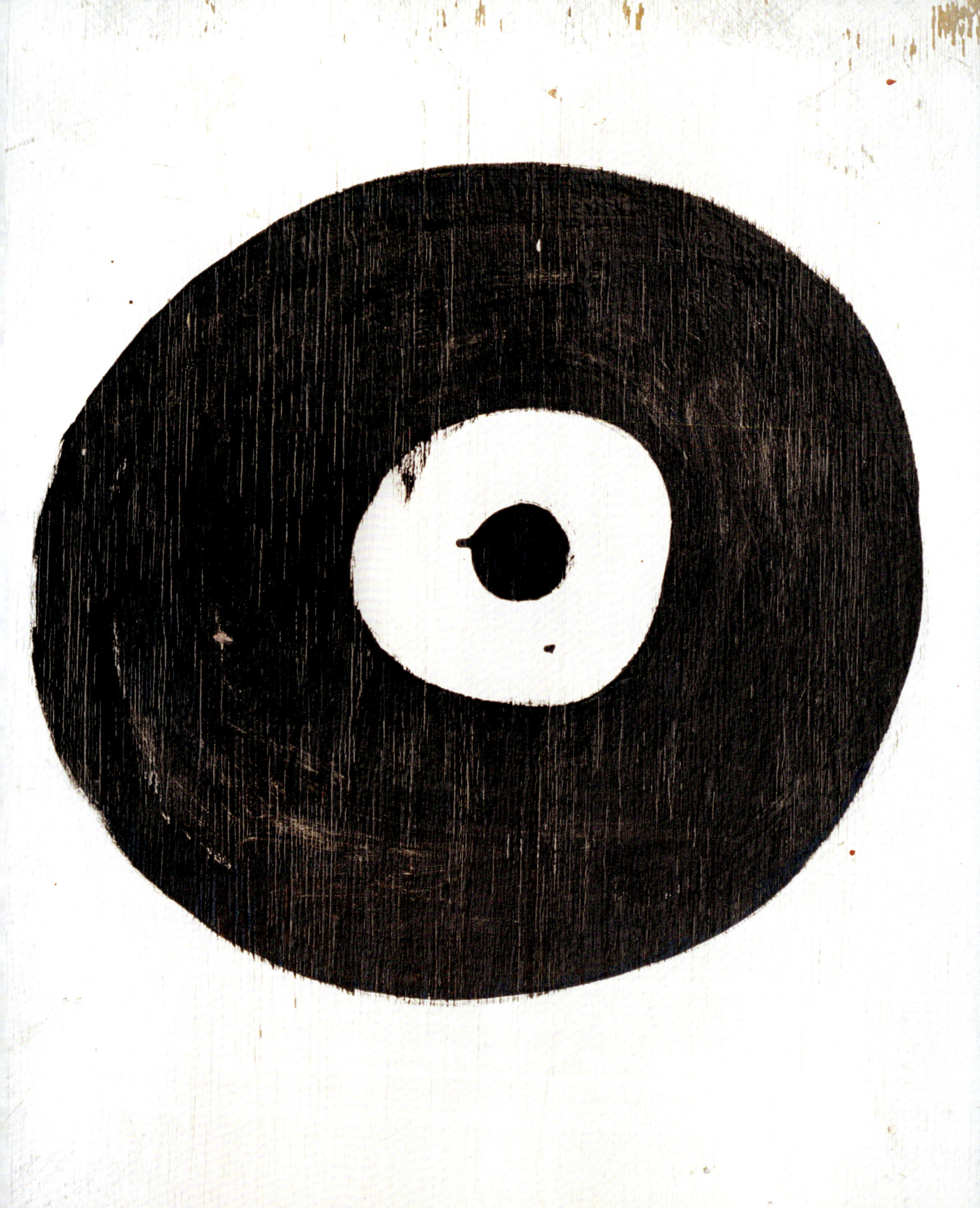

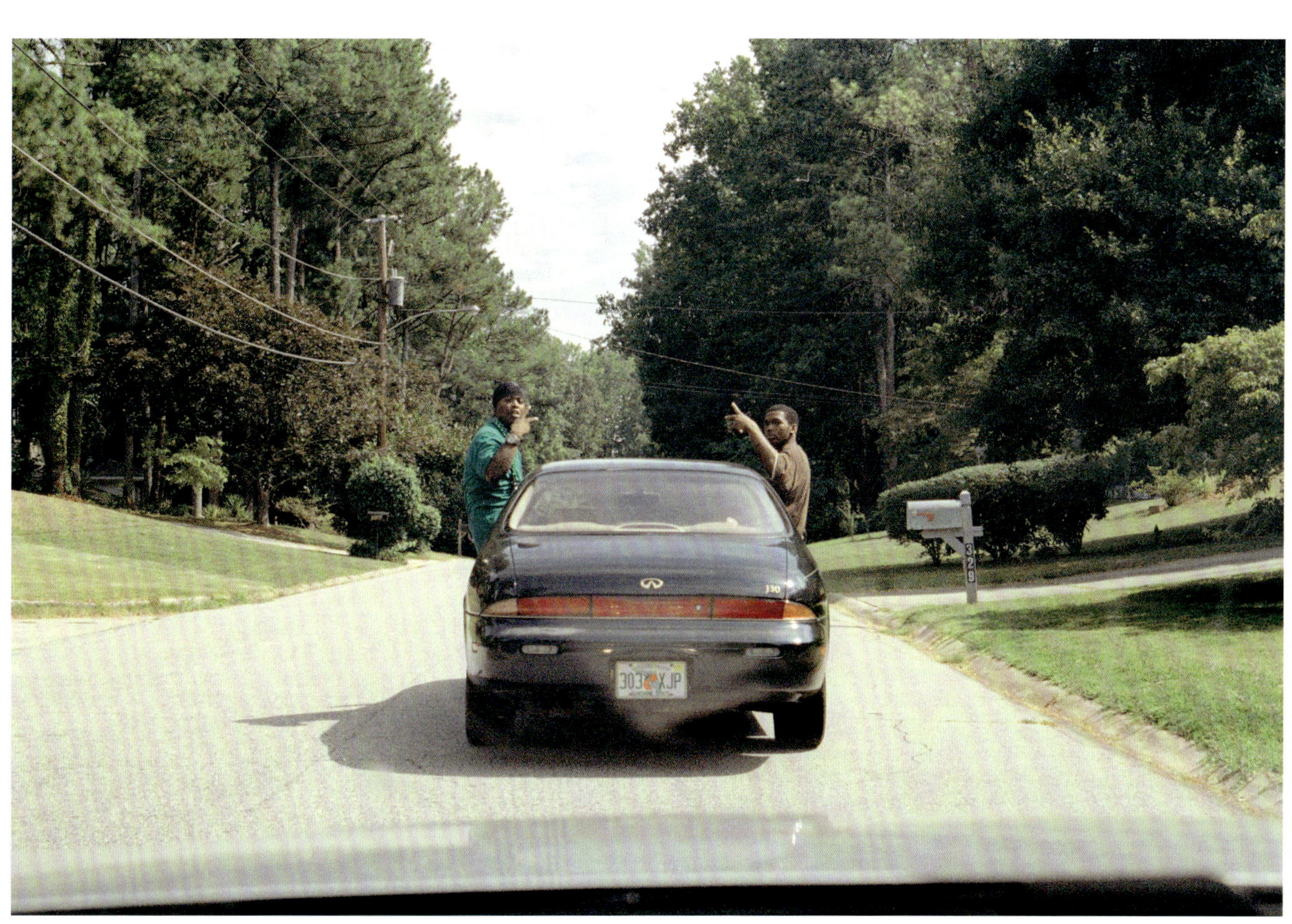
303 XJP

People talk a lot about Atlanta hip-hop, but almost never about the Atlanta sound, which makes sense, because there isn't one. Which is to say, there are plenty: in the 1990s, to those of us outside the city, Atlanta hip-hop seemed ubiquitous but marginal, an irresistible and incoherent jumble of club and street and radio. Atlanta was the home of the influential "So So Def Bass All-Stars" compilation, though it was inspired by Miami Bass. (It spawned "My Boo," by Ghost Town DJs, which cracked the Top 40 and remains a dance floor perennial.) Atlanta was the home of OutKast and Goodie Mob and their Dungeon Family—hip-hop mainstays who preferred to portray themselves as dissidents. Atlanta was the home of the futuristic girl-group TLC, whose hybrid hits anticipated the rise of electronic hip-pop in the '00s. And Atlanta was the home of Jermaine Dupri, a music mogul with an ear for novelty. If New York was hip-hop central, dominated by serious rappers and serious money, Atlanta provided a lovable alternative: a bit more raw, a lot more fun.

Then the New York hip-hop machine stalled (50 Cent was just about the only new hip-hop star the city produced in the '00s), and Atlanta became the hip-hop capital by default—the place where you could hear the next hit first, the place where kids and grown folks alike still seemed excited about hip-hop, the place where you could get the best mixtapes. But the hip-hop elite never quite adapted to this new state of affairs: the major labels were still based in New York, and so were the big music magazines. Perhaps as a consequence, you got the pleasant feeling that no one was in charge; Atlanta had its share of elder statesmen (including Dupri and Lil Jon and the guys from OutKast and DJ Greg Street, from V-103, and DJ Drama, the mixtape entrepreneur), but none of them seemed interested in dictating the sound of Atlanta hip-hop or in policing its borders. Even as the subgenres multiplied—crunk, trap, snap, swag, whatever—and YouTube dances took off and boys' jeans started getting skinnier, the backlash never arrived. You didn't hear many people talking about a return to authentic, old-fashioned Atlanta hip-hop, maybe because they knew that there had never been any such thing. When the new thing started to seem played out, the only solution was to find a newer one.

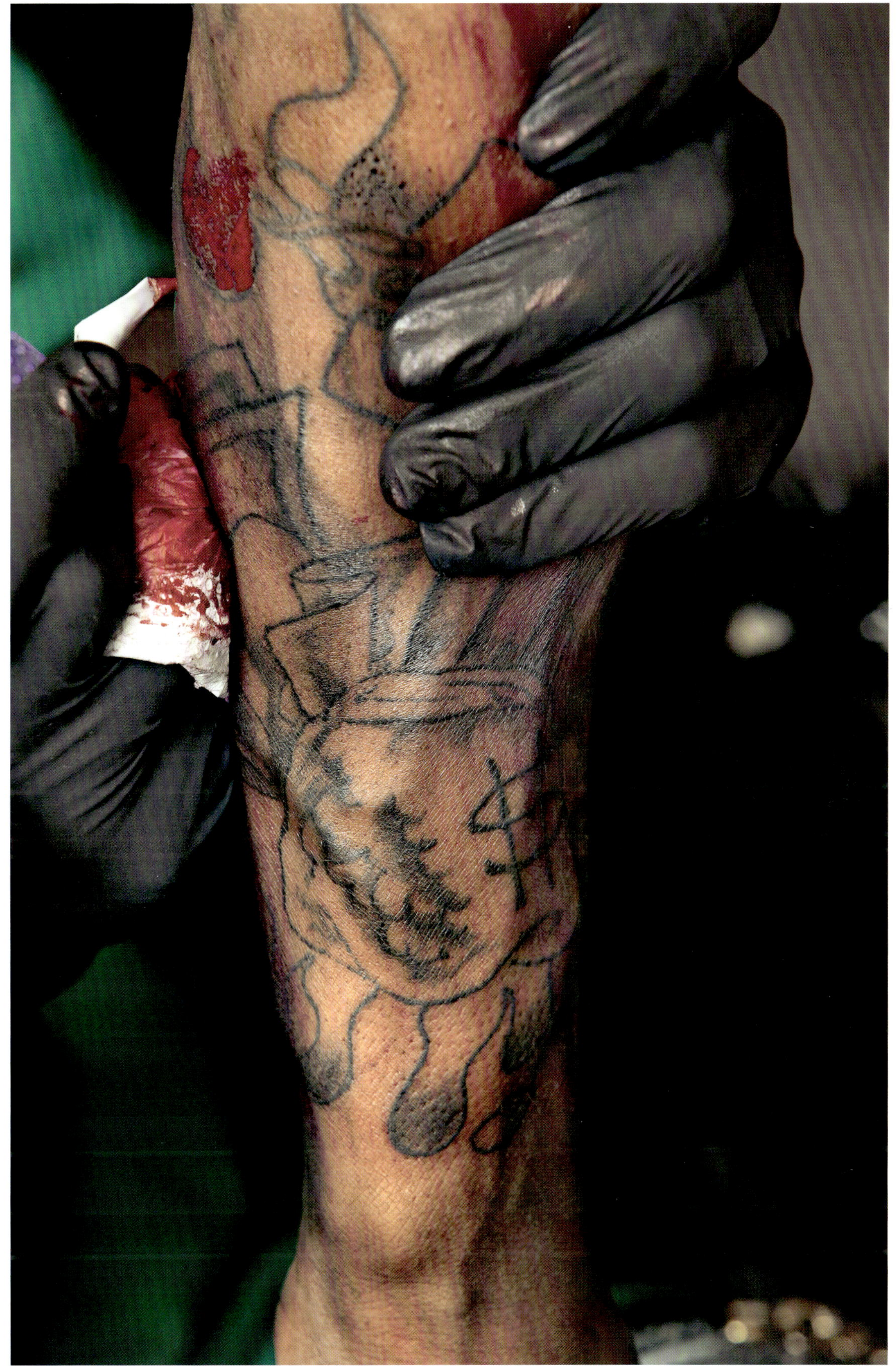

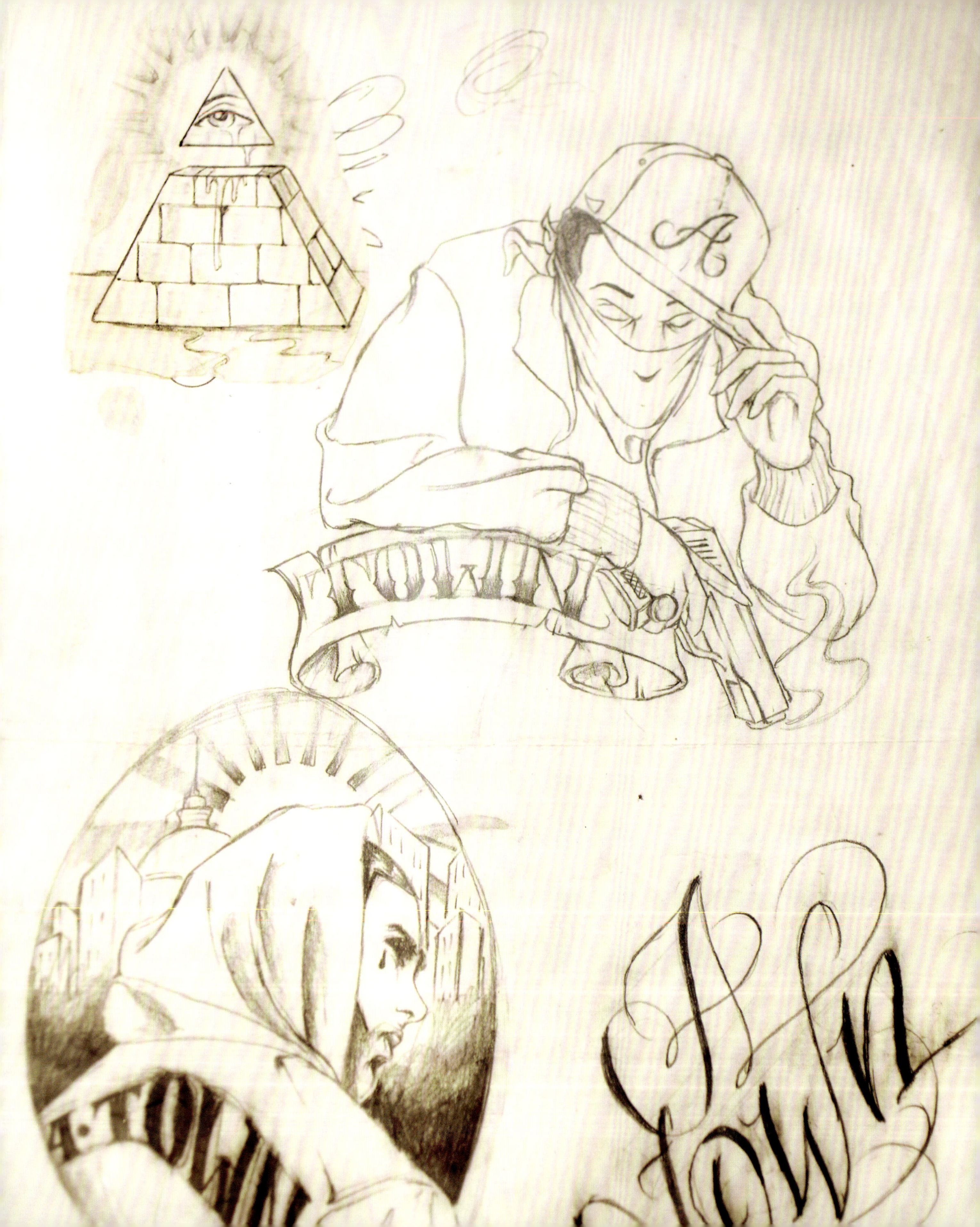

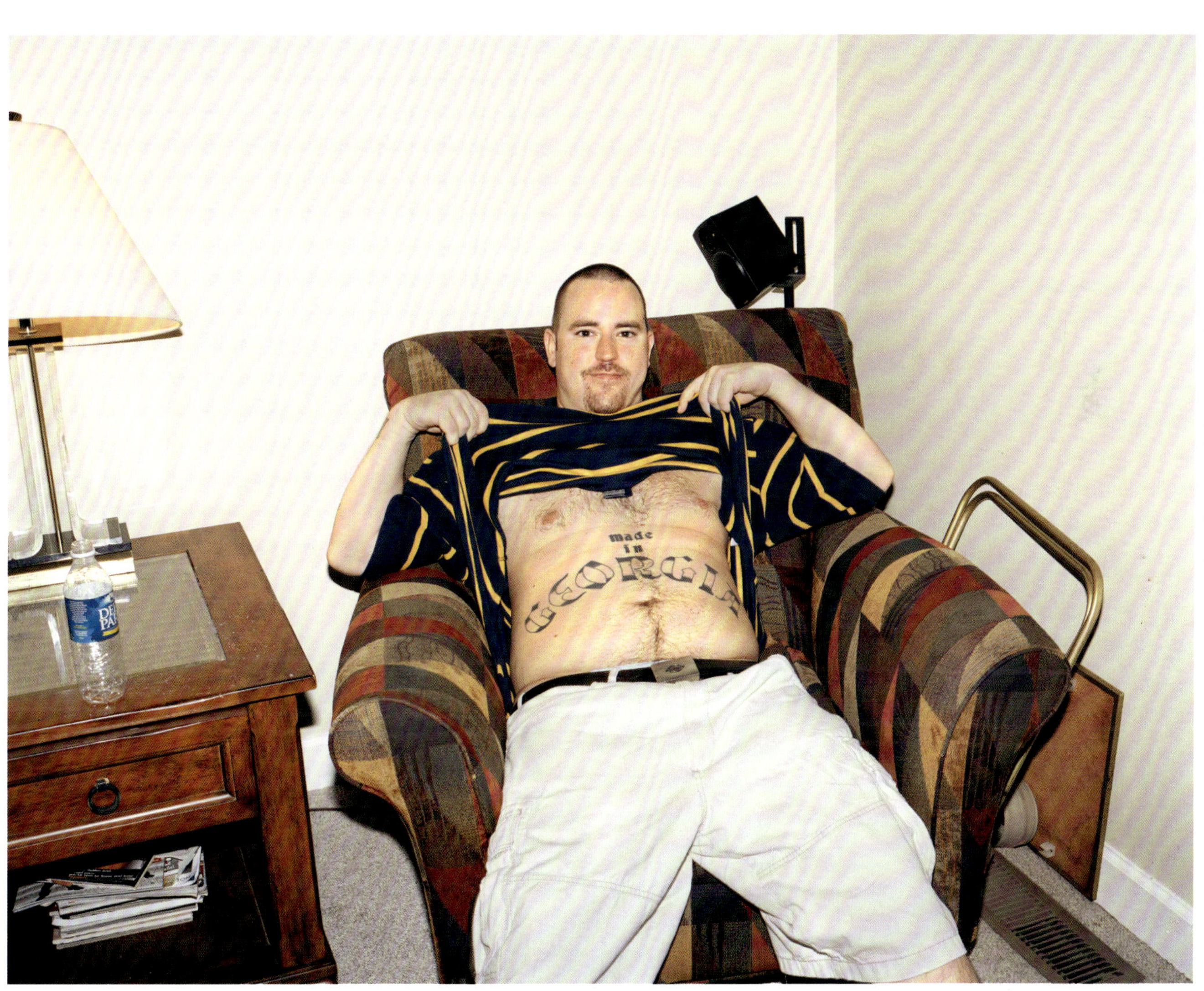

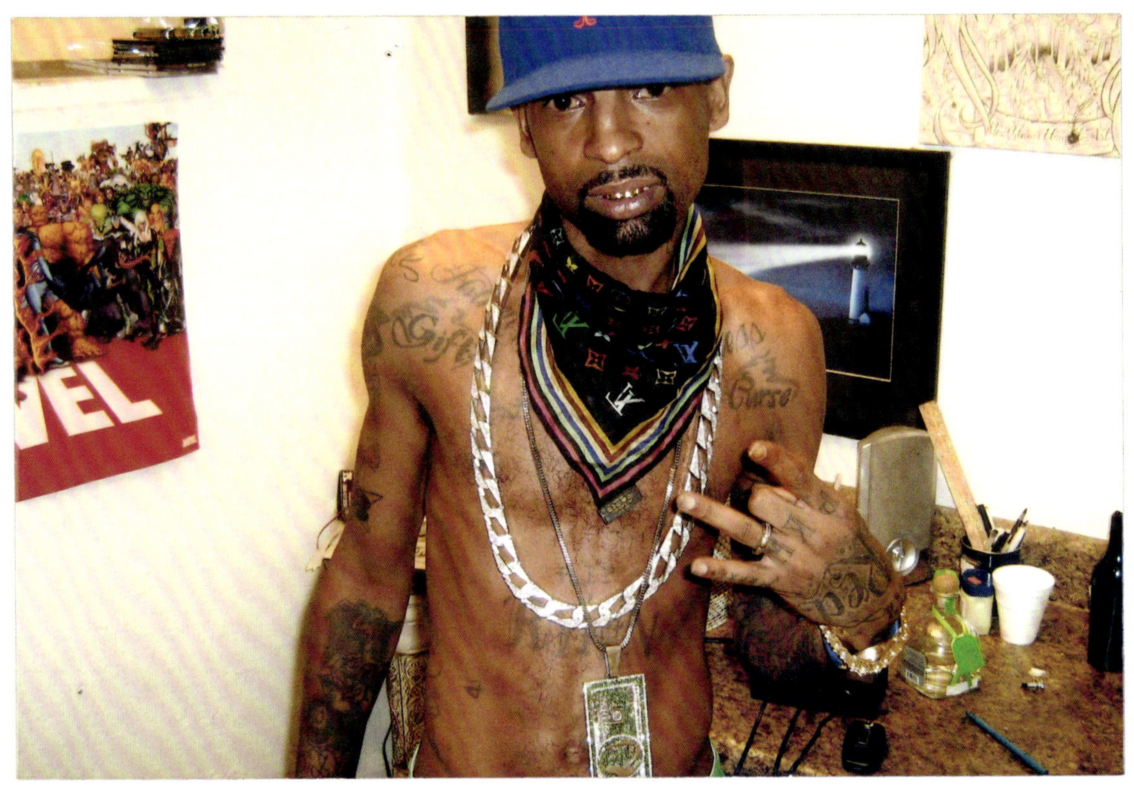

tattoo artist
named
MR. MONEY

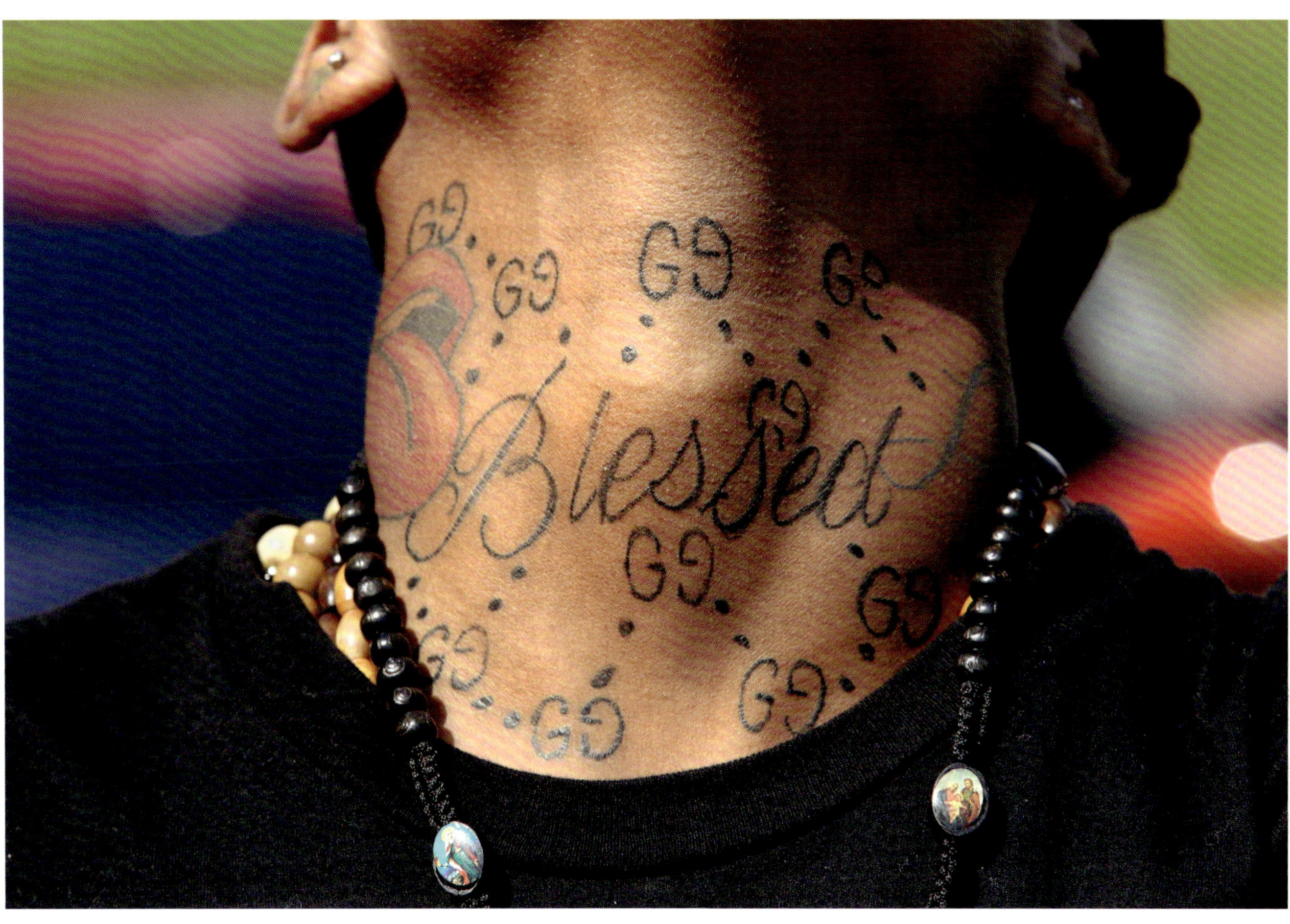

THE THING ABOUT SWAG

--

In the '00s, Atlanta hip-hop churned through subgenres, and at the decade's end, "swag" emerged as the not-quite-logical conclusion: an abbreviation of "swagger," an evocation of style and guts, and a kind of nongenre, or metagenre. "Swag" includes the neo-snap star Soulja Boy ("Hopped up out the bed, turned my swag on") and the trap-rap stalwart Young Jeezy ("One thing about me, yeah I got swag"). "Swag" was the perfect word for Gucci Mane, who saw no reason to pick between street music and club music—no reason why he couldn't be thugged-out and silly at the same time. (He once wore a diamond-encrusted Bart Simpson pendant, just about daring his enemies to try something funny.)

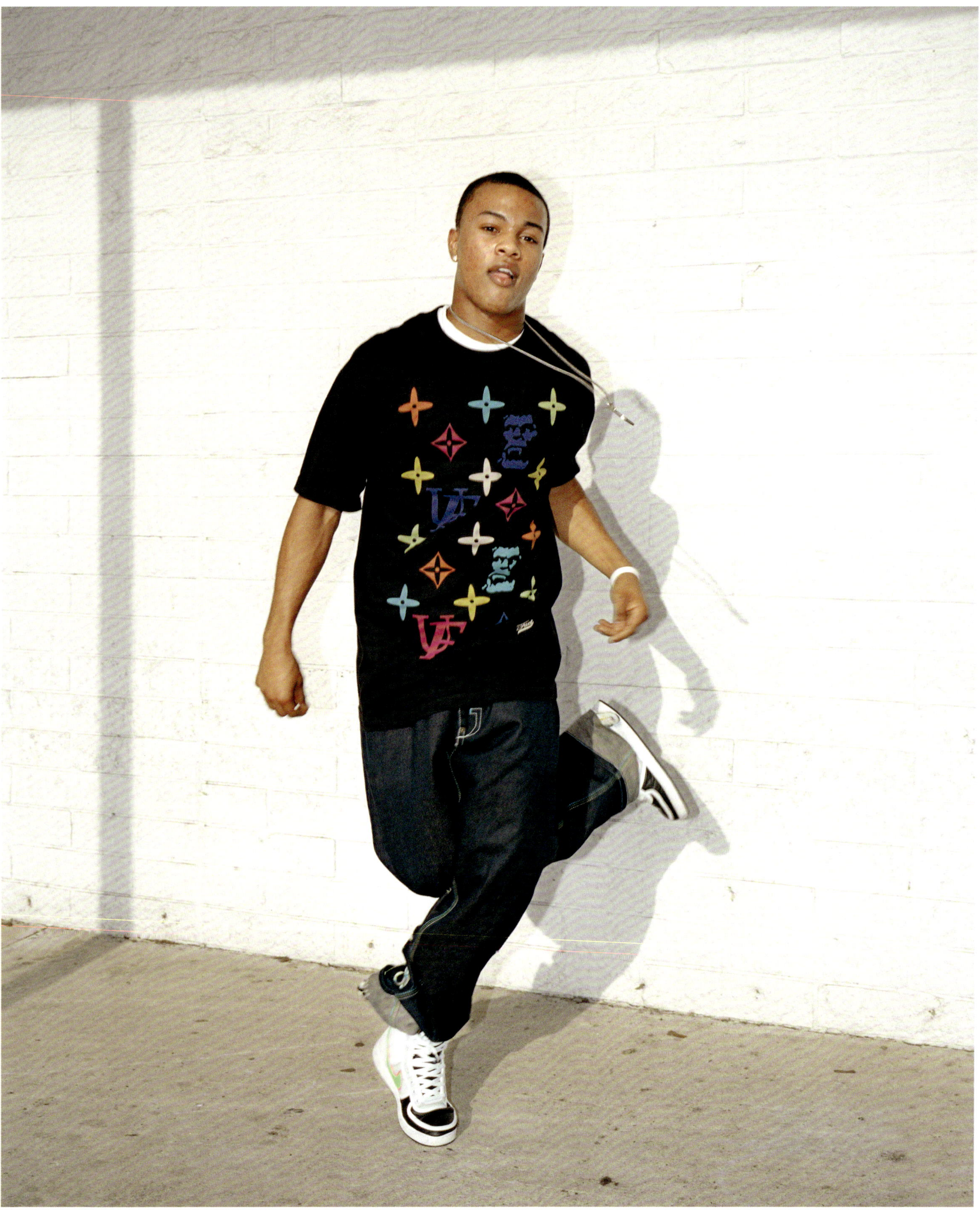

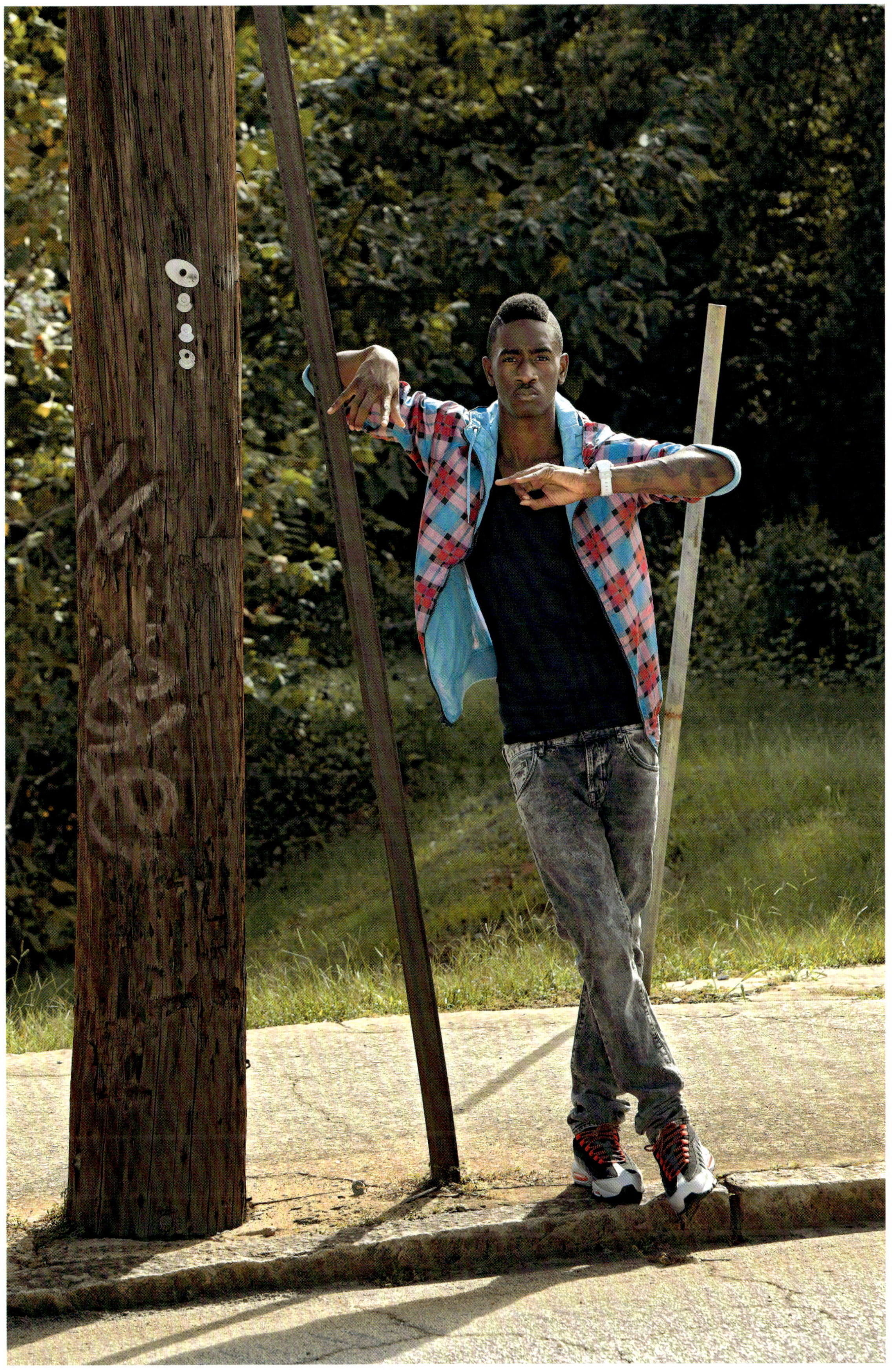

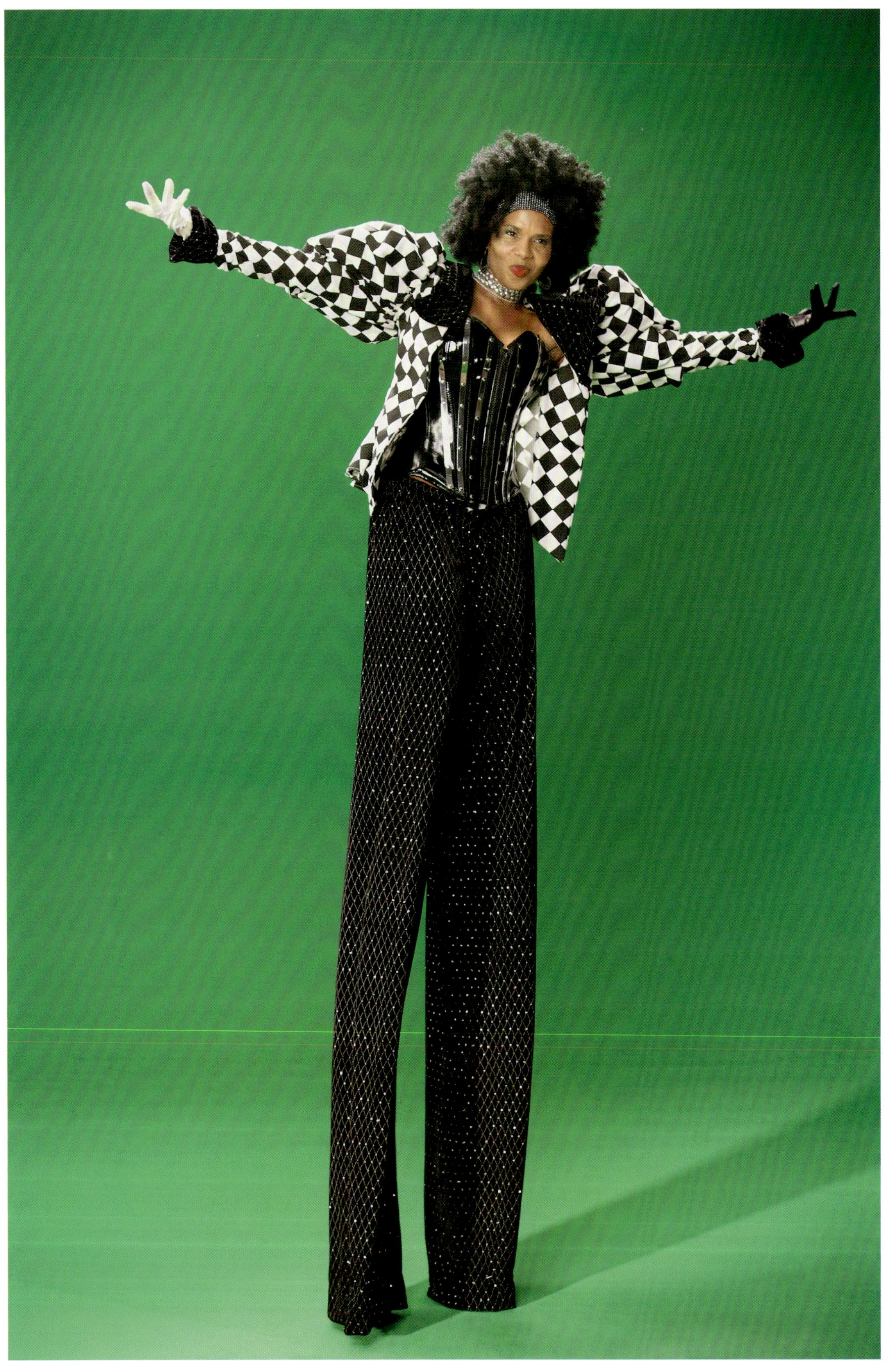

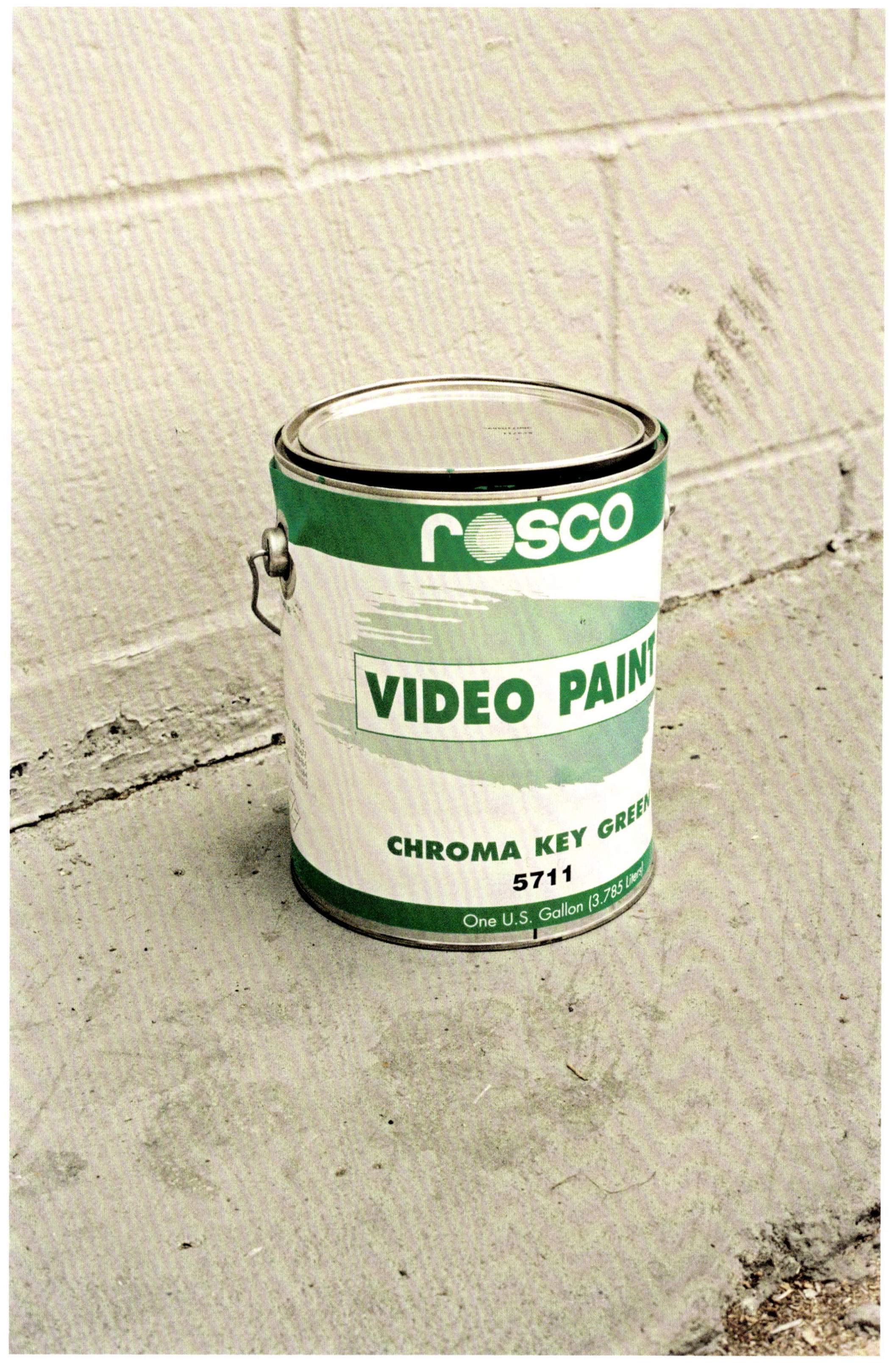

rosco
VIDEO PAINT
CHROMA KEY GREEN
5711
One U.S. Gallon (3.785 Liters)

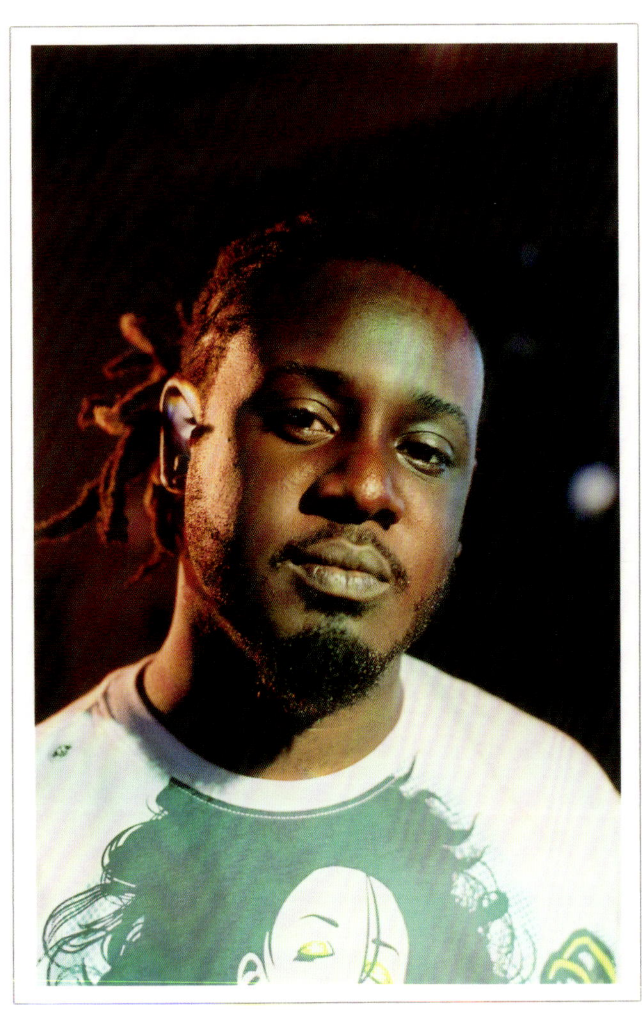

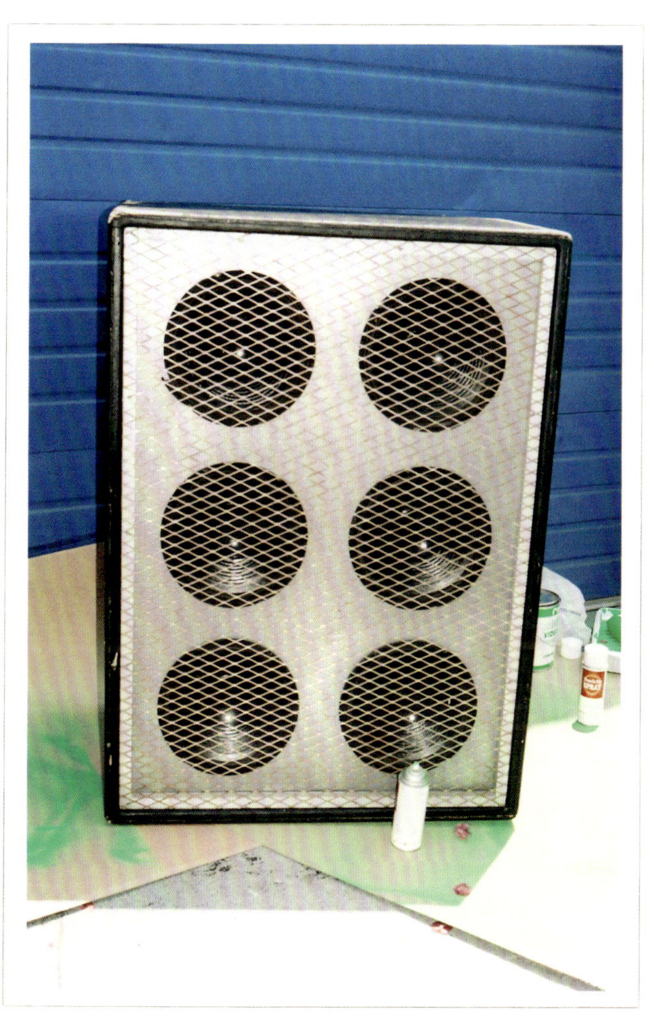
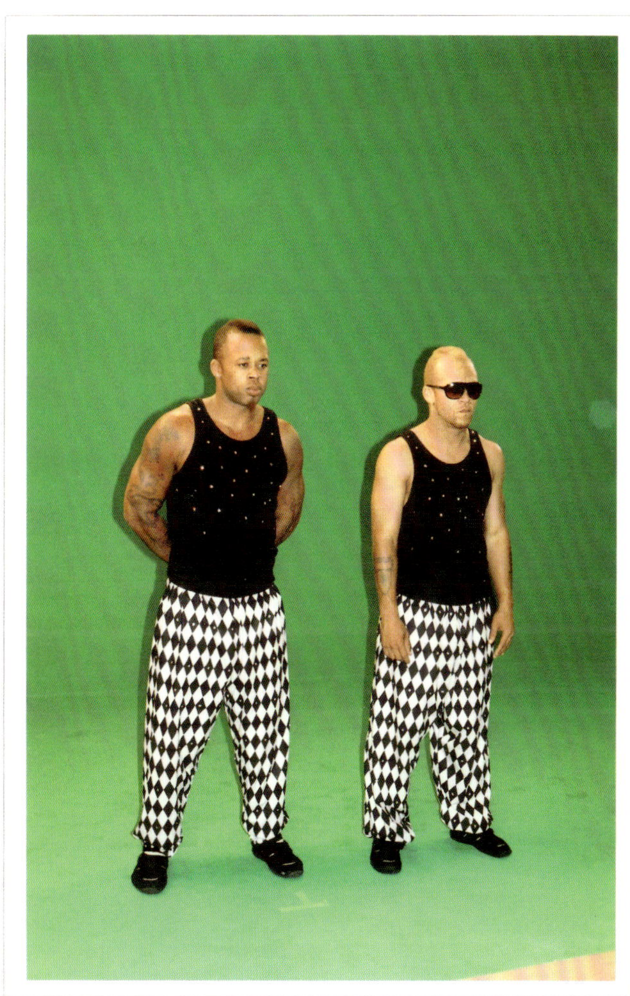

Travis Porter is a trio, and the members—Quez, the animated leader; Ali, the self-styled ladies' man; and Strap, the slickest rapper—tumble into a makeshift photo studio, where Michael Schmelling has set up his camera and a backdrop. There's a half-pipe in the back, and though none of the three can skate, they want to give it a try, and they take turns daring each other to drop in.

The members of Travis Porter met in high school, and they graduated in 2008, which helps explain why it seems like they never left. They started out hard—"Bang bang, shoot 'em up, kill 'em," as Quez remembers it—but then they gravitated toward a more playful style, at around the same time that other kids in the city were making a similar journey. They left behind baggy clothes, too, and Ali remembers his conversion in racial terms. "I'm looking at the white people, and how they was dressing," he says. "And I was liking it. I started dressing like it, just called it, black boy white boy—looking white." Though even now, they look less preppie than they think they do.

In 2008, they released a mixtape called *Im a Differenter,* which they promoted online and in clubs; one of the best tracks was "Stupid Ad-Libs," in which the chorus is merely a list of other Atlanta rappers' catchphrases. More mixtapes followed and, eventually, a local hit: "All the Way Turnt Up," which was one of the biggest songs of the summer in 2009; it had a chorus perfect for shouting along, and a blaring beat (it mimicked heralding trumpets) that didn't sound like anything else on the radio. Unfortunately, it was a collaboration with another rapper, Roscoe Dash, who split with the group not long after the song started to catch on. Which meant they had to start over, find a new potential hit, wait for it to catch on.

Their manager was there: a sharp twenty-something white guy who calls himself CEO Charlie and whose business-casual self-presentation couldn't possibly be confused with white-boy swag. The group hadn't signed with a major label, but he had a plan. "Soulja Boy would upload a video to YouTube, and it would get about forty thousand views in the first week," he said. "We upload a video to YouTube, and we get about five thousand in the first week. So we've gotta grow eight times more, 'til we need to sign a record deal."

Everyone went outside to the street, for some more photographs. The guys posed in their not-quite-matching skinny jeans and American Eagle sweaters. The scene caught the attention of two men across the road—hip-hop fans from a slightly earlier generation, perhaps. Evidently, they hadn't been converted to skinny jeans. "If it ain't saggin', it ain't swaggin'," one of them yelled. "I don't need no swag," the Travis Porter guys yelled back, almost in unison, and they craned to see who they were yelling at. Finally, one of the men broke the tension: "I'm just fuckin' with you, dog," he said. Quez reached deep into his pocket, pulled out a wad of bills, and held it high as the guys walked off.

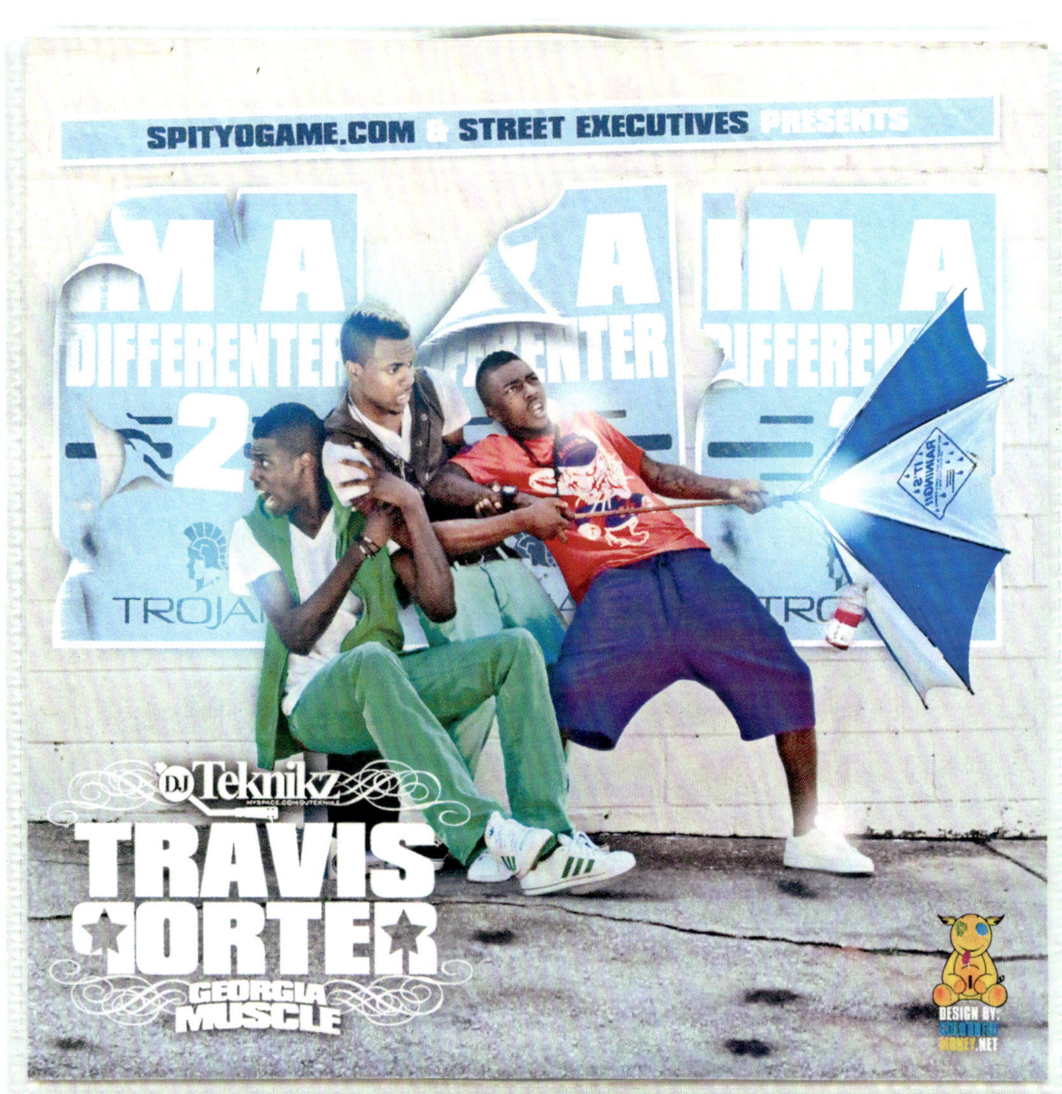

SPITYOGAME.COM & STREET EXECUTIVES PRESENTS
IM A DIFFERENTER 2
DJ Teknikz
TRAVIS PORTER
GEORGIA MUSCLE
DESIGN BY:

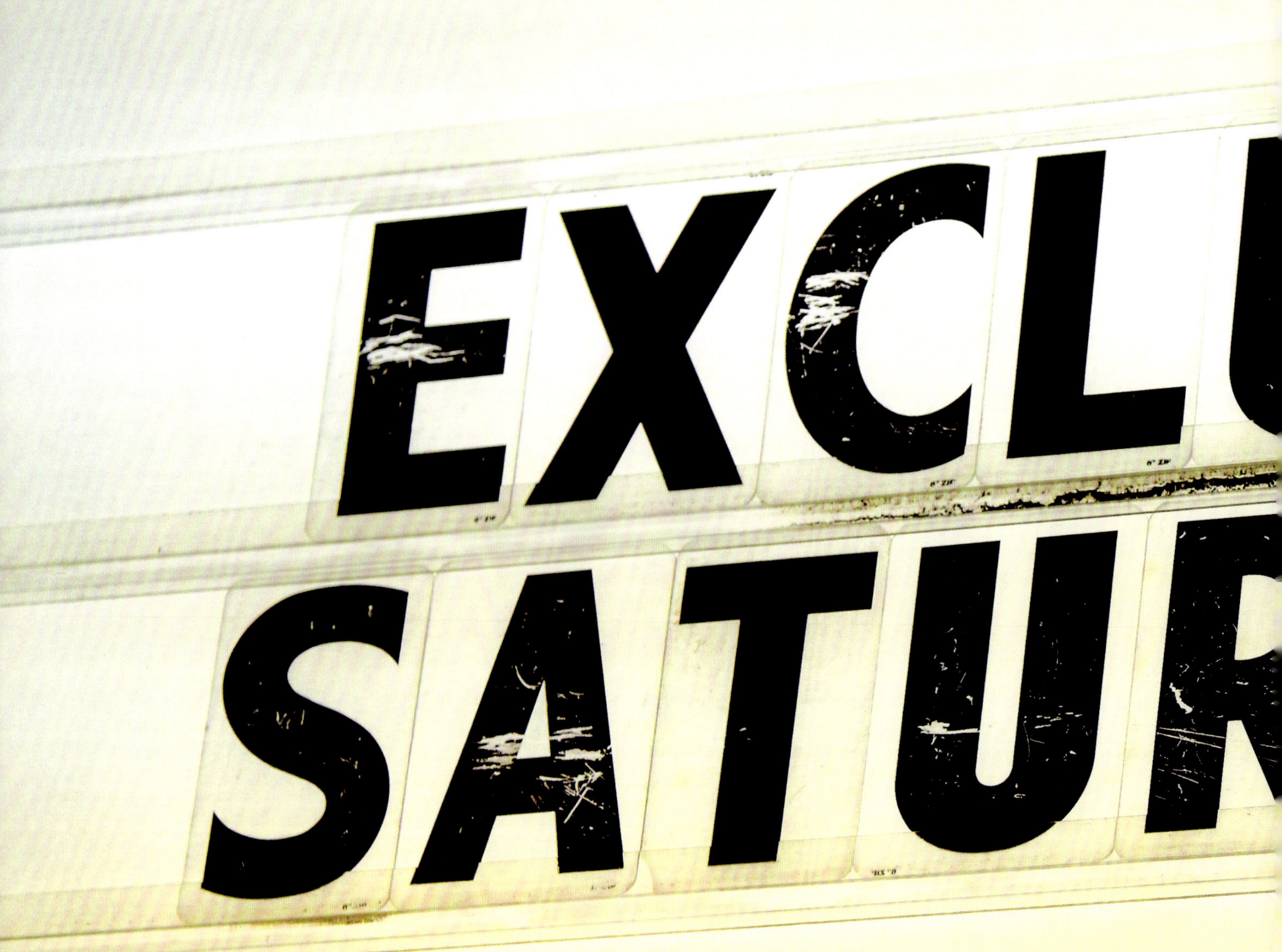
EXCLU
SATUR

USIVE
DAYS

club ritz

lavish lounge

the velvet room

club miami

~~club miami~~

studio 72

opera

posie palace

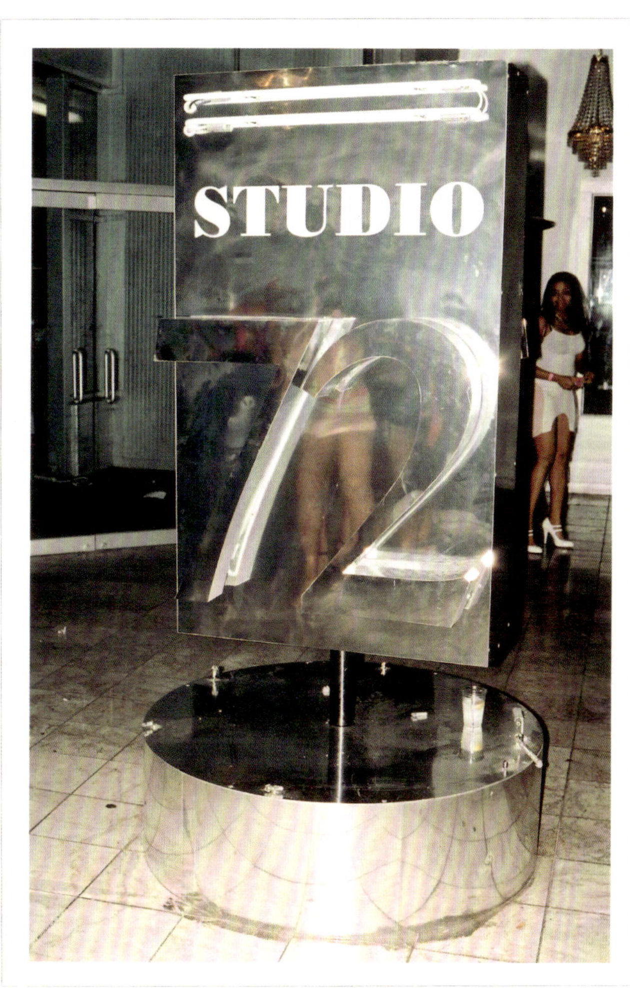

STUDIO
72

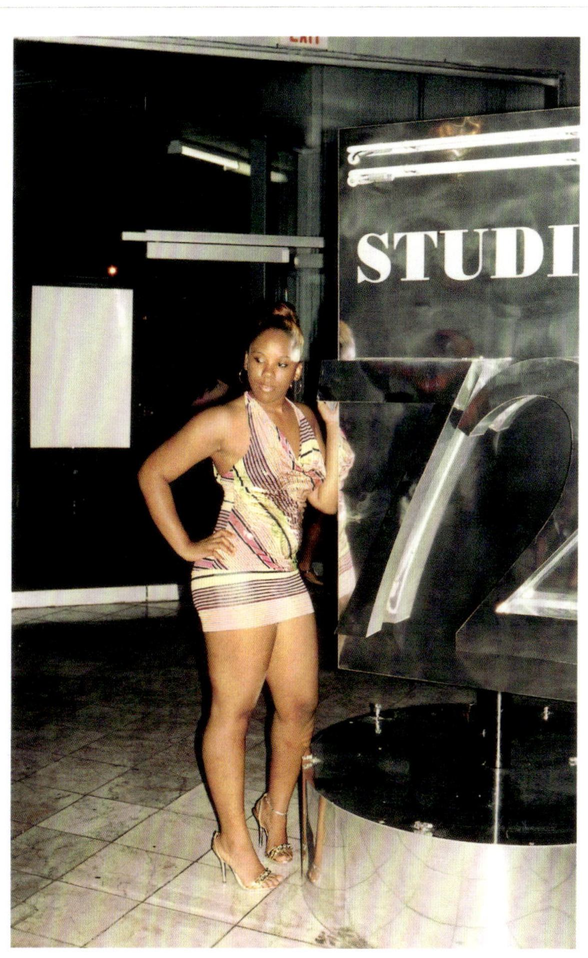

STUDI
72

Sunday night in July at an office park in Decatur, dark except for one doorway and some car headlights and maybe a flashlight that one of the security guys is holding. There are teenagers lined up to get in, and possibly some preteenagers. Each one will be frisked, will pay ten dollars, will pass through the bright lobby and into the party. It's a big room, and raw: cinder block walls, corrugated-metal ceiling, cement floor. (The woman who owns it advertises it as a gym and, less plausibly, a banquet facility.) There's a low stage against one wall, with barely enough room for the DJ, and not nearly enough room for the emcees, who take their wireless microphones deep into the crowd. There are kids everywhere, but you can only see them in the bright blips from a small strobe light.

The kids are clustering around a video camera, rapping lyrics into the lens. ("What I just said, girl, do it on the dick, age ain't shit/I done got a little older, me or your man, baby girl, take a pic.") The girls are wearing tiny T-shirts and tinier shorts, and the boys are mainly shirtless; they come together waist to waist, with the boy facing the girl and the girl facing away, convulsing in unison. Some couples retreat to the walls, which provide a bit of privacy and, more important, leverage. The boys stand up straight, and at first you might not notice the girls in front, touching their toes and pressing backward. After dancing with a boy for a few minutes, one girl suddenly turns to give him a quick kiss. It's shocking, somehow.

Everyone knows every song, though they don't all get the same response. Newer is generally better: "O Let's Do It," the breakthrough hit by Waka Flocka Flame, is the sound of the summer, or one of them, and the kids explode as soon as they hear the cell phone chirp in the introduction. "Up Thru Dere," a year-old club favorite by the Shop Boyz, meets with unanimous approval, but the DJ follows it with "My Hood," a four-year-old Young Jeezy track, which doesn't survive past the first verse. "Knuck If You Buck," by Crime Mob,

is designed to start fights, and on this night it works fine: the grinding stops and security guards rush into the crowd, trying to separate two groups of boys. One kid tries to square off with a guard, who reaches for something; you can see the flash of a Taser as the kid is carried out and his antagonists celebrate.

One of the emcees vows, or threatens, to play nothing but songs for the ladies until people calm down. But as club brawls go, this one seems pretty tame, perhaps because of the partygoers' youth, or their seeming sobriety—the makeshift concession stand is selling nothing but bottles of water, for a dollar apiece. The emcee's name is Fly Guy Fred, and he is white-boy swag from toe to head: red low-top Chuck Taylors, distressed jeans, white tank top, red plastic sunglasses, mohawk. All night he delivers public service announcements, which may or may not be fake. "Myaqueesha, your mama is outside with the damn police," he says, between songs. "And she got a belt, too."

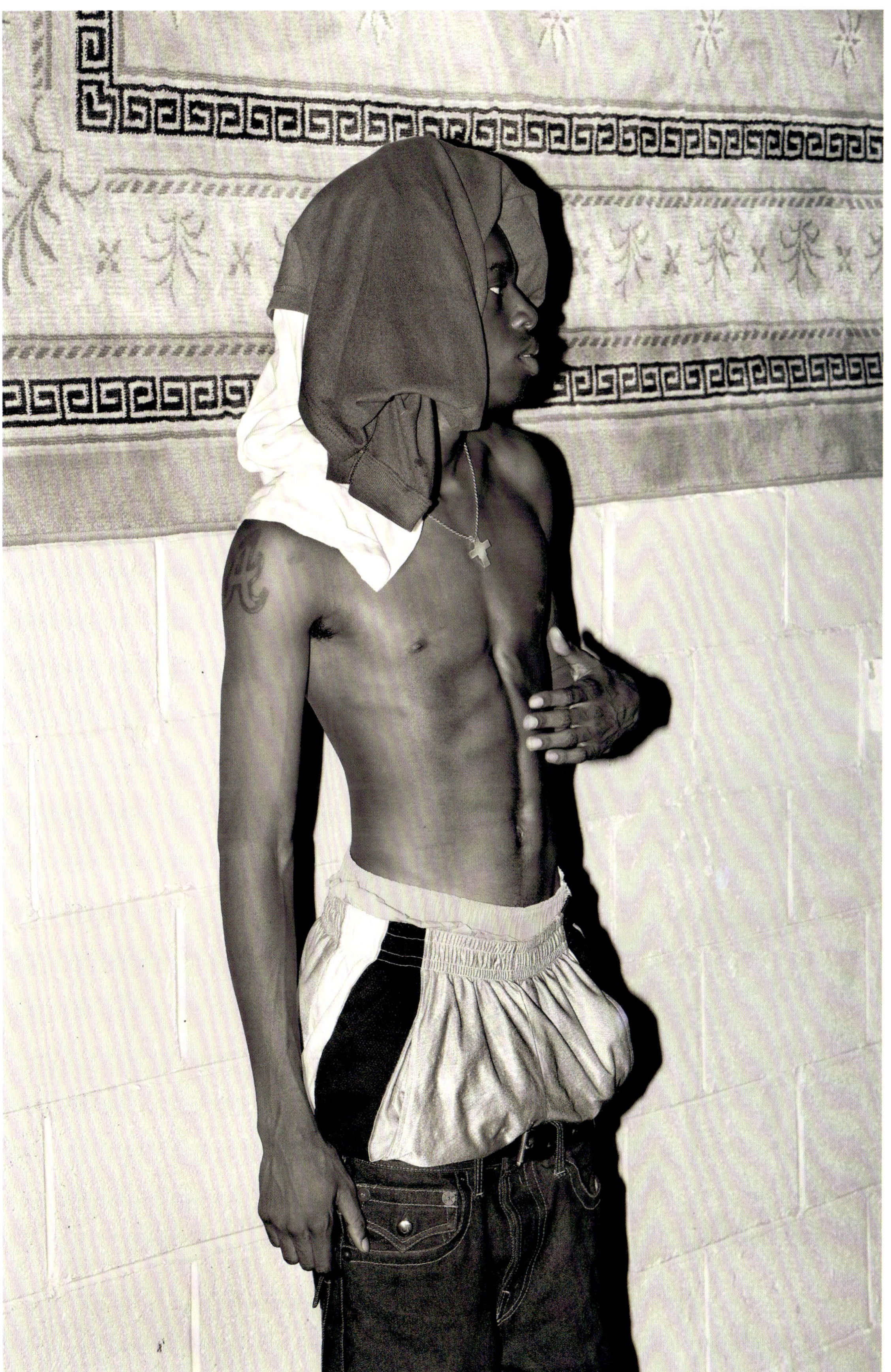

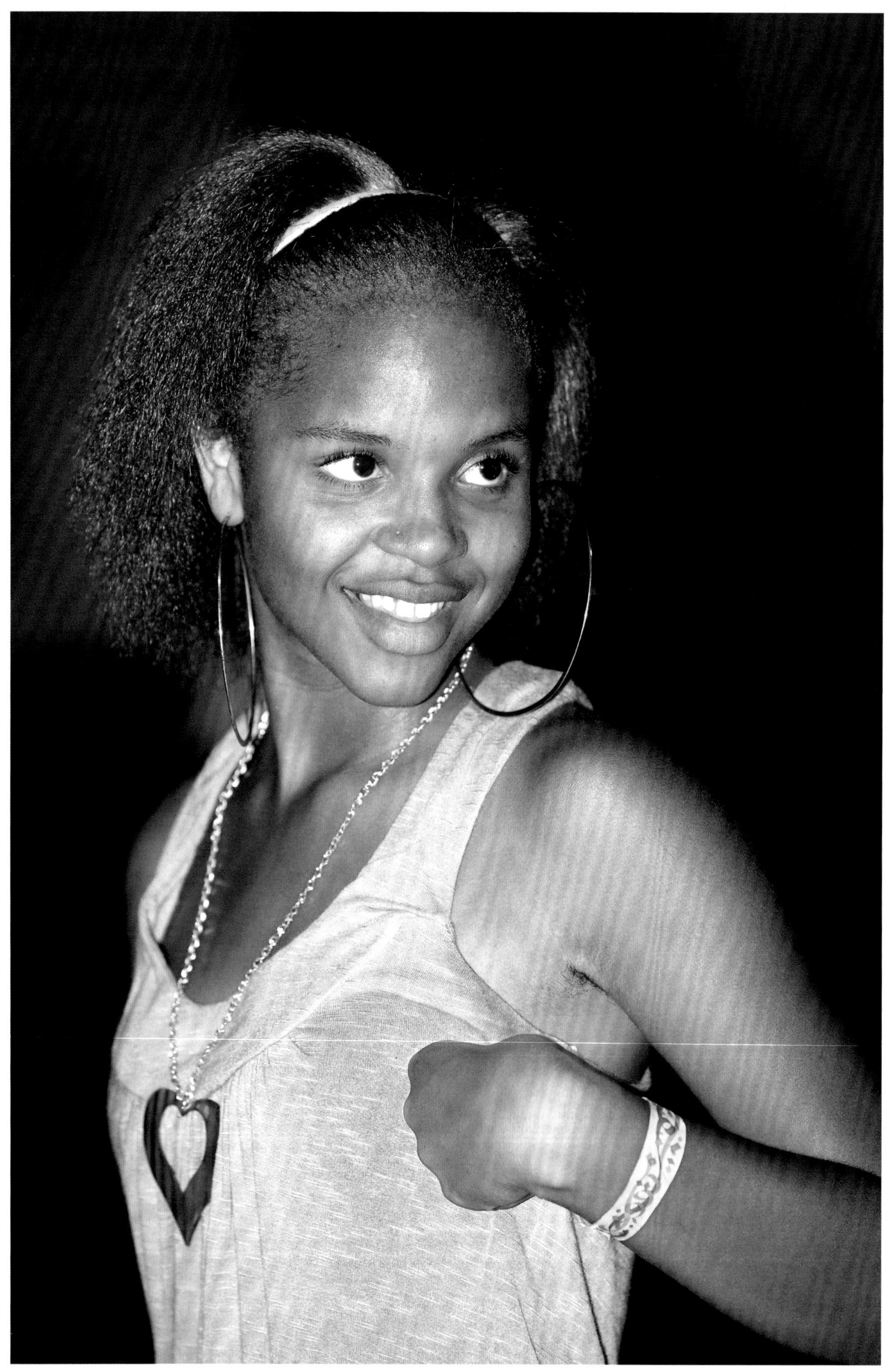

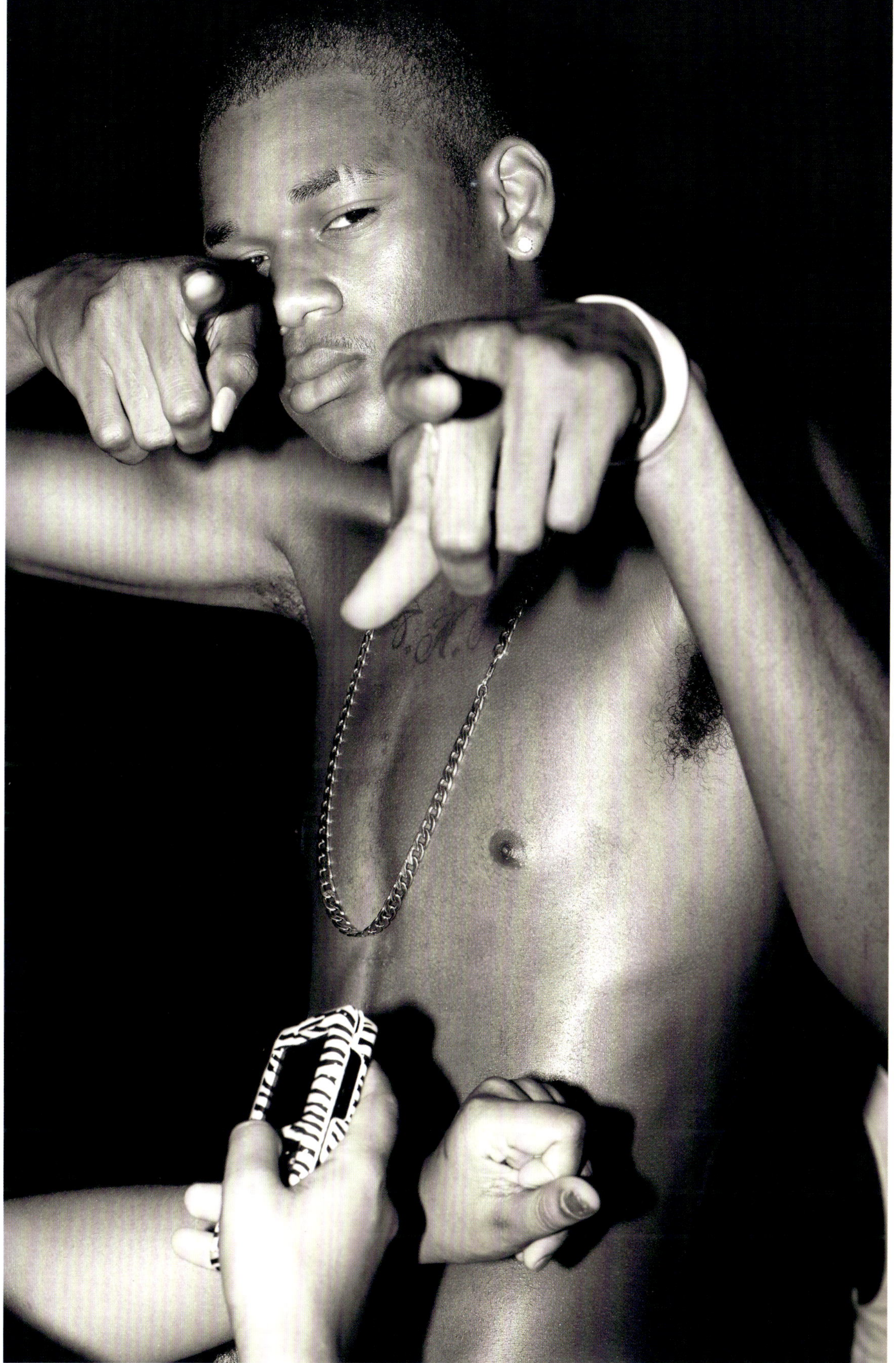

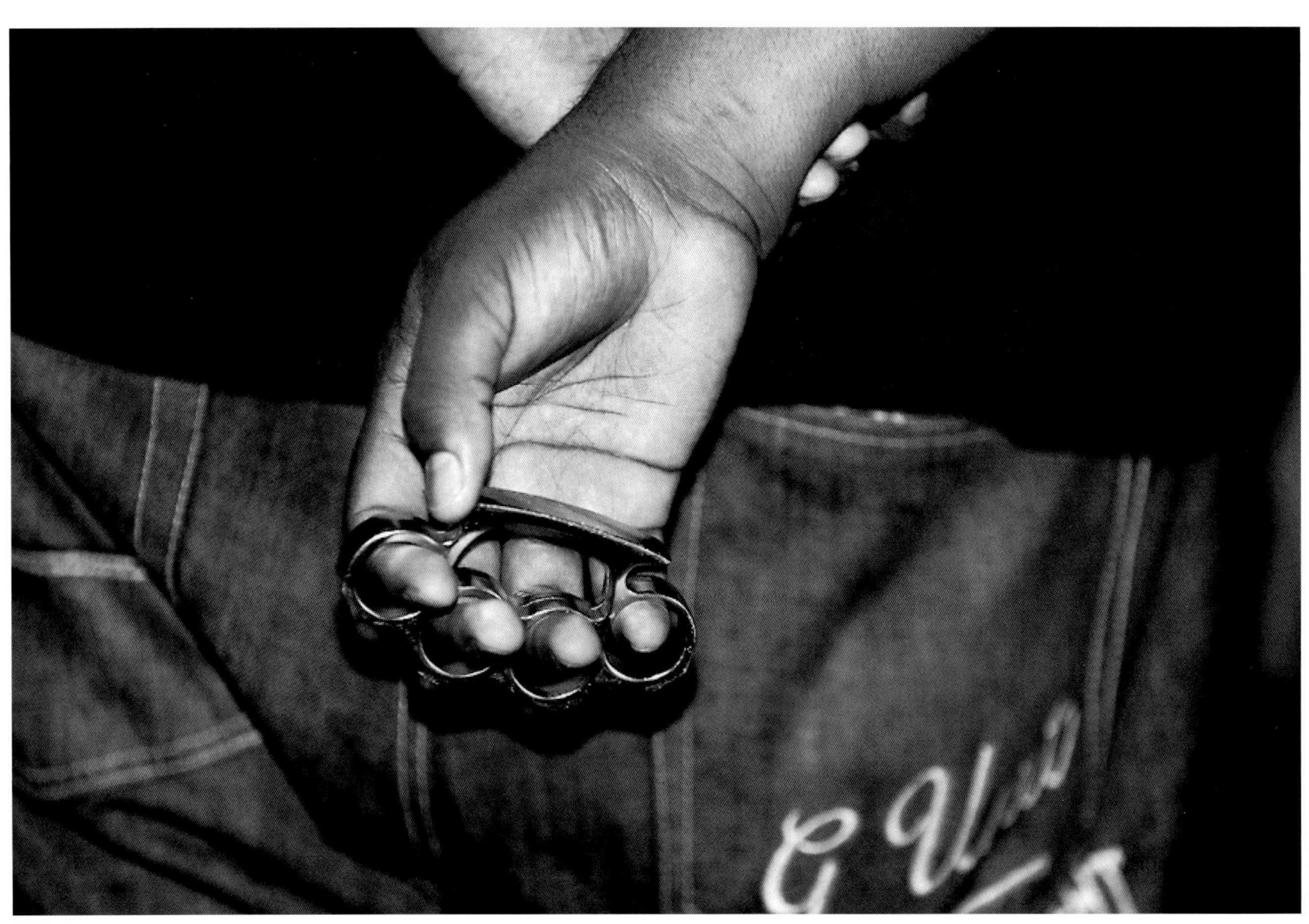

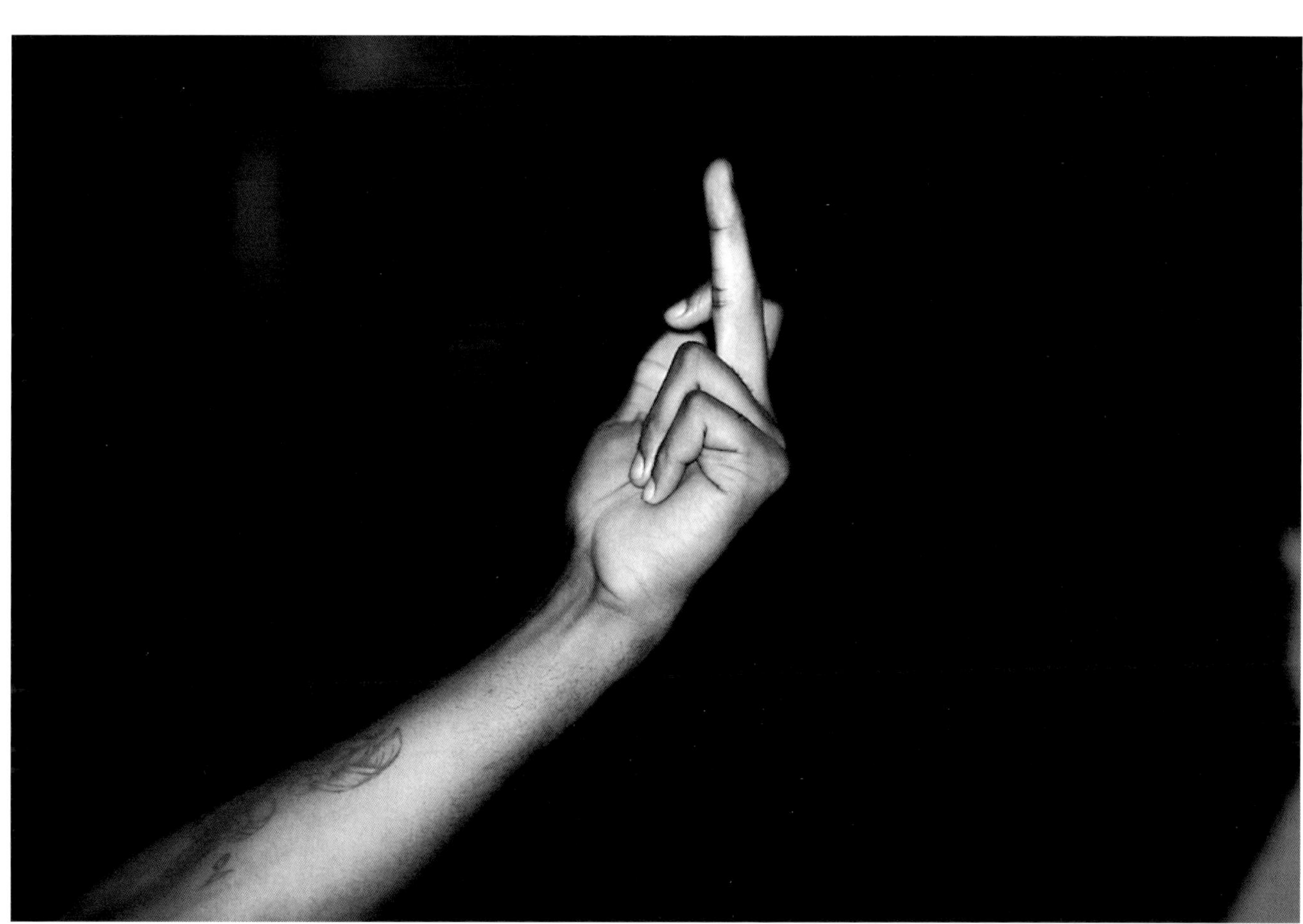

JUL 1, 2009: 10:22 PM

MEGA PARTY #8!: FOAM FEST 3!(Wet Dreams Edition) DIS SUNDAY@ FUSION - FOAM PARTY & PAJAMA PARTY! EVERY1 FREE TIL 1030! 1125 Park Central Blvd DECATUR

JUL 3, 2009: 2:20 PM

PARTY RECAP: LEVIS & LEGGINGS=POPPIN! >>STUDIO 72=TURNT THE F*CK UP! >>DOLLORAMA @FUSION=STR8 MADNESS! & NOW A *FREE* FOR ALL NEW YEARS DAY @ FUSION!

OCT 10, 2009: 9:32 PM

"ThE bLaCk Out" {LIGHTS OUT EDITION} SUNDAY @ FUSION!! only (($5)) til 11p in BLACK or w/TEXT! - 1125 Park Central Blvd Decatur (NO SKOOL MONDAY)FWD

DEC 12, 2009: 10:02 PM

GuCcI MaNe ALBUM RELEASE PARTY! 2NITE decemBURR 12th @FUSION [ALBUM GIVEAWAYS ALL NITE!] EVERYONE $5 TIL 10:45 W/TXT

JUL 3, 2009: 2:20 PM

SHOW THIS TXT: "BaTtLe Of ThE TwErK part 2" TONIGHT @ FUSION! LADIES FREE TIL 10:30 & $7 AFTA w/TXT - 1125 Park Central Blvd DECATUR

AUG 17, 2009: 9:08 PM

Ladies.. get ur BIKINI TOPS ready! Fellas..get ur crew together! FUSION IS GOIN HAMM 2MRW NITE!! (Now Opens @ 9:30! FUSION, WHERE ATL PARTYS.. FOR FREE

SEP 3, 2009: 9:40 PM

BREAKING NEWS!! PLZ FWD::FRIDAY BOREDOM IS OVER!!

JUL 17, 2009: 10:21 PM

((OFF DA BONZ)) 2MRW (Thurs) >One NIght Only<LADIES FREE TIL 12! "REGAL PERFORMIN "Convince Me" LIVE! also GETAWAY BOYZ, MSGOHAM & COVERGIRL - 3614 Hwy 42

SEP 22, 2009: 8:11 PM

1 of 2 FRM: Ent@c.tms g8.com MSG:DESTINATION SATURDAY HAS ARRIVED & THE ONLY PLACE TO BE 2NITE IS DREAMS ATL FOR FREE ENTRY TXT UR NAME & (Con't0 2 of 2 GUESTS BY 8(End)

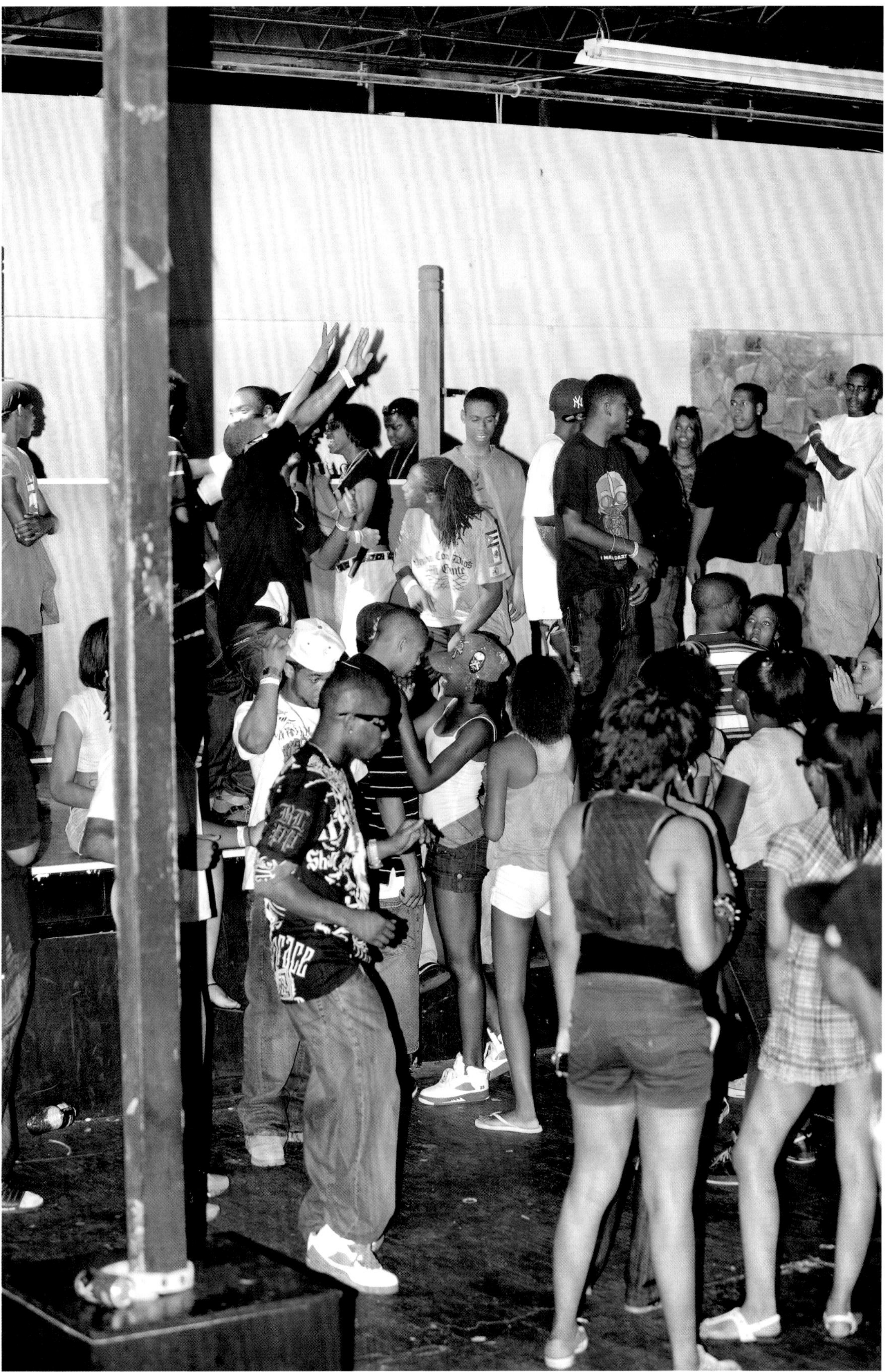

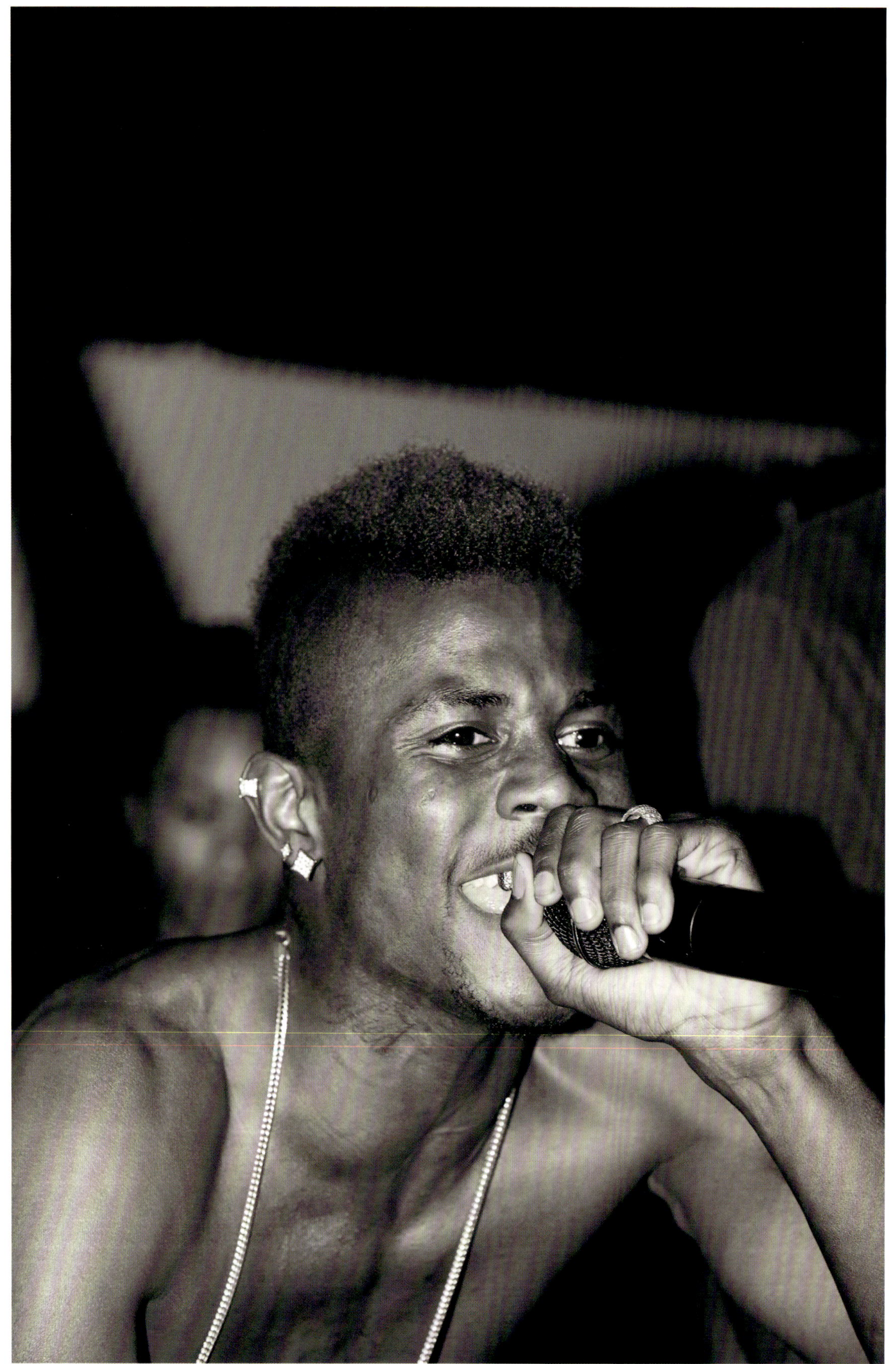

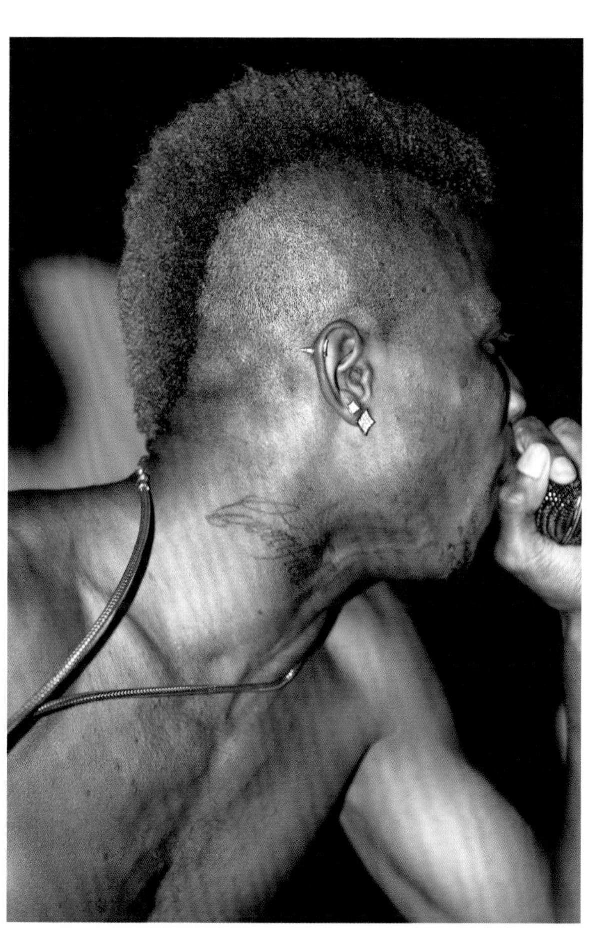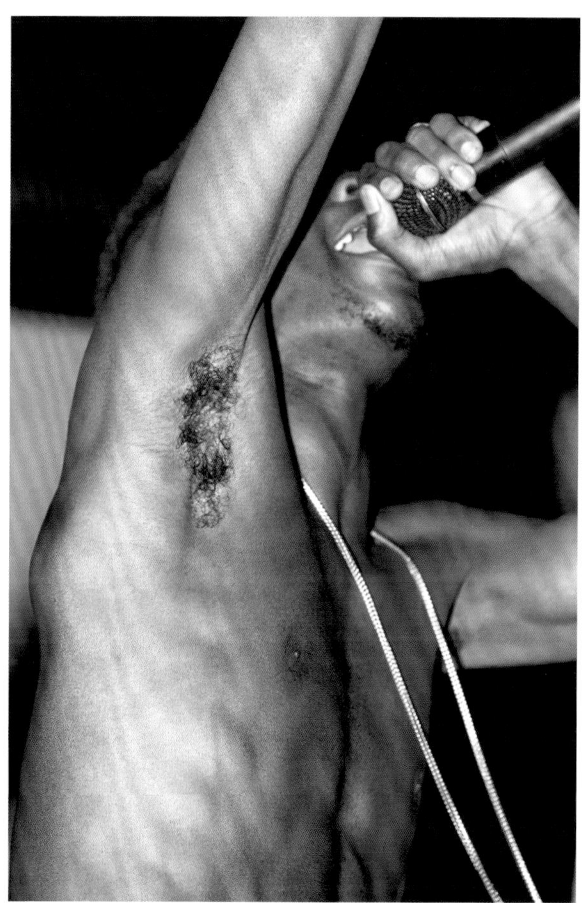

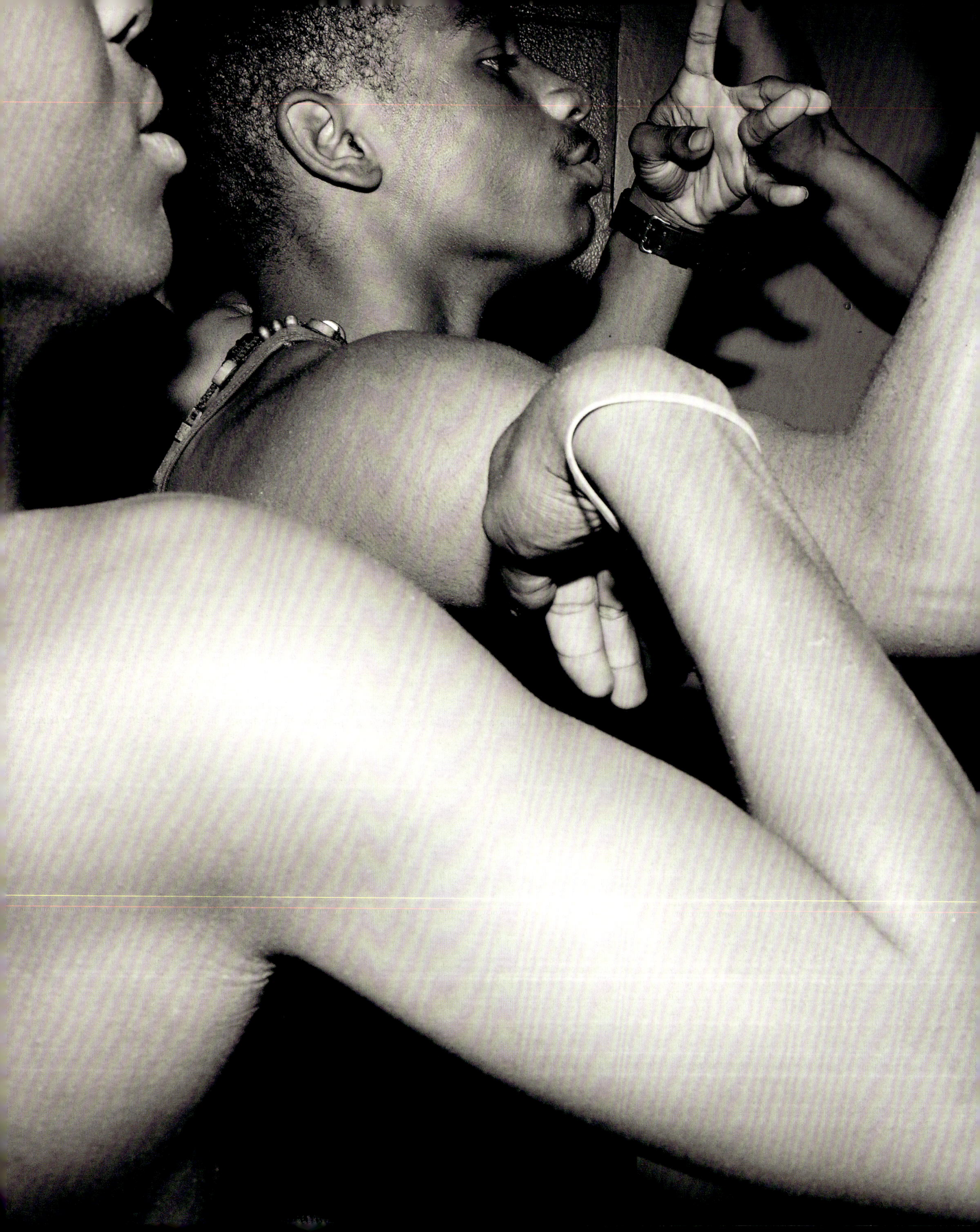

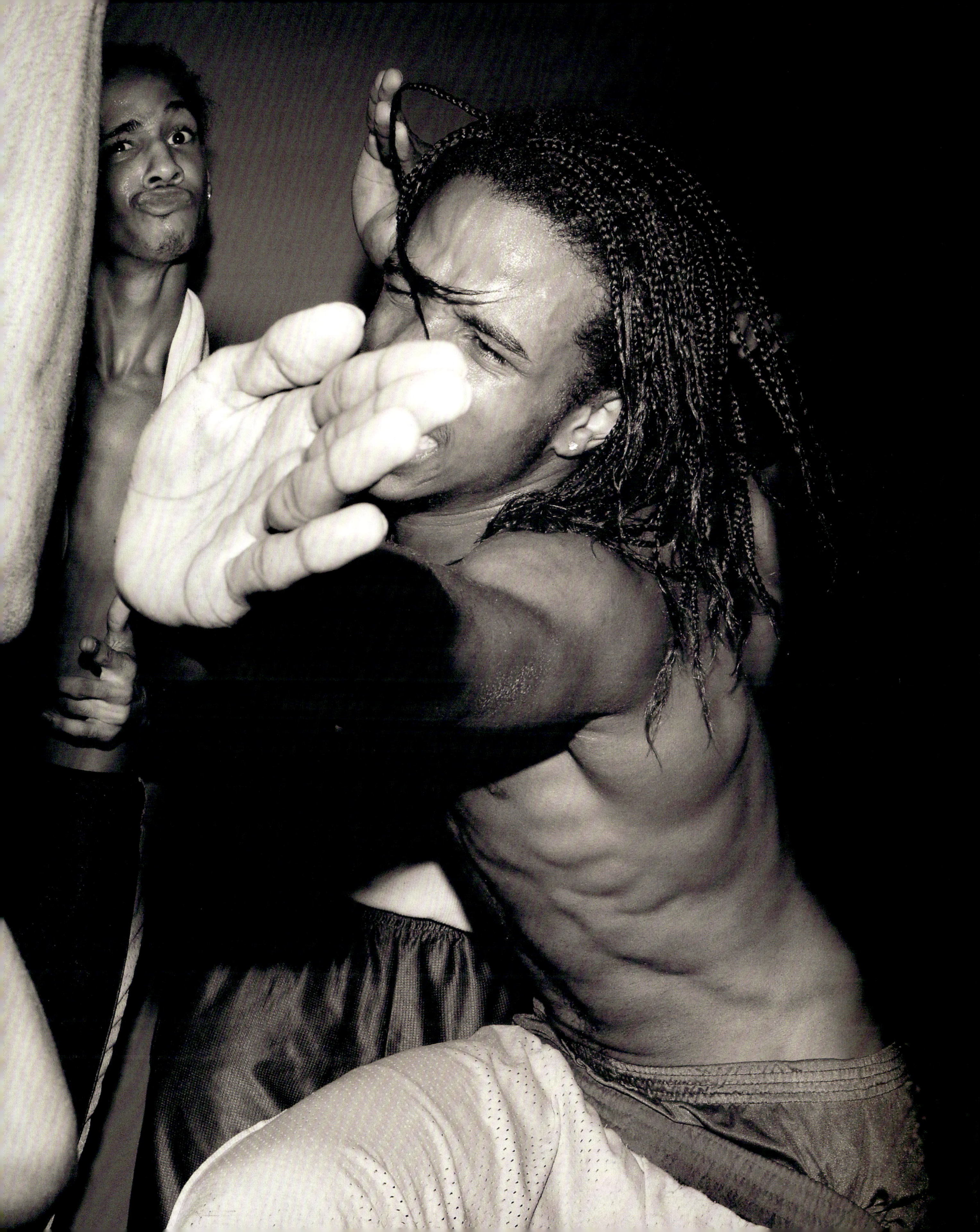

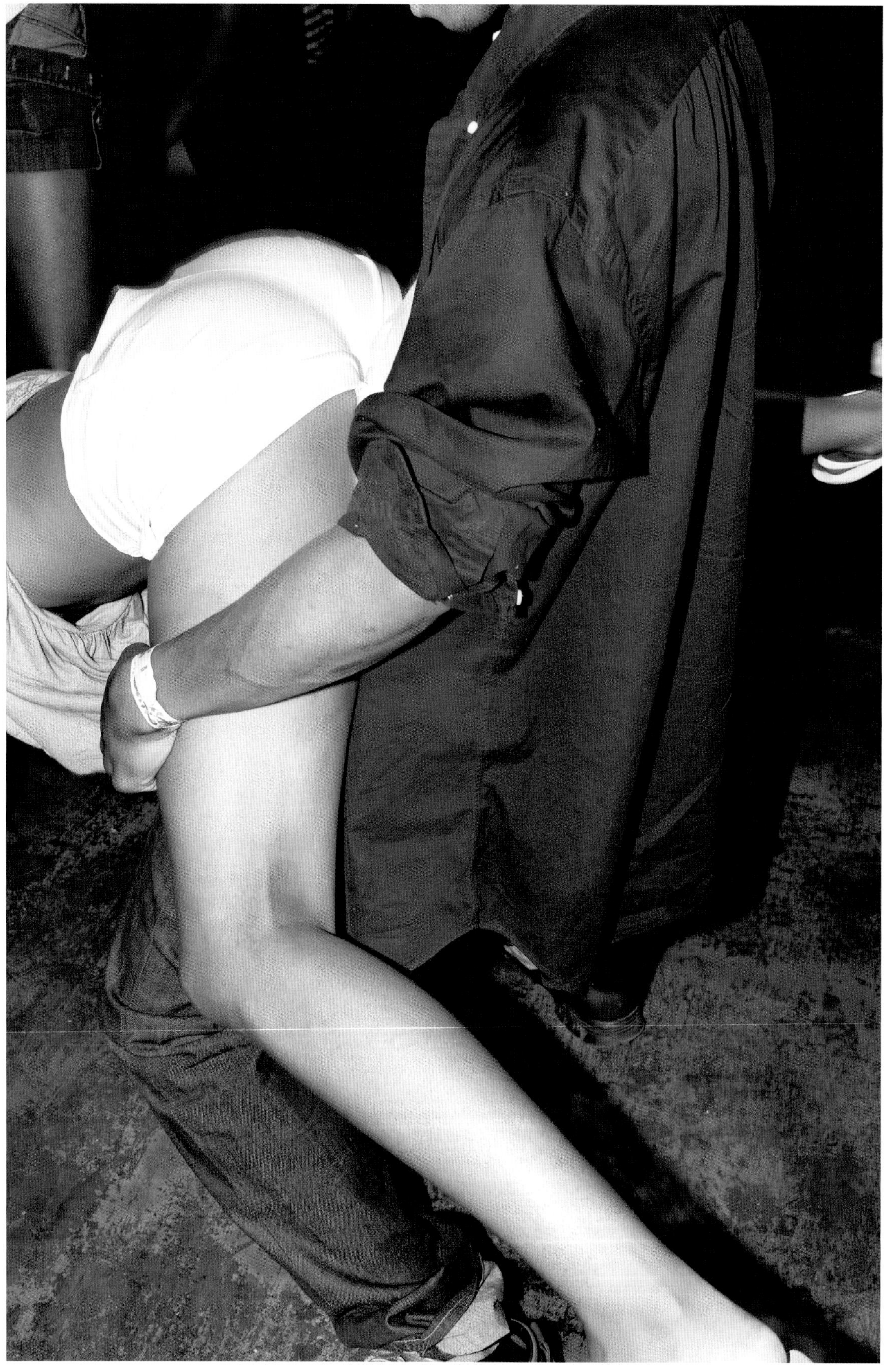

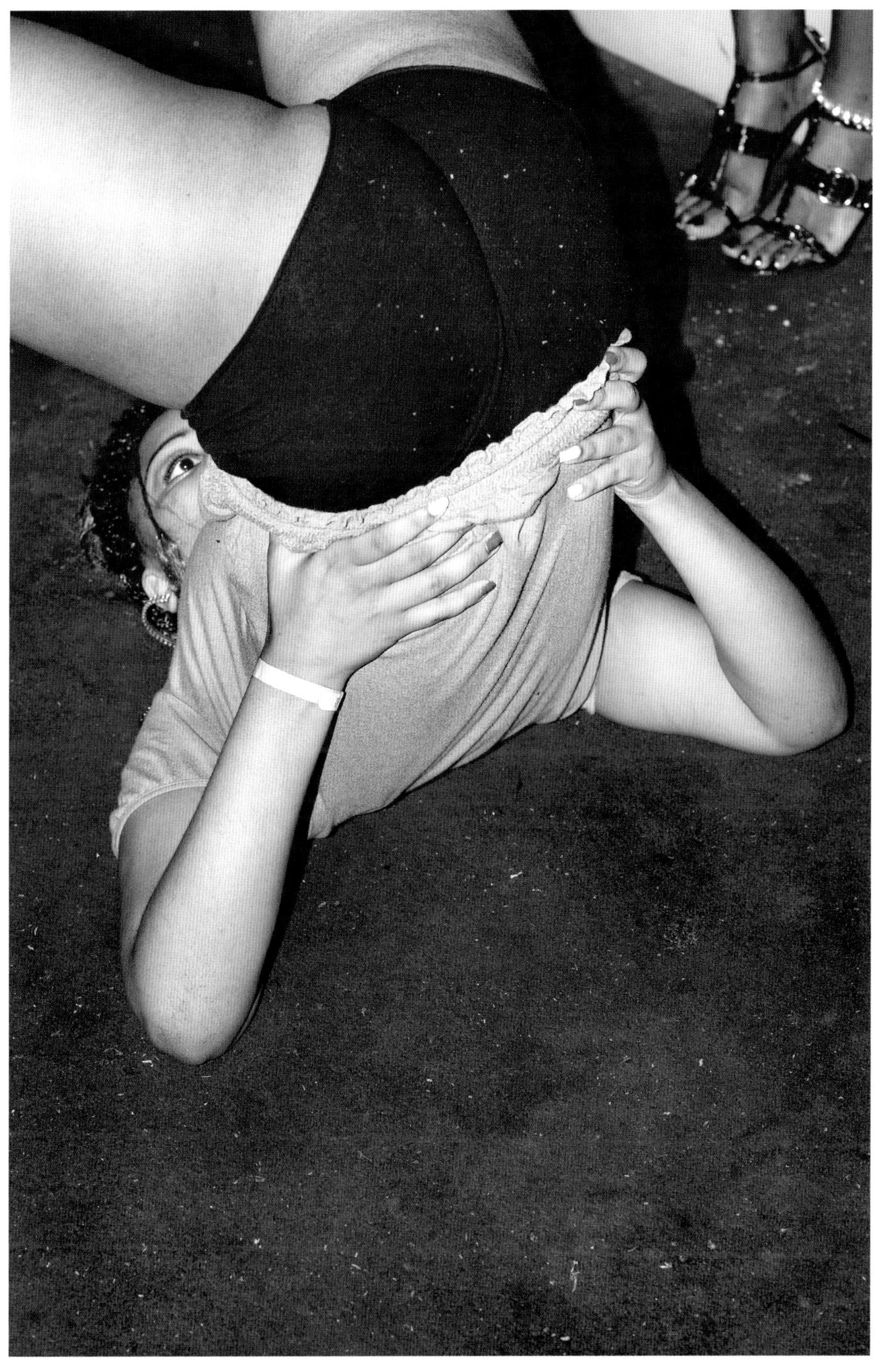

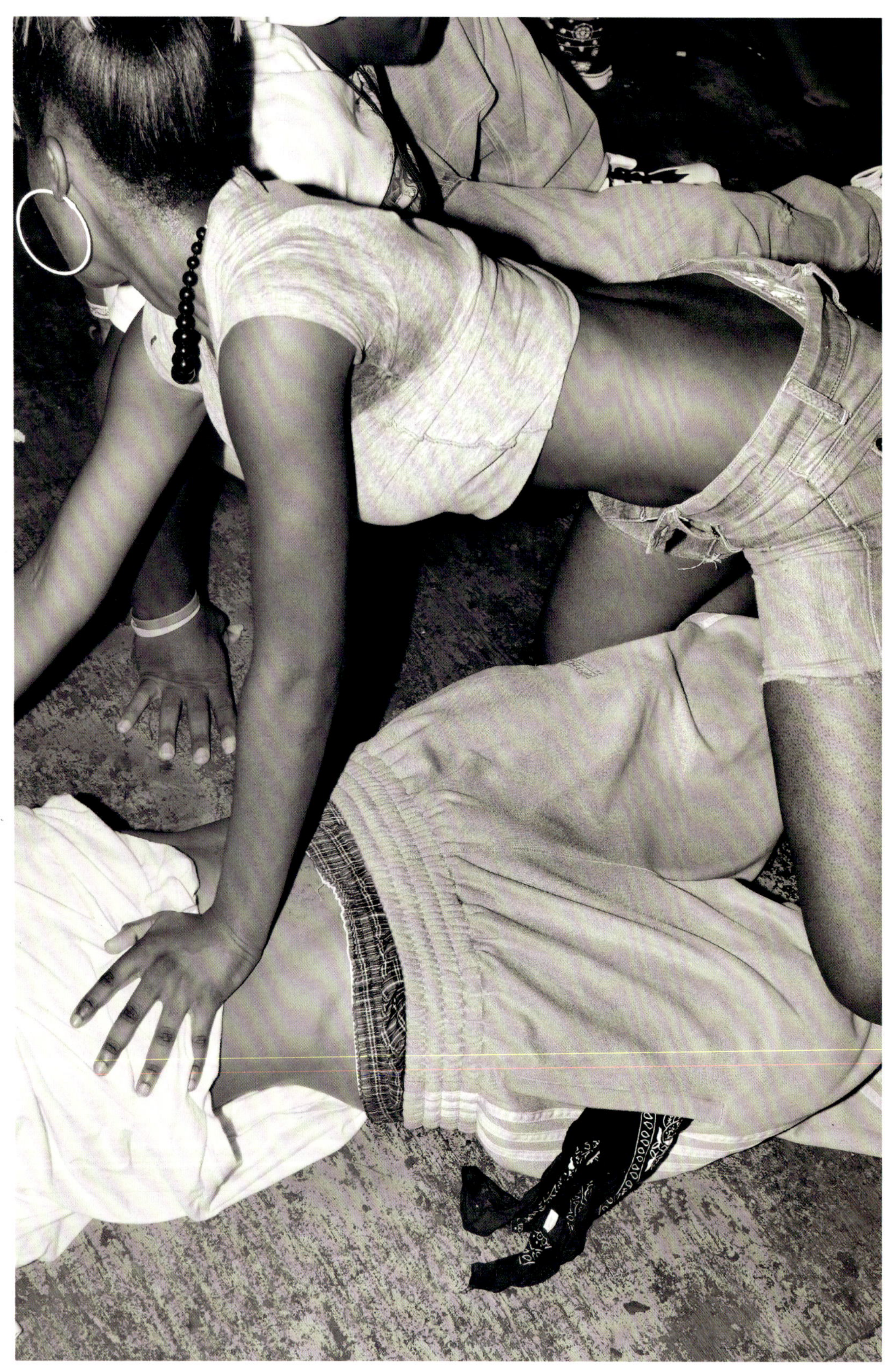

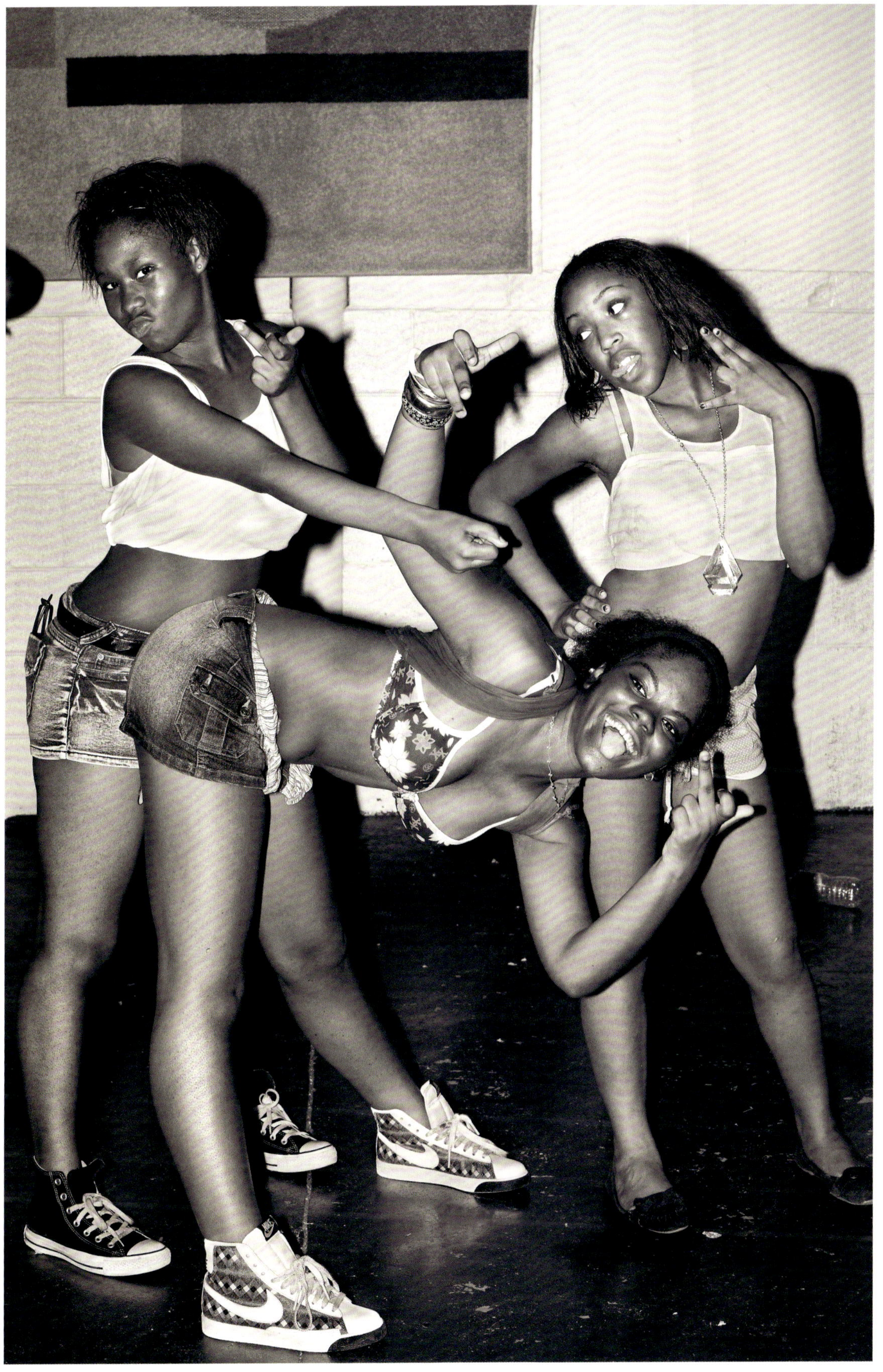

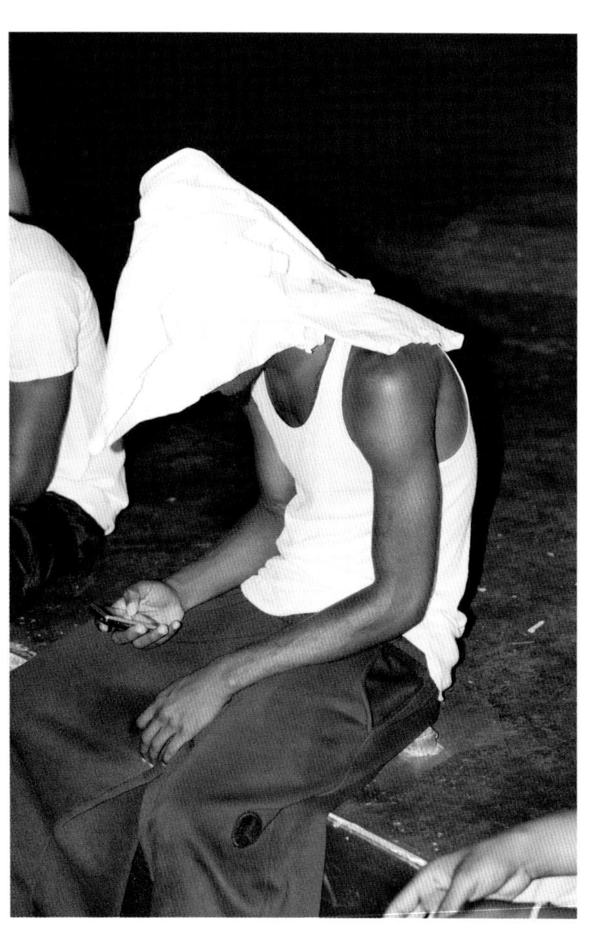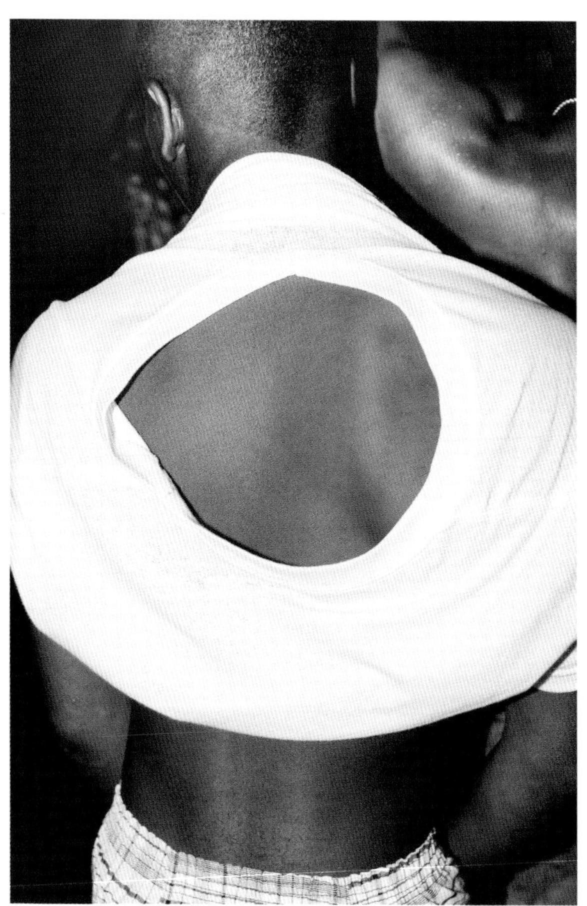

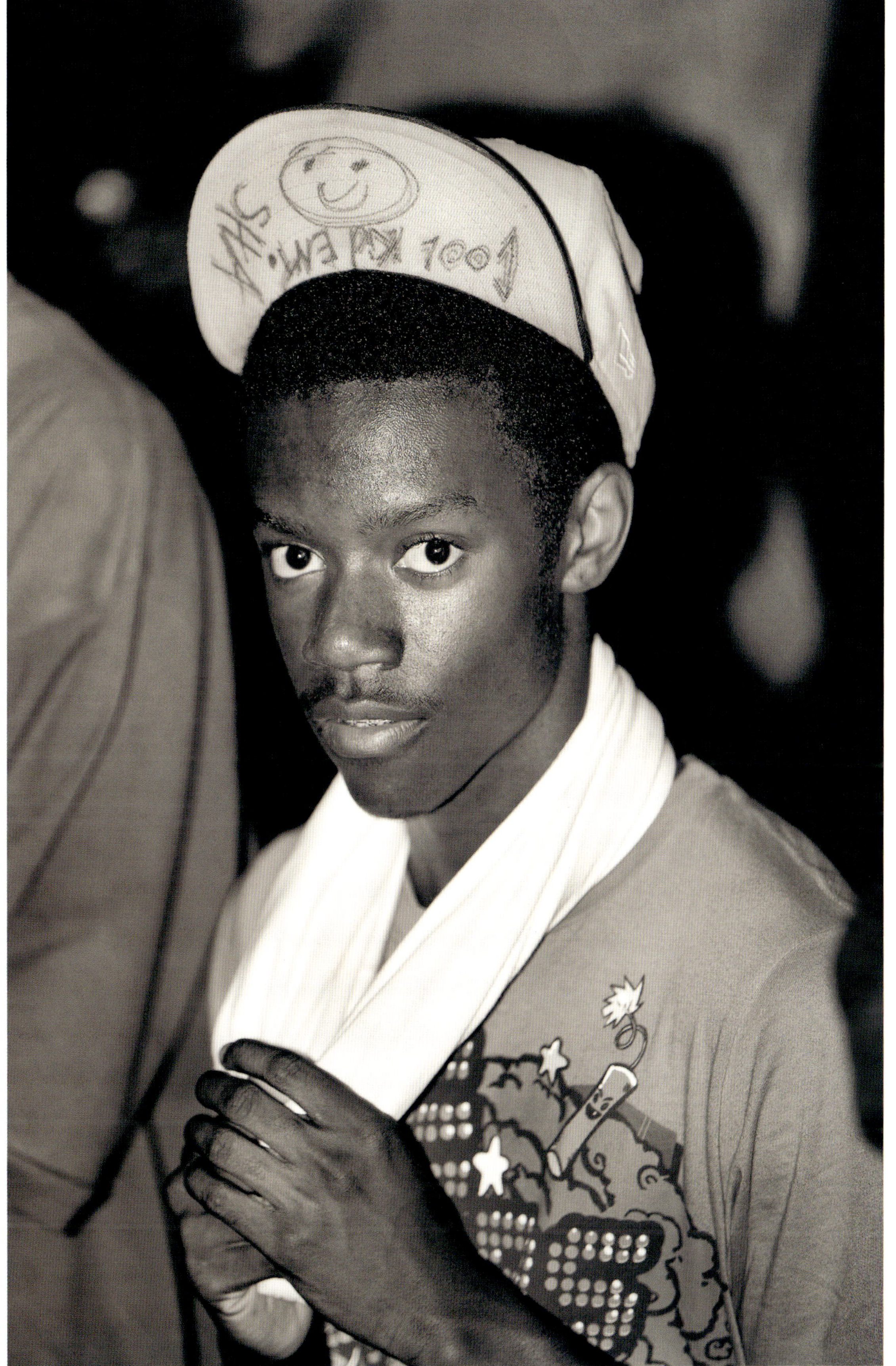
Cool Kid Em • Shea
100

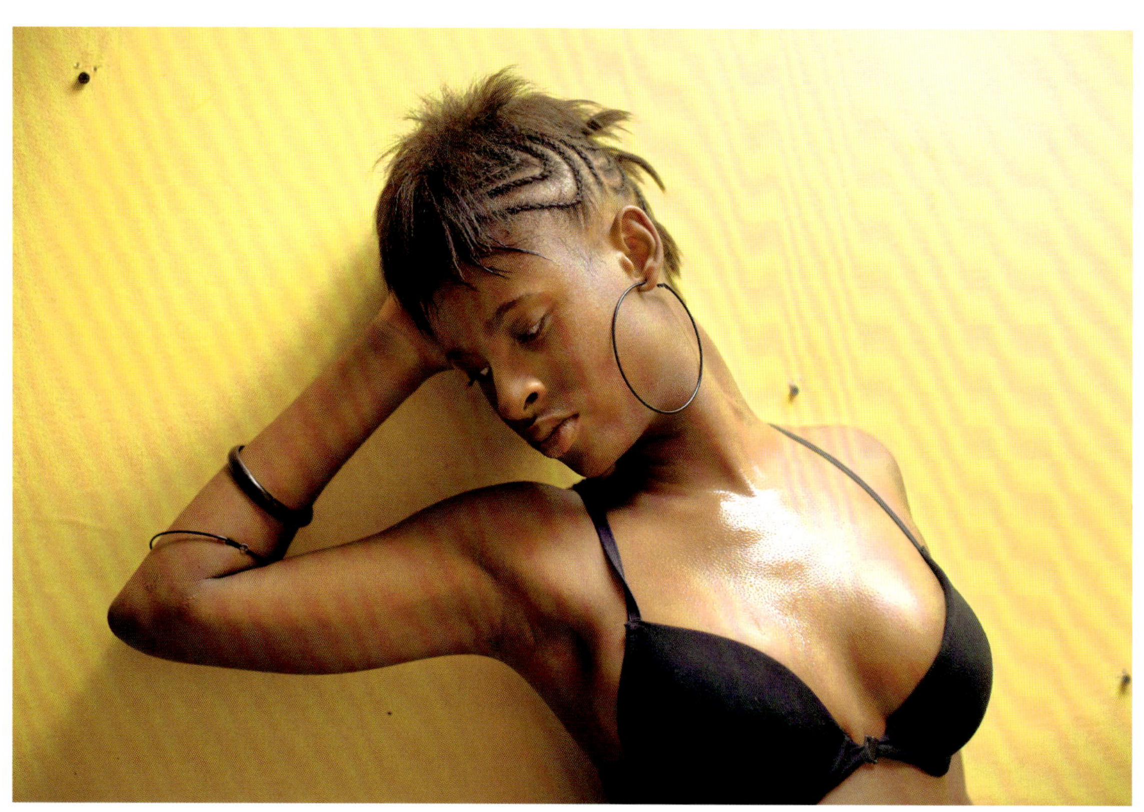

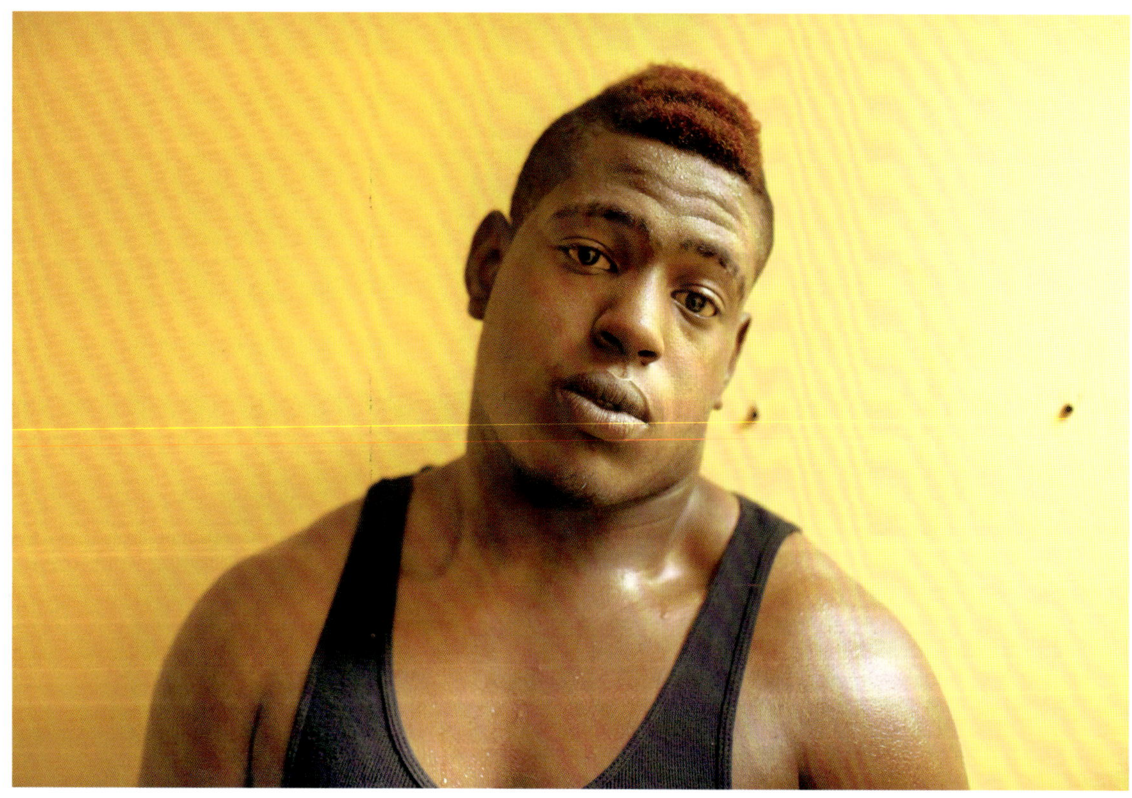

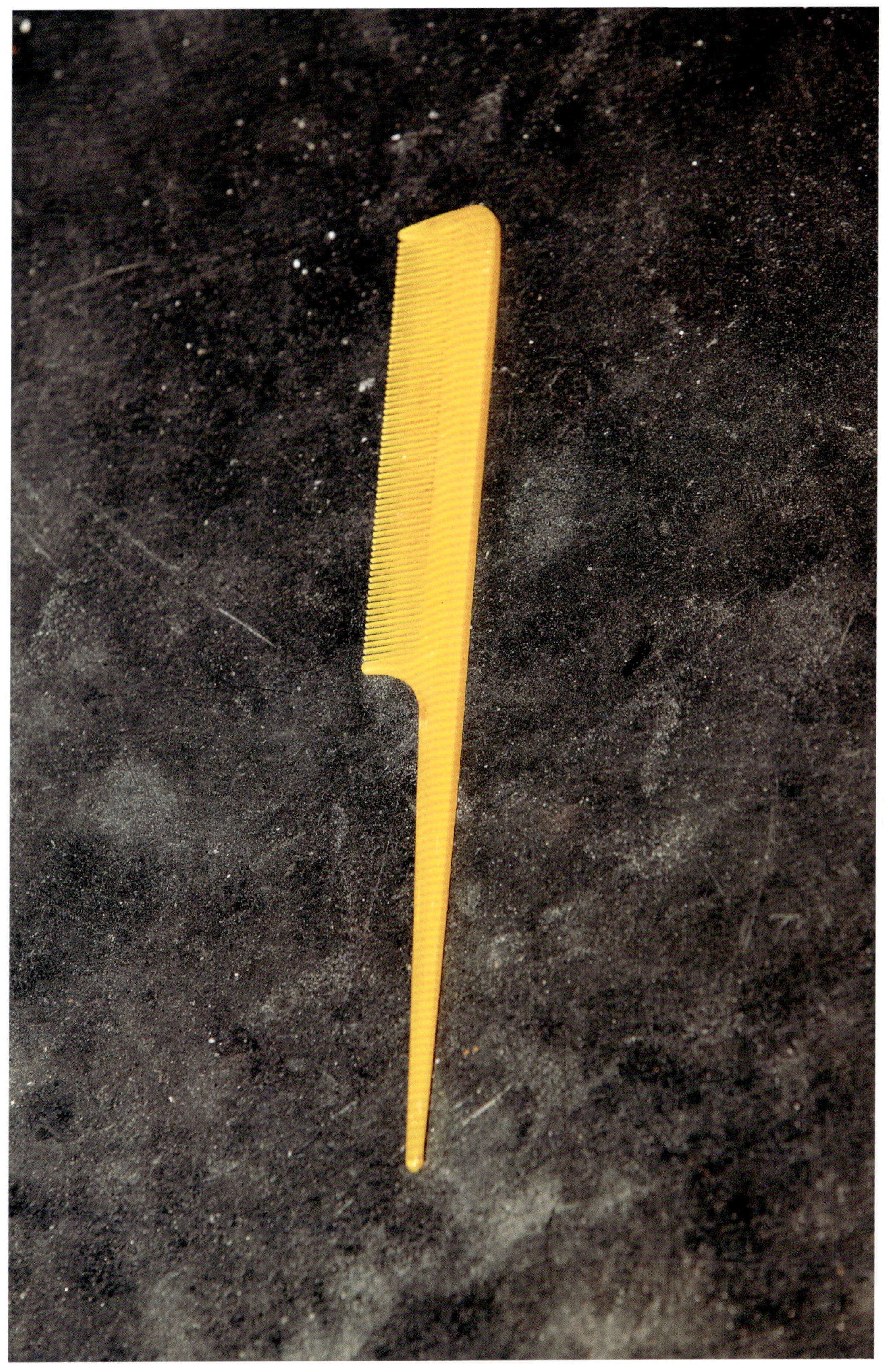

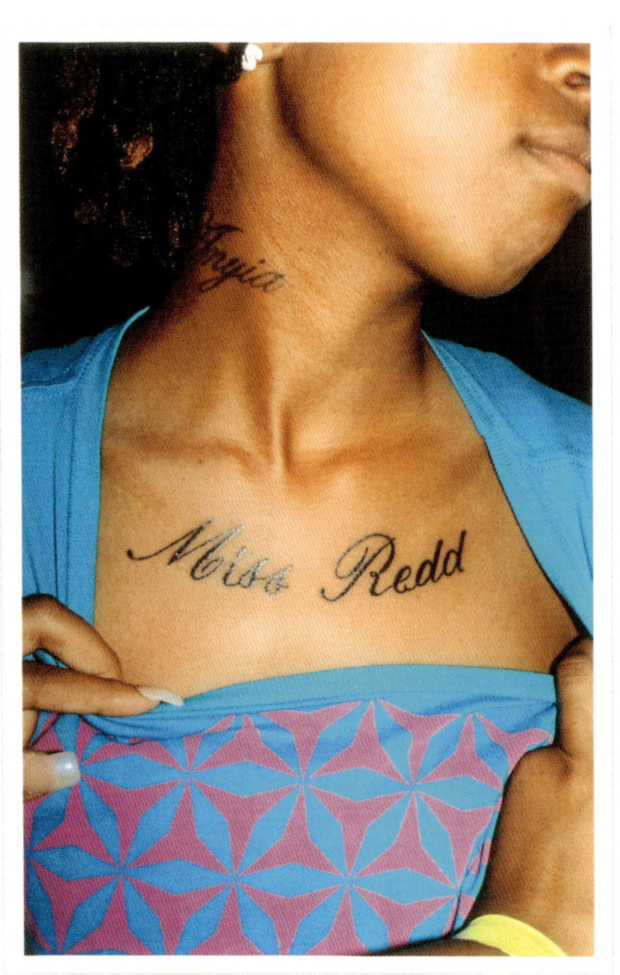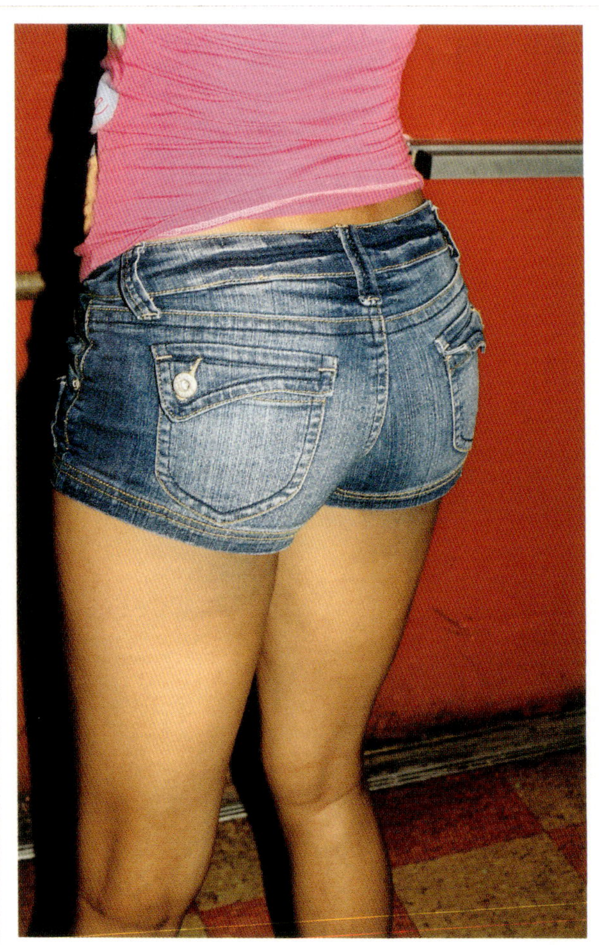

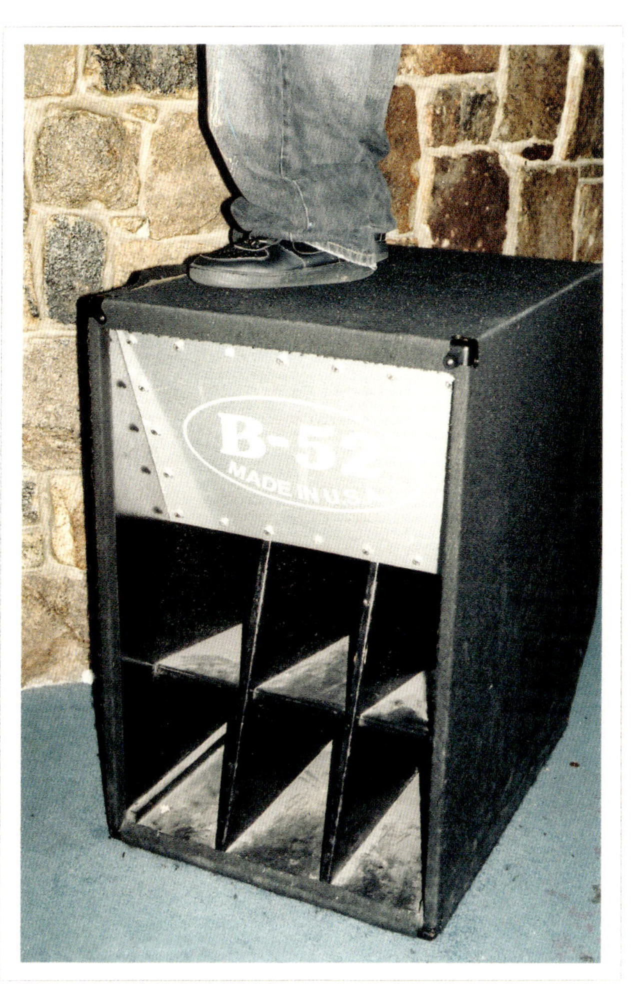

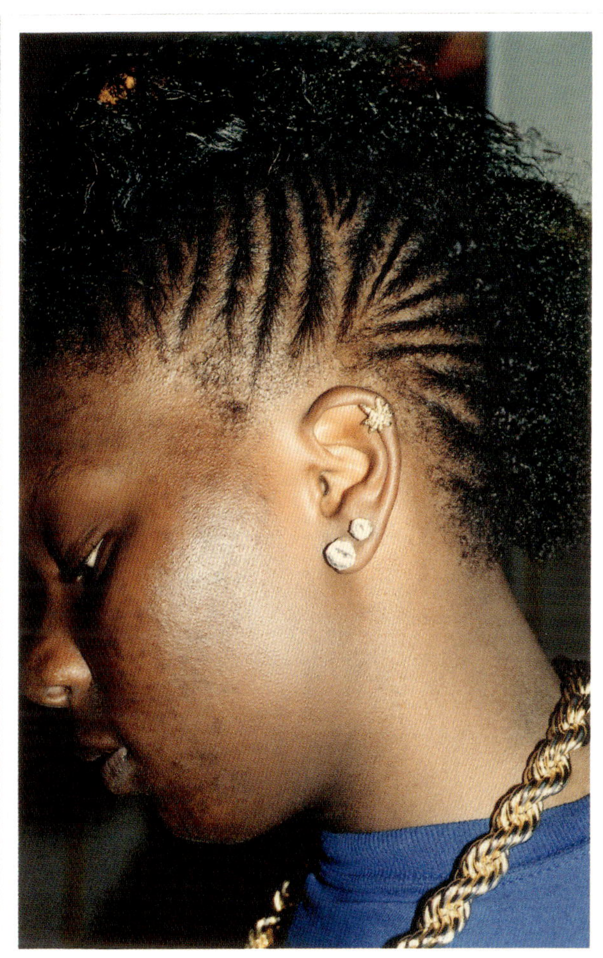

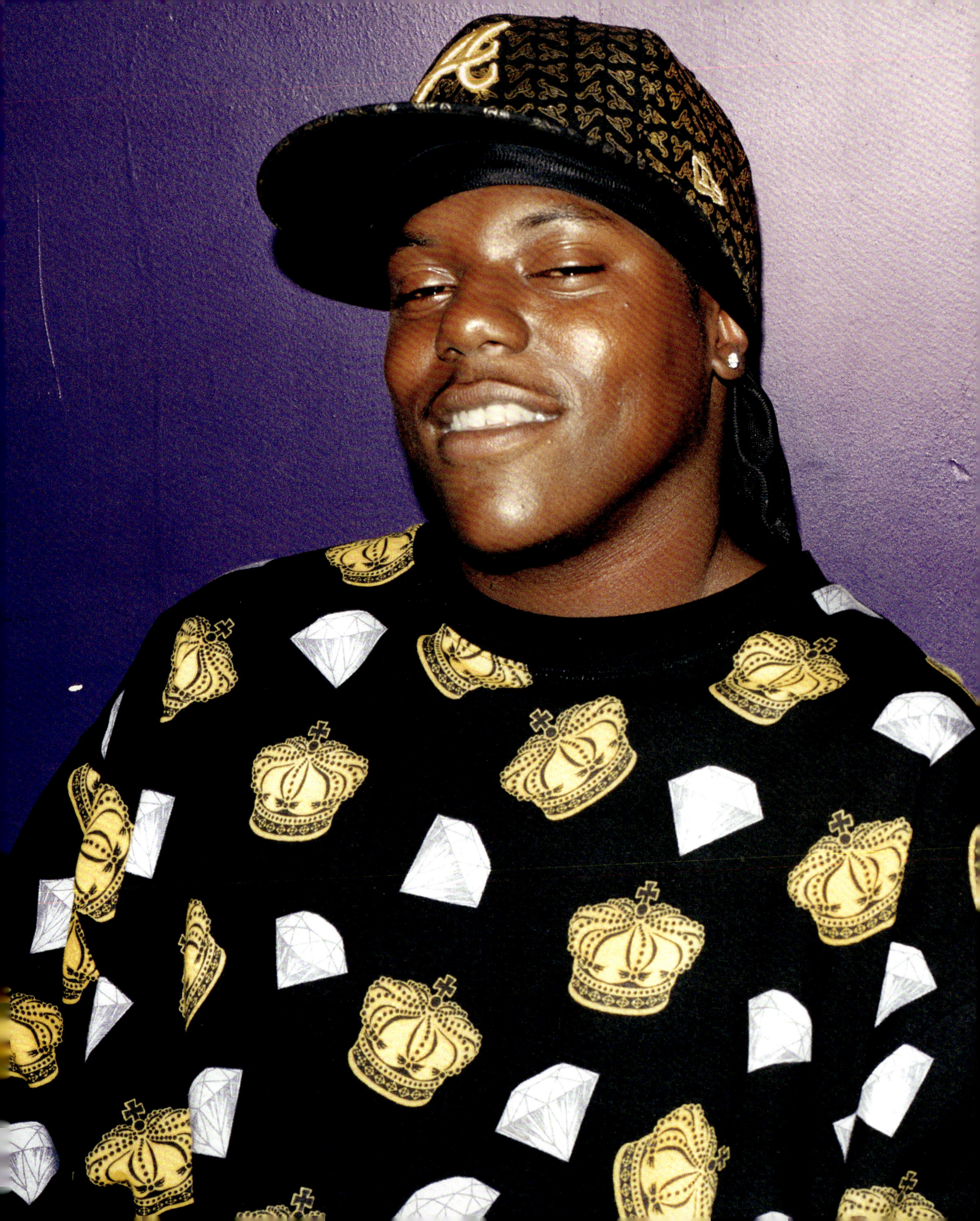

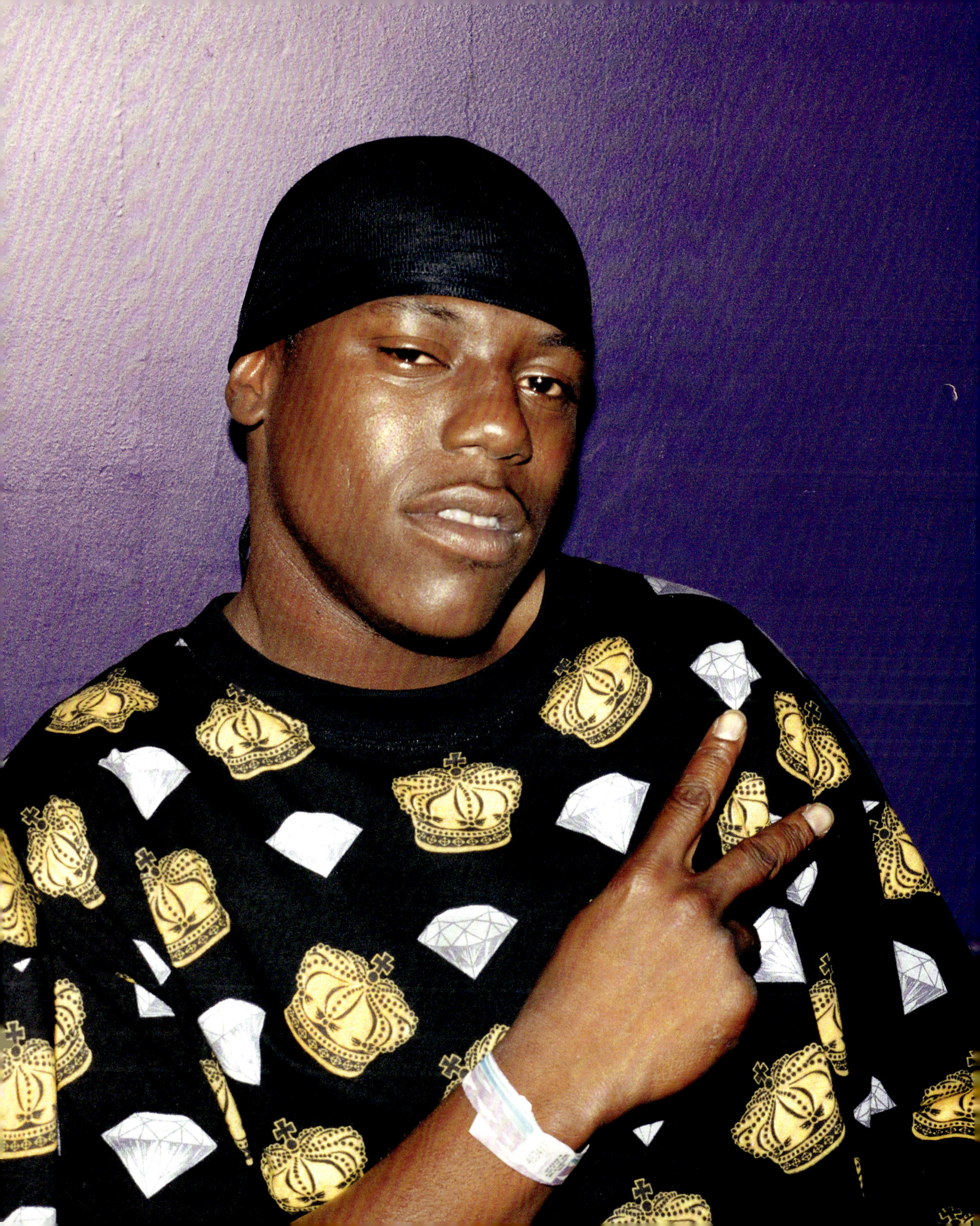

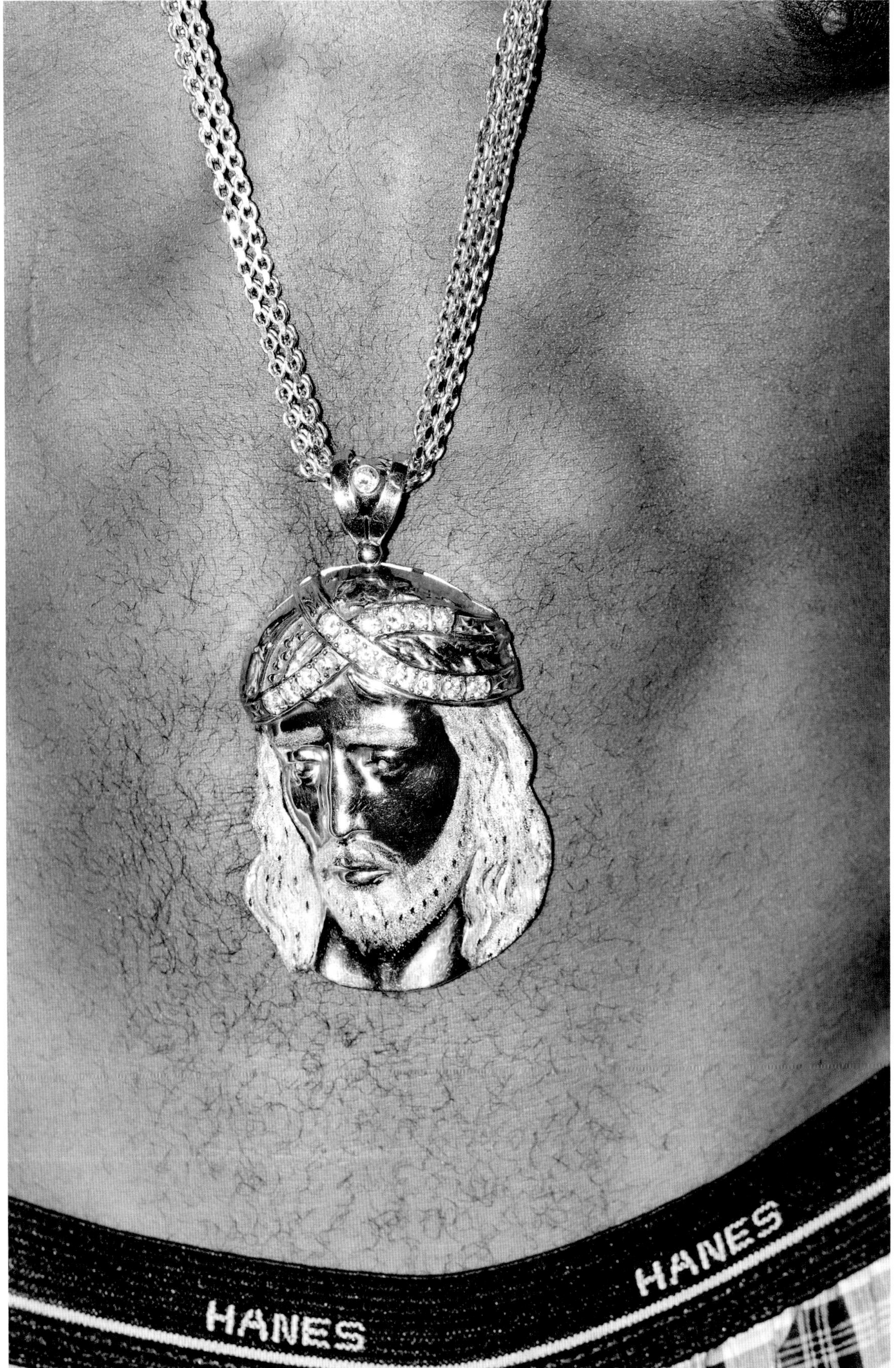

HANES
HANES
HANES

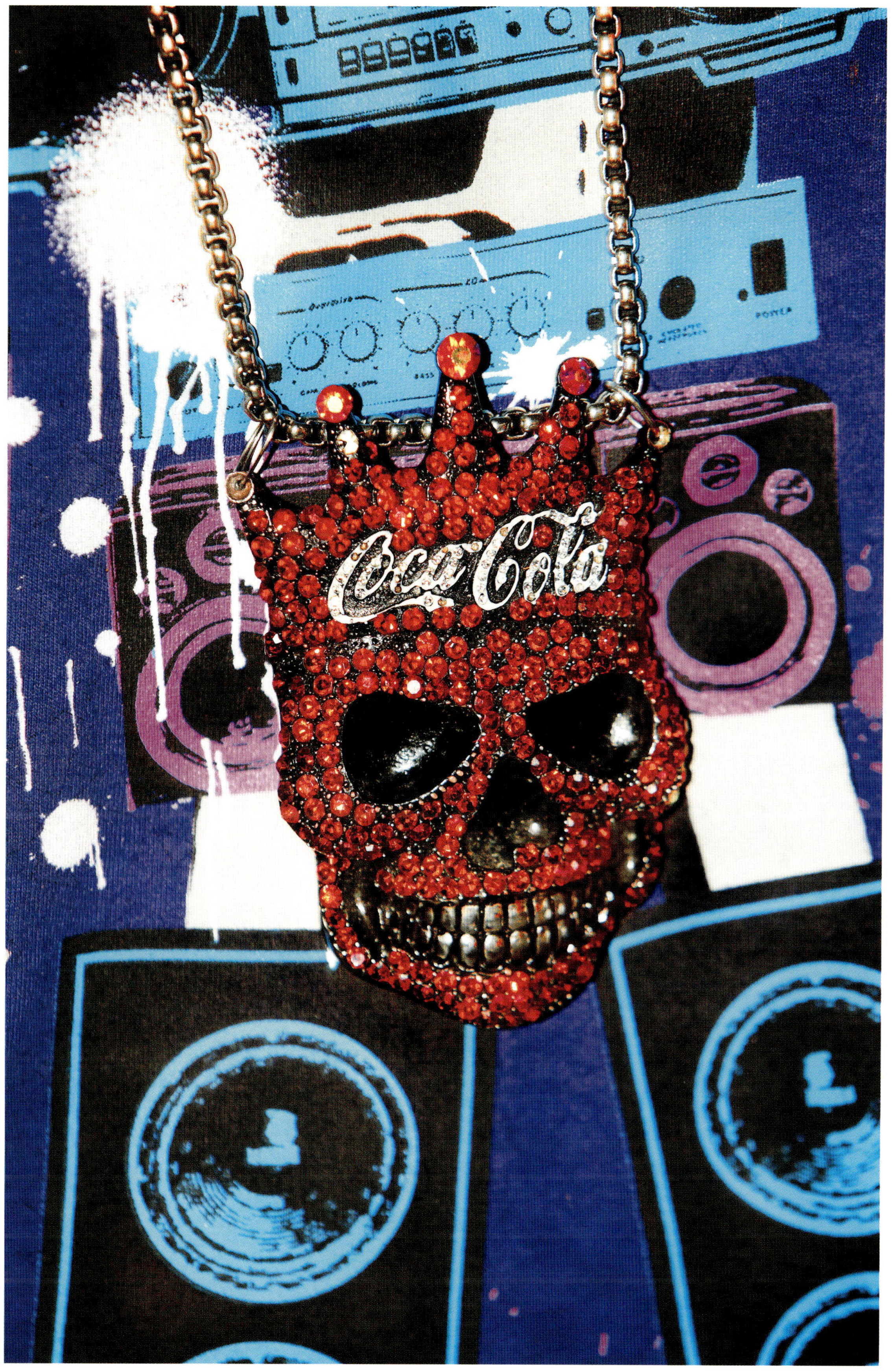

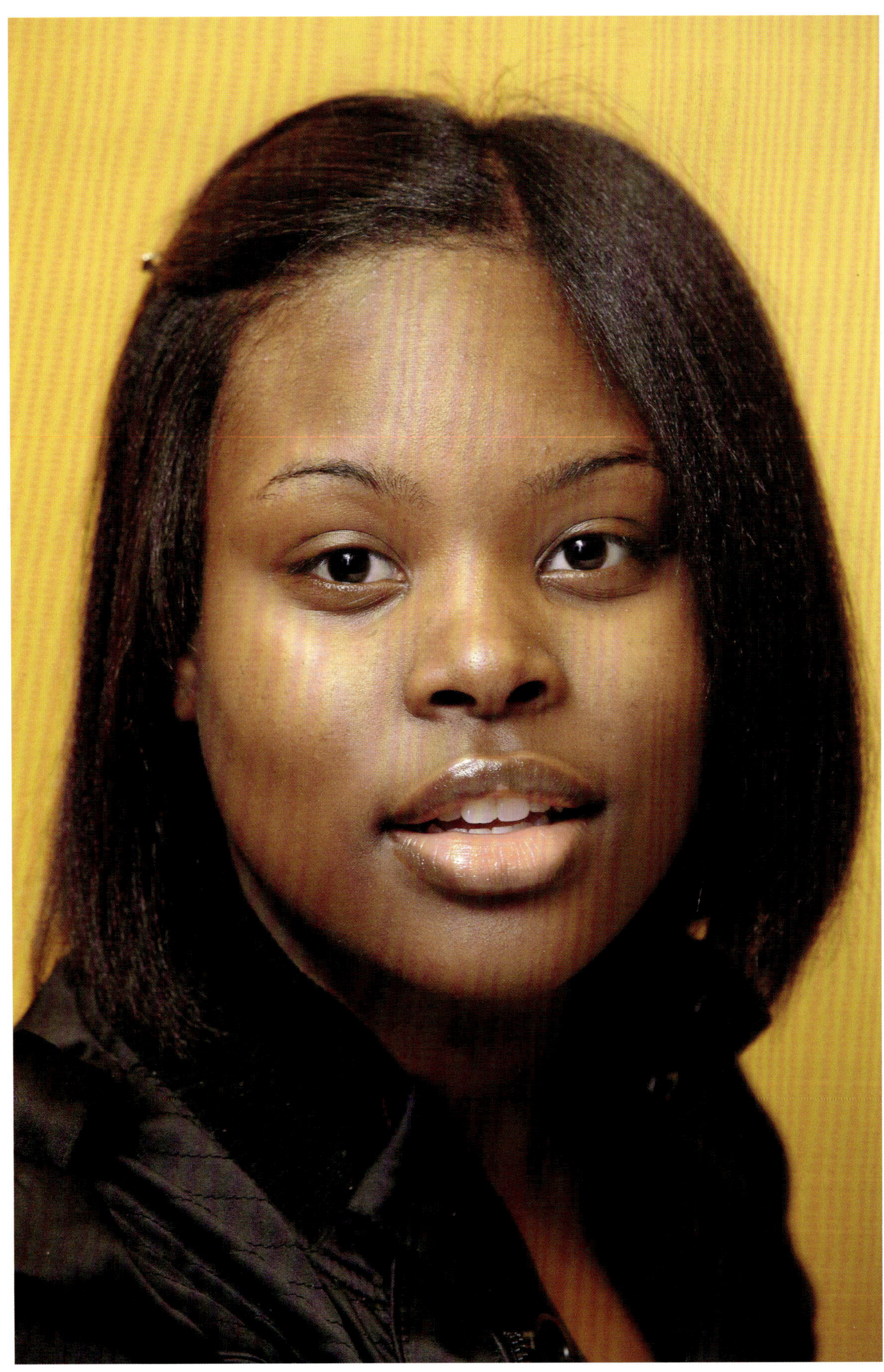

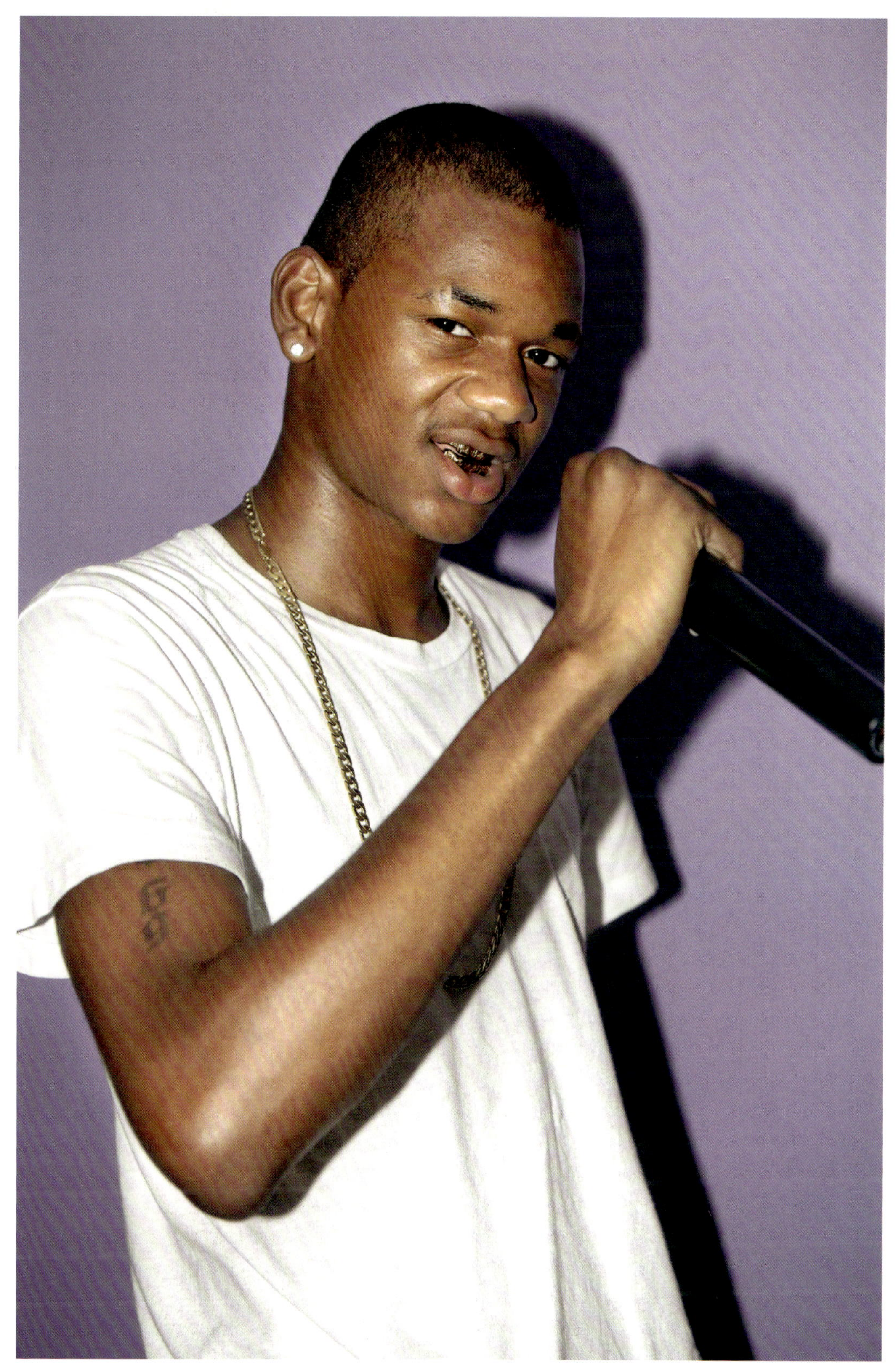

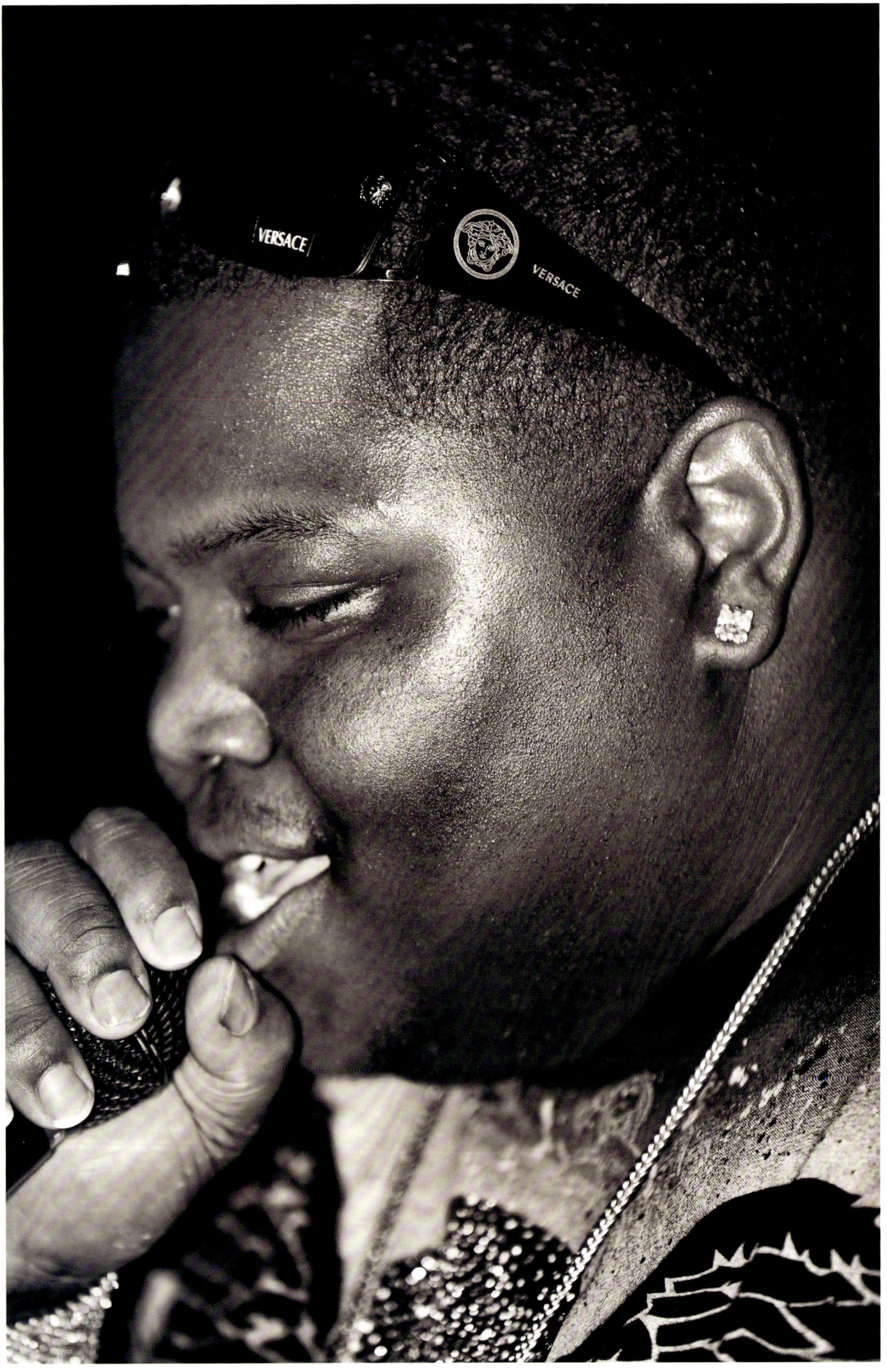
VERSACE
VERSACE

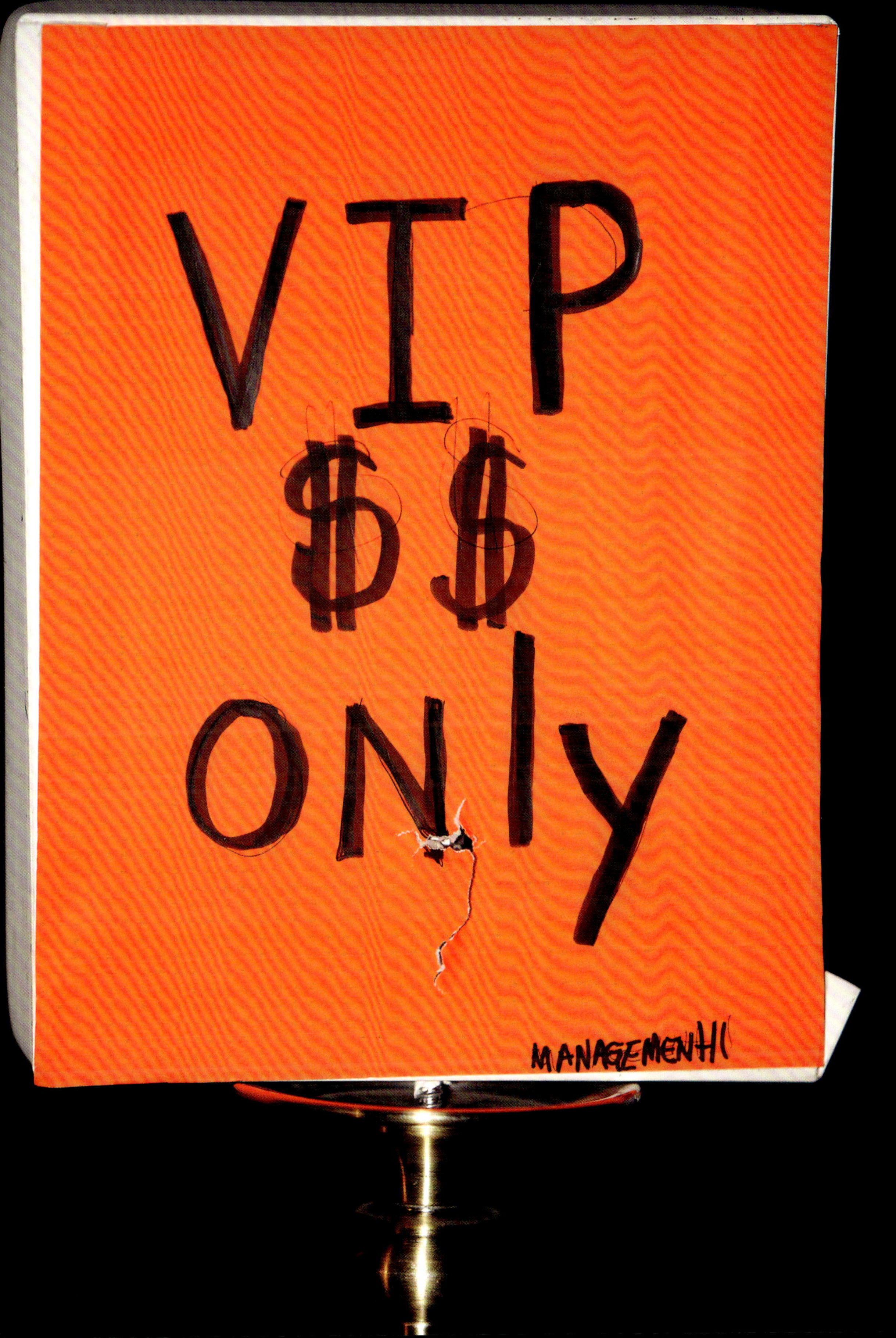

VIP
$$
ONLY
MANAGEMENT

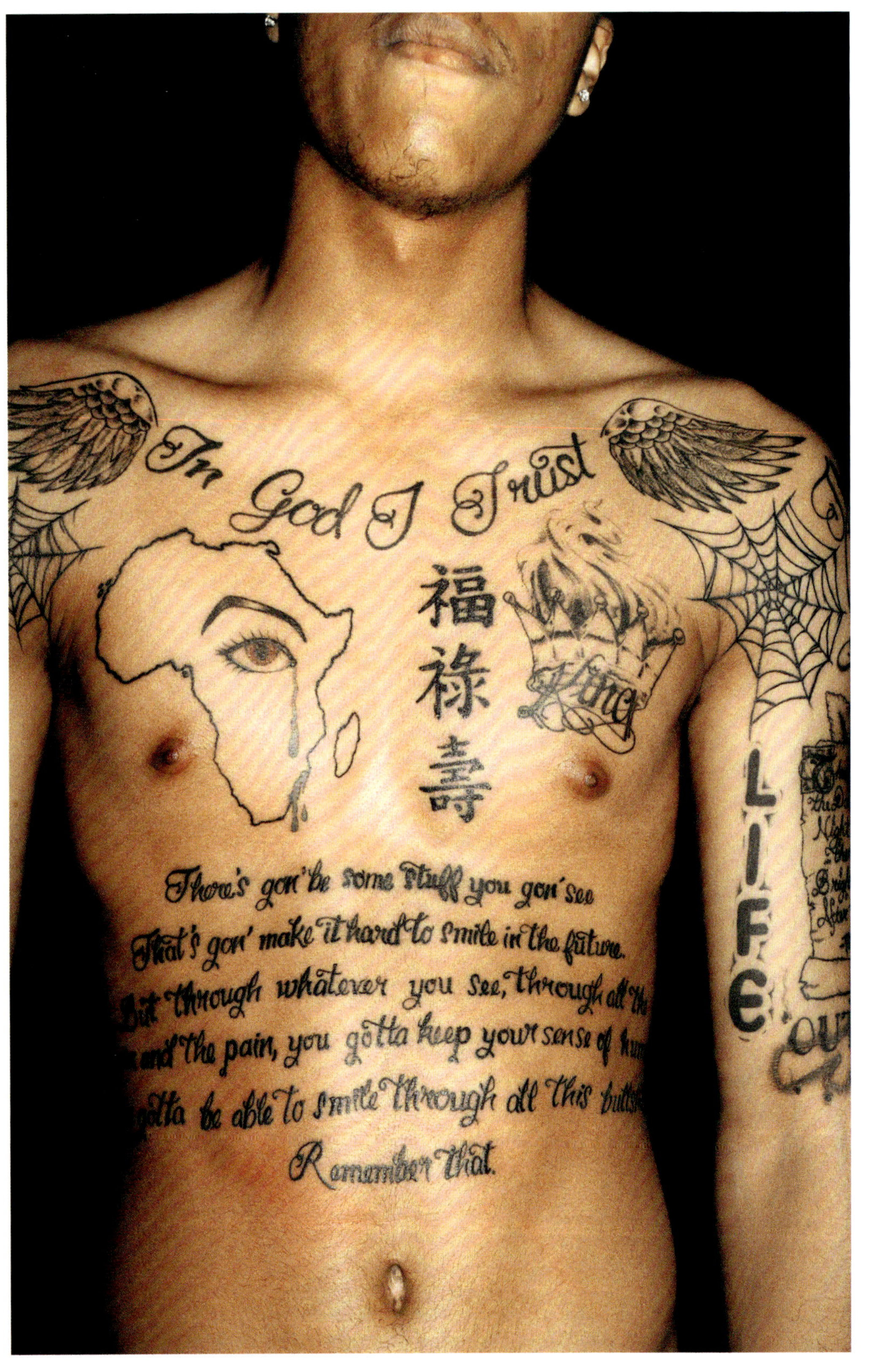
In God I Trust
KING
LIFE
OUT
There's gon' be some stuff you gon' see
That's gon' make it hard to smile in the future.
But through whatever you see, through all the
and the pain, you gotta keep your sense of hum
gotta be able to smile through all this bullsh
Remember That.

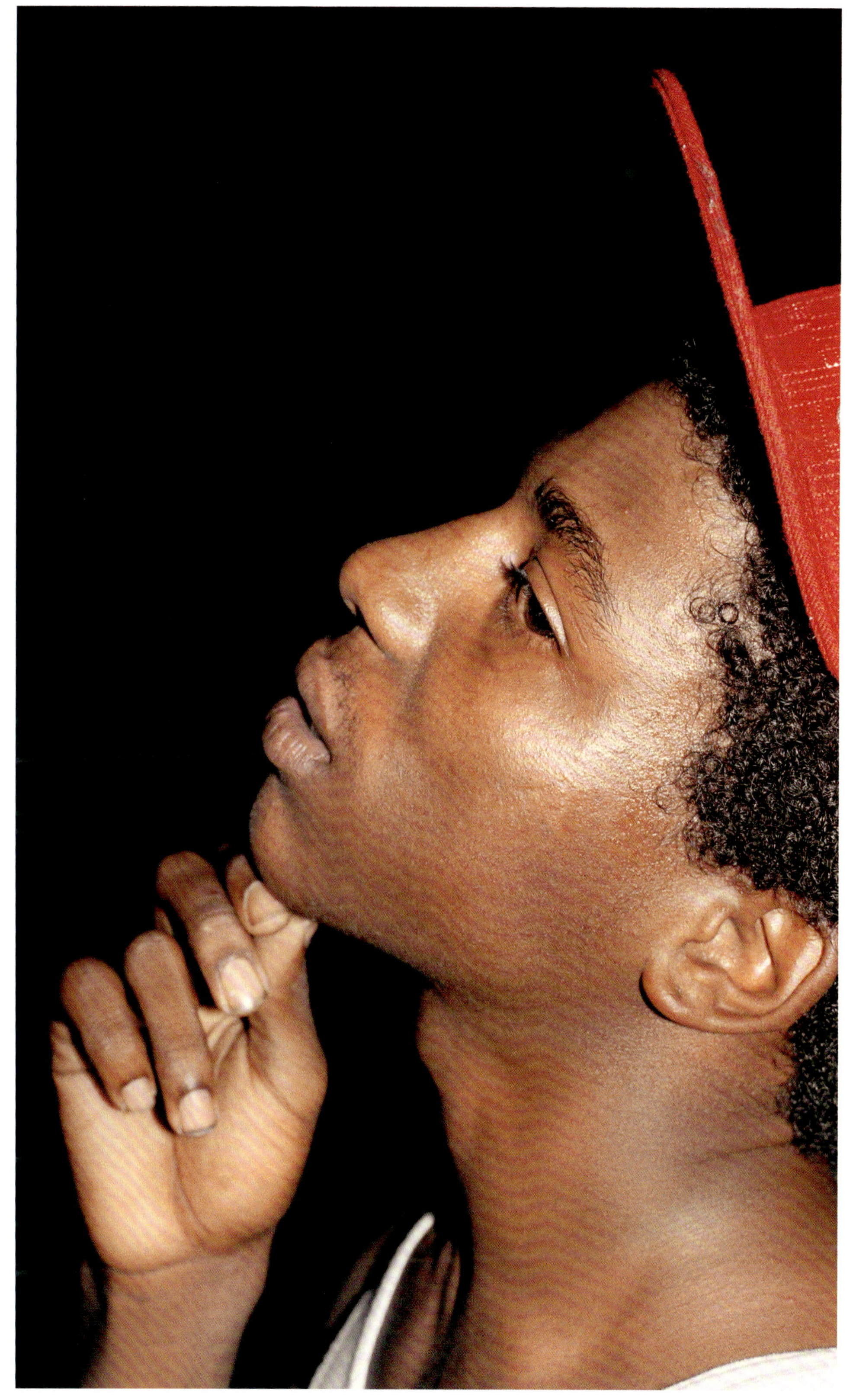

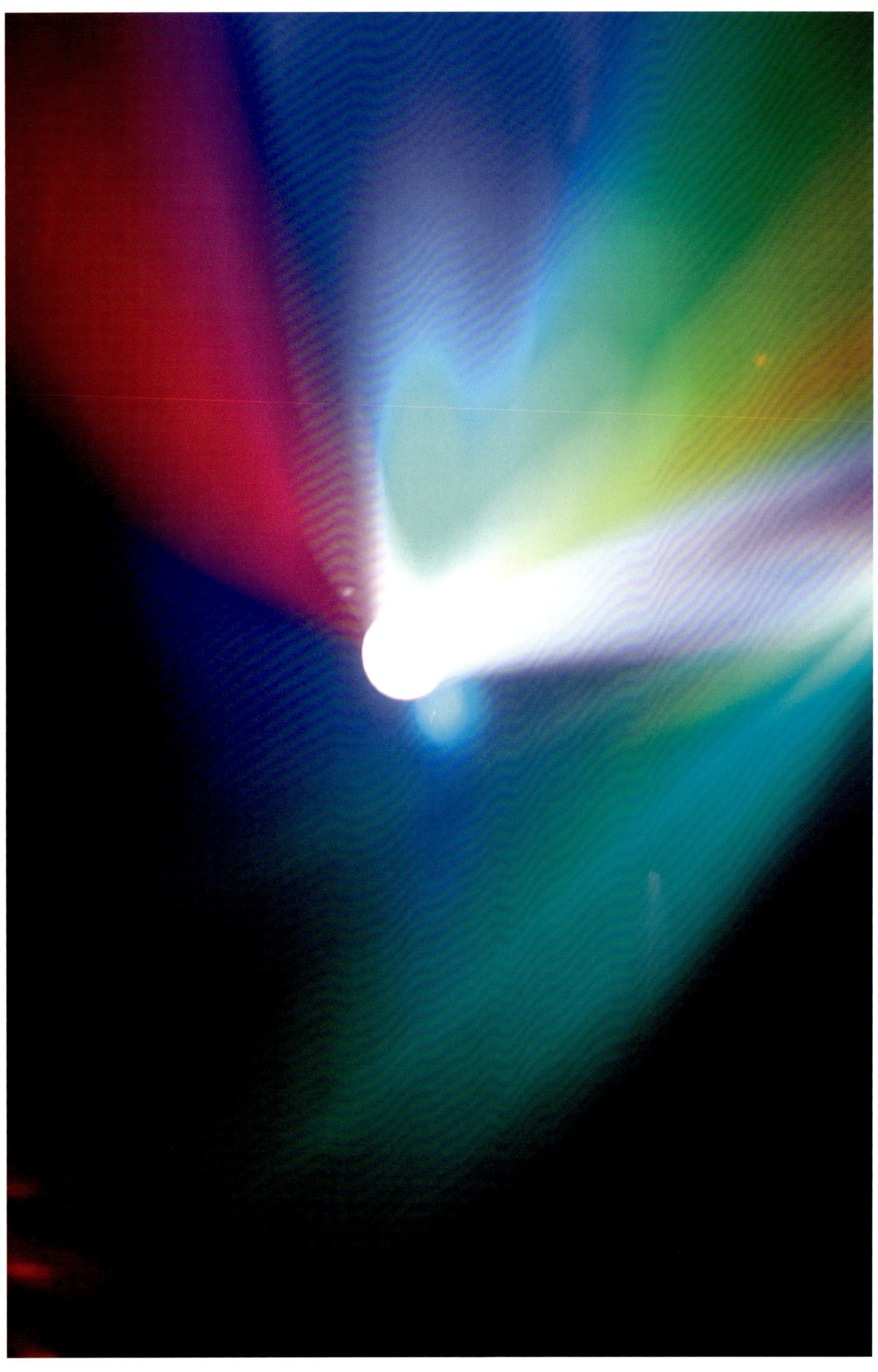

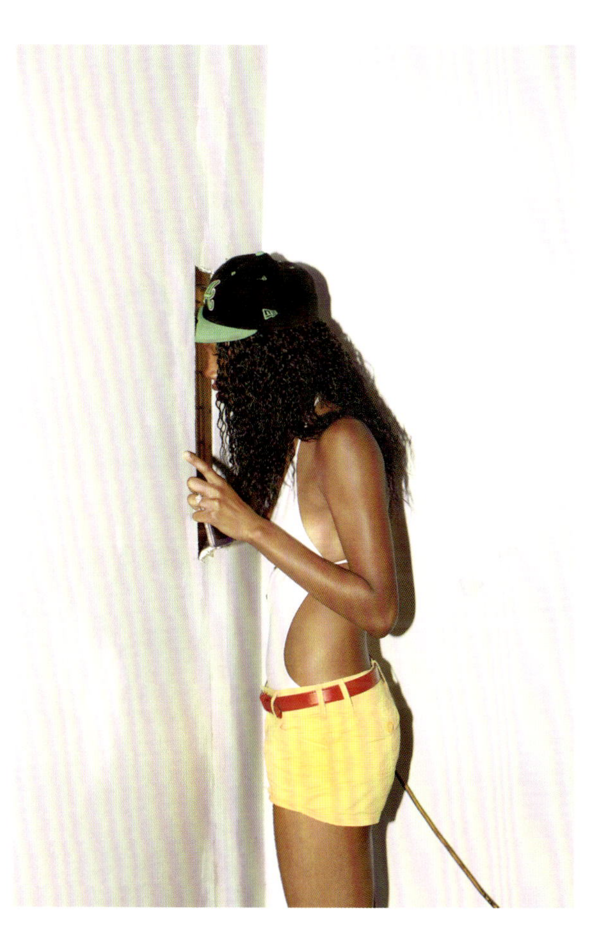
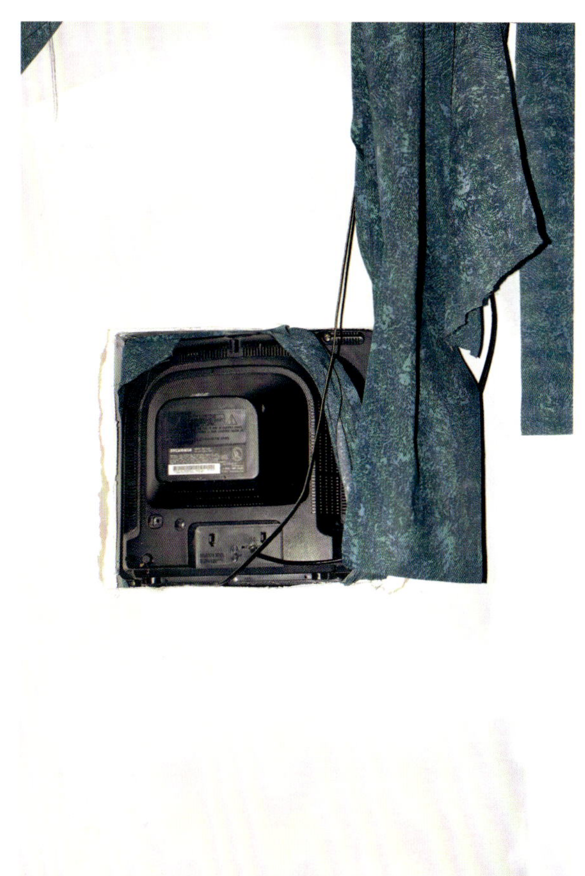

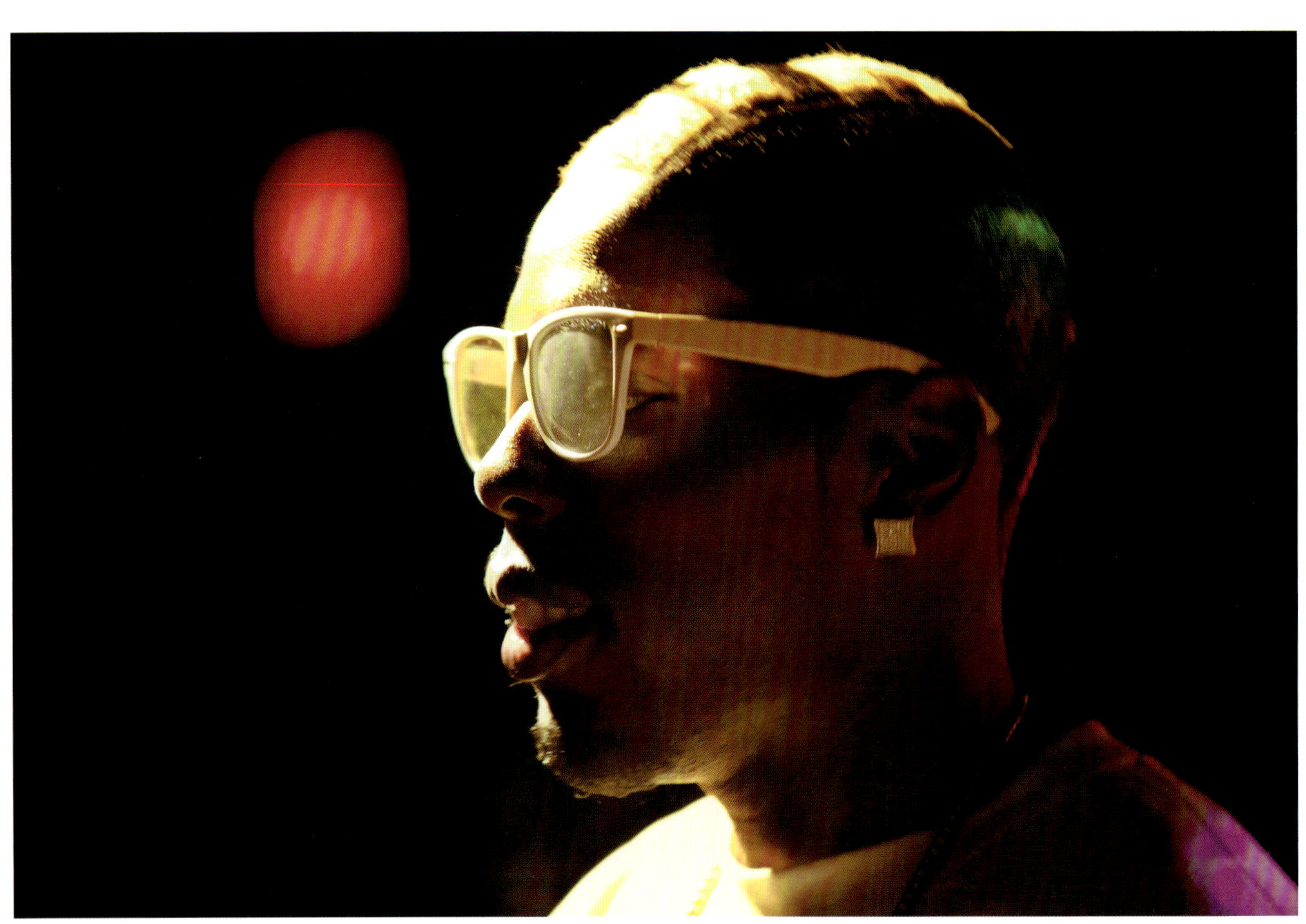

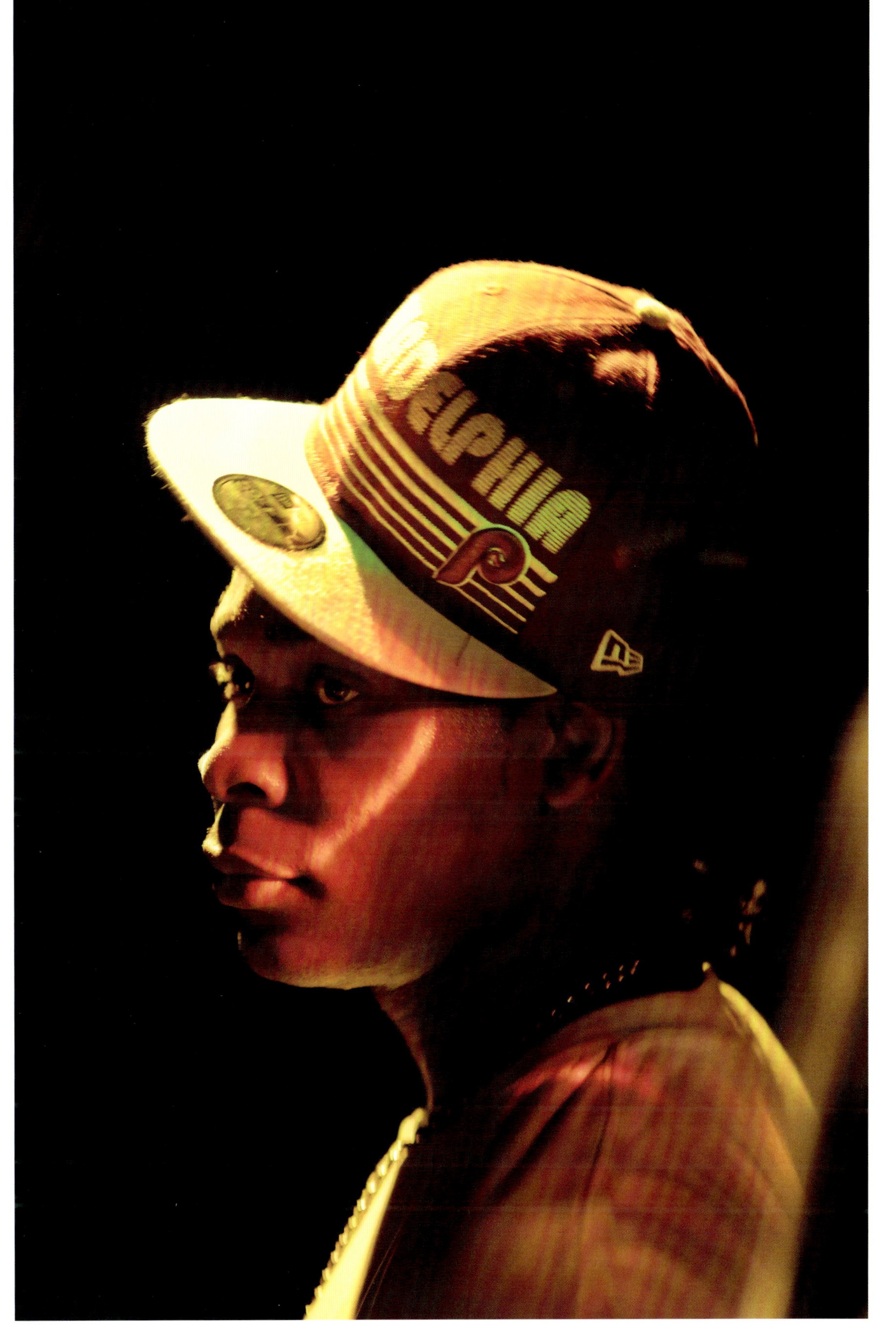

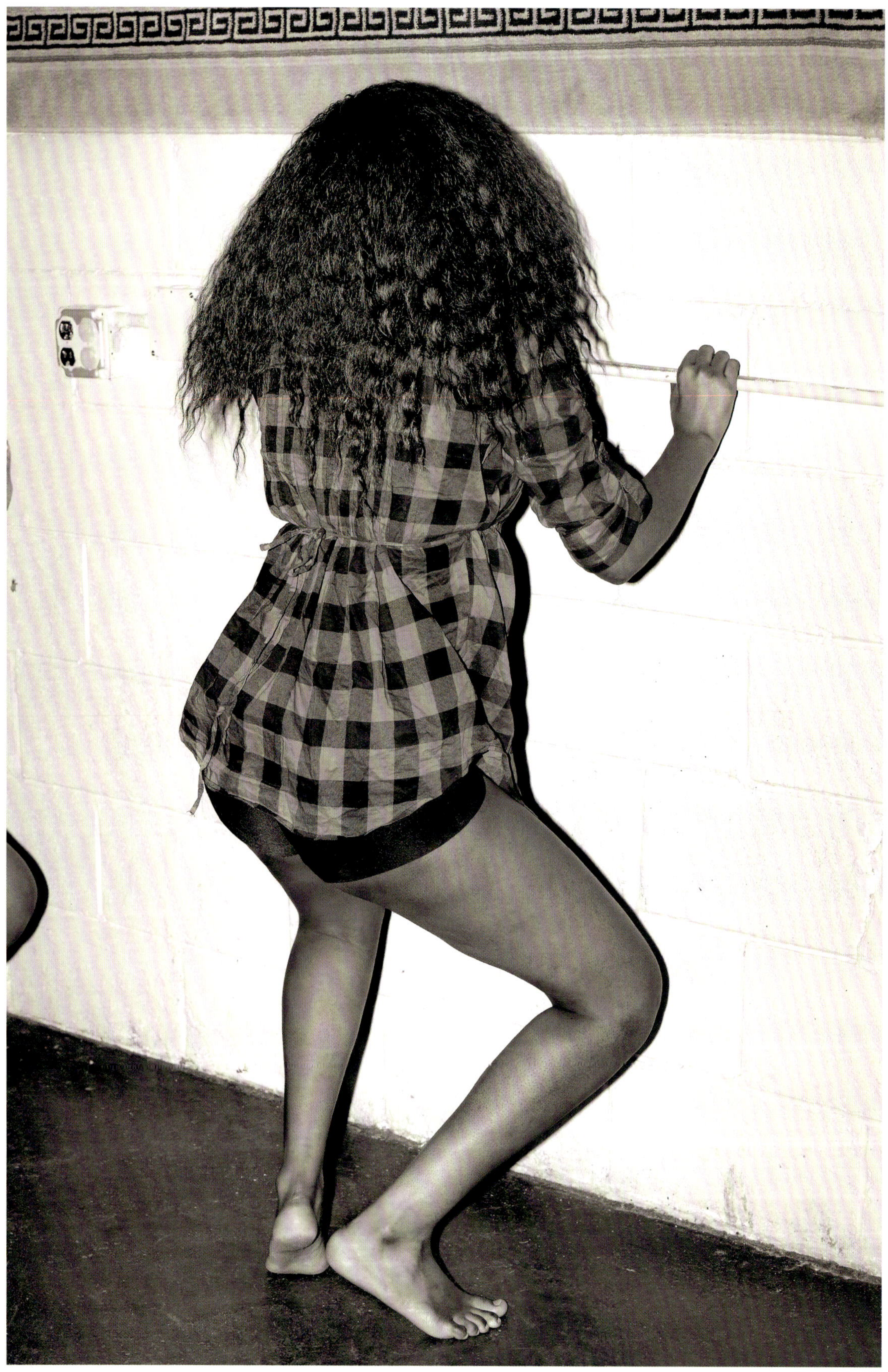

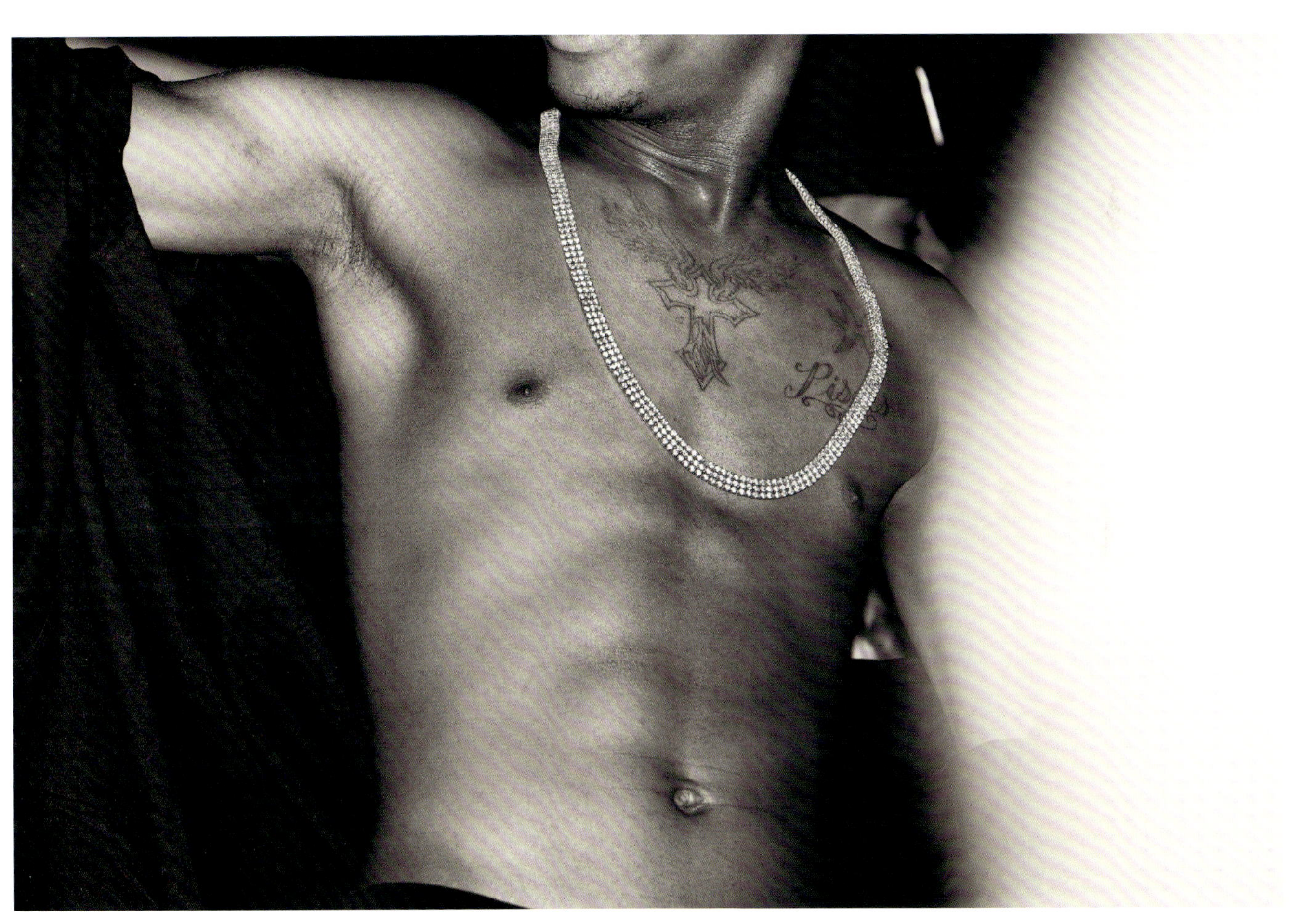

TEEN PARTY, DECATUR

--

OCTOBER

Sunday night in October at a different office park—girls' night, this time in a repurposed cheerleading center, just as bare-bones. The sign outside says "Black Out," with an arrow composed of seven flashing lights. It's even harder to see, and two-thirds of the space has been curtained off; if you're not careful, you'll step on somebody, not necessarily somebody standing up. Outside, a girl is crying and shouting, and the security guards listen to her without saying much. There's no way she's getting back in.

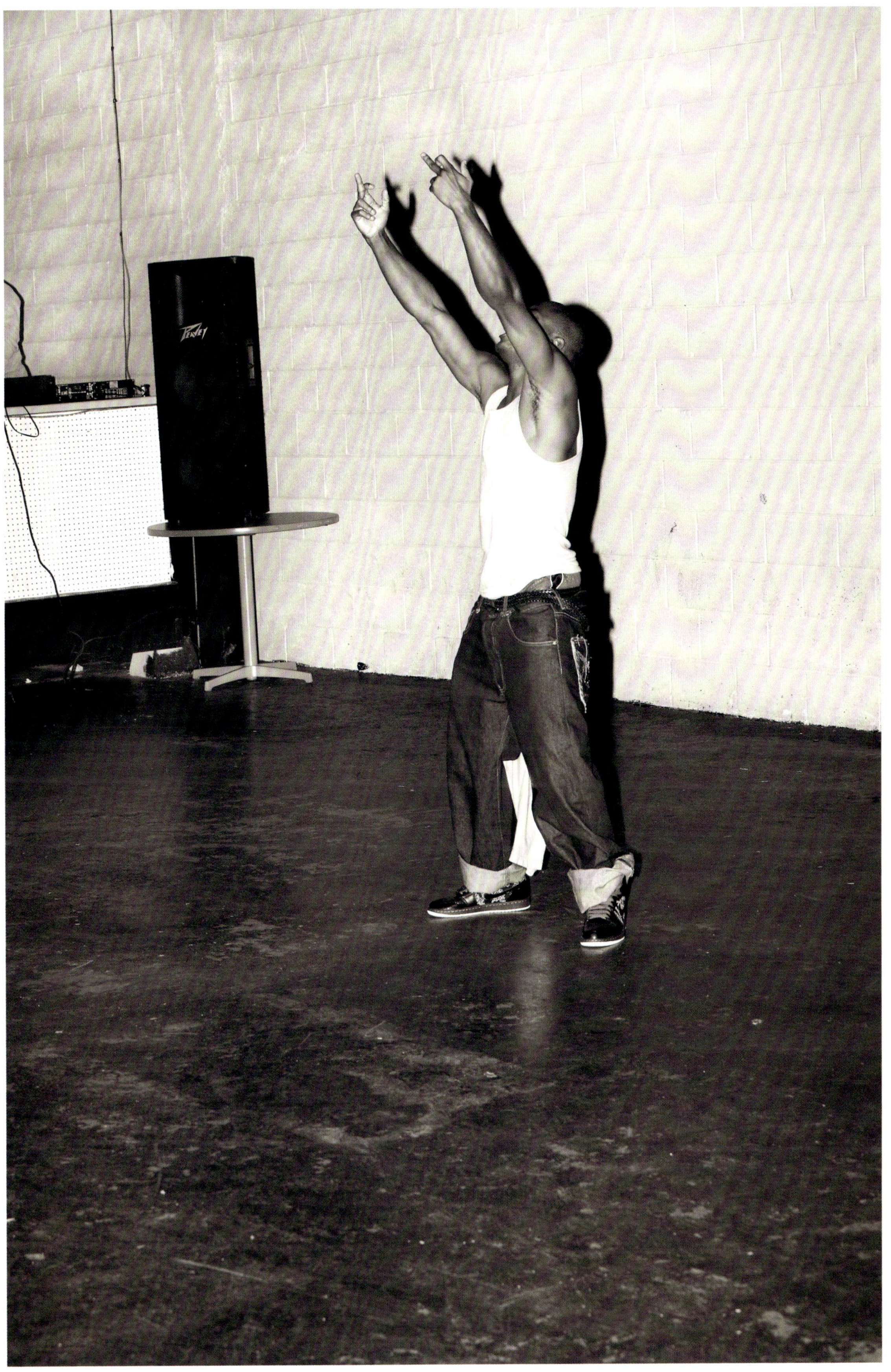

deja-vu

star ~~caramel~~

beauty ~~caramel~~

peaches

prada   caramel

barbie

blue

stallion

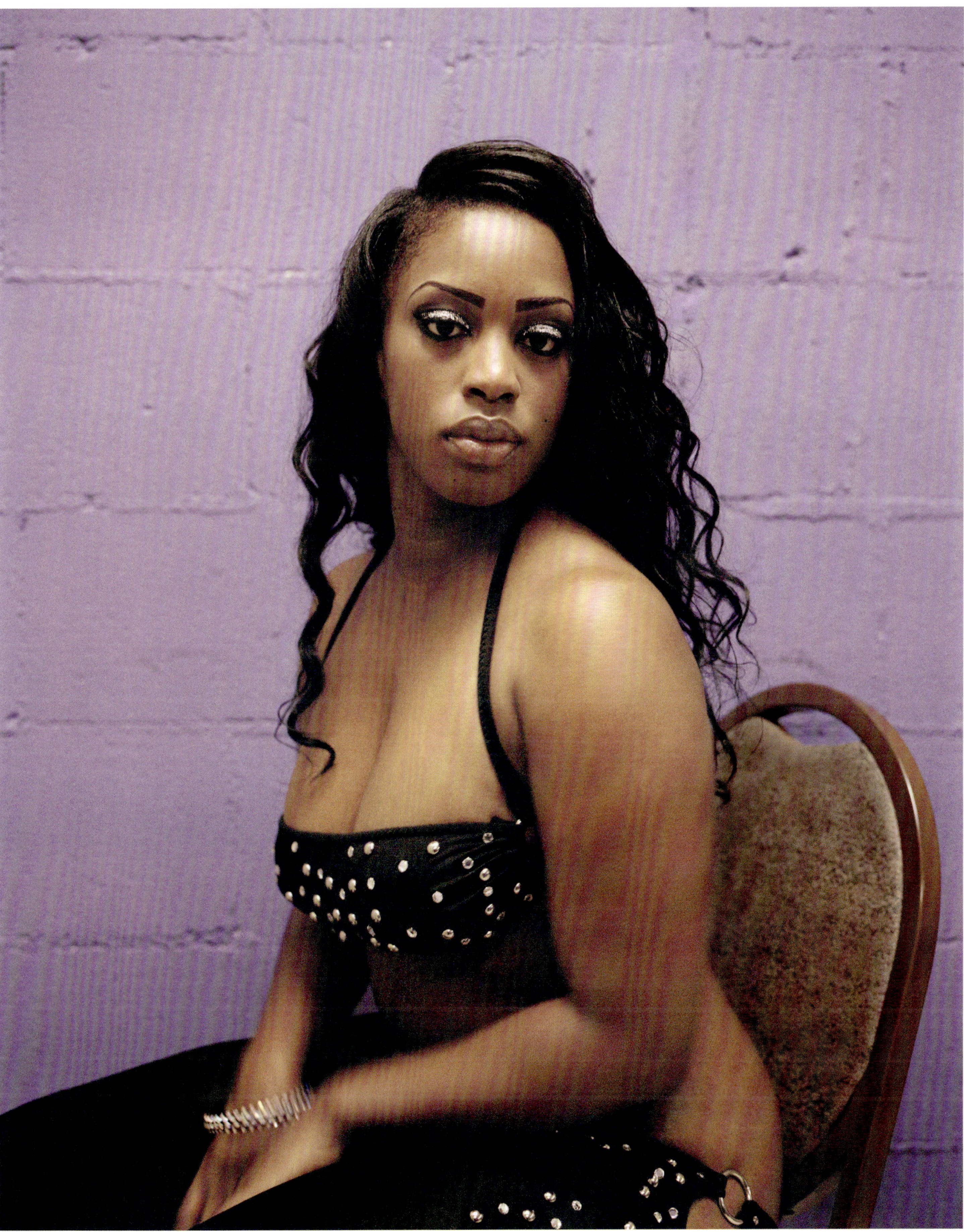

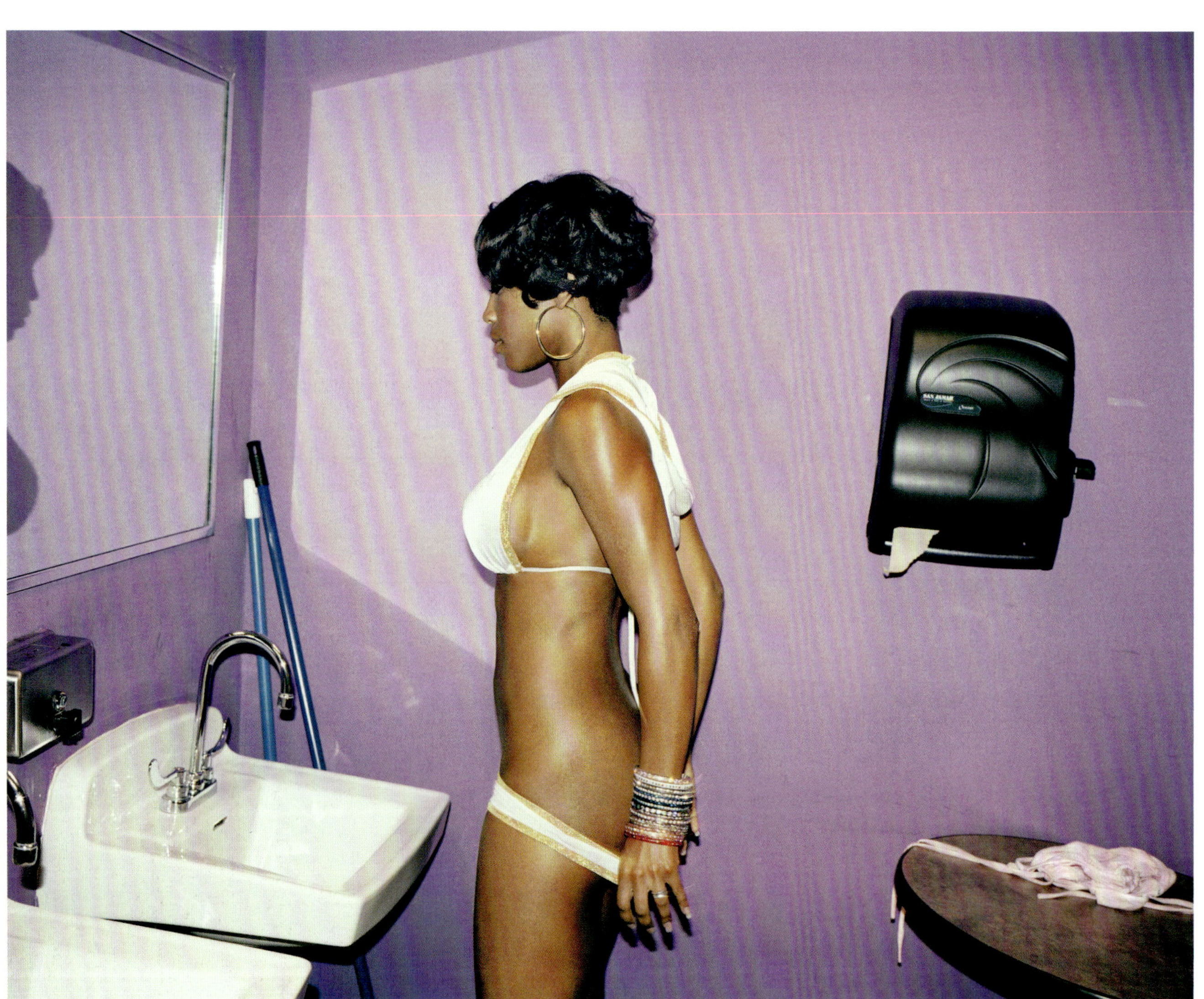

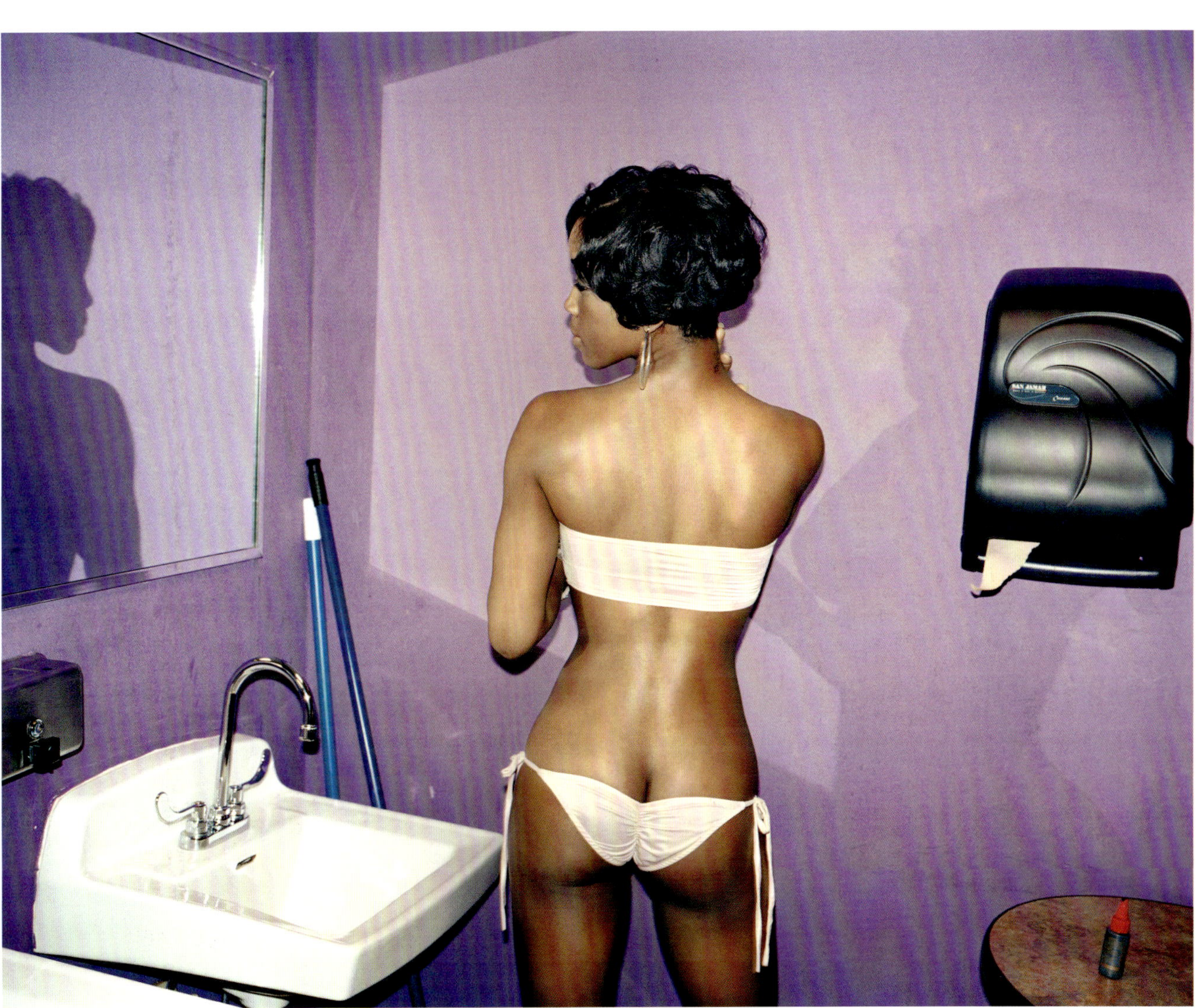

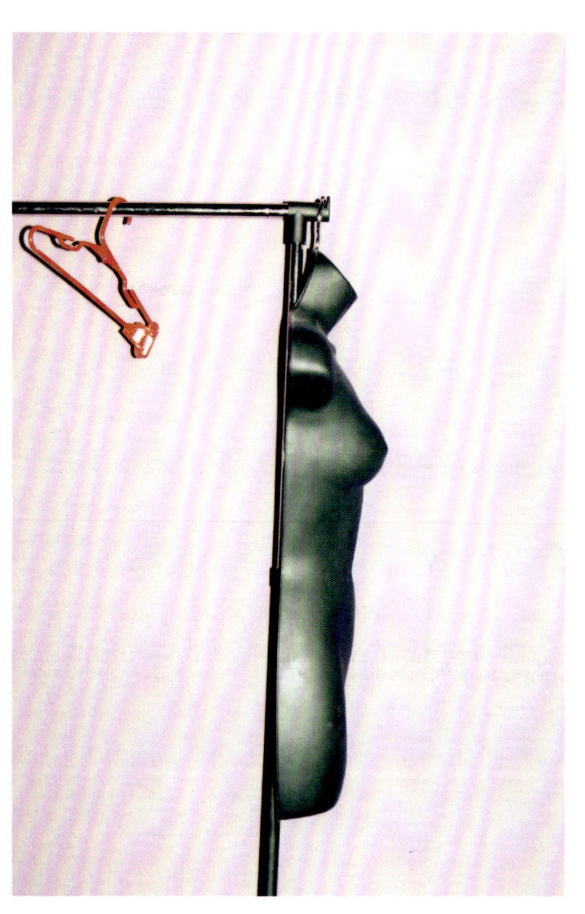
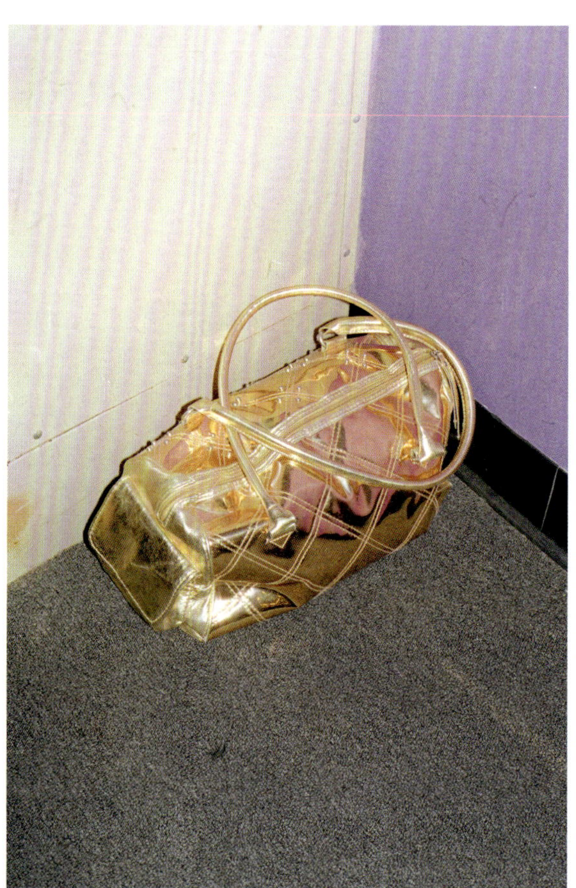

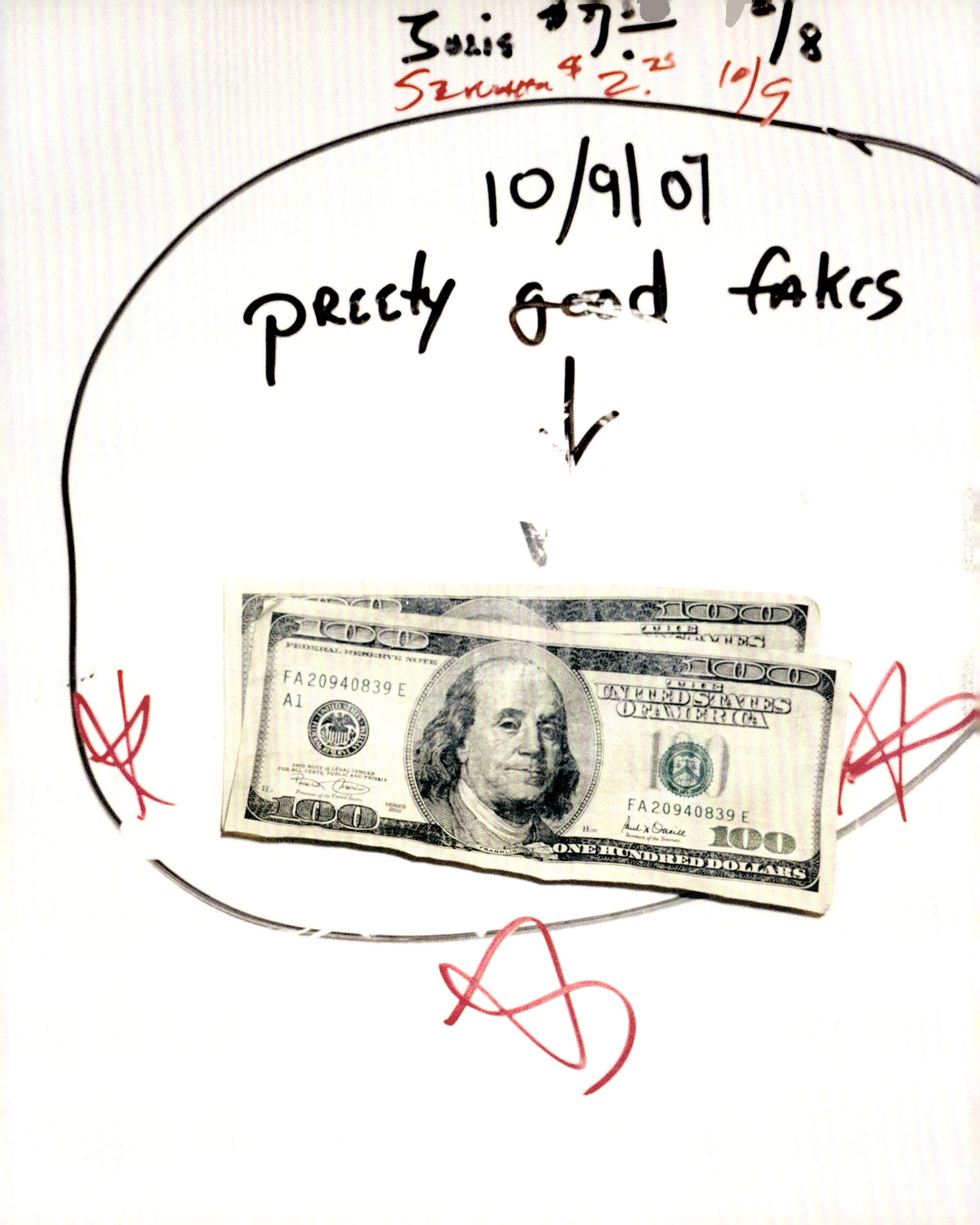

10/9/01

preety good fakes

↓

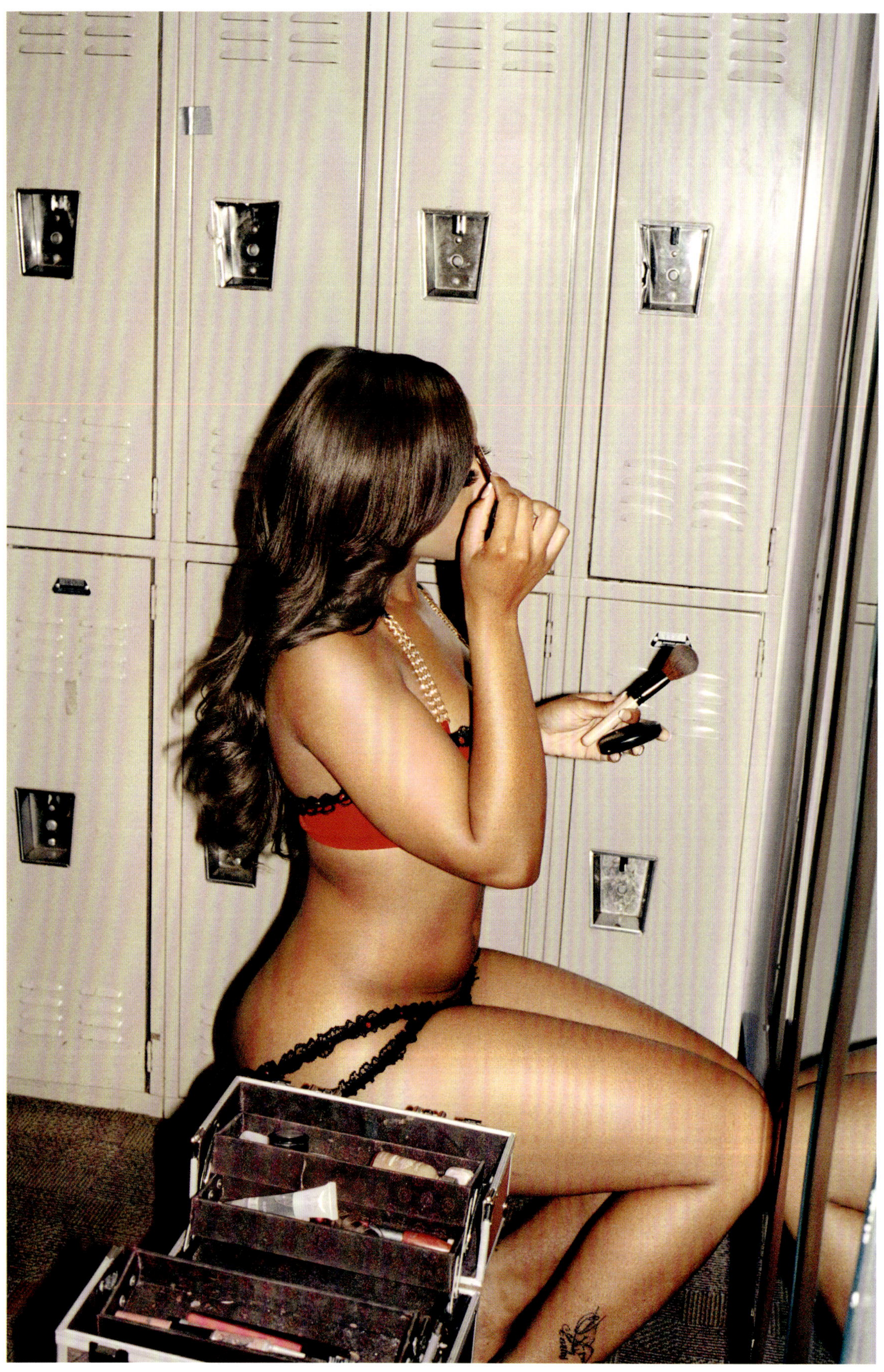

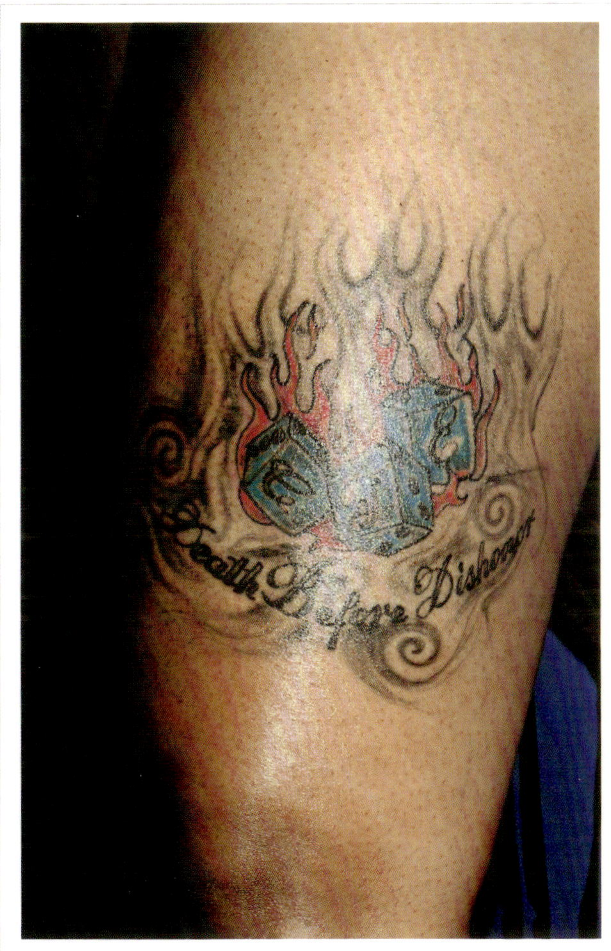

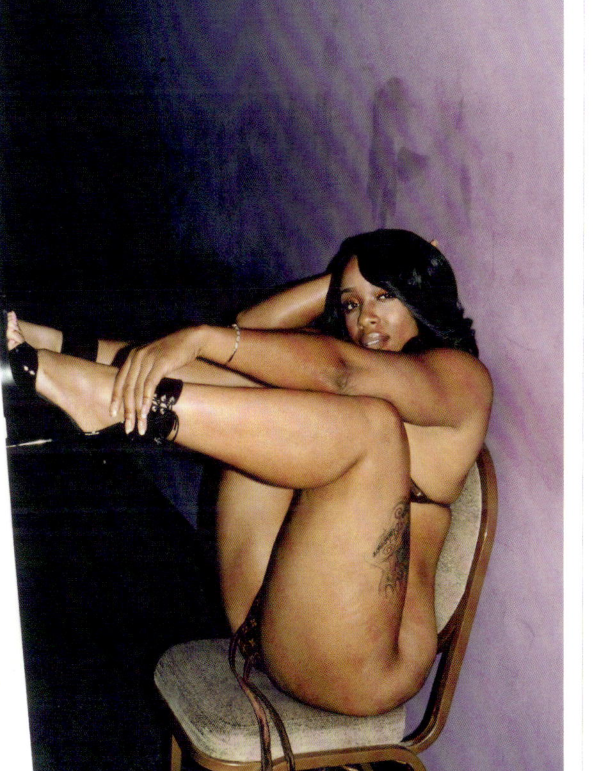

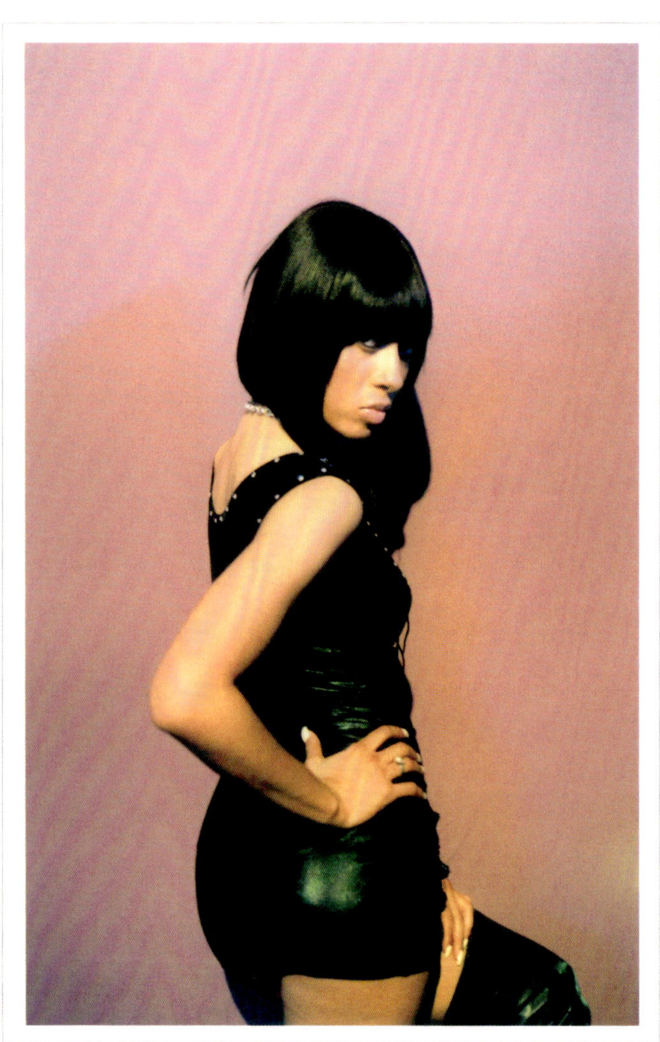

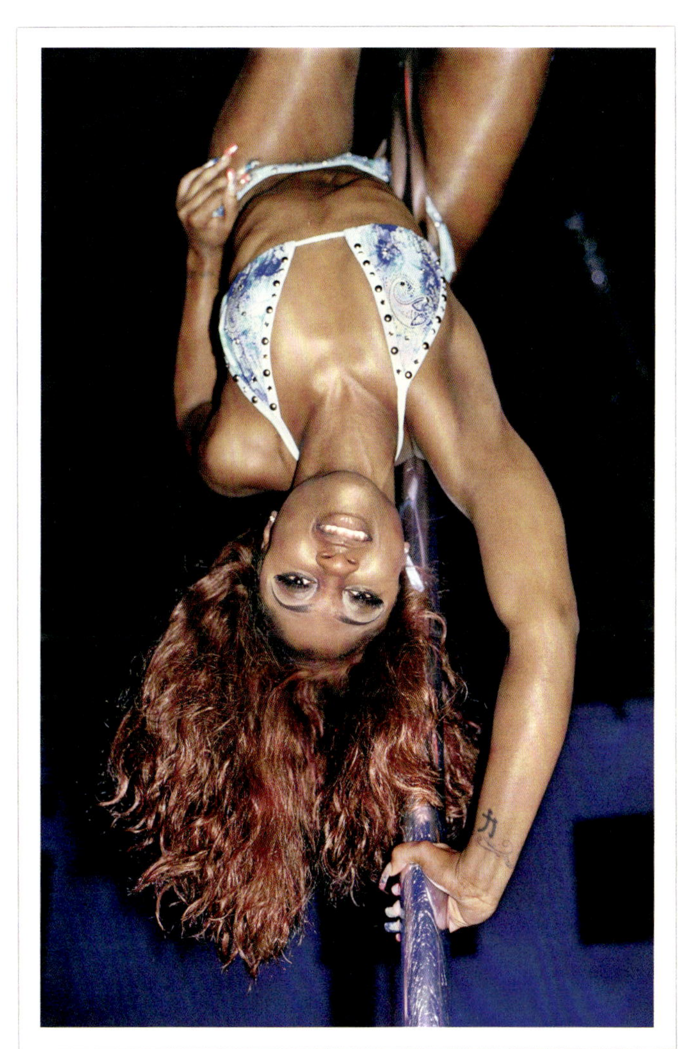

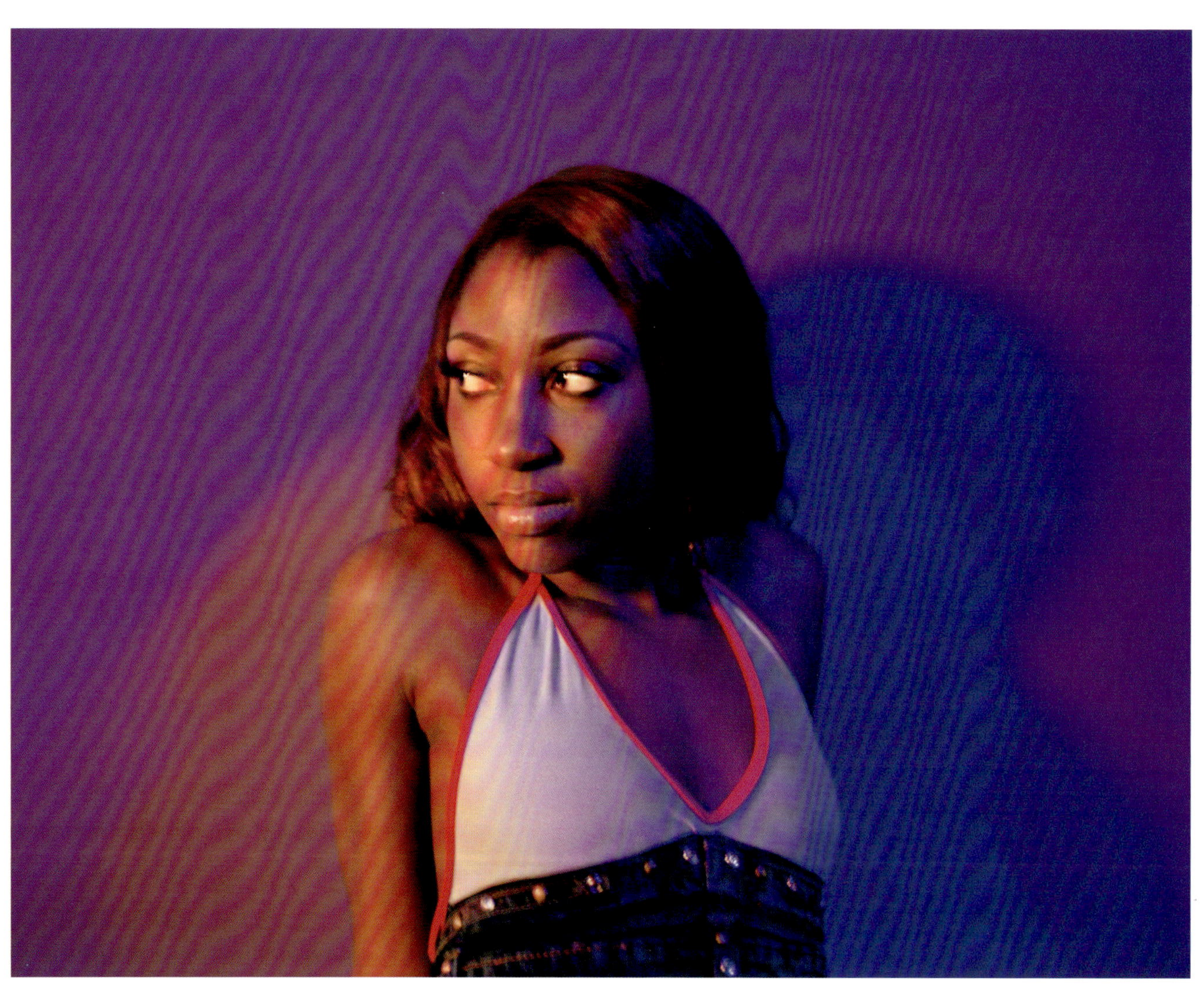

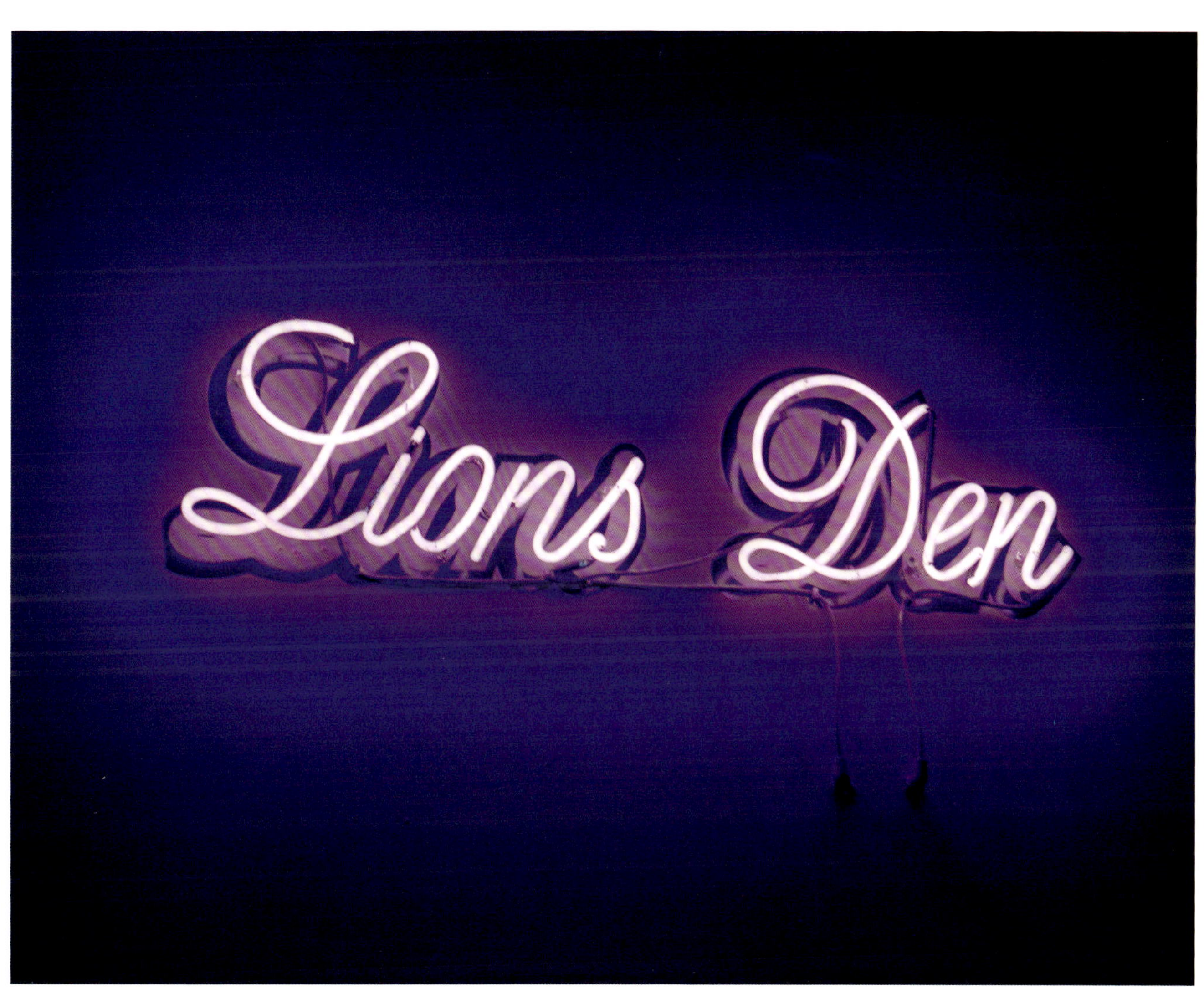
Lions Den

--

In 2009, every club and radio station in Atlanta seemed to be playing "Wasted," one of a blizzard of singles by Gucci Mane, who was born in Alabama but grew up in Atlanta—he was the hottest rapper in the city and had been for nearly two years. It's a track about getting wasted, but it's also a track about the word "wasted," a familiar slang term that retains a strong cultural connotation: it's something white people say and do. When Gucci Mane says, "Party, party, party—let's all get wasted," he's having a particular kind of fun: he is delivering a friendly parody of white folks. The guest rapper is Plies, who makes the point explicit, drawling, "I don't wear tight jeans like the white boys/ But I do get wasted like the white boys." In the video, a white rock band bashes away, totally inaudible—they're just there to provide some authenticity.

They call this "white-boy swag," or sometimes, "rock-star swag": a hip-hop version of white-rocker chic. Plies comes from Florida, but in Atlanta lots of hip-hop kids do wear tight pants and wallet chains in tribute to rock 'n' roll, or perhaps some surreal and abstract idea of it. This isn't just Atlanta: Lil Wayne, from New Orleans (but based in Miami), spent years toting an electric guitar to concerts, building anticipation for his rock album; the Los Angeles subgenre known as jerk music is also full of boys in snug trousers and bright colors. But in Atlanta, where the hip-hop industry dwarfs its pop and rock counterparts, there's something particularly provocative about the way white-boy swag inverts the old stereotypes—it calls to mind a half-imaginary world where white people have the best clothes, the best parties, the most fun.

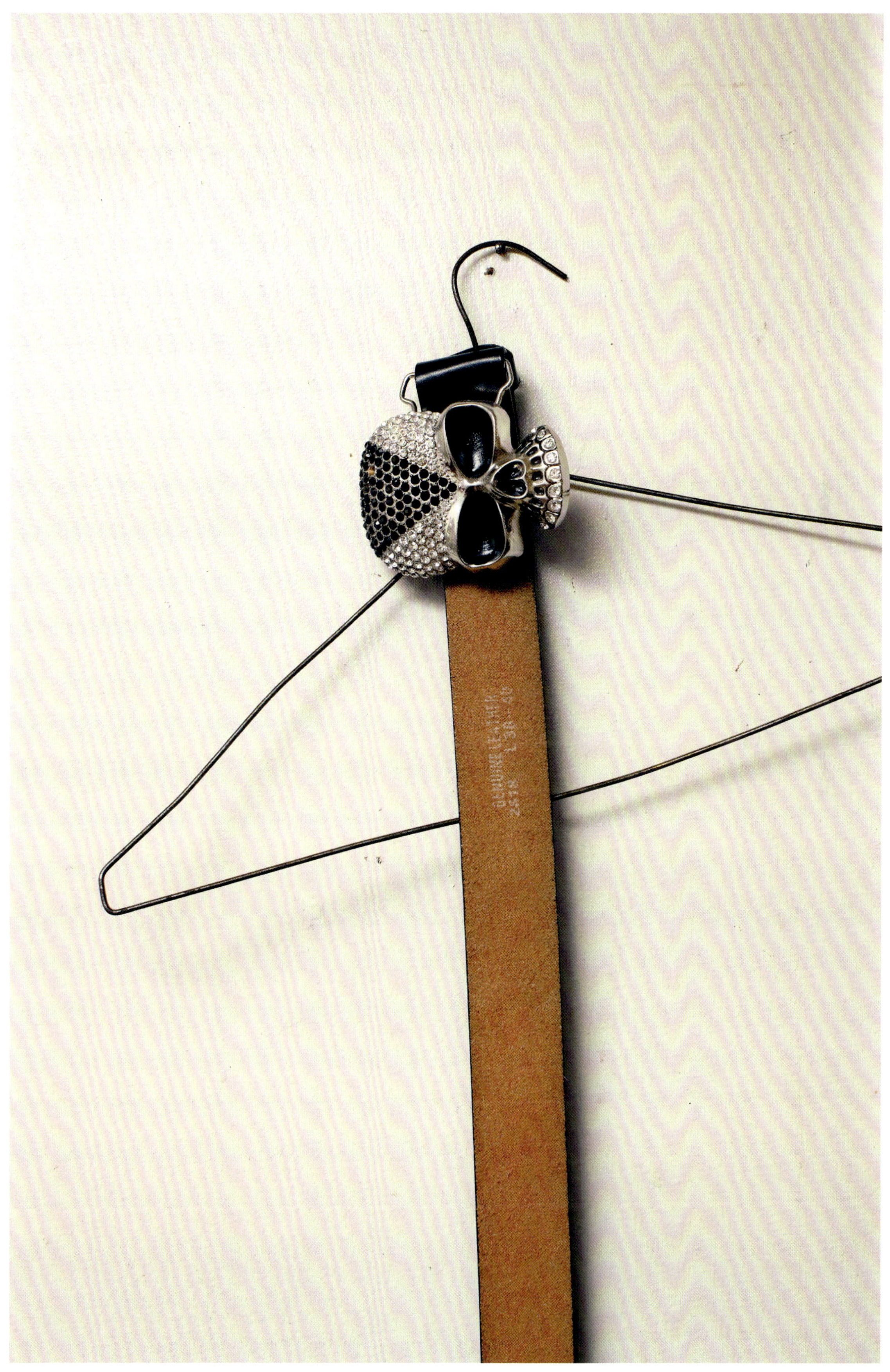

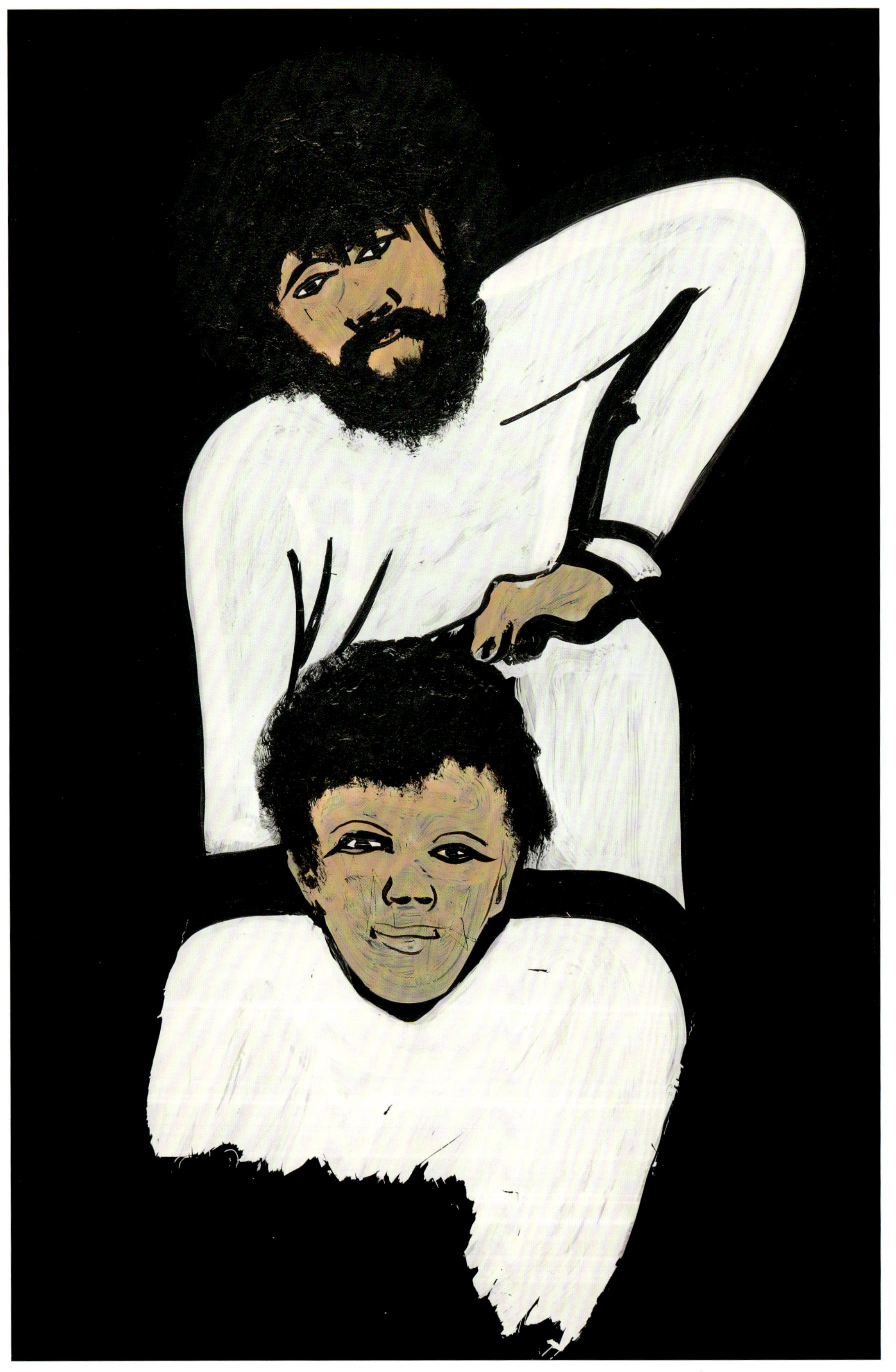

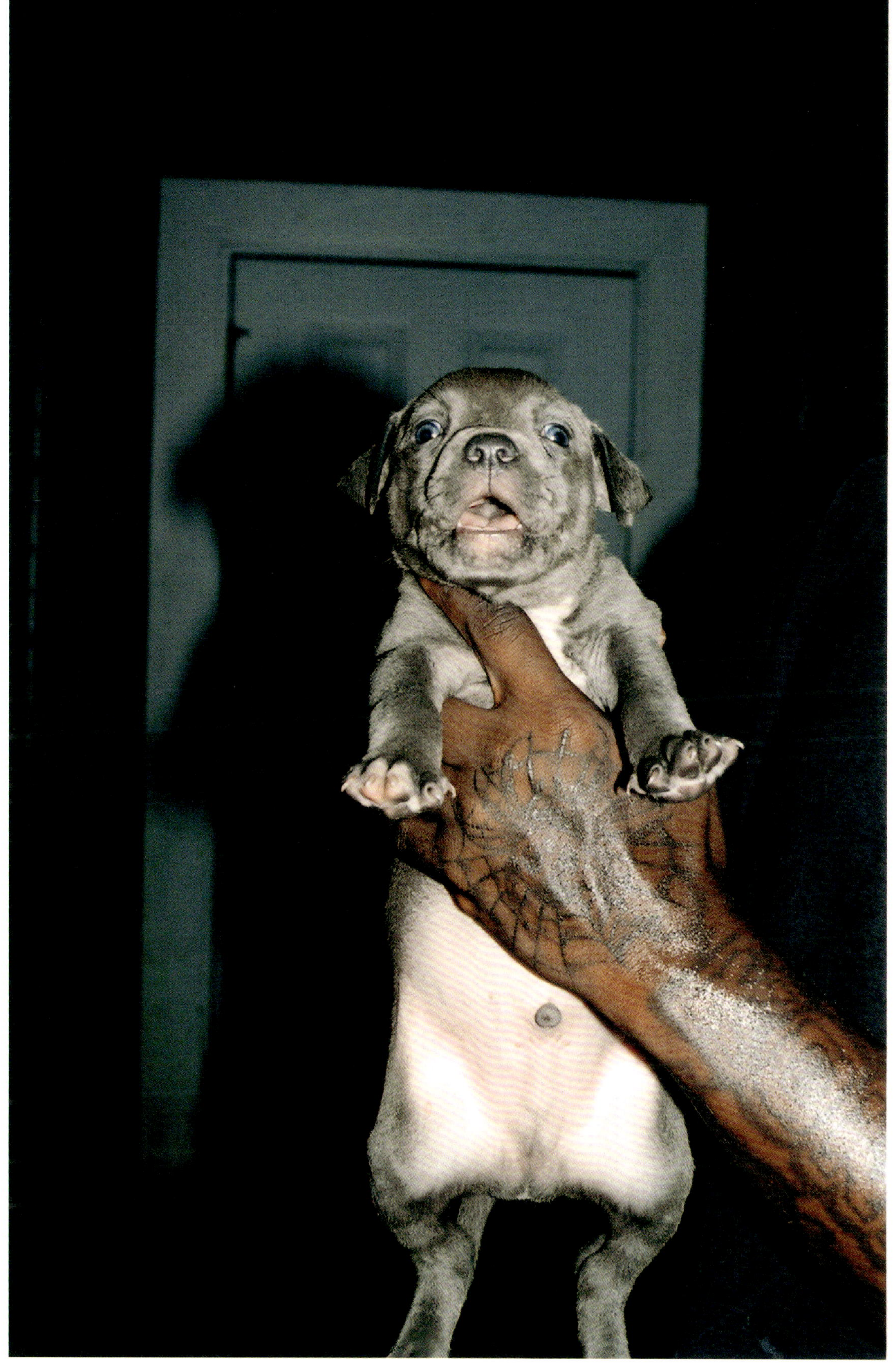

homicide boyz #:

tko

bam-bam AKA
young dred

lil texas

gangsta black AKA k.o.

chris AKA KA$H

flip AKA fliperache

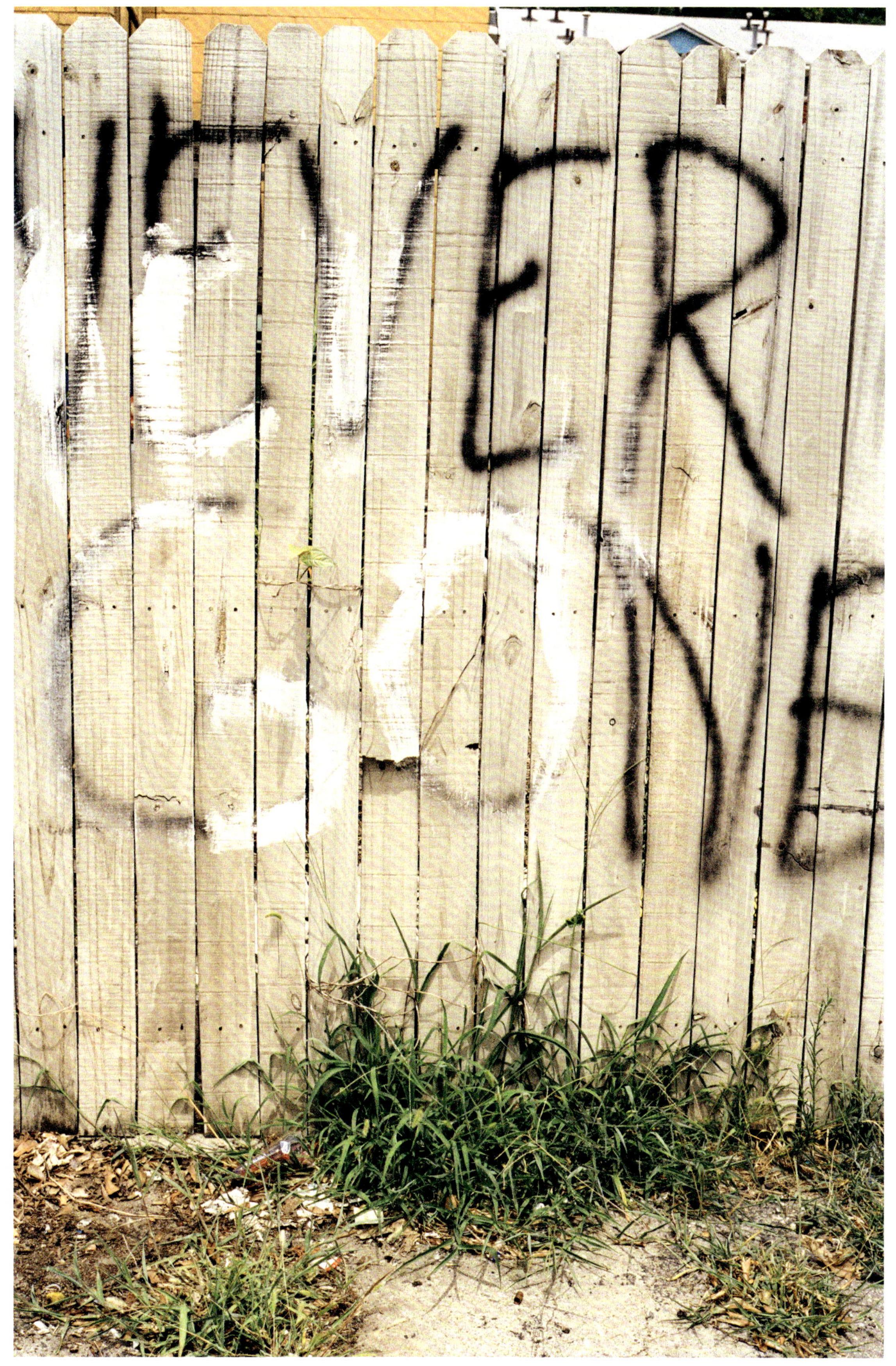

--

Crime Mob by Crime Mob arrived in 2004, showing six teenagers on the cover: four boys in enormous white T-shirts, two girls in tight tops and white sneakers. And it was just about perfect: a gleeful, youthful take on the ultra-rowdy hip-hop subgenre known as crunk. They came from Ellenwood, southeast of the city, and their breakthrough hit was "Knuck If You Buck"—four minutes of eerie chimes and hard kick drums and trash talk. ("Yeah, we knuckin' and buckin' and ready to fight/I betcha I'm-a throw them things so haters best to think twice.") The album sold a few hundred thousand copies, and it also included "Stilettos (Pumps)," which showed off the two girls, Diamond and Princess; they shouted, "We rocking stilettos, ho," as if that were the fulfillment of a lifelong dream, or maybe the dream itself, still unfulfilled. It was over within a few years: one member went to prison for child molestation; a second album spawned a hit but sold poorly; Diamond went solo; crunk went away. Now how long until they're rediscovered?

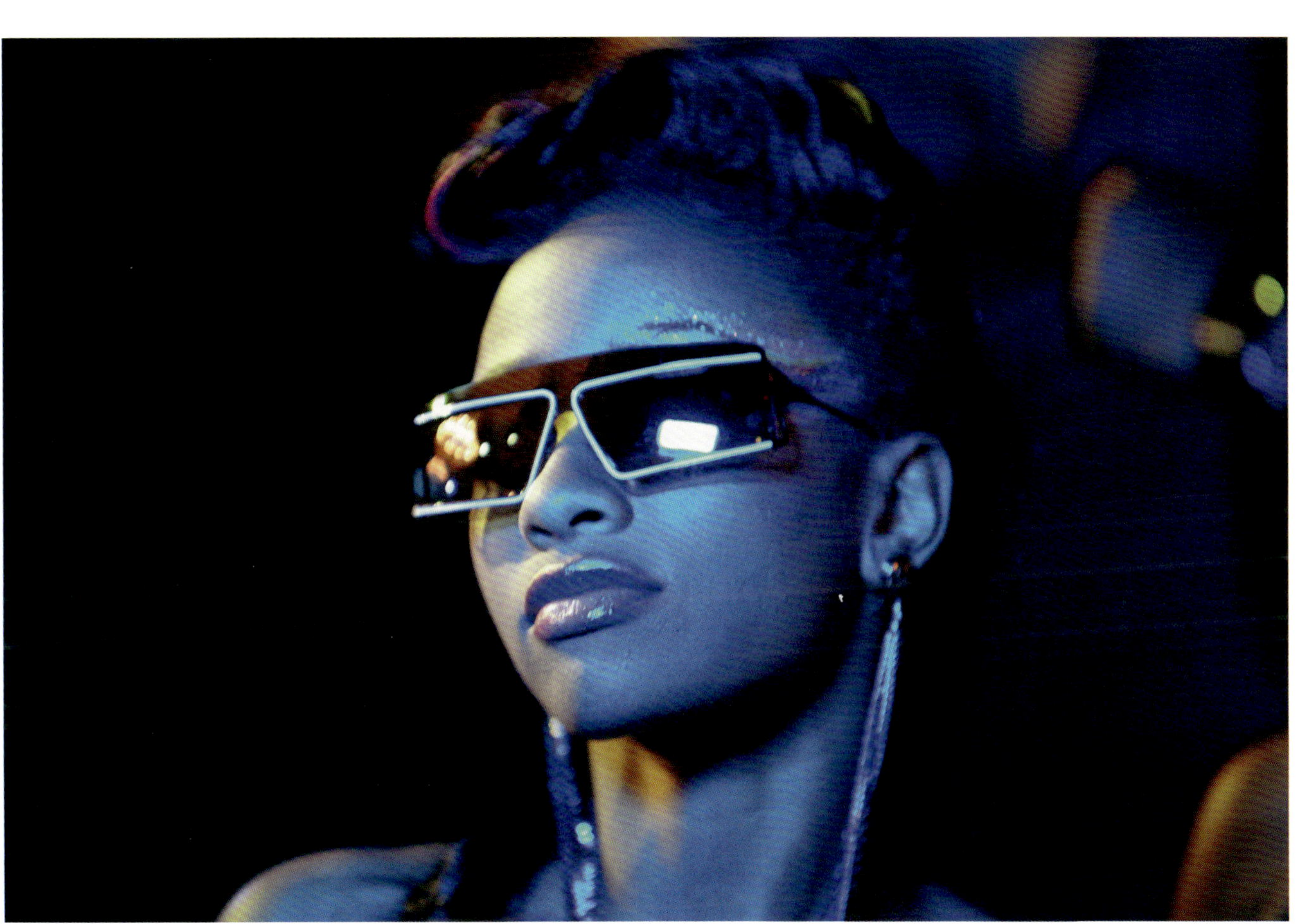

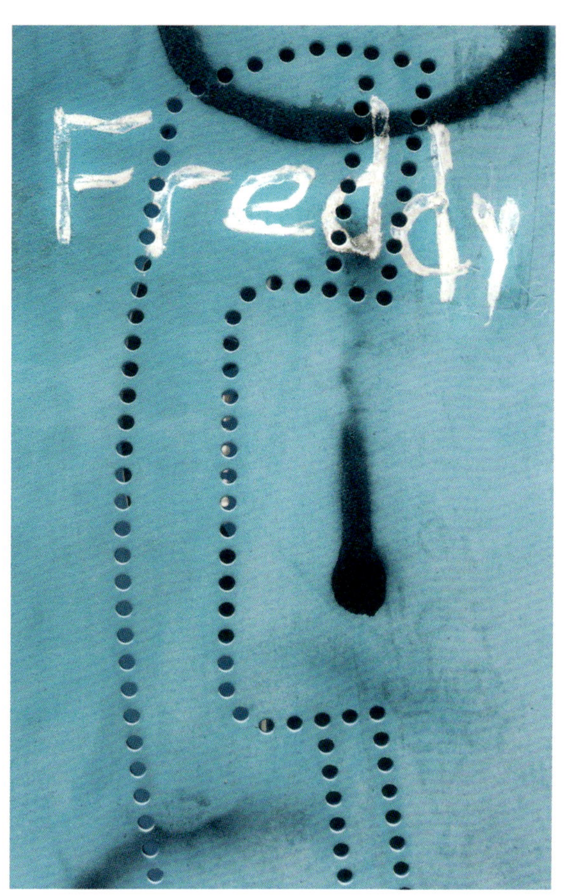
Freddy
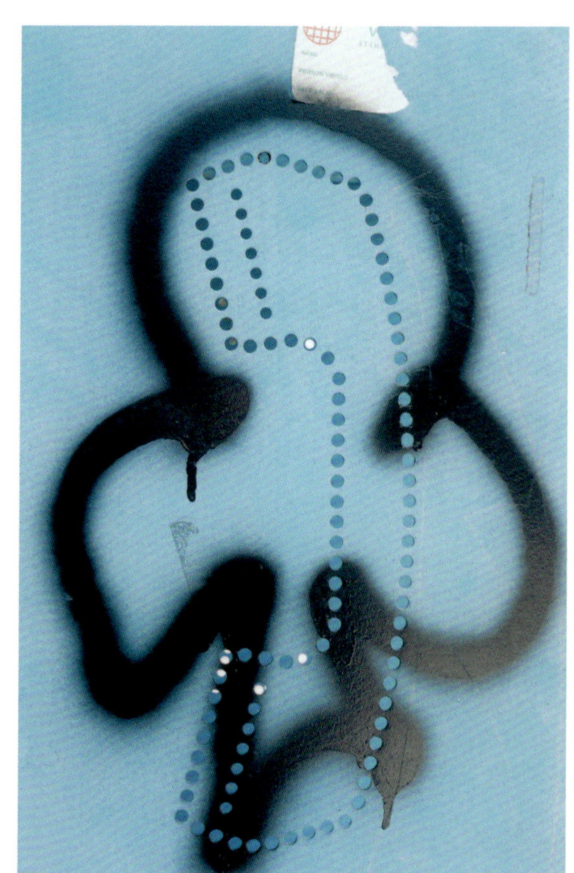
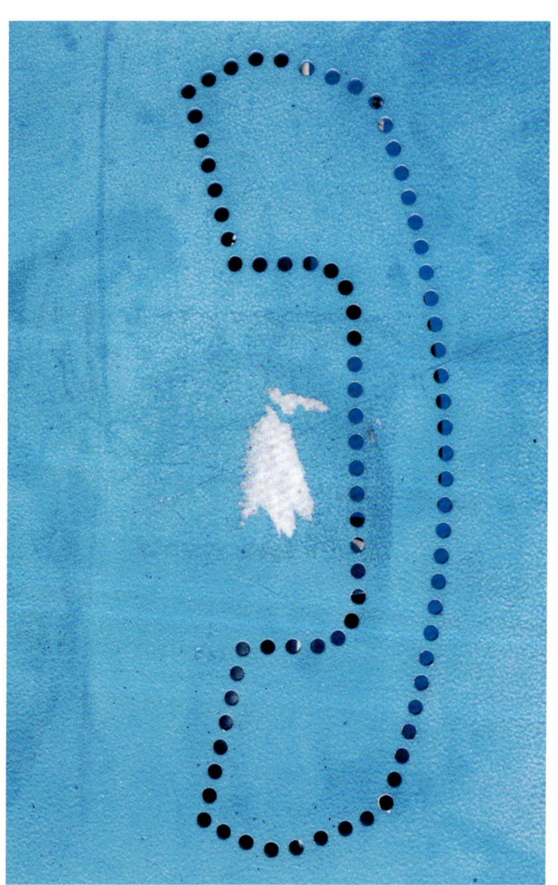
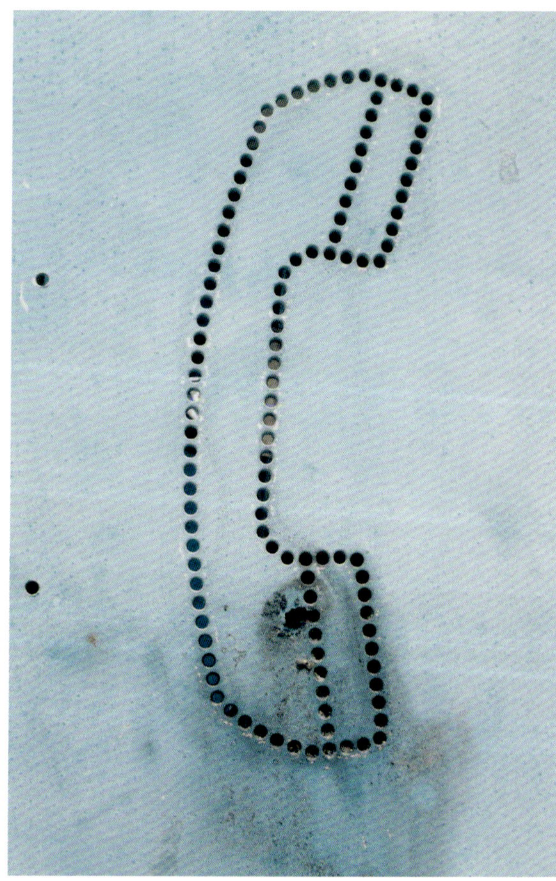

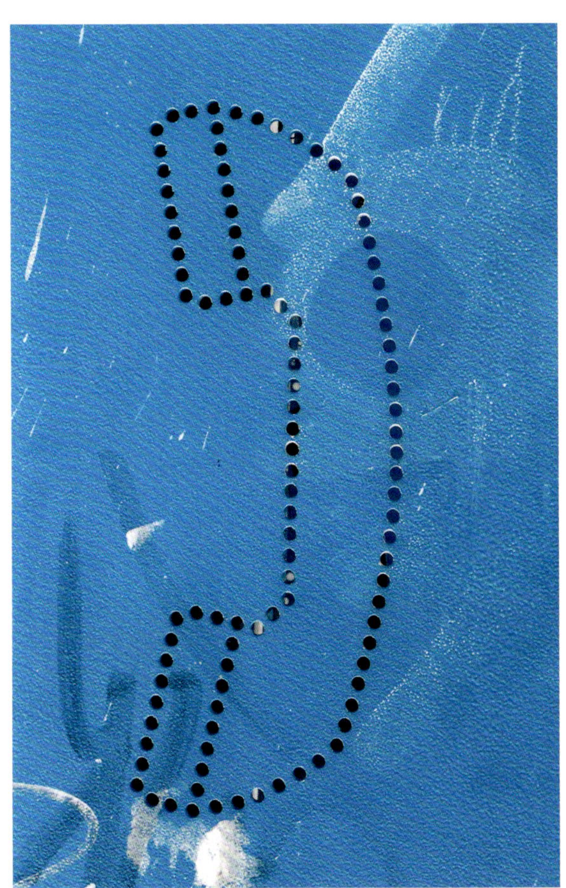

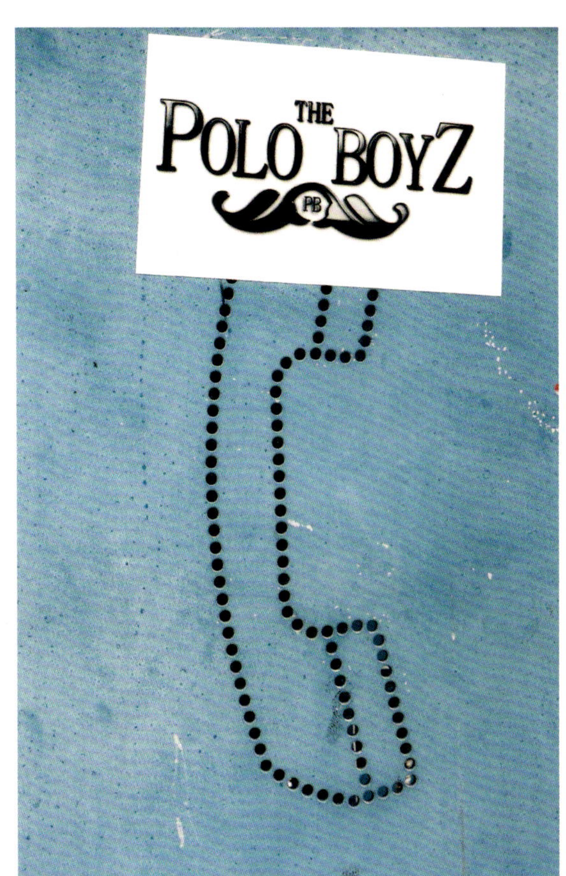

THE
POLO BOYZ
PB

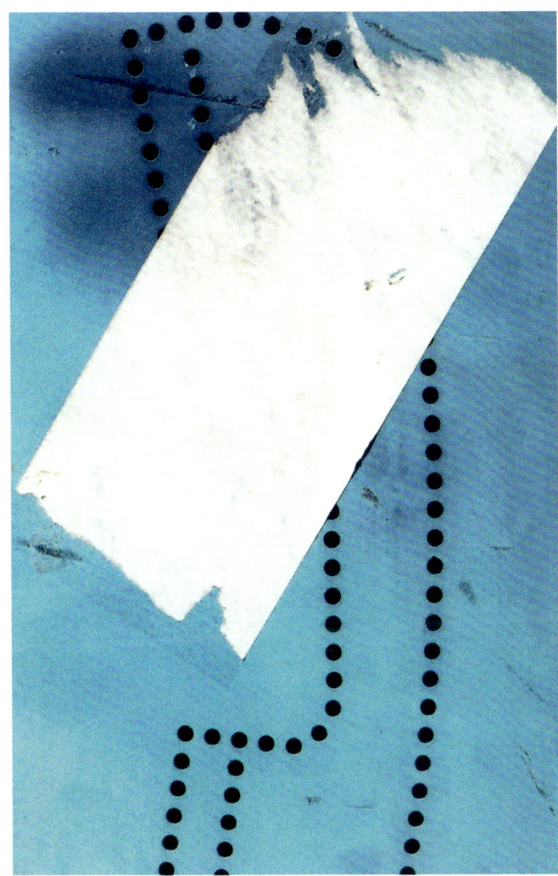

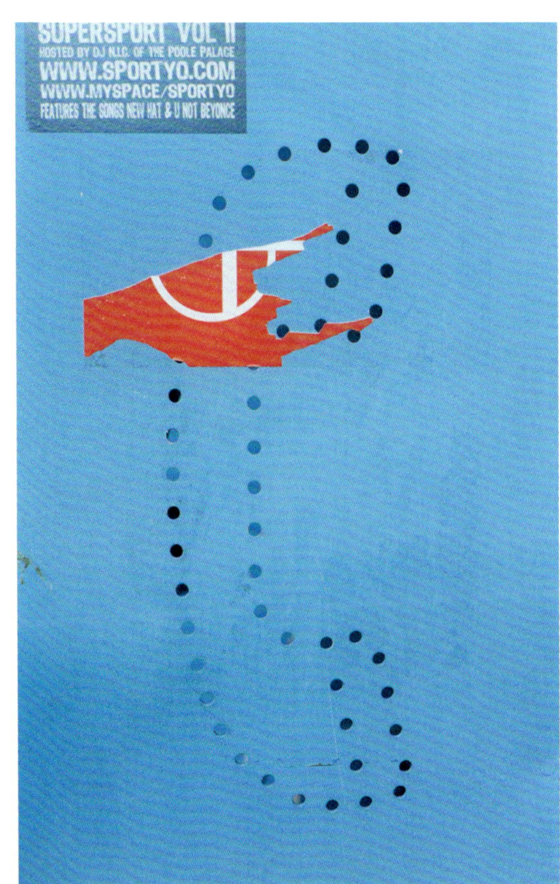

SUPERSPORT VOL II
HOSTED BY DJ N.I.C. OF THE POODLE PALACE
WWW.SPORTYO.COM
WWW.MYSPACE/SPORTYO
FEATURES THE SONGS NEW HAT & U NOT BEYONCE

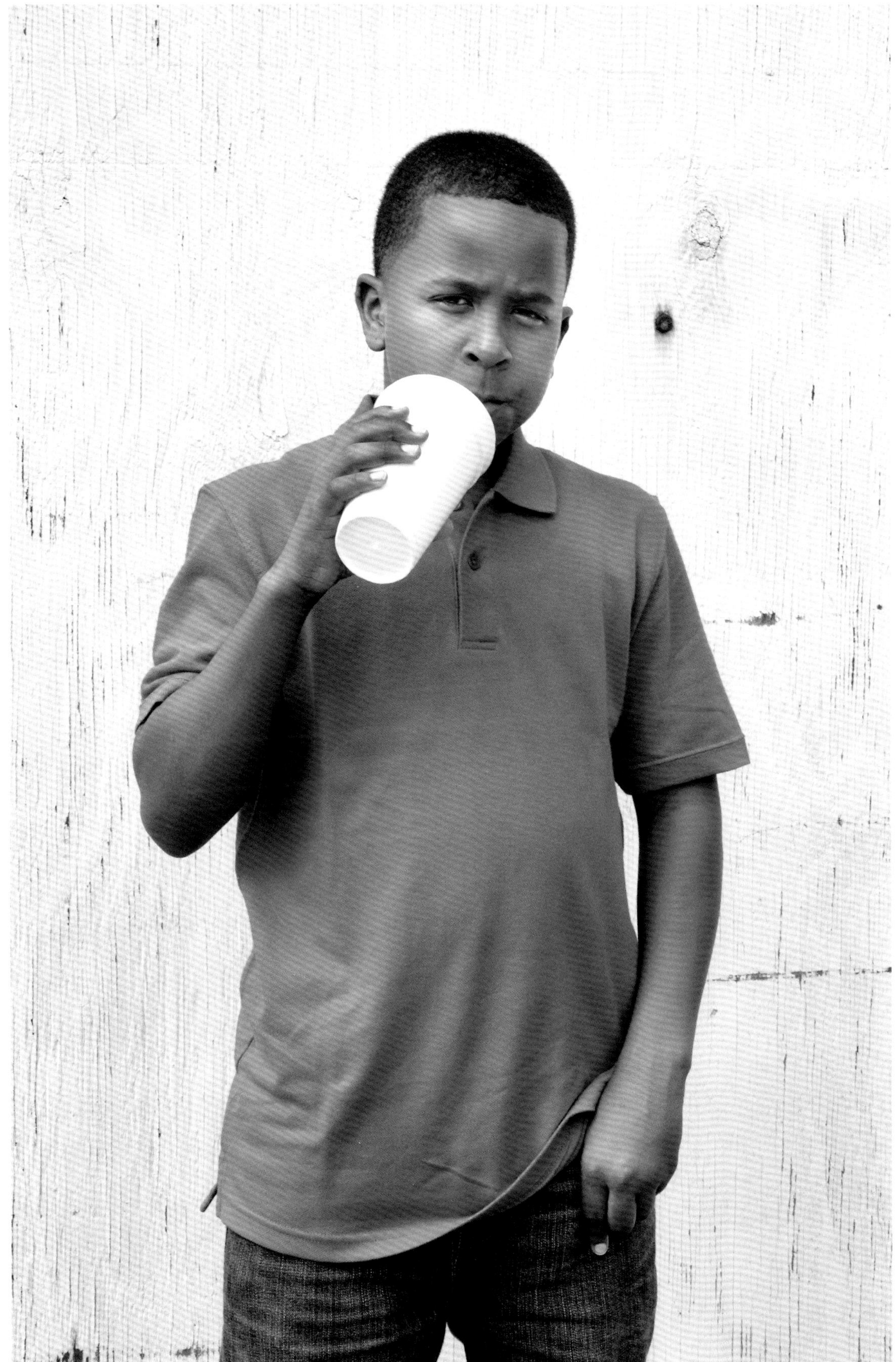

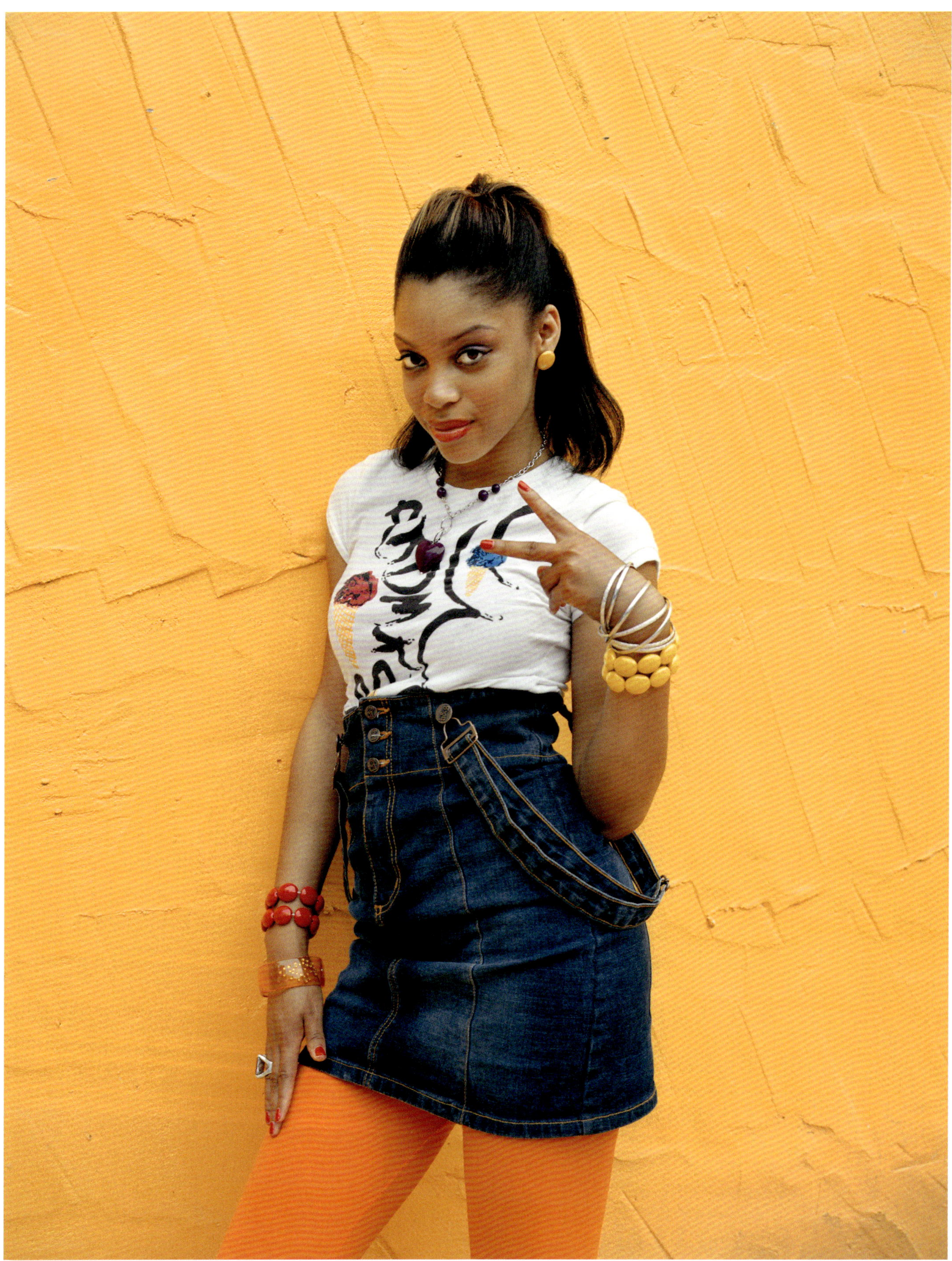

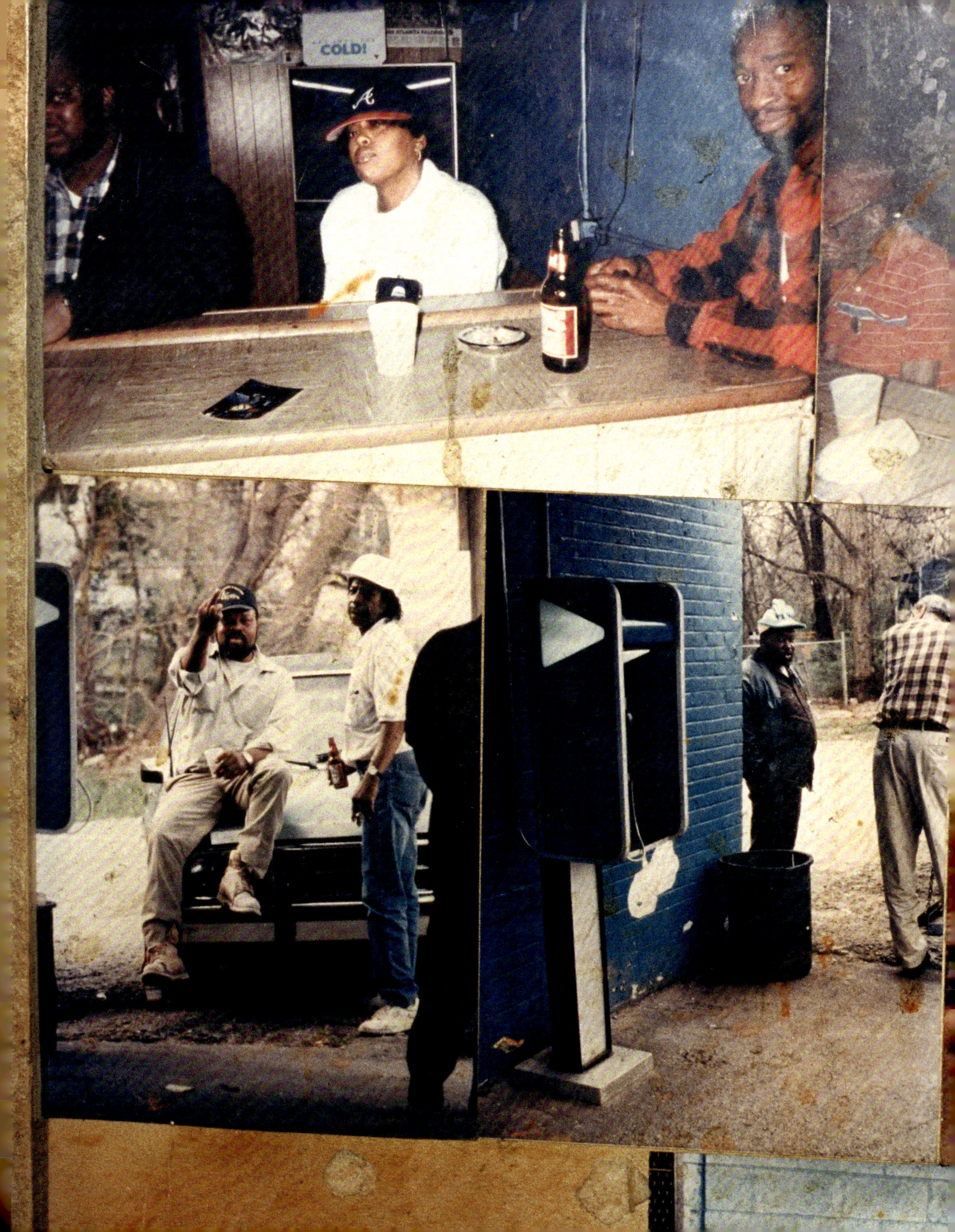

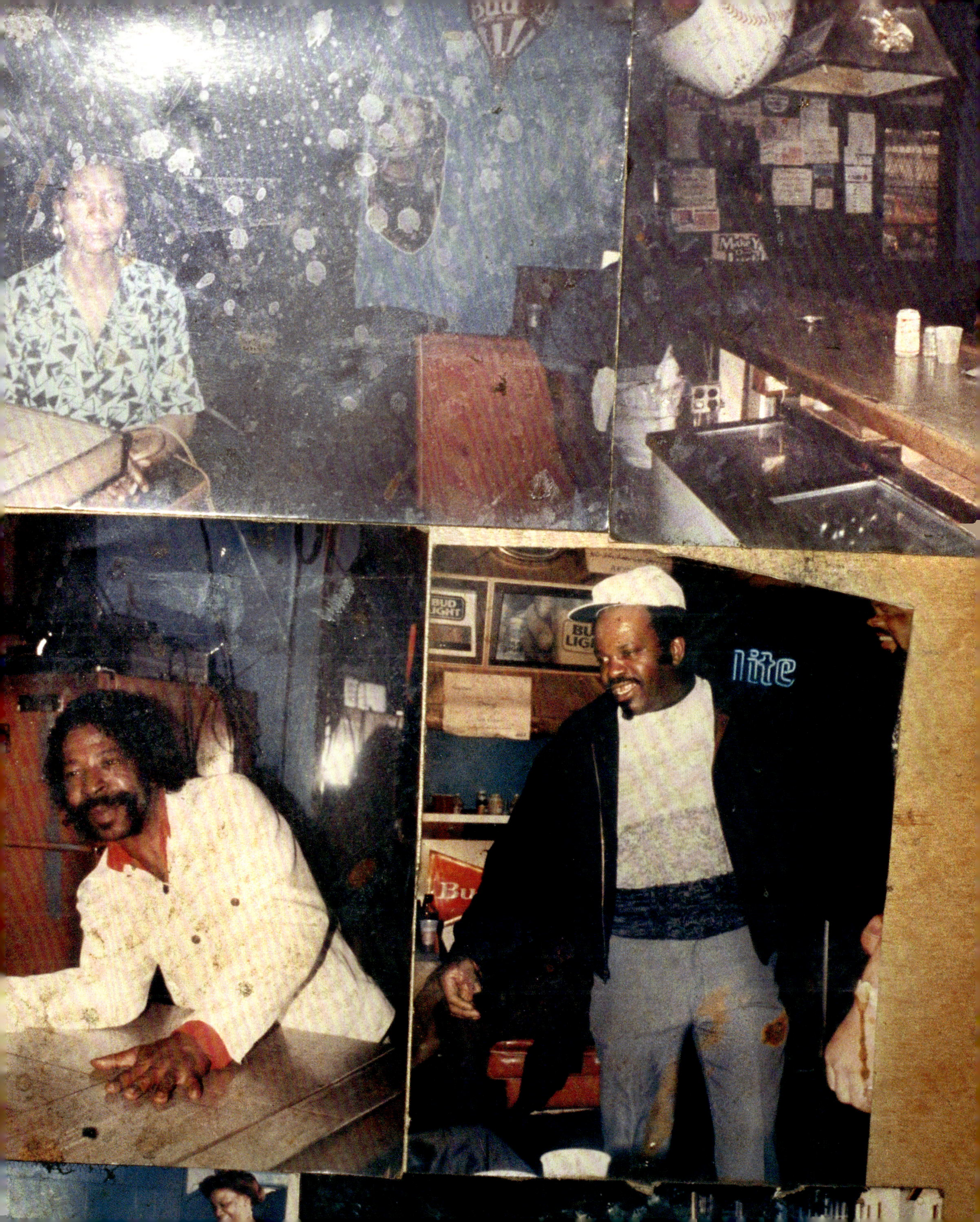

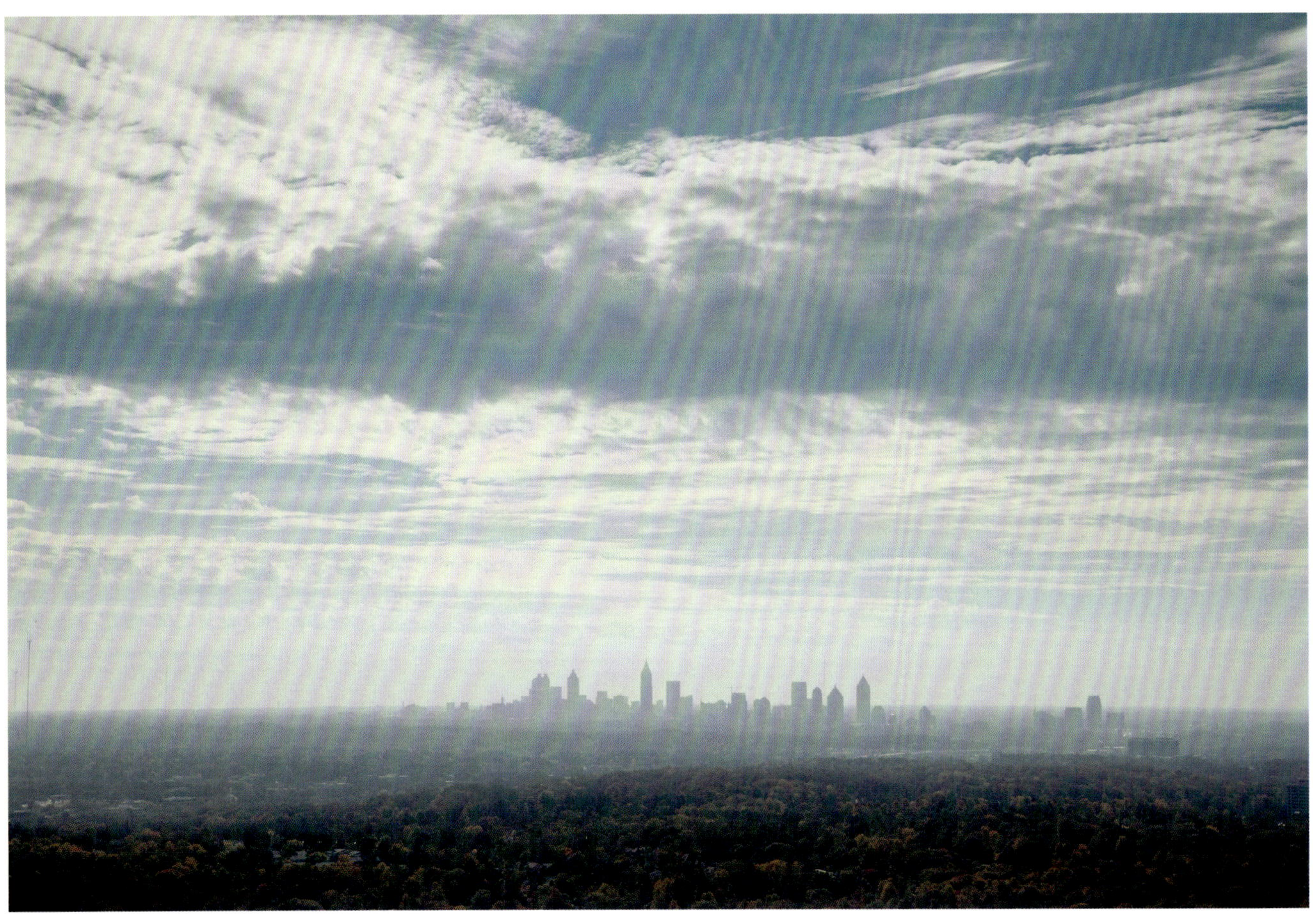

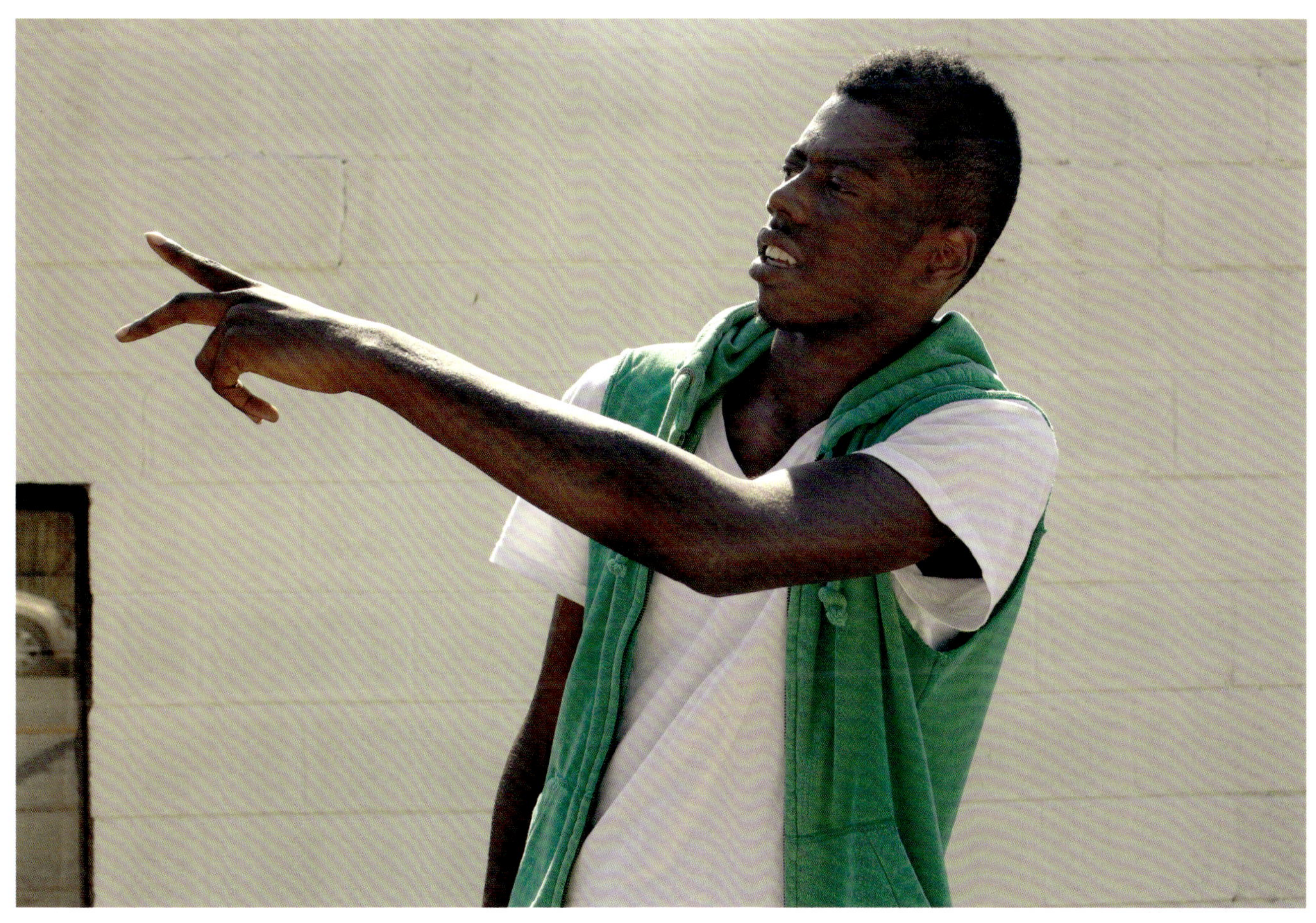

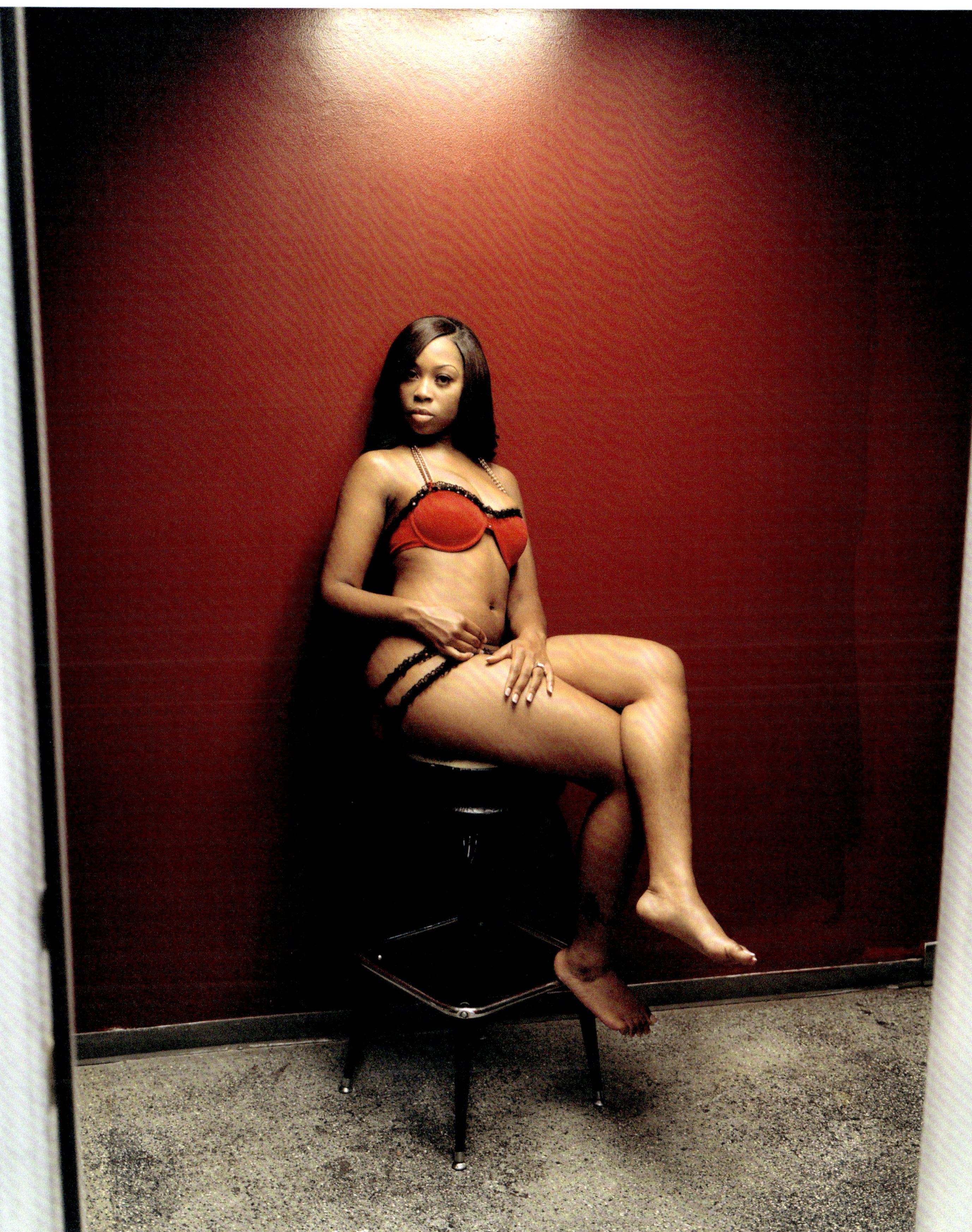

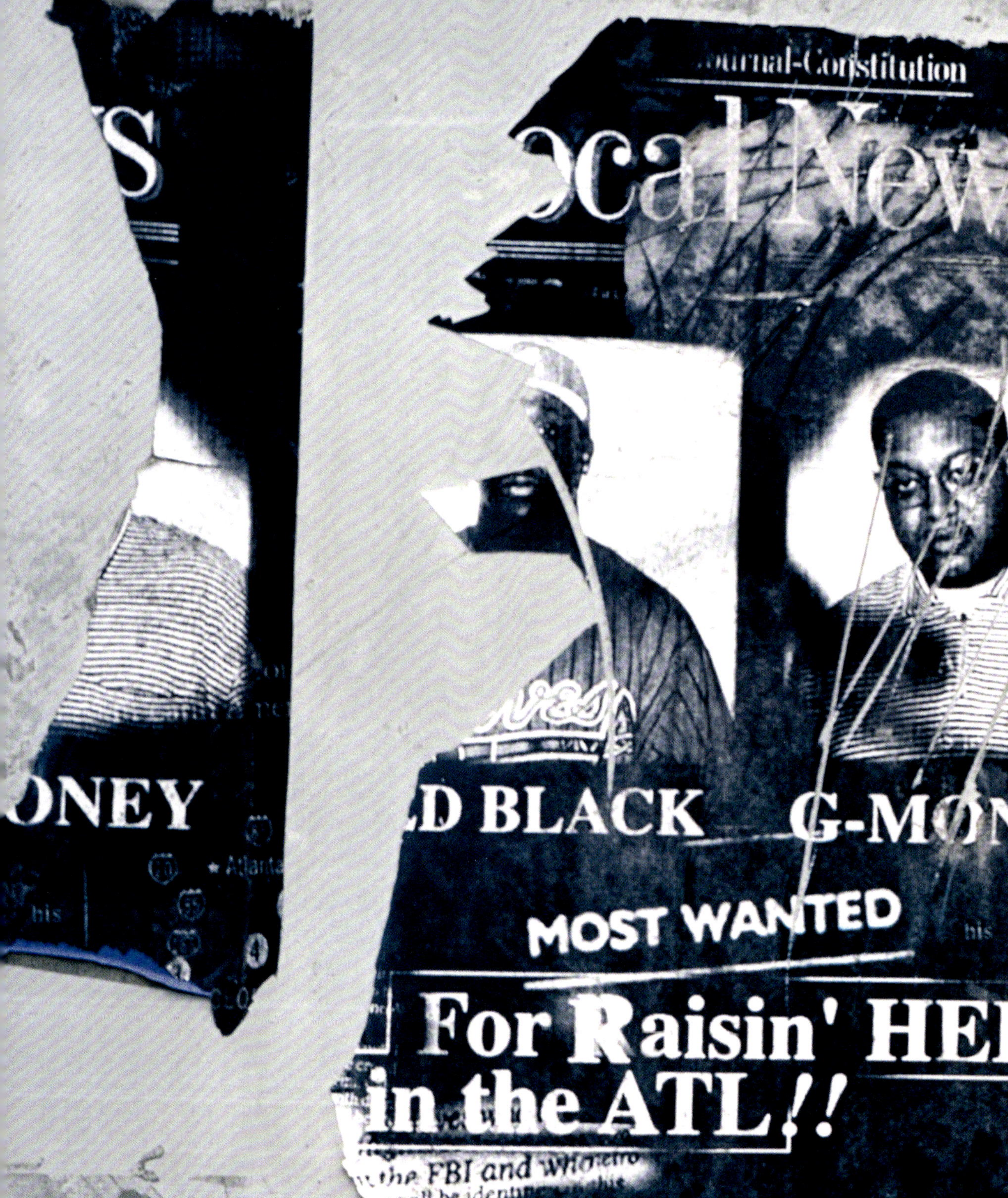
Journal-Constitution
ocal News
LD BLACK   G-MONEY
MOST WANTED
For Raisin' HELL
in the ATL!!
ONEY
the FBI and W
will be identi
Please ca
lp agents
ecounts fears
Palmore wa
which
0-322-66
-66

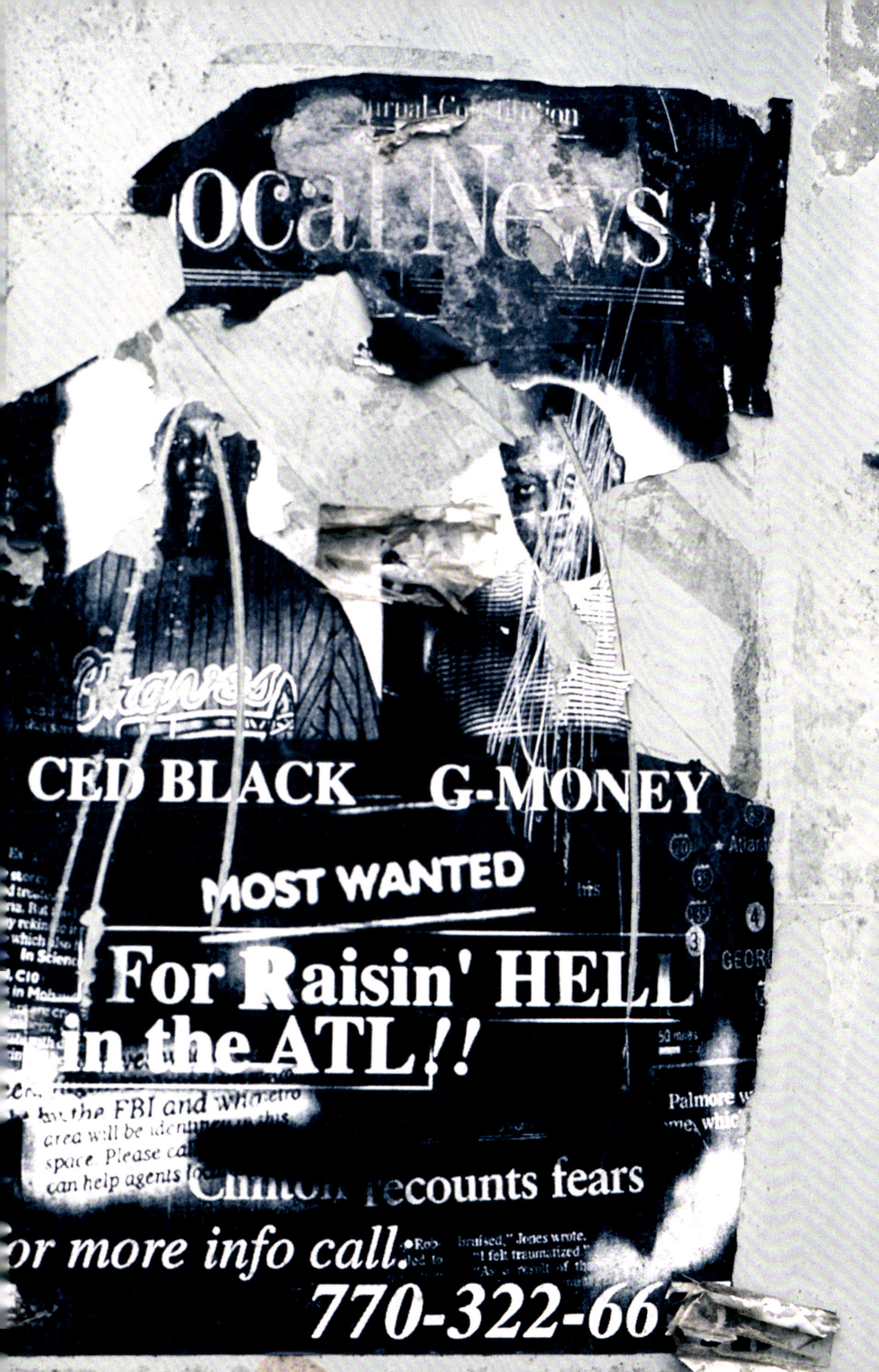

Local News
CED BLACK   G-MONEY
MOST WANTED
For Raisin' HELL
in the ATL!!
or more info call:
770-322-667

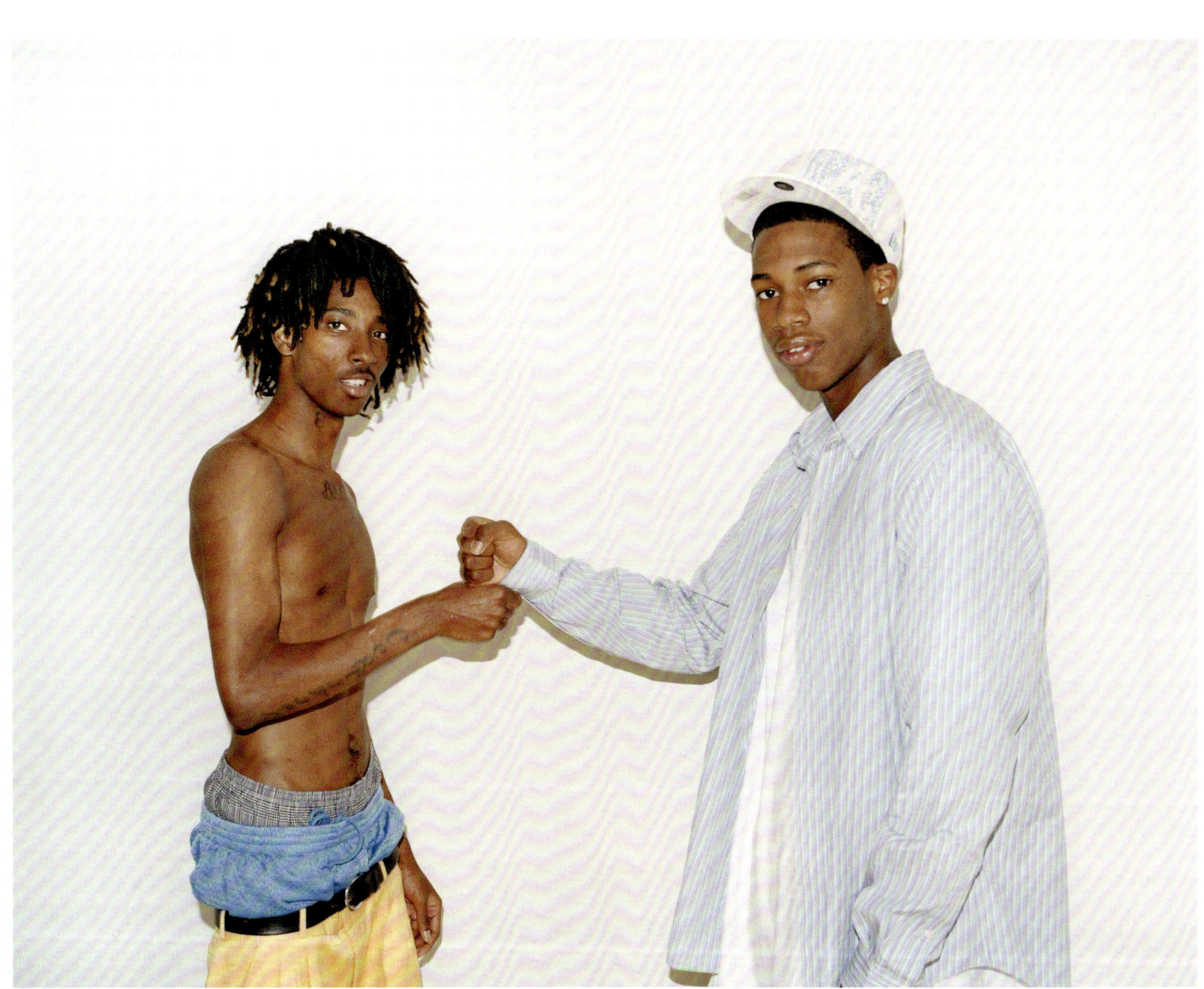

APPENDIX

Atlanta is the catchphrase capital of the world, and Radric "Gucci Mane" Davis is its eccentric mayor. Never mind that he had to pump a Fulton County Jail pay phone to get our November 2009 interview done; he was still governing the airwaves from inside anyway, with irresistible party starters like "Wasted" and "Lemonade" from his album The State vs. Radric Davis *getting constant radio play. There are a few hassles that come with a jailhouse interview— Gucci Mane had to hang up and call me back when time ran out on our first call—but there were collateral benefits, too. The drink-and-drug enthusiast seemed uncharacteristically cogent, attentive, focused ... maybe the right word, actually, is "sober."*

For starters I want to break down some of your slang and where it comes from. There's a track on your new album called "Lemonade." What's that about?

Well when I say "lemon" or "lemonade," that just refers to the color yellow. I talk about yellow-bone girls. I have a yellow-painted Lamborghini. I wear a lot of canary yellow diamonds. Yellow clothing: yellow hats, yellow shoes, yellow Polo shirts, yellow Polo socks. Things of that nature. All the yellow stuff that's in my world.

You've gotten famous for your ad-libs. You call out "Gucci!" in a playful voice or say "Brrrrr . . ."

That just comes from me having fun in the studio. When I'm not working on my album—when I'm working on my mixtape stuff and just having fun with it—I'll come up with some of the ad-libs. Then I'll take it from there and implement some of the best ones when I'm working on serious songs like my features or songs for my own album.

A lot of the heat you've picked up over the course of your career has come from mixtape songs. Can you talk about the role of the mixtape in Atlanta?

Most artists in Atlanta don't put out a lot of mixtapes. Instead, there are a lot of mixtape DJs that compile songs. Atlanta's known for a lot of singles—catchy little songs from one-hit-wonder groups. As soon as a DJ hears a song poppin' in the club from an independent artist or record label, he'll grab that song and put it on a collage of other songs that sound like that. The mixtapes'll have both artists that are established and artists that are unknown. So the DJs are always looking for the next hot song.

Me, I utilize all those DJs. I'll give them a *bunch* of my songs. Most of the established artists in Atlanta, they'll mostly wait until they droppin' an album to put out a mixtape. They'll let people be hungry and thirsty for they songs. And that can be great financially. But me, I like to record a lot, so I have to use that to my advantage. It generates a lot of shows, and a lot of those songs make it to the radio so there's a lot of publishing [royalties], too. So it's a way for me to generate income as well.

Some people try to keep some downtime between their releases, but you tend to flood the market.

Yeah, I don't keep any downtime. I go to the club a lot just on my leisure time, even when I'm not doing concerts. And I always like to hear *me* in the club. If I'm not hearing a lot of me? Then I'm losing. That's just how I feel. I like that feelin' of being there and actually seeing the visual of people rockin' to my stuff. Or people comin' to me and saying, "They played your stuff last night and everybody was grooving to it. All the girls were partying to it and all the guys were fuckin' with it."

There's a really specific club culture in Atlanta. Can you break that down?

I feel like Atlanta is known for being the strip club capital of the world, especially on the African-American side. A lot of people come to Atlanta from all over the country— all over the world, really—just for that. So if you can get something poppin' just there in the strip clubs, and all the dancers are liking it and requesting it while they workin', then all these people are taking it back with them to wherever they might be from. And who knows who's in the club that night? You might get the ear of a prominent record executive who will seek you out. That's a proven formula in Atlanta that works.

You said you go to the club a lot— when you say "the club," do you mean strip clubs, dance clubs, or both?

I go to all kinds of clubs. I been goin' to the strip clubs since I was a teenager, all the dance clubs, all the fancy bougie clubs, the reggae clubs, the white clubs, the straight hood clubs. I see what's going on at all those different places and use that as a tool for making music. Plus there are all those different people—it's fun to mix in with them.

Do you have an easy time socializing with just about anyone?

I have a *very* easy time. I love to party and I know how to party so I have a very easy time with any race, any creed . . . I can do it with the best of them.

What have the hot nights been at the strip clubs recently?

Atlanta is the only place I know in the country that does Two Dollar Tuesdays. You know, two dollar to get into the club, two dollar drinks all night. It's a lot of clubs in Atlanta that run Two Dollar Tuesday. So on Tuesday nights in Atlanta, a lot of people perform. And Tuesday is mostly an off night for artists. There's Monday at Magic City where a lot of people go to drink and throw money and see those dancers, but on Tuesday you can go see a live performance from very established artists from Atlanta or somewhere around the country. And then definitely Friday at any hood spots—its goin' down. The weekend at the strip clubs— it's goin' down. And definitely Thursdays with, like, the bougie clubs.

What's the current state of car culture in Atlanta? For a long time it was about classics, but—

It's still kinna like that in a way. On a hood scale. In the neighborhoods, a lot of street guys can't go buy a Ferrari. It'd raise too many red flags. So they might go spend the same amount they'd spend on a Mercedes-Benz S550 on a Chevrolet,

because that goes unnoticed. That's why I feel like a lot of people get classics in Atlanta. They got the money to buy whatever they want to buy, but they don't want all that attention. They'll spend $100,000, $150,000, $200,000 on an old school instead of buying this new car from a dealer- ship that'll raise all these red flags.

But as far as rappers and enter- tainers go, new schools are at an all-time high. You can see a Bugatti at the club, Ferrarris, Lamborghinis, Phantoms, Porsches. I got a couple of those myself—and I got a couple old schools—so I like to mix it up. I got a nice little car collection myself.

What old schools do you have right now?

I got a '74 Oldsmobile, a Corvette, and that's it as far as the old schools. But they're all the way. I spent about a hundred on both of 'em.

The car itself costs a fraction of that right?

Oh yeah. When I got my Oldsmobile, honestly I paid $9,000 for it. But I done painted it, I done went through everything under the hood of it, I done redone the interior to snow white, put a sun roof in it, twenty- six-inch rims on it, crazy sound system in it. At first it was red, but I just repainted it green.

You've got some jail time ahead of you for parole violations. Do you have a date when you're going in yet?

I'm already in. I'm calling you now from jail.

No way!

Yeah!

You already started?

I already started.

I had no idea.

I been in jail eleven days.

Wow. So you're just getting it done then, huh?

Yeah. I just want to get in and out of here. Hey, it just said I only have one minute left to talk to you so I'm just going to call you right back in twenty seconds so we can finish our interview.

Is that cool?

Yeah that's cool!

[Gucci hangs up. Phone rings five minutes later.]

Hello?

Whattup big dog.

What do you do every day while you're locked up just to keep from going crazy?

A lot of reading, a hell of a lot of writing. I try to talk to all these inmates in here. I talk to them about how they can remain positive, and help them think about what they're gonna do when they get out.

Have you already had some of those conversations?

Oh yeah, definitely. A lot of young folks look up to me and they got no clue, and no direction. I just chal- lenge them to start thinking about what they want to do, at least as a start.

Where are you? Fulton County?

Fulton County Jail, general popula- tion with everybody else.

Do people hit you up because they figure you've got money?

It ain't no secret I've got money, so they can't hit me up. This is my third rodeo here, unfortunately. I been locked up over ten times in my life and arrested more than that. That ain't nothing to be proud of, but I know how to come in here and handle it, then get back to the street.
—

*ANDRÉ 3000

--

OutKast's André "Three Stacks" Benjamin does exactly what he wants, when he wants. He dropped out of high school to focus on making music. He quit smoking weed and drinking after OutKast's 1994 debut album Southernplayalisticadillacmuzik. He quit touring after OutKast's fourth album, Stankonia. He quit the duo's fashion venture, OutKast Clothing Co., and he quit its record label, Aquemini. He's often been accused of quitting OutKast, and he's threatened to quit music entirely. Public appearances are few and far between, and he almost never agrees to interviews. Yet despite his increasingly reclusive nature, he remains a looming presence in hip-hop through fawning references from fans like Lil Wayne and Kanye West. And whenever a new verse by André 3000 appears—rare and exotic as they are—it's nothing short of an event. I caught up with André by phone in August of 2008; he was in Atlanta, driving his car and fueling up at the gas station.

What were you and Big Boi listening to when you met back at Tri-Cities High School in Atlanta?

We listened to everything from KMD's "Peach Fuzz" to Too $hort to Poison Clan to Ghetto Boys to Tribe Called Quest to Das EFX. Das EFX, to me—a lot of people laughed at them—but to me Das EFX was probably one of the most creative things to come out of New York back then. They were like gods to me and Big Boi. In high school, those were our idols. And Souls of Mischief were our idols—you can hear their influence on the first album.

What were the two of you into wearing back then?

I guess you call them tennis sweaters, shorts with no socks, and Timberlands. Not even the boots; we wore the dock shoes.

What did the other kids at Tri-Cities think of y'all dressing like that?

The girls thought it was cool. The guys—some of 'em—thought it was cool. Tri-Cities was between two projects. College Park projects on one side and then Montel Homes on another side. So we going to school dressing prep, and half the school is split into the soul side of things, and half the school is into the prep side of things. And also kids knew us as the guys listening to Grand Puba and Tribe Called Quest. Our school thought of those as odd rap groups, when, you know, Too $hort and N.W.A. was goin' on.

So there was a little friction there.

Yeah.

When you dropped out of Tri-Cities and started spending time at the Dungeon, where Organized Noize was based, what effect did that have on you? Especially being around older guys?

Yeah, we were a couple years younger. It just gave me more focus because I could dedicate my time to the music, whereas before we'd have to meet after school and start throwin' some rhymes back and forth. The Dungeon gave me time to just be there all day listening to music.

Plus you started producing, too, right? It was beats, music, the full package.

Right, exactly.

What are your memories from the 1995 Source Awards? When OutKast won Best New Artist and famously got booed?

I just remember that it was the opposite of what's going on now. Now, you go to New York and all the music sounds Southern. Even New York rappers are rappin' on Southern beats, and hiring Southern people to be on their songs. Back then, the South was so uncool. It was, "They country, they slow, they can't rap." So at the awards, I think it was Salt-N-Pepa who opened the envelope—

Yeah, it was Salt-N-Pepa.

Even they were surprised. They were almost like, "Who is this?" It was a time when Southern music was not ever even heard. That's why I think it was clever of Organized Noize to name the first album *Southernplayalisticadillacmuzik,* because it was the first time that the Southern lifestyle was broadcast nationally. If you look at what was goin' on at the time, we came out with Nas. We came out with Biggie. We came out with Wu Tang. As far as rhyming and being from the South? We couldn't mess around. All of our contemporaries made us better. Nowadays, the competition for a lot of the kids in the South is just their neighborhood. It's not the same. Me and Big Boi started out *rhyming*. We were just rhyming kids.

When you got onstage to accept the award, you said, "The South got something to say." The audio is right there at the end of *Aquemini*. Was that a reaction to the energy in the room, or did you plan it out?

It was the energy in the room. As OutKast, we performed in the Tunnel—and that was back when the Tunnel was the Tunnel. It was *the* New York hip-hop club. There was razor blades in fifty guys' mouths in there. The Tunnel was the place it really went down. So I knew what the temperament was. We were going against the times. I knew there was gonna be a backlash. So I was just trying to say, "Man we spent all our time, and put all our energy into this. How can y'all say that y'all are the only people that can do this kind of music? We got lives too that we can talk about. Just because we're from a certain region doesn't mean we can be discounted." So "The South got something to say" was a precursor to what's going on now. I'm just happy to be part of a crew that was about rhymin'. Of course we do some of the best partyin', and some of the best dancin', and snappin', and poppin'—which we all love—but a lot of the guys grew up listening to me and Big Boi. And it was rhyme focused.

Do you hear some people who are following in that rhyme-focused tradition, instead of just snappin' and poppin'?

To be honest, I just got back to Atlanta last night. I haven't been back to Atlanta in years. I hear stuff every now and then that kinna tweaks my ear, but I don't even know the artists' names or anything. We in a time now where street hop is more important than rhymin'. One day this girl and I were listening to a famous artist—I'm not gonna say who—but we were listening to one of his songs, and he's a classic, he's considered a rhyme god. And he comes on the radio and the girl from Atlanta's like, "He sayin' too many words at one time." *[laughs]* That lets me know that simplicity is reigning supreme right now. If a kid can sing along to it, or it doesn't take too much to think about it . . . that's where it's at right now. The rapper is not popular right now. But I can say an artist like Lil Wayne is finding a really great balance in it. He's a great rapper, but he entertains too, so he's finding a great balance in it.

Let's talk about you and Big Boi starting to go your separate ways. Everyone looks at *Speakerboxxx/The Love Below*. But Big Boi told me, "When Dré left high school, I was still in school. So he'd be at the Dungeon all day, and I'd come after school and try to catch up."

Right.

And then later he said, "I had a kid when I was twenty years old, and that's when Dré was in the studio all the time working on production. So I was trying to start a family, and then I'd go try to catch up."

Right, I mean, that's totally true. Our whole writing process has never been, "Okay, let's sit down and write this song." Every rhyme that we've done has been personal. And it is true, he took the smarter route, which I should have done. I should have finished high school with my class. I did go back to finish while we were working on *ATLiens*. But if I would've stayed focused in high school, then I could've focused on *ATLiens* a little bit more. Anyway, our whole writing process has always been personal. We're always coming together and comparing notes, but it's never been "Let's go tit for tat," or "Let me write this for you and you write this for me." I'm just now finding out fourteen years later that a lot of artists don't write their own raps! *[laughs]* I'm like, "Really?! Are you serious?! Aww man, that is *crazy*!" I never knew that! That's like somebody writing Edgar Allan Poe's shit. Anyway, as far as the production goes, right after *Southernplayalisticadillacmuzik*, I took my money and started buying equipment. I started buyin' beat machines, bass guitars, keyboards, and I started to produce.

Where did you set that up?

In my dad's house—I was still living with my dad. And so some of my first tracks ended up making it onto *ATLiens*. When it says "Produced by OutKast" or "Produced by Earthtone III," those were really my tracks. But I mean, I just thought you said it was by everybody. It's funny, I was having the same conversation with Q-Tip. Because he did a lot of the Tribe Called Quest songs.

Do you wish you had put your name alone on it?

Nah, I don't really, because it probably would've changed things. And I do realize that's what really breaks groups up is when people try to take credit: Who's important? Who's not important? The high school spirit—when everybody's just in it together and you don't care—that's the cool thing.

And credit is one thing, but when you start becoming an adult, and when I had a kid, and when Big Boi had a kid, you start saying, "Aww man, I gotta split a song three ways that I did completely by myself? Aww man, that's not right!" And that's when things start to change. That started to happen, but me and Big Boi have always stayed cool. And even when I was doing beats, I'd send Big Boi the beats and he'd write to 'em. And he'd come up with a lot of the choruses. So it was a partnership. You know, we had a cool thing. And it's still that way. But once I started to explore more—and once the songs started to get more out there and people couldn't understand it—that's when I felt like I was in this small lil' box alone. So I started to kinna root for myself. *[laughs]*

When did you start to feel that way?

Around *Aquemini,* I think. To be honest, it was growing pains. If we've been doing things one way since we were kids, and then I start doing these other songs, and I'm changing my voice, and singing these melodies . . . I don't blame him, you know? Big Boi comes into the studio and says, "Yeah man, I just don't know. People don't like when you be changing your voice." To me, I'm almost like a kid, and that's your parent saying, "I don't like the drawing you just did." So now, when I'm gonna draw, I'm gonna go draw in the closet, you know? I'm gonna paint looking over my shoulder to make sure nobody's gonna tear it down.

Because you really cared when he said those things.

Yeah, yeah. I mean, with *The Love Below* thing . . . how can you sing "I hope that you're the one; if not, you are the prototype" with all your homeboys in the studio? And a lot of those songs were songs I'd recorded at home as a side thing for a movie I was doing at the time with Bryan Barber. But when I went to the record label, they said, "We don't want to put out a solo album." So that's when we started to do the whole *Speakerboxxx/ The Love Below* thing.

You guys always seem to be pushing up against what the label wants.

Yeah, but at the same time, if nobody's around saying, "Okay, we want to put this out at a certain time," I could sit around for years. I see the importance of all of it. You just gotta figure out how to work in those parameters.

Recently when you've been recording solo, are there things that you miss about the collaboration?

Big Boi was always my . . . I guess you would call it my normal man's ear. I would get his true reaction. I remember playing "Hey Ya" for him for the first time. I gave Big Boi and Killer Mike a copy, and they rode around some of the slummiest neighborhoods in Atlanta playin' "Hey Ya." *[laughs]* And they came back and said, "Dré, this shit is *jammin'*." So I knew, "Okay, if they can listen to it, I can put it out." And to be honest, our whole chemistry always worked because Big Boi made what I was doin' acceptable. And what I was doing made what Big Boi was doing extraordinary. And it was a cool balance.

One key to the staying power of OutKast's songs is that the choruses are usually routed in a metaphor that can be interpreted many ways.

Right. We never had a formula. Take "Bombs Over Baghdad." That song started with just those three words first. It didn't have a beat, it didn't have a tempo. Nuthin'. I wrote those words down on a piece of paper in London after hearing it on the news. I heard the newscaster say, *[English accent]* "Blah blah blah bombs over Baghdad." And I was like, "Aww man!" *[laughs]* "Bombs over Baghdad" sounds real good together; it just rolls off the tongue. So all I knew is that it would be the name of a song. At the time, we were on tour for *Aquemini,* and I had my studio equipment set up in the back of the bus. So I'm beating on the [drum] machine and I had this rhythm going. At the time, I wanted to shake things up. I wanted it to sound urgent. So I was working on this beat that I had called "IFOs/UFOs." That was just something to write on the disc itself so I could remember what I was working on.

What did it stand for?

"Identified Flying Objects" and "Unidentified Flying Objects."

Oh right. Got it.

So the beat was going on, and I had these chords playing, and I started singing this melody, and it turned into the chorus to "Bombs Over Baghdad." Then I wrote a verse, Big Boi wrote a verse. The title was just symbolism. It had nothing to do with the war, but at the same time the war did inspire the title and the song. So then I added a little bridge, and we just kind of worked on it until we felt it was done. I went in [and recorded my vocals], Big Boi went in, we did the guitar solo, and then the bridge, and felt like it was done.

Listening to that story, it just makes me wish you'd spend your time in the recording studio, instead of making a movie with Will Ferrell, or instead of doing a clothing line. What do you say to that?

Yeah ... I mean, I wish I was in the booth, too. *[laughs]* I was talkin' to a homeboy the other night and I was like, "*Man,* I wish I had an album to put out right now." I nod to people like Pharrell, Timbaland, and Lil Wayne for their work ethic. That's all they do! I'm not like that. I might write a verse every three months! I do it when I feel it, and I've always been that way.

The rule of thumb in hip-hop is stay relevant, but you've always disappeared.

But now it's harder to do that. We're in the Internet age and everything is faster, faster, faster. I wish I could write a verse every night, but I think I have nuthin' to say. And that's how you end up just talking about yourself, which I don't want to do. That's why it's been a blessing that people like DJ Unk and DJ Drama would call me and say, "Hey man, I wonder if you could check this out and maybe give me a verse on it." They've been my blessings and my saviors. Because people could've easily forgotten about André 3000. And what's funny is that some people don't even know André 3000. They just know Three Stacks. That lets you know how stayin' relevant is really important. What if I tried to put out an album and I hadn't done anything in five years? No remixes, nothing. It would be hard for a younger generation to relate to me.

What's the state of your solo album?

I don't want to put out an album just to put out an album. So I've been tinkering with what I want to say. Then there's little beats that I've been getting from people here and there, and I've done some of my own production. But I need to hear some new music. I wanna hear new sounds. I might have to dig deep and try to find something.

Do you still feel like you've got something left to prove?

Oh, definitely. You always have something to prove, even if it's to yourself. But I'm thirty-three years old, and the things I rhyme about may not be the same things that a twenty-year-old wants to hear. So there's mid-rap crisis goin' on.
--

*LUDACRIS
--

With all due respect to OutKast, Ludacris is Atlanta hip-hop's most successful and reliable crossover star. His rapid-fire (but easily decipherable) flow and hilariously raunchy lyrics have led to sales of more than seventeen million albums in the United States alone. He's also starred in films including 2 Fast 2 Furious, Hustle & Flow, *and* Crash, *which won the 2006 Academy Award for Best Picture. In February of 2010, I caught him on the phone in a moment of downtime during a world tour with the Black Eyed Peas. At the time, his hit "How Low" was riding high atop the urban radio charts.*

Everybody knows you as Ludacris. But a lot of people don't know that you also had a successful career as a disc jockey on the Atlanta radio station Hot 97.5 under the name Chris Lova Lova. How did you first get on the radio and how did the Chris Lova Lova persona develop?

Well, I started rapping at like nine years old. But before that really took off, I used to host all the open mics and talent contests around Atlanta. Eventually, I got a tip that they were opening a rap radio station in town and I was like, "Man, that's the perfect place for me to find a job or an opening for myself." Because there are so many artists and producers that come through the radio stations. So it was a means to an end and a plan that I had— I wanted to go there and develop myself. Of course, as a rapper I was Ludacris. But when I got a job up there on the morning show, they didn't want that to be my radio name. They said, "You can keep that, and we're going to try to come up with a radio name for you." That's where Chris Lova Lova came from.

That was in the late '90s, and it was a particularly interesting moment in Atlanta—right when the city was beginning to evolve into the capital of hip-hop. What was it like being in the middle of that vortex?

It felt great, man! Atlanta really was the new Motown. You had the whole LaFace Records thing going on as well as So So Def and Rowdy; it was like the music mecca, man. You couldn't go anywhere without knowing someone or knowing someone who knew someone.

As Chris Lova Lova, your partner on air was known as Poon Daddy. How did you two meet?

We were the two youngest guys at the station—

—who talked a lot of shit.

Right. In the beginning, he was doing promotions and I was doing interning. They put us together, and it was magic. We *were* the demographic. We lived the life. All we needed was to learn the technical aspects of operating the board. Getting our own show was simple from there.

Atlanta still has its own specific radio culture. As someone who's been all over the country promoting your music, what's unique about the scene in Atlanta?

It's particular because, like I said, it's the mecca. It's the hip-hop Hollywood—or Hollyhood as I like to call it. But everyone lives there, so anybody could come by the station on any given day, anybody could call up. Somebody's always got an album or a show to promote. Now there are reality shows going on in Atlanta, too. There's all this madness going on here, and radio works hand in hand with all of it.

What is it about Atlanta radio that will allow sixteen-year-olds making music out of a sewn-together studio in a trap somewhere to get heavy rotation?

There's a hard-core fan base here. That's the essence. The fans make it what it is. All those songs you're talking about come from a hustler's mentality. They're about having a dream, making it out of a certain situation, and getting money. And in Atlanta, Georgia, that's what fans like to hear in the car, that's what they like to hear in the club . . . so radio has to respect it.

At this point you're an international music star and a Hollywood movie star. Do you feel like your music is still fundamentally rooted in Atlanta?

Oh man, absolutely. It's in everything I do: the heavy bass lines, the infectious hooks, even the "How Low" record is derived from bass music. I live in Atlanta. I have homes in other places, but if I'm not doing anything specific, I'm here. There's no mistaking it. I still live in College Park. The same city where I went to school.

--

*BIG BOI

--

First and foremost, OutKast's Antwan Patton prides himself on being a team player. He's the unofficial brand ambassador of OutKast and of a subsection of Atlanta hip-hop that Big Boi lovingly calls, simply, "the funk." What's the funk? It's hip-hop of a lineage that Big traces from Bob Marley to Parliament to UGK, and it ignores party-oriented trends like crunk and snap to focus on live instrumentation and flawlessly thorough rhyming. While André 3000 is largely MIA these days, Big Boi unblinkingly soldiers on without him and can usually be found at Stankonia Studios, the recording house that he and André bought from Bobby Brown out of foreclosure. Every single OutKast album has largely been recorded there—even before the duo owned the deed. This interview, which focuses on the early days of OutKast, was conducted in August of 2008 at the W Hotel in Midtown Manhattan.

What was high school like for you?

I'd just moved to Atlanta—I got there at the beginning of tenth grade.

You moved up from Savannah, Georgia, right? What moved your family up?

It was just me. I used to come up from Savannah in the summer and live with my auntie. I started hanging around with the fellas in the neighborhood and used to do things like cut somebody's grass for ten dollars—anything to get a little money. Back then the dream job was to work at Six Flags. *Anything* to work at Six Flags. But that summer my auntie wanted me to stay in Atlanta to help out with her son. He was maybe six or seven years old by then, and it was just the two of them. I saw it as an opportunity—I'd been back and forth all my life—so I was like, cool. They had just merged a whole bunch of schools to make Tri-Cities High School, so you had everybody there: people from the projects—Montel Homes—middle-class kids, suburban kids, the whole nine yards. And I was always into the books, always sharp. So that's where I met Dré. I had classes with our homeboy Sutton, and he introduced me to the rest of the crew. We'd all hook up around lunch periods: Sutton, Dré, Preston, and another homeboy named Silk. I was like, "Oh, okay, it's a squad!"

What drew you all together?

We were all preps. Before it was Gucci we'd wear Birks, corduroys, Polo, tennis sweaters, tennis rackets . . .

You'd carry tennis rackets to school?

Yeah! We were full-on prep. Everybody at school had their own style, and all the while you got these gangs from all different places and projects. The gangs didn't like that prettyboy shit. Because the girls loved us, and we'd be friends with the girlfriends of some of the dudes in the gangs. But, anyway, that's what kind of drew us together: school, girls, clothes, and tapes. The music was a big thing that brought us together.

How'd you start rapping?

Well, one day me and my brother caught the train out to Lenox Mall to go window-shopping, and we saw Dré on the train by himself with his headphones on.

Who did Dré live with at the time?

It was his dad's house, but his dad was never home. I was like, "Man, this guy cool! He got his own apartment!" His dad had so many old records, so we'd listen to music, and at the time Dré was painting—he was airbrushing. So we started airbrushing on our jeans. From there, we continued a little friendship, and one day we left school and went back to my aunt's house and were just looking at *MTV Raps*. We're just sitting around and he's like, "Man, we need to start ourselves a group." "I'm like, Hell yeah!" And Dré's like, "Man, I'm for real. I'm dead ass serious. We need to start us a group." I was like, "Shit! Let's do it!" Even then, we had the "Say No to Drugs" raps and stuff like that, but we didn't know we had the gift like that.

How'd you start the group from there?

So we're sitting there like, "Let's get us a name." We decided on the name Two Shades Deep—you know, two shades of brown. I was like, "All right, what's your name gonna be?" Dré's like, "I'm going to be the Black Wolf." I said, "Shit, I could be the Black Dog." Man, it was Black Dog, Black Wolf. That day we started writing records. From then on, every day at school it'd be like, "I got some shit, I got some lines." And we'd go rhyme for rhyme, just raw, man. Every day we'd rehearse our raps and memorize them. You know that line, "Every day we'd look up at the ceiling, watching ceiling fans go round, trying to catch a feeling off instrumentals"? That's real, man. It was in my auntie's kitchen. Just walking around the table with the fan turning above us, memorizing that shit.

What did the rest of the clique think when you and Dré formed a group?

They were like, "That's hard!" But at the time, they was really on some "We need to get some bread *now*" shit. Them boys ended up robbing a liquor store on Highway 85 and Riverdale Road. Both our homeboys been in since that day—since the tenth grade. Armed robbery. One of our homeboys, Silk, got out maybe five years ago. But Sutton's still in there.

Wait, so y'all have been making music for fifteen years and he's still in jail?

Still in jail.

Where were you that day?

I think I was in school. My auntie didn't want my grades to slip when I moved, and when I came up to Atlanta my GPA was 3.68. She was like, "You have to keep your GPA or you got to go back to Savannah." So I stayed out of trouble like that.

So from there, you and Dré started hitting the local open mics?

Yup. A place called Club Ritz opened on West End and that was our first time getting on the microphone. There was a local TV show called *Atlanta Jams*—different artists would come to the different clubs and they'd broadcast the show. We were like, "Shit, we want to go up there." So we went up to Club Ritz on an open mic night. I think we were the second ones to go on. The shit was crazy because they only had one hardwired mic that we had to pass back and forth. Somebody gave us a little bit of reefer, man, and we were trying to roll that shit up in toilet tissue. It was burning funny and we were trying to rap and smoke at the same time. We were cracking each other up, passing the mic and the joint back and forth.

So what happened to the "Say No to Drugs" raps? Y'all weren't doing weed and pistols raps yet, were you?

Oh yeah, that's what it was. Gritty and grimy—that's what we fell into. It was just gutter hip-hop. We were into girls, and then everybody's got that side to 'em where you don't take no shit.

What were y'all rapping over? Somebody else's instrumental?

Anybody's instrumental! As a matter of fact, I believe it was Marvin Gaye's "After the Dance." We had our homeboy DJ Win loop up a tape for us. We killed that shit.

You guys were still in high school when you got a record deal, so things must have moved quickly from there.

Well there was this girl named Bianca that we knew, and she worked at the beauty supply store that Rico Wade from Organized Noize managed—it was a beauty supply store and a movie rental store. Through her we heard some beats that Rico did, and we'd never heard no track like that before. People would leave us some shit on some tapes, but Rico had real beats, real sounds, new original shit. We said to Bianca, "Man you should set up a meeting with us." One day she said, "Okay."

What did Rico have going at that point?

They had a group called UBoys. Atlanta was all about dance competitions at the time, and this group was a singing and dancing group. They were the baddest in Atlanta, you know what

I'm saying? I'm talking about the perms and big waves. That shit was gangster as hell—them boys were running the whole city. At the time me and Dré had bald heads, Champion sweatshirts, cut-off T-shirts with different sneakers and shit. So we went up to the beauty supply store to meet Rico, and Big Gipp pulled up in an Isuzu Trooper. We had our favorite song, the "What's the Scenario" remix, on a tape, so Gipp put that in and we just started rapping. At that point we'd been doing months and months of just long, drawn-out raps. We just ran our raps all the way down, and it was ferocious. Rico was like, "Okay, I'm fucking with y'all. Y'all need to come back to the house." So later that night he brought us to the Dungeon.

What were you thinking the first time you went to the Dungeon?

Rico lived with his mom and two sisters, and then he had all his equipment in the basement. That was the Dungeon. The basement wasn't finished—it was red clay dirt, dust, wooden steps, rats running across the floor, everything. I was like, "How the fuck can they sleep up there with this music on this loud?" Everybody was like, "His mom cool as hell." After that, we was there every day.

Were y'all in eleventh grade then?

Yeah, it was late tenth grade, maybe early eleventh. Everybody else was four or five years older than us and had already graduated. Once we got there, man, it was just all about the music. I stayed going to school, but after a while Dré was like, "Man, fuck that school." He stopped going to school altogether, and just stayed over there all the time.

Were y'all calling yourselves Out-Kast yet?

No. We didn't become OutKast until like the middle of eleventh grade when a singing group stole our name and started calling themselves Four Shades Deep. We were like, "Man, that's some biting-ass shit." That singing group turned out to be Jagged Edge. We were like, "Cool, whatever. We're going to get us a new name, and ain't nobody going to take this shit." Everybody started looking in the dictionary until we hit on OutKast and thought, "That's it." That was that, and nobody could take that shit. So thank you, Jagged Edge!
--

*SHAWTY LO
--

If you trust Carlos Walker's own telling, his transition from convicted cocaine trafficker to the architect of Atlanta's snap music craze was almost accidental. And snap is so simple you almost believe him: the songs are characterized by slow tempos, skeletal beats, and finger snaps where there should be snare drums. The lyrics usually combine simple boasts with directives about a new dance craze—you know, "Girl shake that laffy taffy." It's been called the death of hip-hop; it's also been called a symphony in four sounds. Either way, snap has morphed and so has Shawty Lo's career. He spearheaded snap as the leader of a group called D4L; he's now a solo artist who's hugely popular in the region, if not across the nation. We spoke via telephone just days before Christmas of 2009. He was at the Georgia Dome hosting a charity event along with a member of the Atlanta Falcons.

What part of Atlanta are you from?

I was born and raised in Fulton County. I was raised off of Bankhead Highway in the project Bowen Homes.

What are the associations that come along with Bowen Homes?

Well, it's always been kind of negative, man. But I was born and raised there. Bowen Homes is just a rough area with a big crime rate. They just closed it down probably 'bout like seven months ago.

Were you relieved or upset when they shut it down?

It's a negative and a positive, you know? It's where I grew up at and there's a lot of memories left there. But, at the same time, it's a good thing because there's a lot of crime. Now they're tearing down all the projects in Atlanta and moving everybody elsewhere.

How'd you start rapping?

I just came to be a rapper at the end of 2005, really. Not in a million years did I think I'd be a rapper. It was just something I tried out. Before that I was just doing my thing, you know, illegally. I was unfortunate coming out of high school. I did get my GED, but I've been on my own since I was seventeen, when my grandma died. That put me in the streets, and I came into a life of crime. I was into a lot of drugs—not taking drugs, but selling drugs and doing all kinds of stuff.

Around 2003, it was getting like . . . the police were closing in on me. I was trying to get out of the streets, but they ended up catching me. I was facing three cases and like twenty to forty years. I was blessed to just get a year on each case and then God blessed me to come home after a year. I started doing the music, and I been doin' positive stuff since then.

Tell me about D4L coming onto the scene—it was an explosive moment for Atlanta.

Basically, I formed the group D4L around 2003. I went around and got guys from different projects that I knew who could rap good and I made the group. We were already calling ourselves Down 4 Life in the hood anyway. Then, before I got locked up in 2004, we did a song called "Betcha Can't Do It Like Me." Then when I was in jail, they was telling me, "Lo, the song pickin' up!" "Lo, they rappin' your verse and everything in the club!" Then about three or four months before I come home, they was like, "Lo, we got another song called 'Laffy Taffy.'" And I said, "Let me hear it!" I'm listening to it on the phone from jail and I'm like, "That's not it right there." And they was like, "Lo, I'm telling ya—that's it." I just didn't understand "Shake That Laffy Taffy" at that time. But then I come home, and they had a surprise party for me at a club called Vegas Nights in Cobb County. I was just standin' at the top in VIP and the song came on and the whole club went crazy. The song was so explosive, I couldn't believe it. It wasn't the type of rap that I wanted to pursue, but I was like, "Rather than going back to the streets, I can get my money the legal way." And that's what I chose to do.

You didn't love "Laffy Taffy"?

Not at first, but I grew to love it.

A hit's a hit.

Yup. A hit is a hit.

What were your goals when you went solo?

Basically, I didn't try to be happening like that; it just happened like that. I'm really a shy person. I was so shy in the beginning that it took me a minute to finally grow into myself and become the great artist that I am. My first mixtape was the "I'm Da Man" mixtape. Before that, I was getting about $1,500 a show. But when that came out, next thing I know I'm getting about $5,000 a show. That's just off "Let's Get It" and "I'm Da Man." I was eating *good*. That was great for me: coming into the rap game and not having major radio play, just clubs and the street. The next year rolled around, and I come with the "Dunn Dunn" and the "Dey Know" and the "Foolish," and before I ever even dropped an album I was getting over $20,000 a show. People were like, "Shawty Lo, that's the type of music we want to hear from you right there. We know your stuff's for real. We know you from Bankhead. We want to hear from you." So I kept recording and they were like, "Boy you got it! You the *one!*"

--

*THE-DREAM

--
Even if you don't know Terius Nash by his government name—or by his three groundbreaking solo R&B albums as The-Dream—you know his songwriting. In addition to his own hits, and radio staples over the last few years for Mariah Carey, Diddy, and Justin Bieber, Nash penned Rihanna's "Umbrella," and Beyoncé's "Single Ladies." In the Atlanta musical landscape, The-Dream represents the latest in a line of artists stretching from TLC to Usher to Lil Jon who transcended region ("The South") and genre ("urban music") to reimagine and redefine the sound of American pop. "Umbrella" and "Single Ladies" aren't just smash radio hits; they're instant pop-culture history, and two new entries in the national songbook (or at least the playlists of the nation's wedding DJs). In May of 2010, I caught The-Dream on the phone from The London Hotel in New York, where he was promoting his third solo album, Love King. His speaking voice is high and soft, with little cracks in it, as though he's always about to laugh.

I understand you grew up somewhere off Bankhead Highway. True?

That's right. They call it the West Side. The East Side is Decatur, of course, and the South Side is College Park. I grew up on a street called Bicker Road and went to Harper-Archer high school.

When did you start singing?

Let my auntie call it: she went to church a lot and if you were there, you sang. You didn't have to try. It wasn't like, "Hey, I'm the singer! Let's let it rip!" It was just a part of what went on. But singing didn't really start until the eleventh or twelfth grade, when I was a part of a singing group.

What was your group's name?

Oh wow, you're taking me back. We had a couple different names but Decision was one of them for some reason. I forgot how we came up with it.

Amazing. Were you a harmony group?

Definitely. In those days—1996, 1997—you had Boyz II Men out. Dru Hill was out. Jodeci had been out years prior to that and influenced a lot of us. So everything at the time was about harmony.

And I assume you must've danced, too.

Definitely. We did the whole shebang. You couldn't just go up there and Streisand it. The stage presentation, the celebration—it all had to go past just singing. Because everyone that's looking at you can dance—that was the culture. It was like, "You better show me something!"

Did y'all match your outfits up and all that?

Oh yeah. Looking back at it, we did all the corny stuff, but it was dope at that particular time. We was goin' in. Hard. I remember these CTK suits—jogging suits or whatever. That's what Puffy made popular. Puffy and Ma$e had the red ones, and we had different blues and reds. There was also the whole leather phase, the whole Jodeci thing. It was fun, man. It was always talent shows going on and I got a lot of first place trophies back at home.

Were you toying with original song-writing all the way back in high school?

No, I had no idea. That was the sneaky thing—I had no idea what I wanted to be when I grew up. At the time, art was more on my plate. I loved drawing. I was thinking more visually. I knew I had an imagination, but I wasn't thinking about writing songs, so it was a surprise. I didn't notice that was part of me—and that I was actually pretty damn good, too—until after high school.

It sounds like you fell into sing-ing and songwriting as much as you chose it. Take me through how that happened.

Well, I've been working nonstop since I was 13. My grandfather raised me and everything was about, "If you want something, you've got to go work for it." He was a cement mason, and he didn't have the abil-ity to imagine things beyond what he did. Things on TV was just things on TV to him. Not because he lacked imagination, but just because he was from a different generation—and we're in the South. There was just a disconnect: I'm quite sure a grand-father in the South and a grandfa-ther in New York City in the '80s probably had different ideas about whether you could be an entertainer. So when I was younger, it was just about having a job and getting my paycheck every Friday. I was work-ing towards a car, rims, a radio system.

Where'd you work?

Aw man, I worked everywhere. My first job was in a summer program in the eighth grade—I worked at a daycare center. I worked at Six Flags when I was sixteen. I worked at a maga-zine packing plant called The News Group that still exists today. I worked at Equifax, I worked at Dodge/Chrysler doing detailing and changing oil. I was taught that if you wanted something, you had to go to work. So whoever was paying most, that's where I went.

What were the first steps toward you getting a foothold in the music industry?

Before I even started writing, I already knew the structure of songs just from listening to Jodeci or R. Kelly. I knew what a verse was; I knew what a bridge was; I knew what a pre-chorus was; I know what a hook was. And right after high school, the group I was in was still to-gether and we started writing original songs together. We were just doing it for the fun of it, but sud-denly the people before us who did the same thing were riding around in Ferraris and Porsches. So it was like, "Hold up. You can do it like this, and ride around like that?" That's when I began to challenge myself. And I remember in September of 1998, after looking at *The Thomas Crown Affair*, I put a picture of the Bentley Arnage as the screensaver on my Compaq computer. A couple of my friends were like, "Yeah, you're definitely never getting that." But because of *The Thomas Crown Affair* I was like, "However he's living, I want to live like that." So I began to write lights out. I became possessed. From then on, I knew in my head where I was going.

Before you signed a deal as a solo artist were you writing and record-ing demos and passing them around? How does that system work for song-writers in Atlanta?

Everyone in Atlanta does music. It's not even a system, it's just all around you. It was so easy to run into Jermaine at that time; so easy to run into OutKast. It was like being in Hollywood and every car you look in—there's Steven Spielberg. And look over there! Denzel. That's what it was in Atlanta, and it's still like that right now.

The West Side of Atlanta is associ-ated with raw hip-hop: T.I. and Shawty Lo and guys like that. Was R&B always accepted right alongside rap?

I think it was just *music*. Even the bands in the South at the time—we were just musical. And rap was a part of that, too. Thing is, there were rappers in Atlanta before T.I. and before Jeezy and before OutKast, even. It was real songs down there! You may not remember him if you weren't from Atlanta—unless you remember him from Freaknik—but there was this guy Kilo. You know, "There's a white girl in town, name is cocaine . . . " I know it in my head, and when I hear it, I can remember the exact feeling of that time. So there were people putting songs together before the big names we know now. And that was the Atlanta blueprint. That's why it's shaped how it is today.

You still write songs for other people in addition to the songs you record yourself. Without getting you to fax me your tax returns, what's the difference for you financially?

At this stage, both are pretty lucrative. It's not that big of a gap. Of course, if you write a "Single Ladies," the money is going to be different than it is on a "Shawty Is A Ten." Definitely. But I got to write one "Single Ladies" for Beyoncé while I get to write thirteen or fourteen records for myself every year. So it catches up. Right now my publishing company is very happy about this "Baby" record on Justin Bieber.

I bet they are! I hear you live in Buckhead these days. What made you want to move there?

Everybody wants to move to Buckhead, whether they'll say it or not. And that's not just because it's where the rich white people stay. It's because it's the heart of the city—everything is there. If you're not in Buckhead, then you're gonna be in Alpharetta, and that's thirty minutes outside the city. That's not happening for me.

What do you mean when you say "everything's there"?

The malls, the restaurants, the feeling that you can just go right down the street and chill at the park or sit down and eat. Just regular stuff that, growing up, in our neighborhood, my mother couldn't do. That just

wasn't happening. So really it's just about wanting to advance.

I should say here that where I grew up wasn't as bad as it is now. When I was a kid, people like my grandfather and the other older people controlled the kids in the neighborhood and their attitudes and behavior. Back then, if somebody broke into your house, somebody knew about it, and they'd bring your shit back to you. It was a community thing, and that's way different than it is now.

But we've been seeing the houses in Buckhead for years. My grandfather used to drive through and point and say, "Now *that's* a house." And it was almost like a challenge. I could've grown up just wanting the same ole thing I'd seen in my youth, but he made it known that the things he got were bigger than the things he'd previously seen in his lifetime. He showed me the things that I needed to try to achieve—things that were bigger than what he had. So Buckhead is just where I stay.

Are you too busy most of the time to enjoy it?

I can enjoy it. I try to keep my homey vibe. That's who I am—I was the kid that grew up cutting the grass, and if I stay at the house I'm gonna be nailing things and painting walls and whatever else. That's what I do. Like, this Mother's Day, I went out for a drive. Of course, I lost my mother to cancer in '92. So I passed out my favorite wine to the mothers in the neighborhood.

What was their response?

They were like, "Wow! That's really nice!" They all know what I do even though they don't talk about it

very much. Their daughters all tell me, "I know what you do!" But they're dealing with this young guy that lives in this neighborhood where, most of these people, their fathers owned these houses and their grandfathers before them.

Did you already know your neighbors before going around on Mother's Day?

Oh, you know—this is Georgia. They'll wave when I go by and ask how I'm doing, and some have come by the house to bring me things or let me know what's going on in the community. But I was just driving around and if I passed a woman I'd stop and say, "Here you go. Happy Mother's Day!"
--

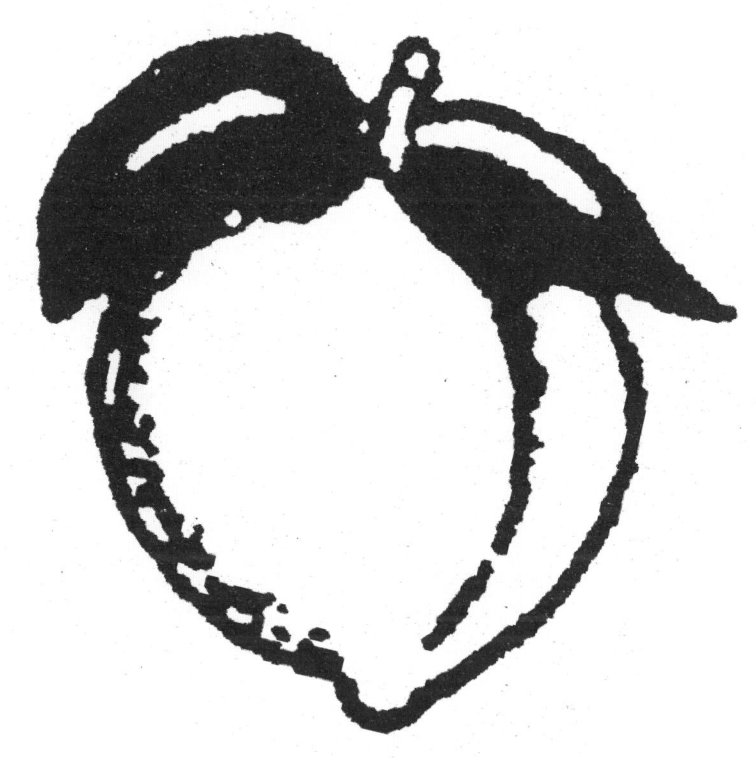

The first thing you do when you get to town is turn on the radio. You fly into Atlanta's Hartsfield-Jackson International Airport, a massive, sprawling structure that matches the sprawl of the city itself. You get into your rental car and put on Hot 107.9, put it in as a preset, and then do the same with V-103, "The People's Station."

In the twenty minutes it takes to get to Midtown, you've flipped between the two stations a dozen times and probably heard every song you'll hear for the next two weeks. Now you know at least half of what they're playing in the clubs, and what the person driving in the car next to you might be listening to. You'll probably get sick of those same ten songs, but that's okay, there's always gonna be a new song next week or next month that will feel like the biggest song in Atlanta, and the biggest song in the world.

This book started out as a conversation about music and photography. My friend Nick and I were trying to figure out an album that we could make a photo book out of. The idea was to make a book that reflected both the content of an album and the context in which the record was made. There were a couple of obvious choices, Terry Allen's *Juarez* or The Mountain Goats' *Tallahassee*. But we kept coming back to OutKast's 1998 record *Aquemini*, an album full of literal imagery and, undeniably, proudly, of a place: Atlanta.

The ghost of *Aquemini* hangs over this book. That record was my introduction to Atlanta—it plays like a piece of theater, or a novel, full of characters and back stories and vignettes and subplots. It was a road map: It told you everything, even what the weather was going to be like. The imagery is so specific, the way a photograph can be.

We wanted to dig into the not-too-distant past and investigate the making of the record, and at the same time photograph the current scene in Atlanta to find out where *Aquemini* was, where it fit in.

We went to the studios where *Aquemini* was recorded, interviewing the people involved, looking for traces of OutKast's music and identity in the music ten years later. We asked everyone we met about OutKast; everybody said that they had grown up listening to them, but you could never hear it in the music. Then we figured that we could look back on the record by looking deeper into what was happening now—looking back by looking forward. So we found kids who were the same age as André and Big Boi were when they were first making records— sixteen, seventeen, or just out of high school. There wasn't a trace of the sound of *Aquemini*—no live music at all, not much of an emphasis on lyrics—but the music and the spirit were just as good, and maybe more fun and more immediate anyway.

I was first drawn to Atlanta for its celebrities, but I found myself going back to photograph the unknown kids who were hustling to make it; looking for that moment right before things happen. There's this spirit of youth and ambition in Atlanta that makes the city so unique—and so interesting to document

The story was whatever was happening now (or then, in 2007). Soulja Boy was exploding, there were a thousand YouTube videos of kids dancing in their living rooms, beats and songs were being made on PCs and uploaded to SoundClick or SpitYoGame. Something new was happening. And something new kept happening, was always happening, keeps happening. The story of Atlanta hip-hop is whatever is happening right now.

Every year that I went back, the scene had shifted. The hairstyles changed, the clothes changed. Mohawks replaced dreads, American Eagle replaced Polo, rubber band chains and fake platinum chains were replaced by rosary beads. One year everyone's talking about Young Jeezy, or about T.I. going to jail, but by the time he's gotten out everyone's talking about Gucci Mane and the time he's doing.

But the old stuff will come back around. It won't be too long before people are sick of swag or trap or whatever comes next, and something else will get distilled from the Atlanta sound, borrowing from the past and the present. A year in Atlanta hip-hop is like five years in any other genre.

Late at night you leave the club smelling like Black & Milds, blunts, and perfume. They can still smoke in the bars down here. You drive around connecting the street names from songs you've heard: Campbellton Road, Headland and Delowe, Old National Highway, Bankhead. You get lost over and over again. There aren't any landmarks in Atlanta, no way to tell which way you're going. But there's always one of those nights when it all comes together and the city makes sense; there's a map of it in your head.

Back on the highway at 4 in the morning and on Q100, DJ Andre is playing techno remixes of Drake and Gucci Mane. In a couple hours, early Sunday morning, the hip-hop stations will be playing gospel 'til noon.
--
MICHAEL SCHMELLING

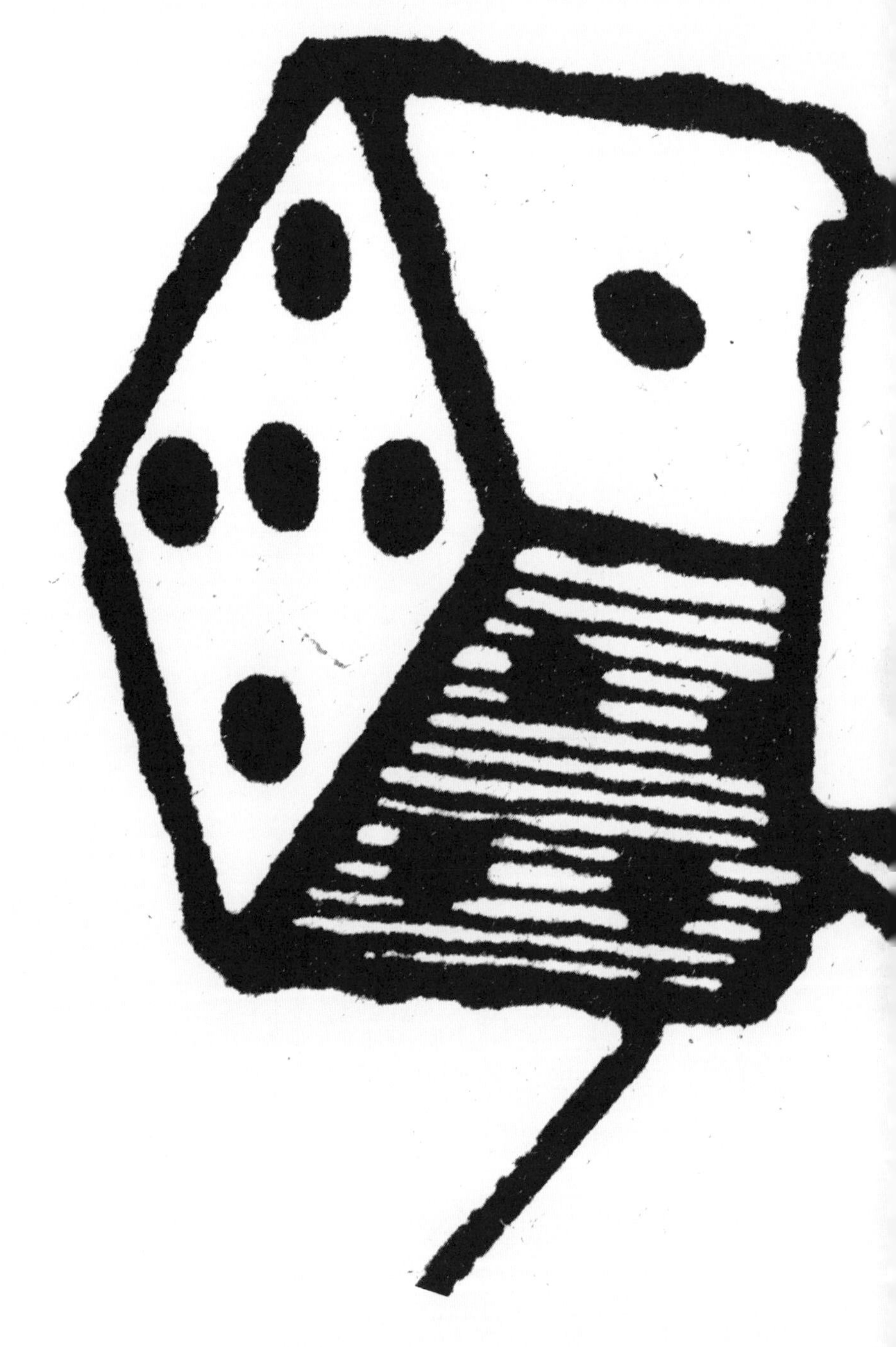

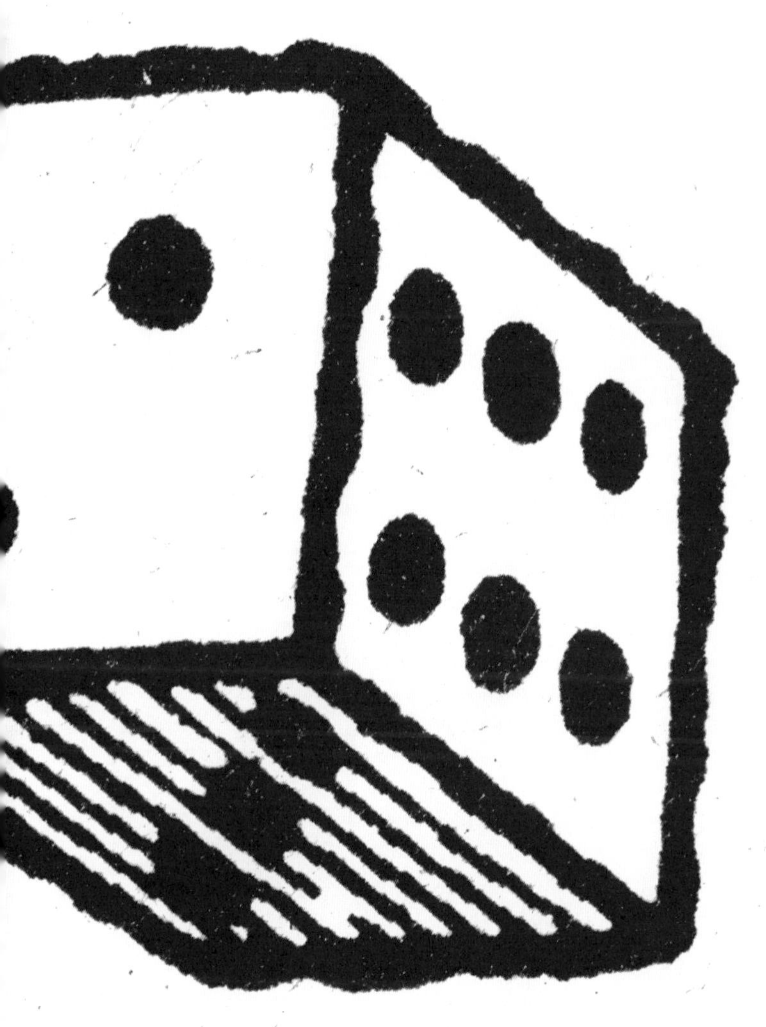

PLATES

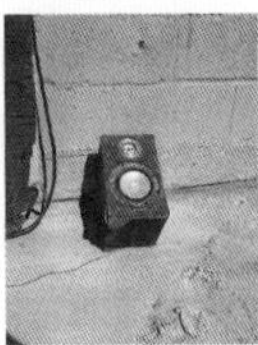

1. There was a barbecque stand near the corner of Joseph E. Lowery Boulevard and Martin Luther King Jr. Drive SW. A speaker leaned against the outside wall. Saturday afternoon, fall 2007.
--

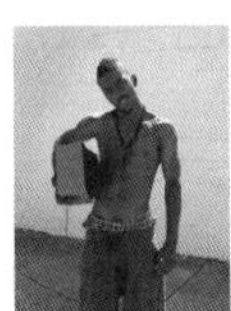

2. Strap pulled out an old speaker from the trunk of the car, July 2009, near Grant Park.
--

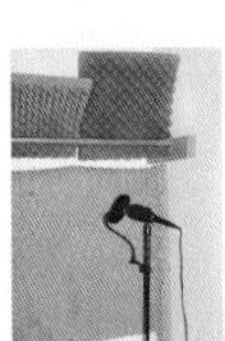

3. Almost every one of the home studios I went to had a closet lined with yellow foam that worked as a sound booth. It seemed like there were three steps to making music at home: get a PC, get a mic, get some foam.
--

4. Make a V or a peace sign, put your thumb between it. Turn it upside down, and it's an A.
--

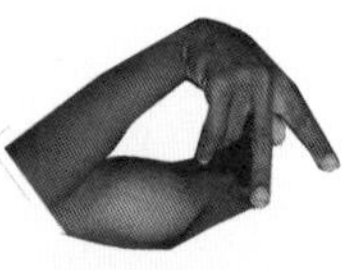

5. Map of Atlanta, 2010.
--

6. List of Street Names, 2010.
--

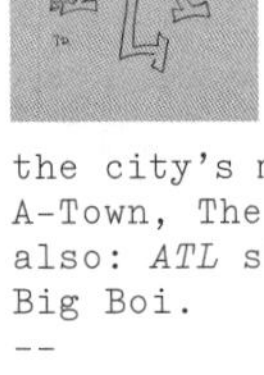

7. ATL graffiti in a gas station bathroom off I-20, probably the Candler Road exit. ATL is both the airport code and one of the city's many nicknames—A-Town, The A, The ATL. See also: *ATL* starring T.I. and Big Boi.
--

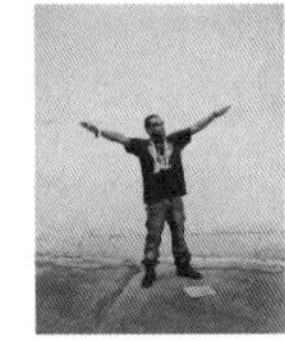

8. Shawty Lo, on Bankhead, Atlanta, 2007.
--

9. Lil Texas was living at his sister's place on the east side of Atlanta. She was in the military, stationed in Iraq. A real estate agent's lock was on the front door.
--

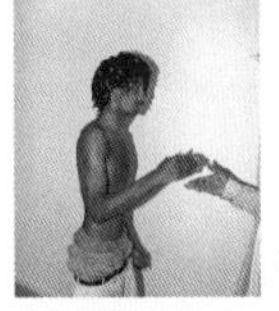

10. A poster-size photo of Rico Wade was propped up against a wall at the Dungeon West, a small studio in the basement of Rico's neo-colonial mansion on the west side. Rico is largely credited with discovering OutKast. There's a story about them taking the MARTA bus to the hair salon where Rico worked and rapping for him. See also: "Am I My Brother's Keeper? The Untold Story of the Dungeon Family," published in *Vibe*, January 2010.
--

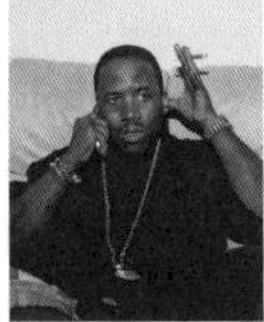

11. Witchdoctor signed a deal with Interscope Records in 1997. His debut record, *A S.W.A.T. Healin' Ritual,* sold 42,500 copies in 1998/99. Sweetwater Creek State Park, 2007.
--

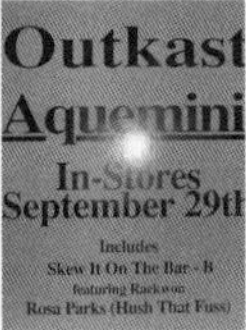

12. Big Boi, one-half of OutKast, in the VIP Lounge of the Body Tap, a strip club in west Atlanta, 2005.
--

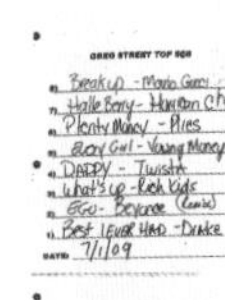

13. OutKast's third record, *Aquemini,* was released in September 1998. It peaked at #2 on the Billboard album charts and sold a million copies within two months.
--

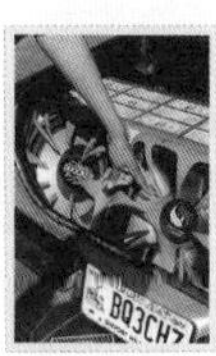

14. Every night, Greg Street plays the top eight songs of the day at 8 PM, on V-103.
--

15. The interior of Tilson's car was upholstered with bright green alligator skin and 371 consecutively numbered one-dollar bills. He didn't say why 371. The dollar bills were also laminated into the car's paint job with a polyurethane coating. Campbellton Road, 2010.
--

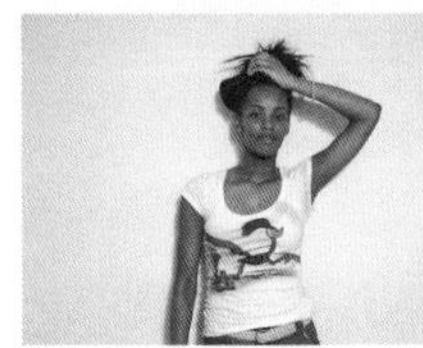

16. The three Roadrunner Girls were recruited by Darnik McAlpin, the producer of the track "Crank That Roadrunner." There's a video of them dancing to the song in his living room. It's been viewed 1,813,646 times on YouTube.
--

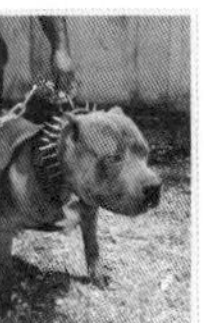
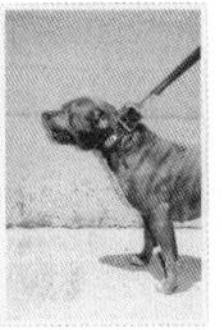

17. Pit bulls, 2008.
--

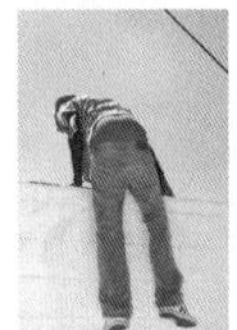

18. Quez, of Travis Porter, 2009.
--

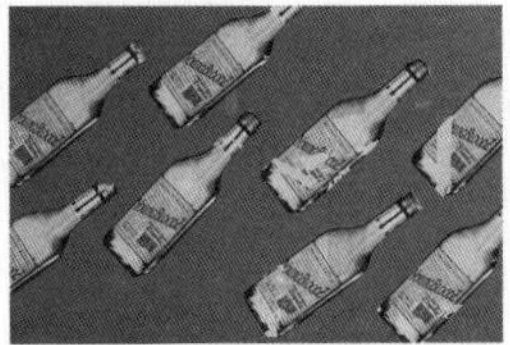

19. Promo stickers for YoungBloodZ's *Drankin' Patnaz,* released in 2003, at the mixtape store next to the Shell gas station off I-20 and Candler Road, 2008.

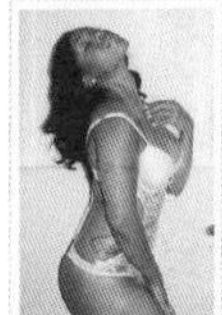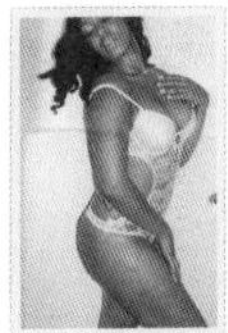

20. Barbie Bentley, Magic City, 2009.
--

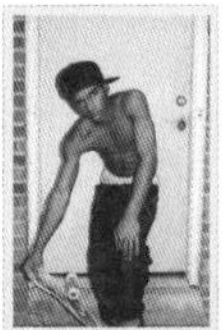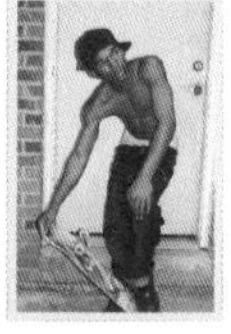

21. Gritz, summer 2009.
--

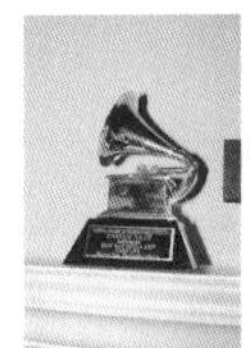

22. T-Pain's 2007 Grammy for cowriting Kanye West's "Good Life," north Atlanta suburbs, 2008.
--

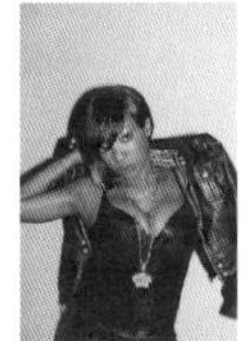

23. Bola, a.k.a. the Black Betty Boop, signed a deal with Grand Hustle when she was fifteen. West side, summer 2009.
--

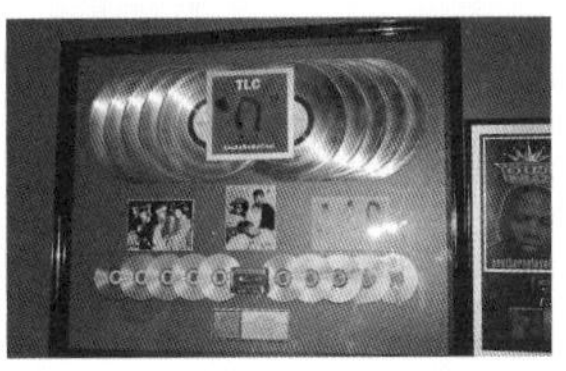

24. By the end of 1995, TLC had sold over five million copies of *Crazy-SexyCool*. The Dungeon East, Decatur, 2007.
--

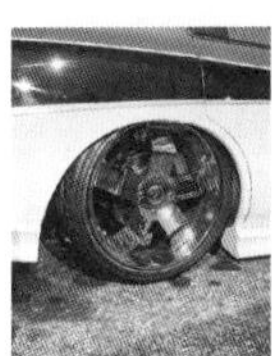

25. Jonesboro, Georgia, 2007.

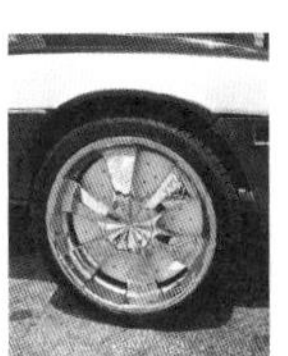

26. University Avenue, Atlanta, 2008.
--

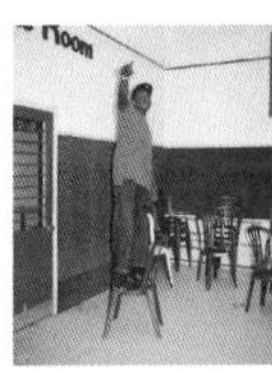

27. Cash Camp did a quick show at the skate rink. The DJ played a couple of their songs, and they rapped along. Kids crowded the stage and stood on chairs to see. All American Skate, summer 2007.
--

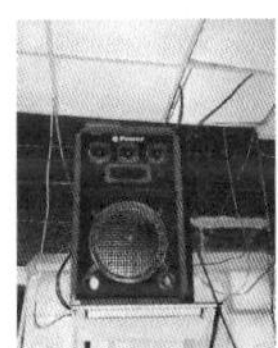

28. The Speakeasy Lounge, University Avenue, 2008.
--

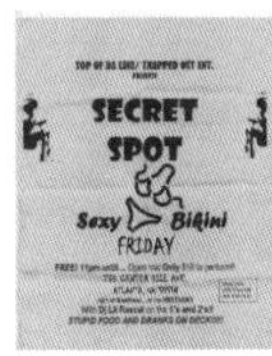

29. Flyer for the Secret Spot, near Bankhead Highway and Hollywood Road, west Atlanta.

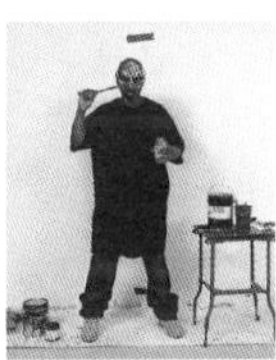

30. People in Atlanta talk about rap's "otherground," hip-hop that comes out of Atlanta but doesn't necessarily fit in with the mainstream rap scene. MF Doom, at his friend's art studio on Howell Mill Road, 2005.
--

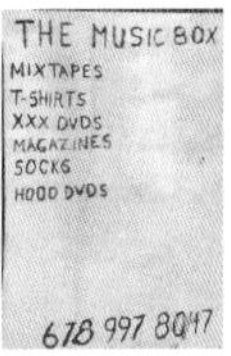

31. J.R. got his start selling mixtapes out of an old shipping container right next to the gas station at I-285 and Bankhead Highway. He moved into a store in a strip mall not far from there in 2009.
--

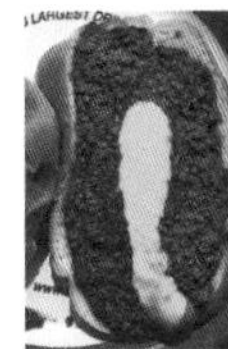

32. The Varsity's Heavy Dog, 2009. See also: the Chili Cheese Slaw Dog at the Varsity and the chili slaw dog at the Oasis Market on Ellsworth Industrial Drive and Chattahoochee Avenue.
--

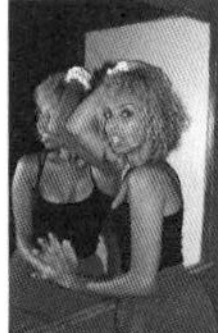

33. Christina's friend had a birthday party at an old recording studio on Hank Aaron Blvd., not far from downtown. I took some pictures of her and her friends out front as they were leaving. They put their shoes up on the bouncer's stool so that I could get a photo of their stilettos.
--

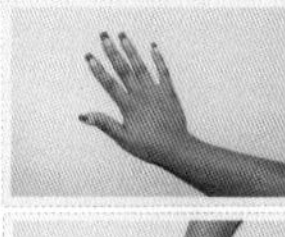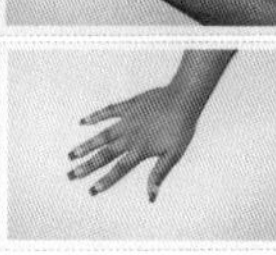

34. Painted fingernails, Fusion, 2009.
--

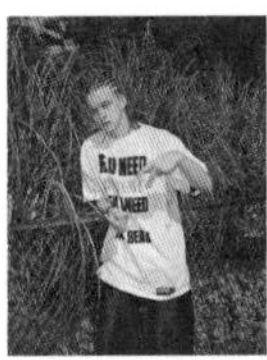

35. Big Boi and his brother James Patton opened a pit bull kennel in Fayetteville.
--

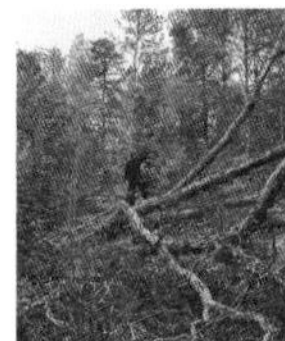

36. Beau Ritter is a twenty-year-old producer and aspiring mogul, the CEO of Outta Control Entertainment. He almost always wears a T-shirt that says "IF U NEED A BEAT DEN U NEED TO CALL BEAU."
--

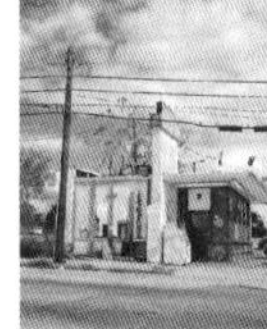

37. Ray Murray is one-third of Organized Noize (along with Rico Wade and Sleepy Brown), the production team that produced/coproduced OutKast's first three records, as well as Goodie Mob's *Soul Food*. He runs the Dungeon East, a Studio near Decatur, where parts of *Aquemini* were recorded.
--

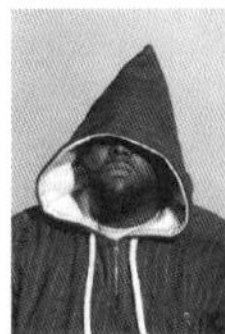

38. King's Food Mart, McDaniel Street, west side, 2007.
--

39. Killer Mike, aka Mike Bigga, 2009.
--

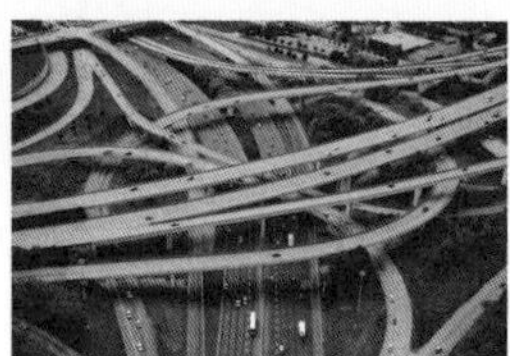

40. I-85/I-75 North/ South meets I-20 East/ West. Atlanta has the fourth worst traffic in the country.
--

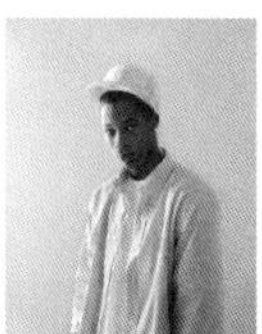

41. Ricardo had just gotten out of jail that day. Fall 2007.
--

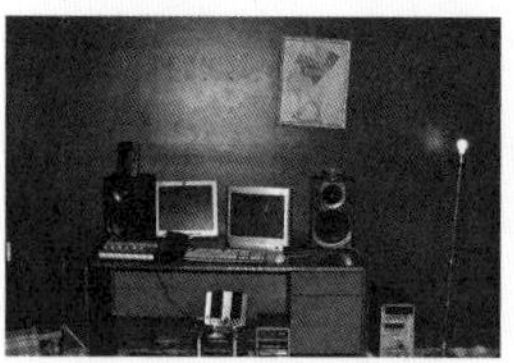

42. Qint and Gritz record out of the back room of Gritz's mother's house on the east side of Atlanta. A Bic pen was stuck in the wall, holding up a crucifix.
--

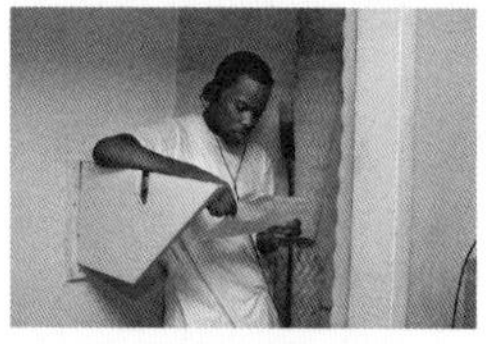

43. Midnight took the door off the hinges and propped it up against the wall. KB got in the booth and put on the head- phones. Midnight restarted the computer and cued up a beat for a song they'd been working on. You could hear a tinny rhythm coming from the headphones.
--

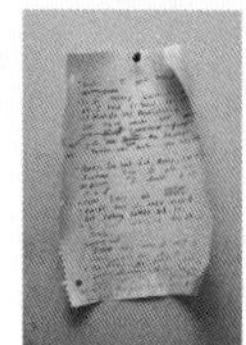

44. KB, Kawan, and Midnight formed 3rd Degree in high school in 2007. Midnight makes most of the beats using Adobe Audition; they record in his bedroom at his sister's place.
--

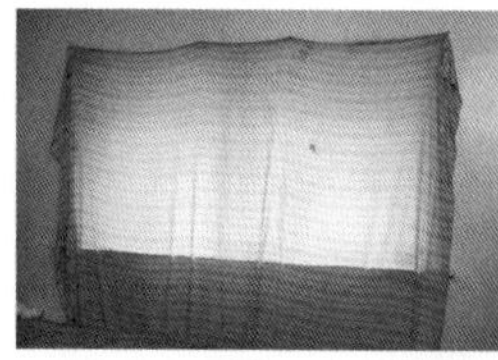

45. The sheet, or the blanket, goes over the window to absorb the sound, and to keep people from looking in.
--

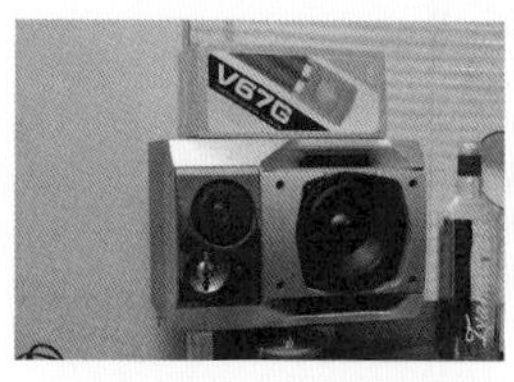

46. The V67G condenser mic costs about a hundred dollars.
--

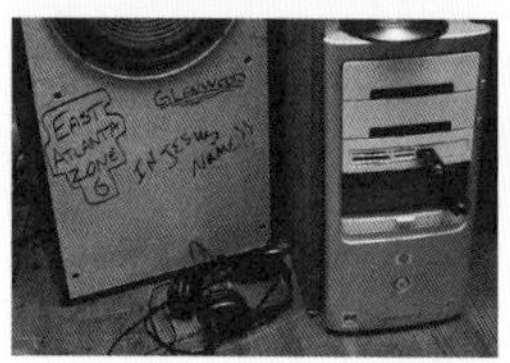

47. Atlanta's police precincts are divided into six separate patrol zones. People say they're from a certain zone, the way you would say what neighborhood you're from.
--

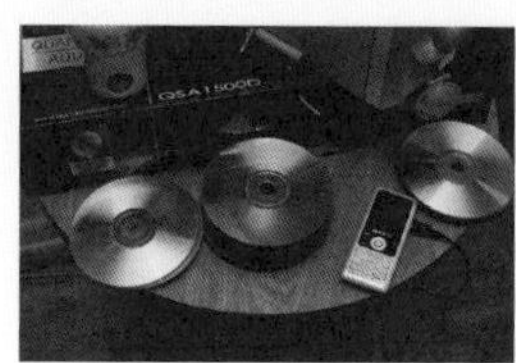

48. Vinyl gave way to tapes, tapes gave way to CDs, CDs gave way to jump drives and iPods.
--

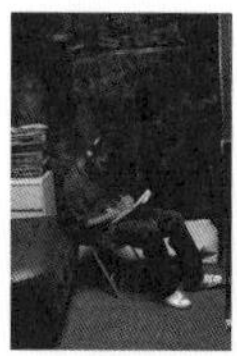

49. Paper Boi lives in a recording studio in East Point.
--

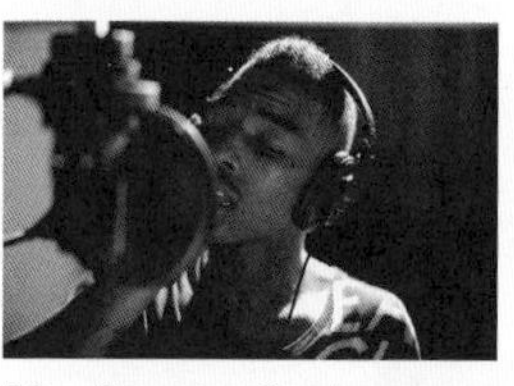

50. Travis Porter recorded their third mixtape at another unassuming office park studio on the north side.
--

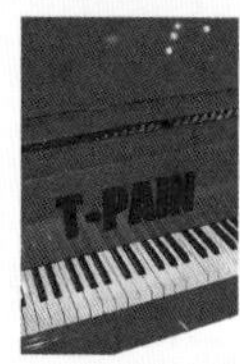

51. T-Pain had a red room in his new house. Red couches, and a red piano so new you could smell the paint.
--

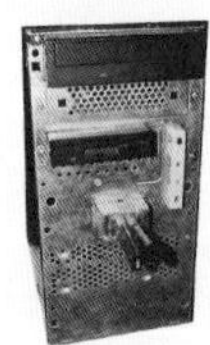

52. Qint built a hard drive tower out of old computer parts in high school.
--

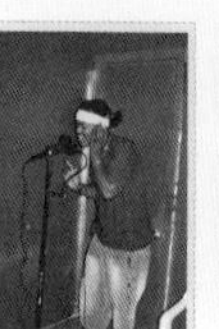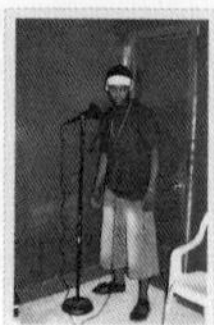

53. Qint was freestyling over a beat coming out of the speakers on the desk. It was so loud in there, Gritz's baby brother, or nephew, kept wandering in, in his diaper. Gritz would pick him up and put him in the other room, but a couple minutes later he'd come back in. Eventually, Gritz got fed up and shut the studio down for the day.
--

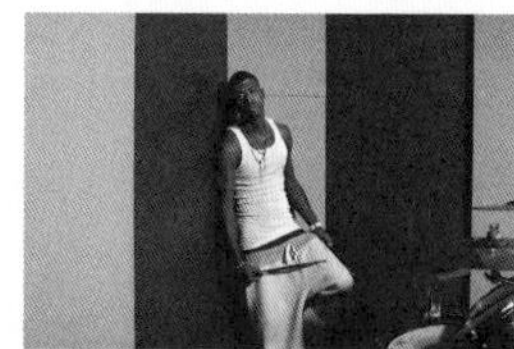

54. Yung LA's "Aint I" was one of the biggest songs of 2009. Grand Hustle Studios, summer 2009.
--

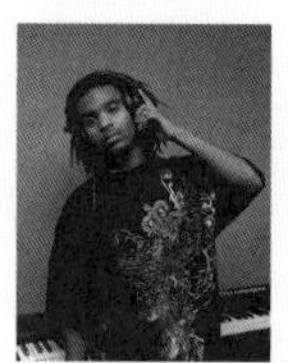

55. Cash Camp was recording at an old office building in Decatur in the summer of 2007. They started out as Soulja Boy's dancers and then had a huge YouTube hit of their own with "Crank That Yank." In the video, the four of them are dancing in a parking lot, each one of them wearing an oversize white T-shirt with an ace, club, heart, or diamond on it. It has 4,839,692 views on YouTube.
--

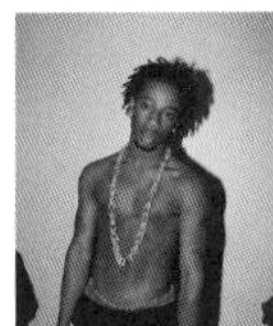

56. Young Jit went solo after Cash Camp broke up.
--

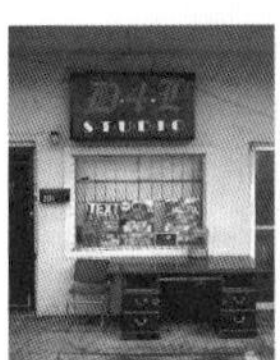

57. East Point, 2009.
--

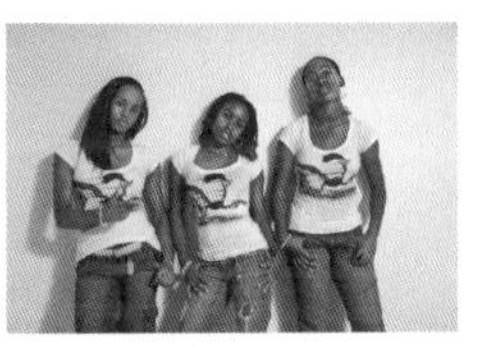

58. D4L's "Laffy Taffy" went #1 in 2006. For a while the group had a store-front studio on Bankhead, across the street from the Poole Palace.
--

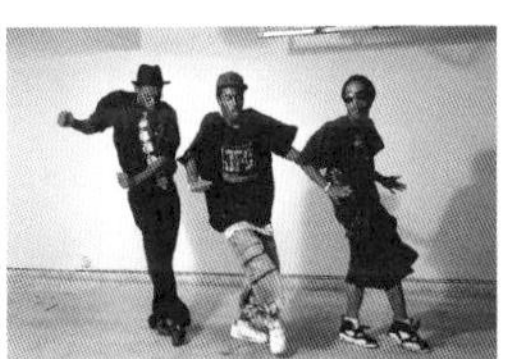

59. The living room looked exactly like the video: beige walls, a light brown rug, and a huge banner for 2 Bold Entertainment that filled the back wall. It was like being on the set of a famous TV show. For the photos, the girls had gotten matching Roadrunner shirts made at the mall.
--

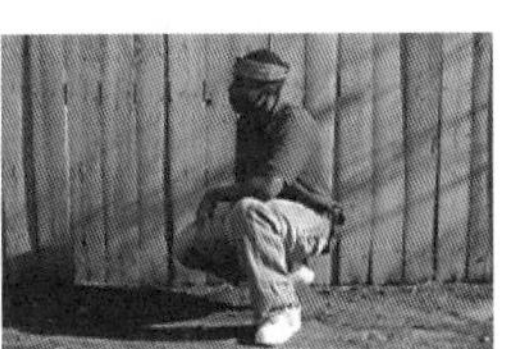

60. The Animations dance crew, 2007.
--

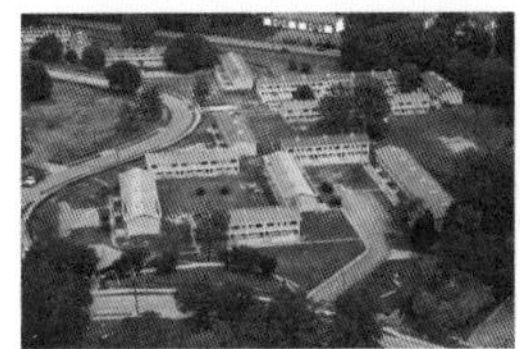

61. Bowen Homes, fall 2009.
--

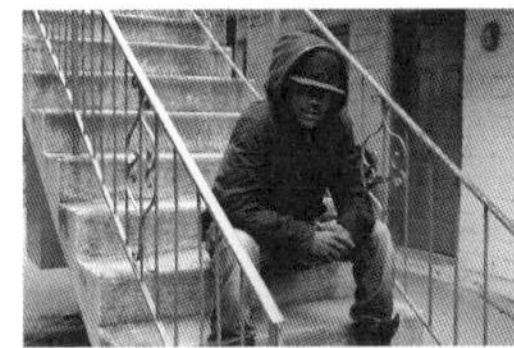

62. Pill walked around his old neighborhood on Auburn Avenue. He'd recently been getting some attention for the video for his song "Trap Goin' Ham." Auburn Ave—"Sweet Auburn"—was the heart of black Atlanta from the late 1800s until the 1960s.
--

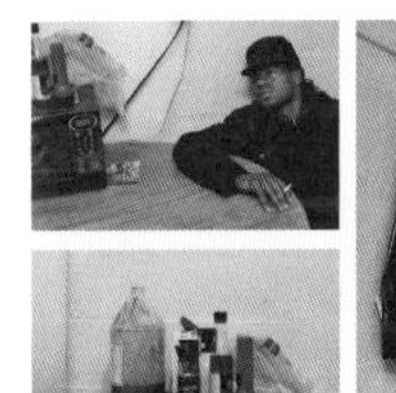

63. A crate of pit bull puppies was in the living room and a giant fake hundred-dollar bill was hanging above the doorway. They cleared the drugs off the kitchen table before you started taking photos. There was a guy with a gun in his pocket and a home-made 4th Ward tattoo on his arm standing next to you.
--

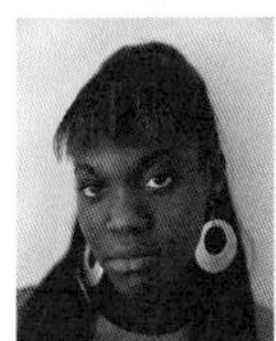

64. Lindsey was part of the all-girl C.A.T. Squad in High School. "Keep Poppin Like Bubblegum" has 1,500 plays on their MySpace page, but no one has logged in since 2008.
--

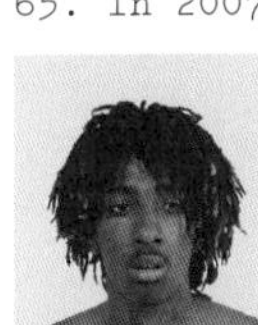

65. In 2007, Lil Texas recorded "From Da A," "On Goose," "Imma Homicide Boi," and a bunch of other amazing homemade songs for a demo tape. He signed a small label deal for fifteen grand, but it went nowhere.
--

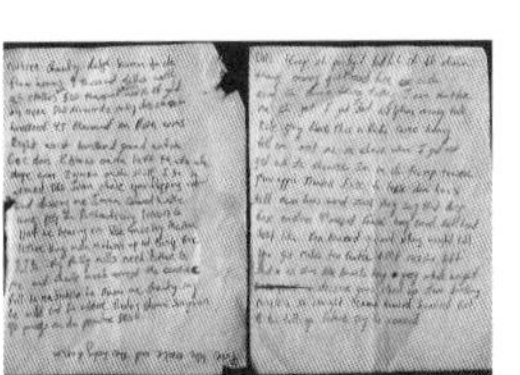

66. Young Dro's lyric sheets, Grand Hustle Studios, 2009.
--

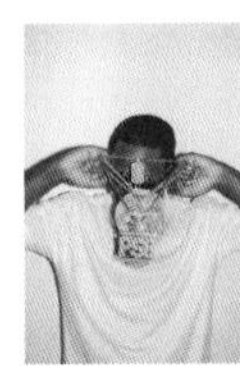

67. Young Dro, 2009.
--

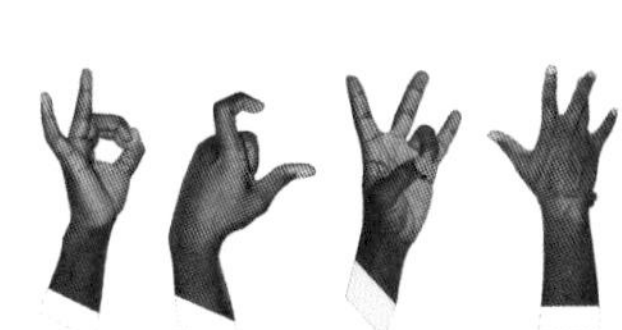

68. Various sets, 2008.
--

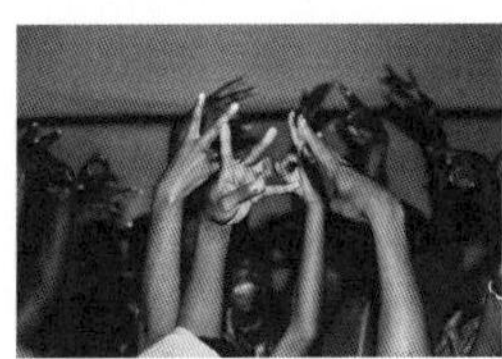

69. A couple of songs always make the place go crazy. Everyone starts throwing their set up, and before long a fight breaks out. It happens almost every time.
--

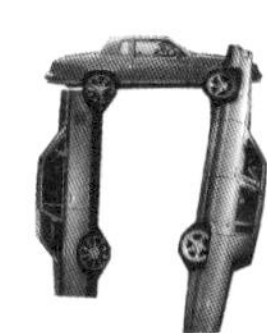

70. *Car Collage #1, 2010.*
--

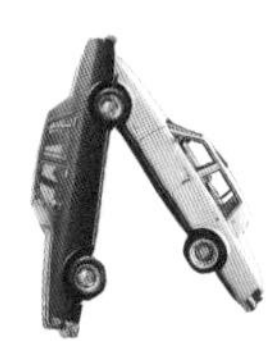

71. *Car Collage #2, 2010*
--.

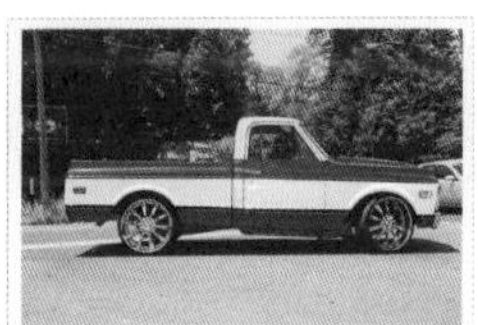

72. Early '70s Chevrolet Custom.
--

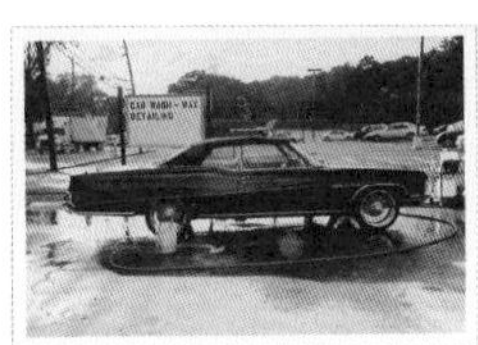

73. 1969 Buick Electra 235 Convertible.
--

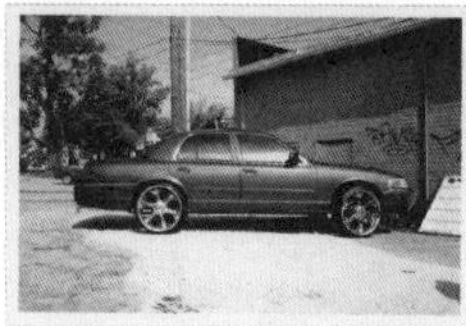

74. Late '90s Ford Crown Victoria.
--

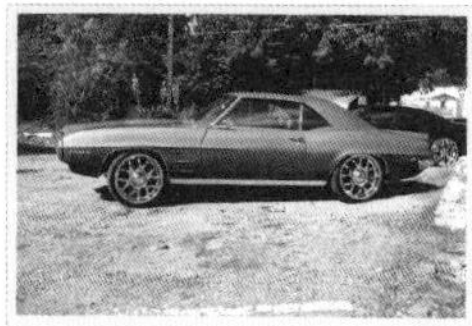

75. Late '60s Pontiac Firebird.
--

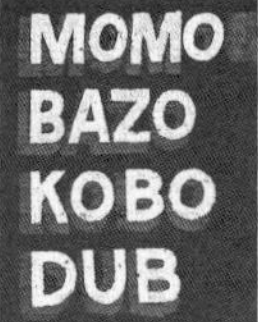

76. A list of rim brands was painted on the wall of a rim-and-tire shop at the corner of Memorial Drive and Moreland Avenue.
--

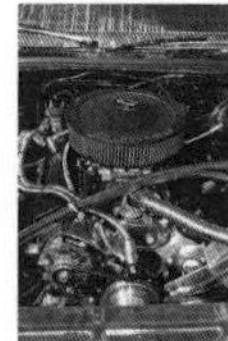

77. Chevy engine, Campbellton Road, 2010.
--

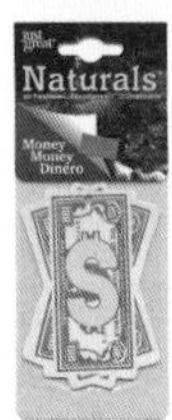

78. Money-scented air freshener, 2008. Yung Ralph's got a song called "Look Like Money" that goes, "'Cause I look like money, smell like money, talk like money, even walk like money."
--

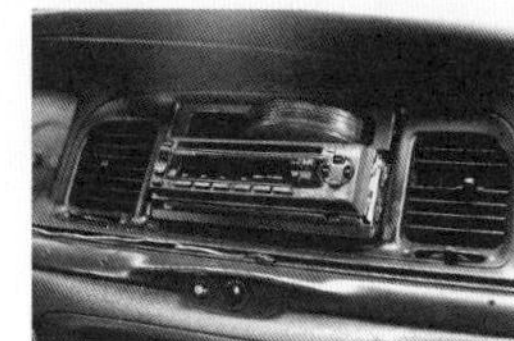

79. CDs got stacked on top of the Kenwood stereo in Midnight's black Crown Vic.
--

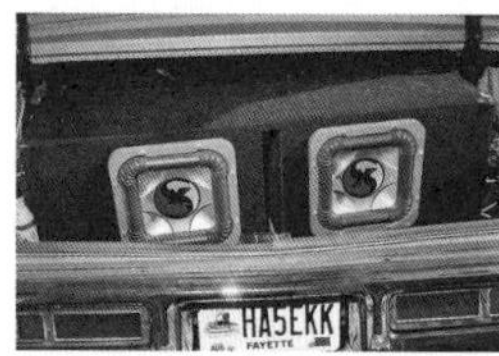

80. A subwoofer in the trunk.
--

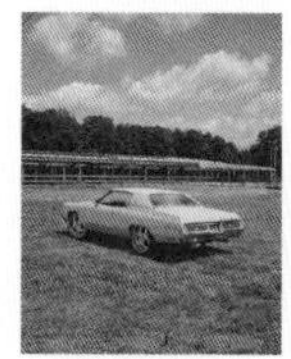

81. Early '70s yellow Chevy Impala.
--

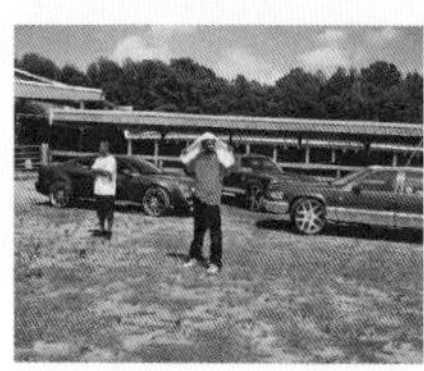

82. Car contest at Ben Hill Day, Ben Hill, Atlanta, 2008.
--

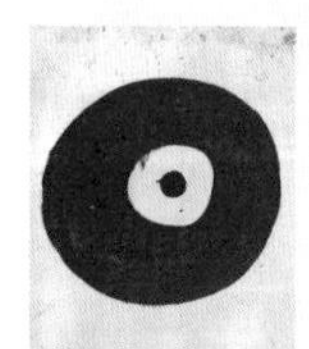

83. Tire and/or record, Bankhead, 2009.
--

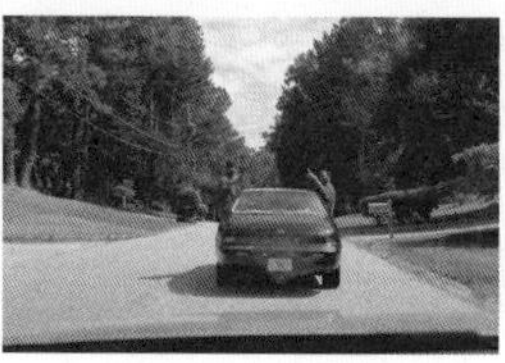

84. Qint and Gritz ghosted the Infinity J30 down side streets on the way to Stonecrest Mall. They walked around the mall and posed for photos in front of their favorite stores. Eventually, we were asked to leave.
--

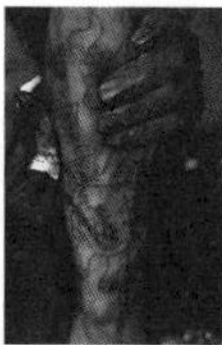

85. The tattoo artist said the biggest tattoos in the last couple of years were musical notes, stars, money bags, and, of course, the Atlanta Braves *A*.
--

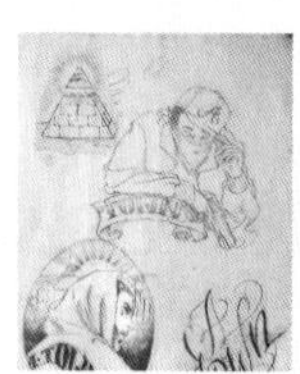

86. The pyramid might as well be an *A*, too.
--

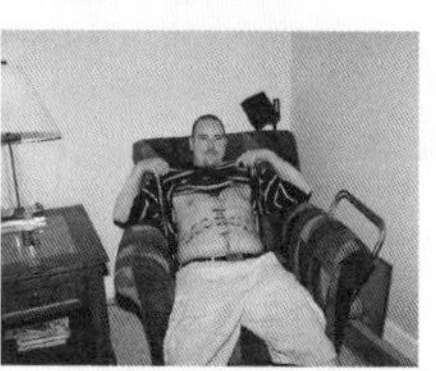

87. Bubba Sparxxx told the magazine writer that if his next record didn't go platinum, he'd retire.
--

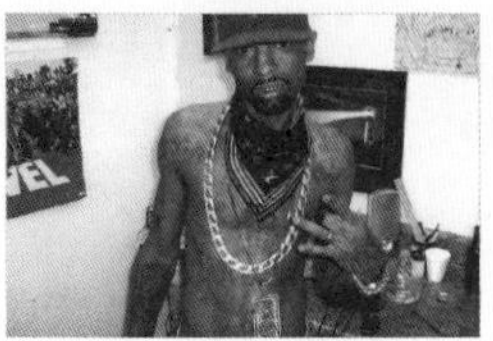

88. Money had his photo taken with Lil Wayne's chain on. He moved from New Orleans to Atlanta and opened up Permanent Emotions Tattoos in College Park. Later, he changed the name to Mardi Gras Tattoos.
--

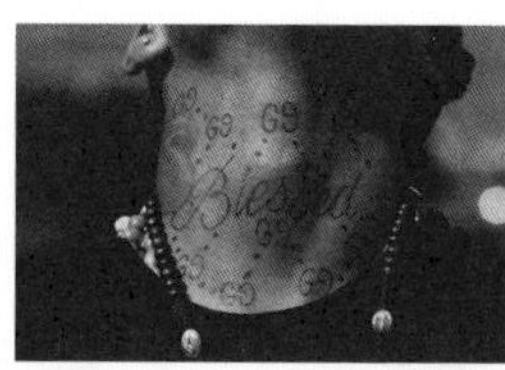

89. The Rich Kids showed up with two new Camaros and lots of brand-new tattoos. Juney's neck was tattooed like a Gucci bag. He was sixteen.
--

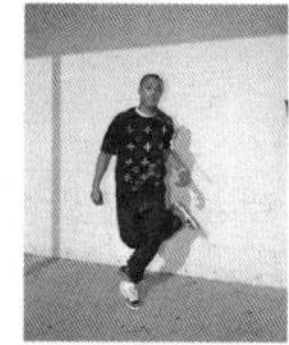

90. Young G had a YouTube hit with "Crank Dat Spongebob," possibly the fastest and most complicated of the crank dances that came out in 2007. It seemed like there was a new dance every day that summer. After Soulja Boy's "Crank Dat Superman" became a hit, a rash of new dances followed: "Crank Dat Peter Pan," "Crank Dat Spiderman," "Crank Dat Batman," "Crank Dat Roosevelt," "Crank Dat Forrest Gump, "Crank Dat Lion King," and so on.
--

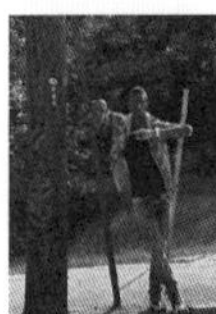

91. Baby Kaelub, summer, 2009.

--

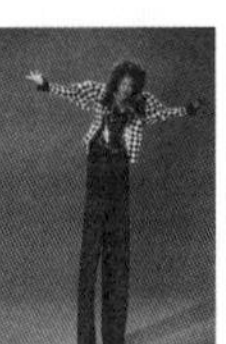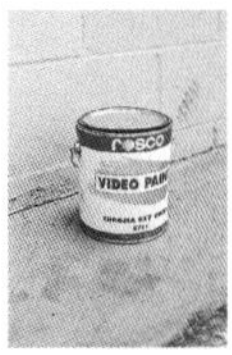

92. We were flown out from Atlanta. They shot the video on a sound stage in LA. The crew painted everything green. A circus crew was hired—tumblers, contortionists, a woman on stilts, and a juggling clown.

--

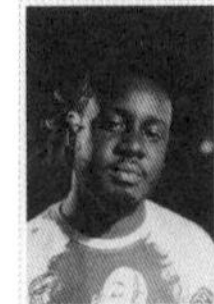

93. T-Pain, July 2008.

--

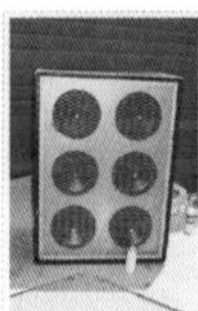

94. Fake speakers, 2008.

--

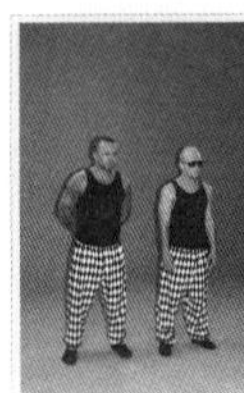

95. Acrobats, 2008.

--

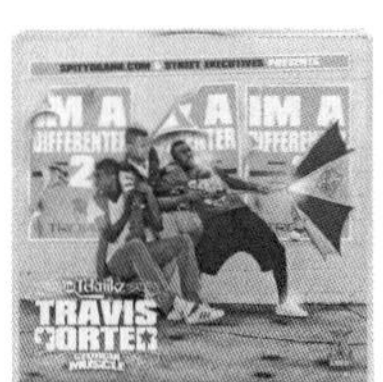

96. The idea was to have the mixtape cover look like the poster for that Paul Rudd movie *Role Models*. CEO Charlie was telling me this over the phone. Paul Rudd is taking a piss on a wall, and the other dude, Seann William Scott, is sitting on a curb drinking a beer. So I found a white wall, and we shot something like that, with a third guy hanging off the top of the wall. The umbrella stuff looked better in the end. I gave Charlie the files, and he sent them off to a kid in Florida who does mixtape designs for a hundred bucks.

--

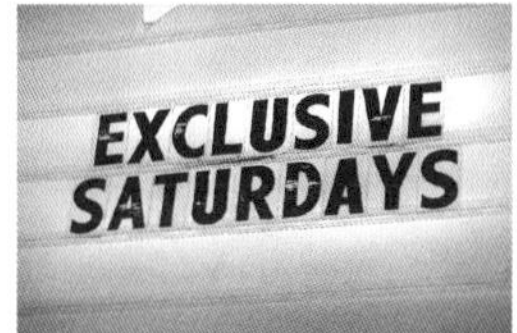

97. Exclusive Saturdays, Two Dollar Tuesdays, Magic City Mondays, Bitch Slap Thursdays, Thirsty Thursdays, Pin Up Sundays.

--

98. *List Of Club Names*, 2010.

--

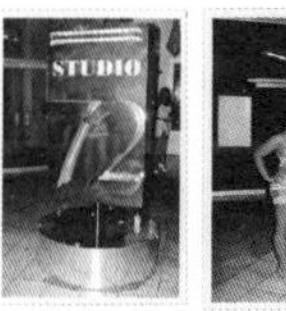

99. The Billionaire Boys hosted a party at Studio 72 every Friday. Birthday parties in the VIP section, a DJ booth crowded with girls in dresses. It seemed like Grey Goose vodka was the only thing anyone was drinking.

--

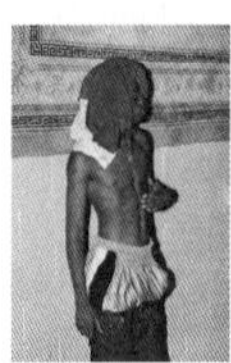

100. Club Fusion, or Fusion, isn't necessarily a club, just the name of the party that's being thrown by the promoters. It happened every Sunday night all summer and then every Saturday night when school started again.

--

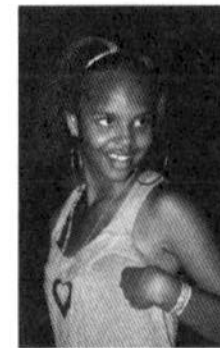

101. Club Lonestar was a cavernous old bar in the back courtyard of a semi-defunct mall out west on Memorial Drive in Stone Mountain. Lil Thrax and another young promoter named Meatball threw some birthday parties out there. By fall of 2009, the club had moved to Buford Highway and the name was changed to Lonestar North.

--

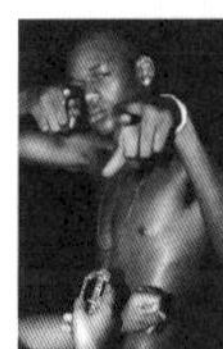

102. Fusion, 2009.

--

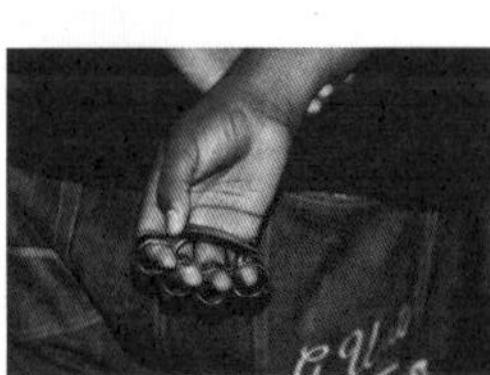

103. Fusion, 2009.

--

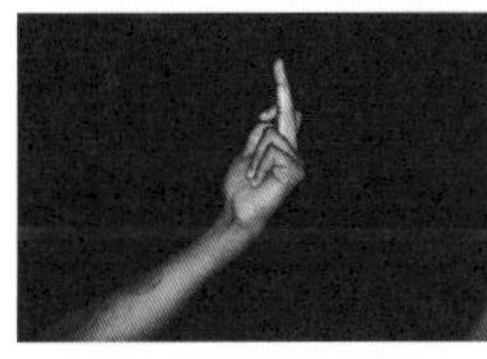

104. Club Caliente, Jimmy Carter Boulevard, Norcross, 2009.

--

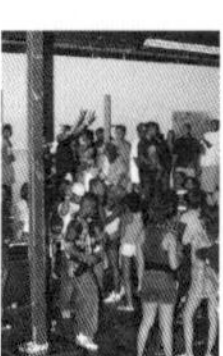

105. Club Lonestar, "Swagg and Surf Affair," hosted by Lil Thrax and Cash Camp, mid-July, 2009.

--

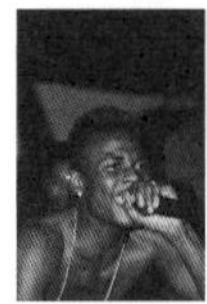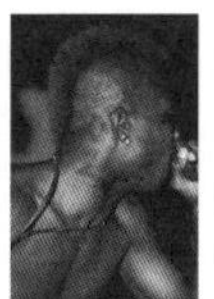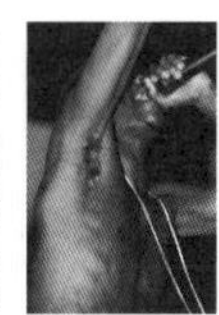

106. Lil Jit of CTC, a.k.a. Certified, playing a show at Lonestar, 2009.

--

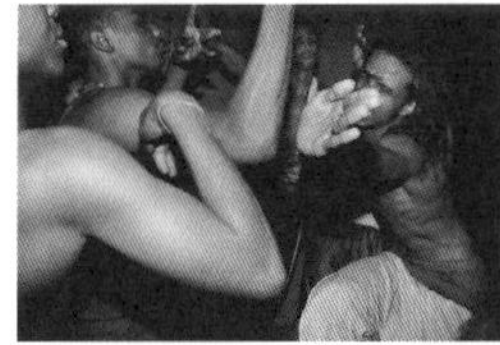

107. Fusion/ The Black Out, 2009.

--

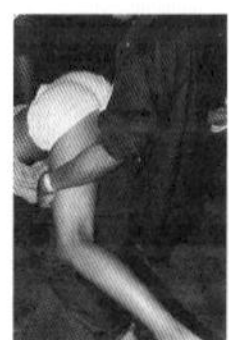

108. Lonestar, 2009.

--

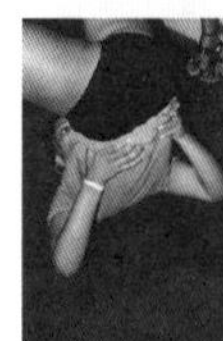

109. Studio 72, 2009.

--

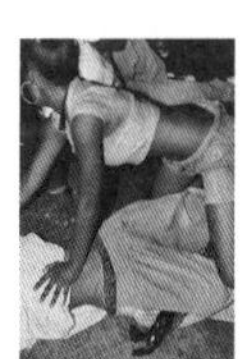

110. Lonestar, 2009.

--

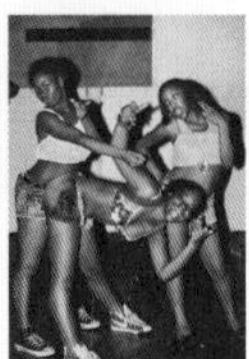

111. Fusion, 2009.
--

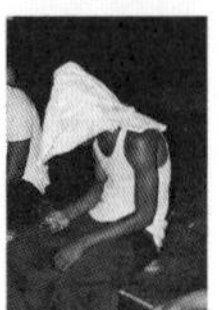

112. Lonestar, 2009.
--

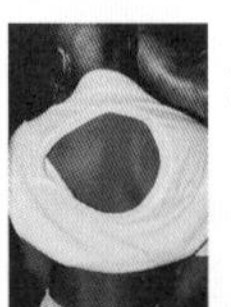

113. Fusion, 2009.
--

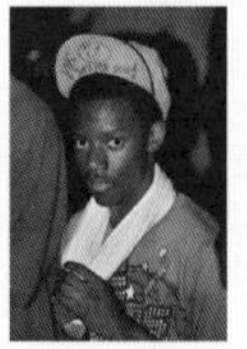

114. Caliente, 2009.
--

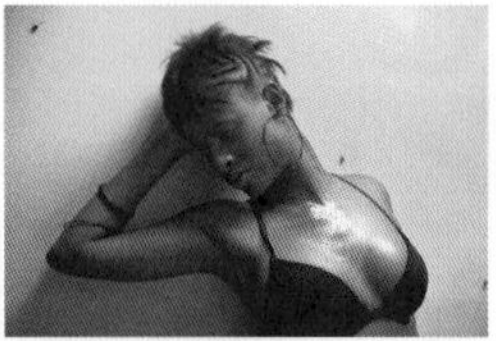

115. Fusion, 2009.
--

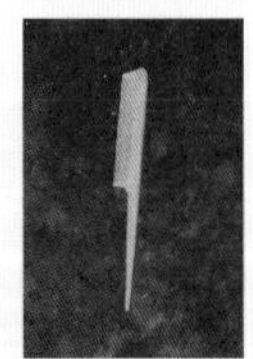

116. Club Crucial, 2010.
--

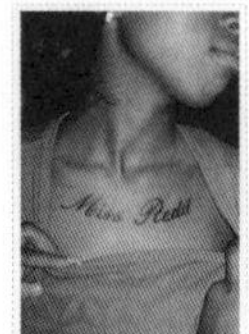

117. The girls who worked at the skate rink showed off their tattoos, and one of them said, "Take a picture of my booty."
--

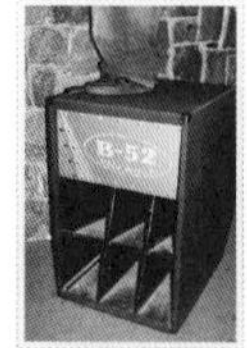
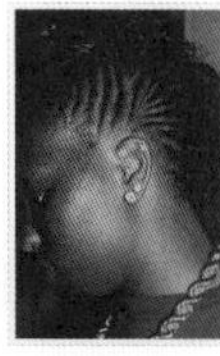

118. All American Skate, 2008.
--

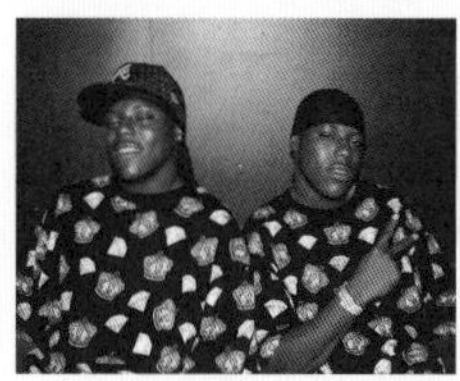

119. In 2006 or 2007, Club Crunk opened up on Moreland Avenue in Avondale Estates. It was a huge old furniture warehouse painted black and red, impossible to fill. A year later the name was changed to Club ICE, and the whole place was painted white. The year after that it closed.
--

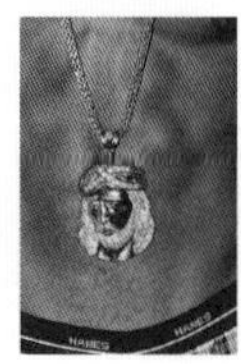

120. Fusion, 2009.
--

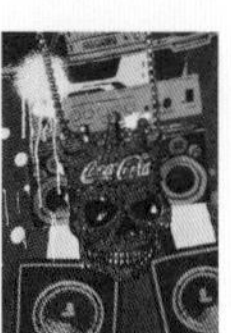

121. Lonestar, 2009.
--

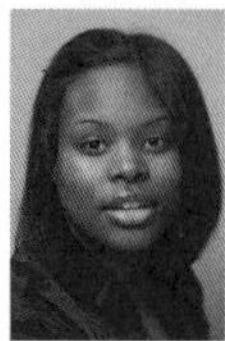

122. There's a constant stream of kids coming in and out of the ad hoc lobby at Fusion. They're catching some air, or fixing their hair before security gets them to move back into the club or out the door.
--

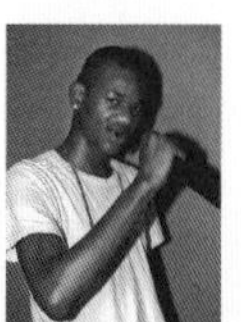

123. Dominique, 2009.
--

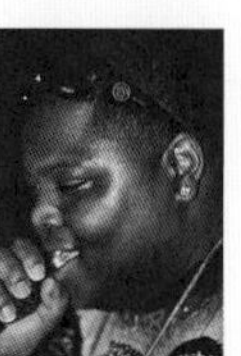

124. Caliente, 2009.
--

125. Lonestar VIP Room, 2009.
--

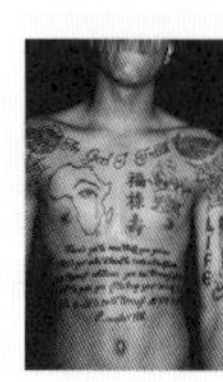

126. Club Hollywood, 2008.
--

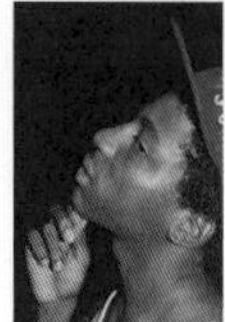

127. The first time I went to Club Caliente in 2008, most of Black Mobb was there, twenty or more, running the place. A year later, I showed all the photos from that night to KB. He said almost every one of them was in jail or had moved away. The cops cracked down hard on Black Mobb. It was always hard to tell if Black Mobb was a rap crew or a gang. They all had matching jackets. KB's aunt threw his away when the cops came looking for him.
--

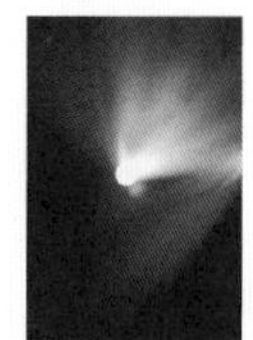

128. Club lights, 2009.
--

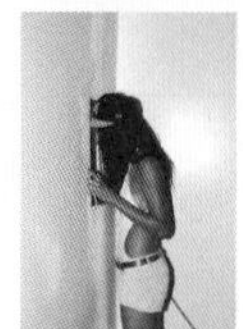
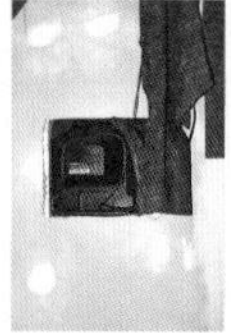

129. The bartenders at the high school parties just serve water and soda, but mostly nothing at all. Lonestar, 2009.
--

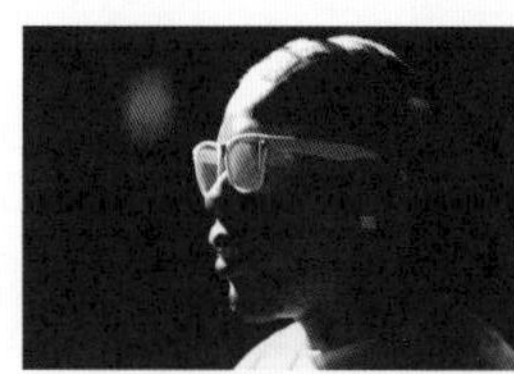

130. G-Baby, Lonestar, 2009.
--

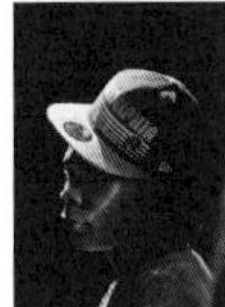

131. Kissinger, Lonestar, 2009.
--

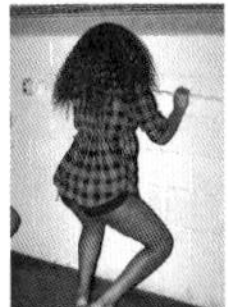

132. Fusion, 2009.
--

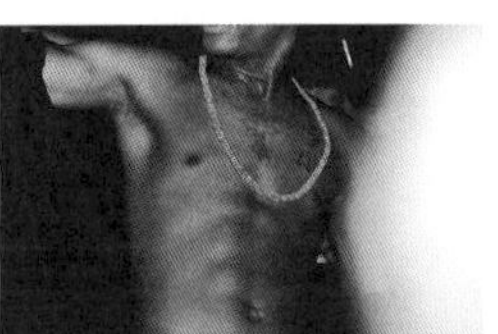

133. Lonestar, 2009.
--

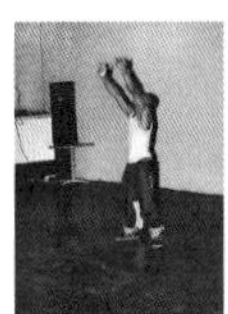

134. Fusion, 2009.
--

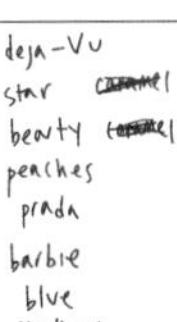

135. *List of Stripper Names*, 2010.
--

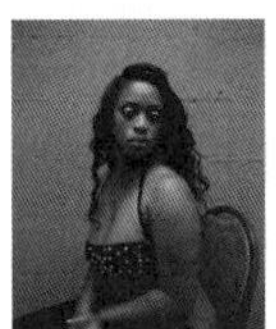

136. Star worked at the Body Tap in 2008 and then at Magic City in 2009.
--

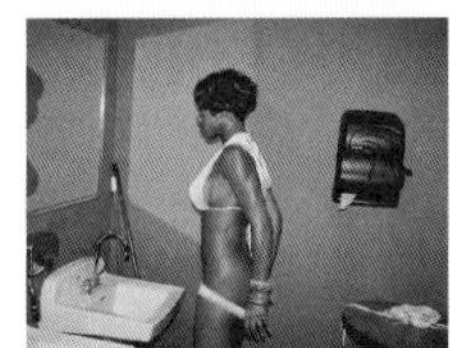

137. Keisha, in the dressing room at The Body Tap, 2008.
--

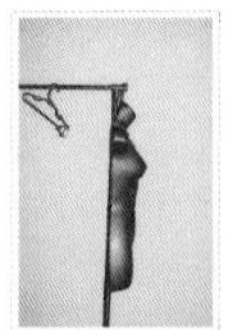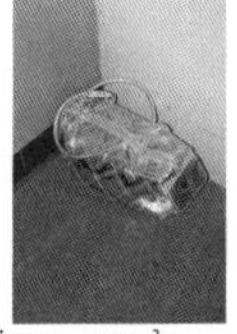

138. Clothing rack and purse, The Body Tap, 2008.
--

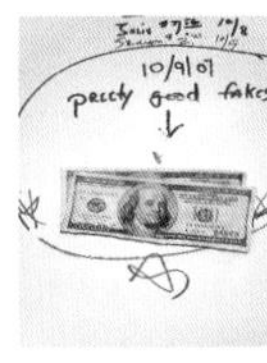

139. Someone passed a couple of fake hun-dred-dollar bills at Magic City, 2008.
--

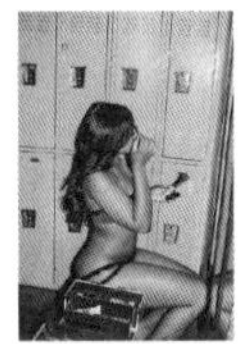

140. Prada, Magic City, 2009.
--

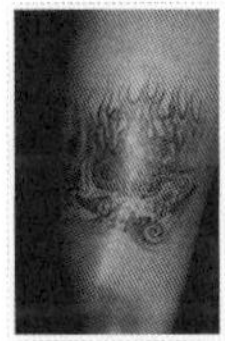

141. Beauty, 2008.
--

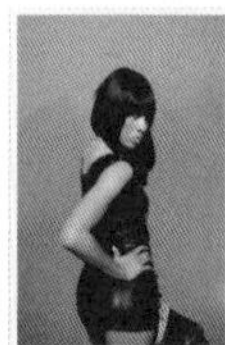

142. Luckie, 2008.
--

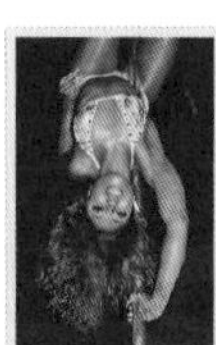

143. The Body Tap closed in 2010. It's now called Stacks.
--

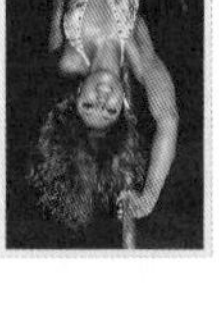

144. The Body Tap, 2008.
--

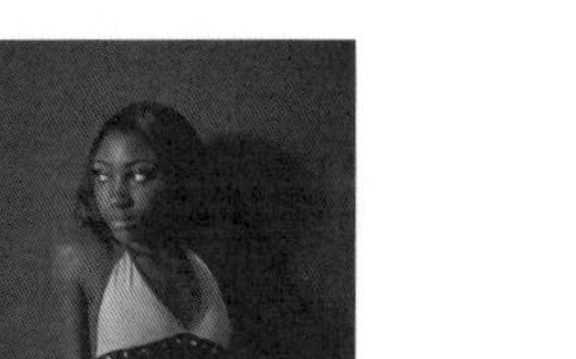

145. Lions Den was the name of one of the VIP rooms at the Body Tap. There's a picture of another neon sign from the club that says "Platinum Level."
--

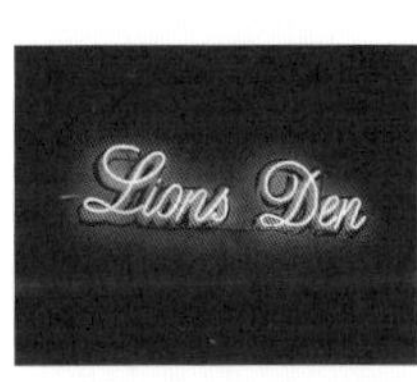

146. Belt buckle, 2009.
--

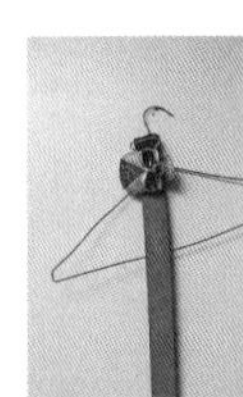

147. Barbershop, Bankhead, 2009.
--

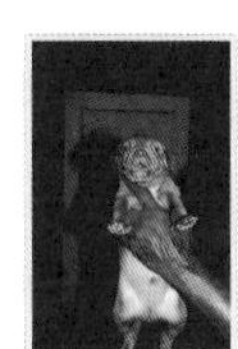

148. Pit bull puppy, 2008.
--

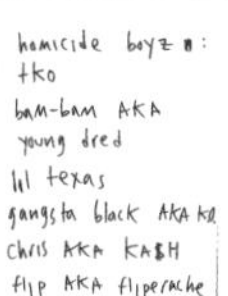

149. *List of Homicide Boyz Members*, 2010.
--

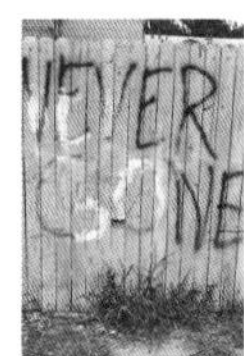

150. Stadium Grocery, Hank Aaron Boulevard, 2009.
--

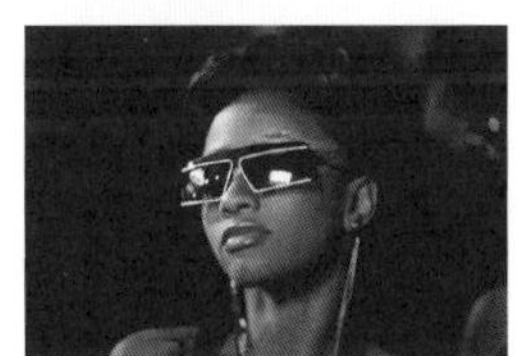

151. In the fall of 2009, Princess, of Crime Mob, shot a video at Opera, one of the bigger clubs in Midtown.
--

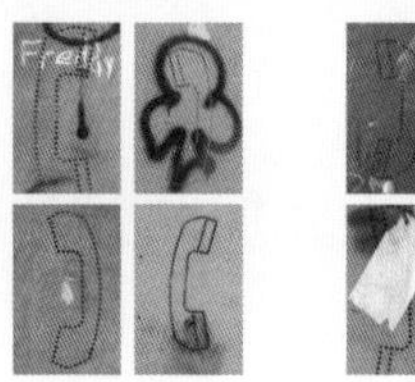

152. All those old songs talk about beepers, and all the old phones that they made calls from are still there.
--

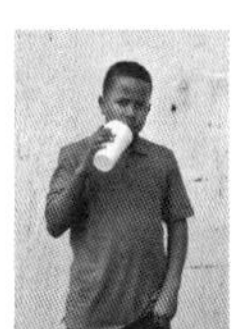

153. Shun had at least a dozen perfect poses; he must've practiced them. He's an R&B prodigy.
--

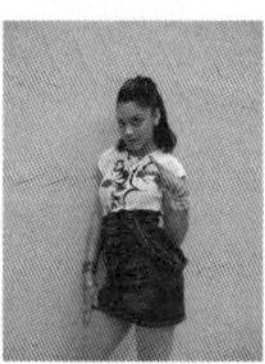

154. Christina and Elasiah met me out on the north side near Chamblee Tucker, near the industrial area out there. They did a bunch of dances for the photos— the Heisman, the Make-Up, and the Rockstar.
--

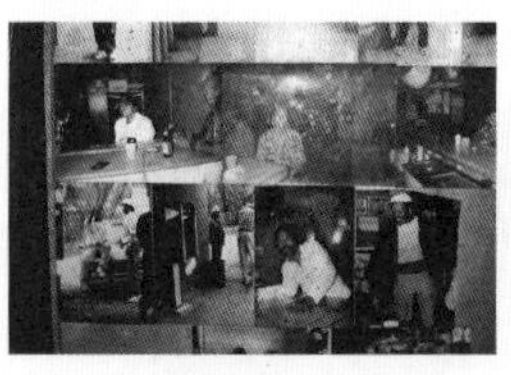

155. Old photos from the Speakeasy, 2008.
--

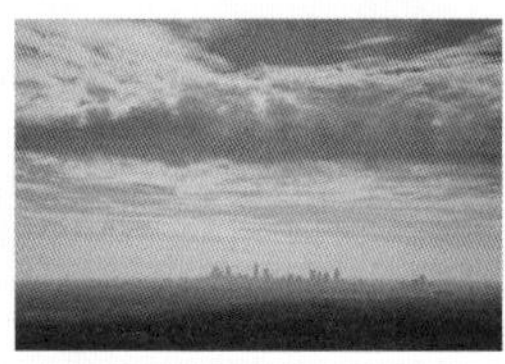

156. Atlanta, 2009.
--

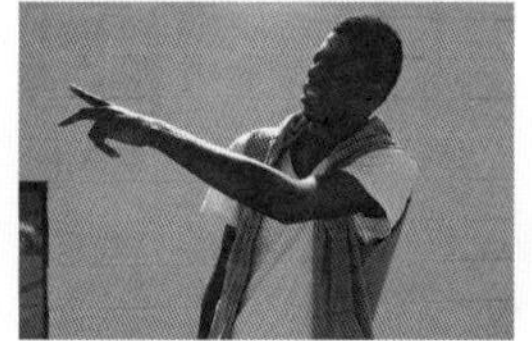

157. Quez, 2009.
--

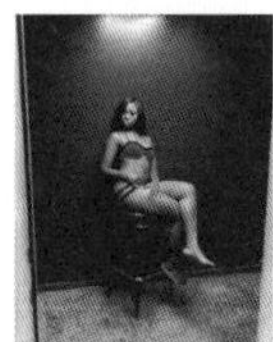

158. Prada, Magic City, 2009.
--

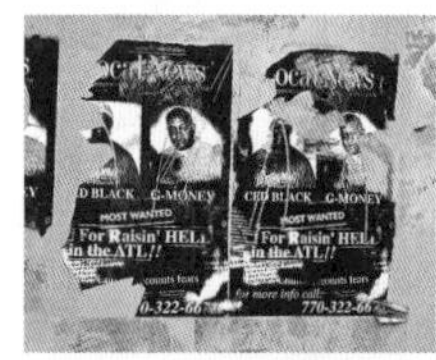

159. You've probably never heard of Ced Black and G-Money and you probably never will.
--

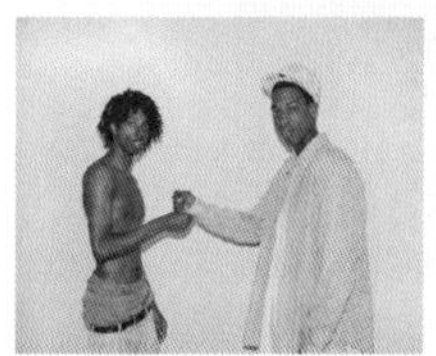

160. Lil Texas and Ricardo, October, 2007.
--

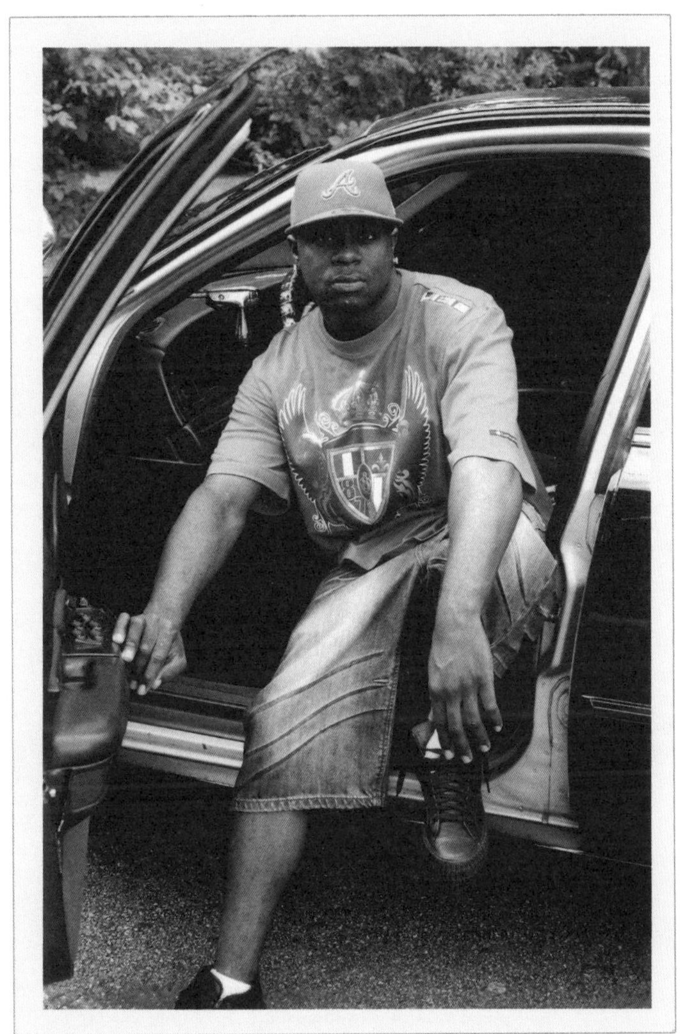

--

JOSHUA "MIDNIGHT" HOLDER
OCTOBER 27, 1987 – MAY 3, 2010

ACKNOWLEDGEMENTS:
--
Thank you, K, Will, Rodrigo, and Nick for collaborating. Thank you to Jen Jenkins and Steve Mockus for your insight and support; and to Julie Pochron, Steve Attardo, Beth Steiner, and Katie Hawthorne xo for making everything look better. To Jason Fulford; Leanne Shapton; Matt Salacuse; Charley Damski; Noel Camardo; Friedrich and Maggy; Jason Nocito; Richard Maxwell; Dave Shaftel; Molly Murray; Sarah Buck; Peter Buchanan-Smith; Sarah, William, and Abby Schmelling; Bobbie Gale; Suzanne LaGasa; Brian Clamp; Aaron Schuman; Ted Harrison; Gabe Tesoriero; Ross Kasovitz; Mario Delgado; Greg Miller; Ian Toombs; Heidi Smith; Eleni Peters; Becca Cohen; and to everyone at Pochron Studios; Chronicle Books; and Rodrigo Corral Design; thank you.

In Atlanta, thanks to KB, Kawan, J Dot and J Roc, Hannah Kang, Alex Young, Julie Pender, Daniel Weidenfeld, Jason Walden, Derek Schklar, Carol Wilson, Ray Murray, Tamiko Hope, Julia Beverly, T-Pain, Killer Mike, CEO Charlie, Julian Cox, William Boling, The Speakeasy, Jay Morel, and Greg Street.

Thanks, especially, to Amy Leavell Bransford, Steve Bransford, Ollie Green, Dave Hughes, and Amantha Walden for their generosity.

AND TO EVERYONE WHO WAS PHOTOGRAPHED, THANK YOU
--

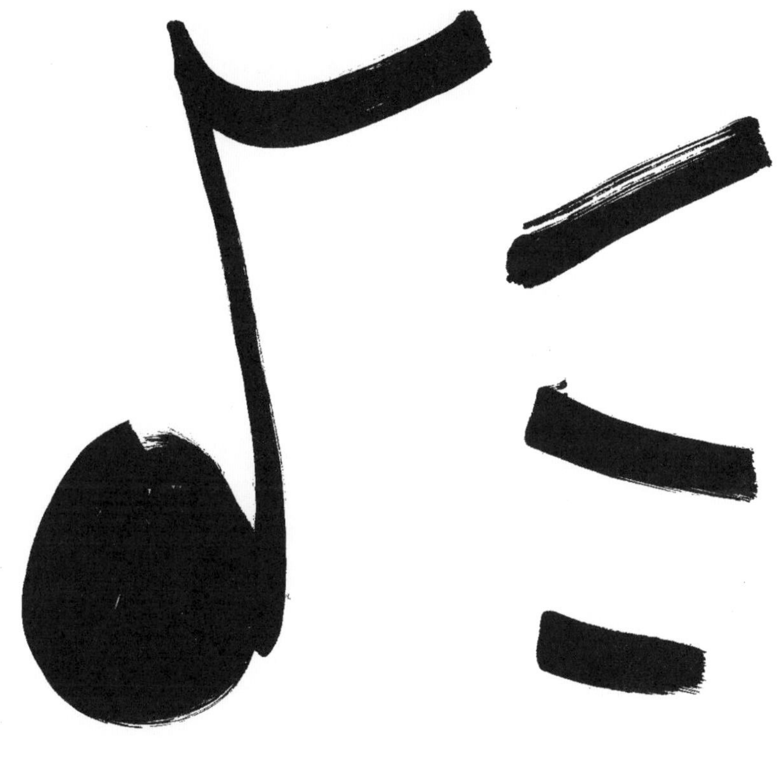

Copyright © 2010 by Michael Schmelling.
All rights reserved.
No part of this book may be reproduced in any form
without written permission from the publisher.

Library of Congress Cataloging-in-Publication Data Schmelling, Michael, 1973-
Atlanta : hip hop and the South / photographs by Michael Schmelling;
text by Kelefa Sanneh ; interviews by Will Welch.
p. cm.
ISBN 978-0-8118-7277-5 (hardcover)
1. Rap (Music)—Georgia—Atlanta—Pictorial works.
2. Hip-hop—Georgia—Atlanta—Pictorial works.
I. Sanneh, Kelefa. II. Welch, Will. III. Title.

ML3531.S37 2010
782.42164909758'231—dc22

2010023536

Manufactured in China
Designed by Rodrigo Corral Design
and Michael Schmelling
Design Assistant: Steve Attardo

10 9 8 7 6 5 4 3 2 1

Chronicle Books LLC
680 Second Street
San Francisco, CA 94107

www.chroniclebooks.com

An online index of songs,
links, videos, and
additional materials accompanies
the publication of *Atlanta*.

--

VISIT
WWW.ATLBOOK.COM
and enter code:
AH54BV7
to download a
mixtape featuring artists
from this book.